Housing Associations
a legal handbook

Dr Christopher Handy OBE is chief executive of the Accord Housing Group and Professor of Governance at Birmingham City University's Business School. He is a Fellow of the Institute of Housing, a member of the British Institute of Management, a board member of Dudley NHS clinical commissioning group and also of Eurhonet a European network of public and social housing organisations. Chris has been chief executive of Accord and its precursors for over 20 years, previously working in other housing organisations and local government. He is on the editorial board of the *Journal of Housing Law*.

John Alder is Emeritus Professor of Law at Newcastle University. He was previously Professor of Law at Keele University prior to which he held teaching posts at Exeter and Birmingham Universities. He has been a board member and chair of housing associations in the West Country, the Midlands and the North East of England. Apart from his work on housing association law, John has published books and articles on constitutional law, administrative law, human rights, legal theory and environmental law.

Available as an eBook at www.lag.org.uk/bookshop/ebooks

The purpose of Legal Action Group is to promote equal access to justice for all members of society who are socially, economically or otherwise disadvantaged. To this end, it seeks to improve law and practice, the administration of justice and legal services.

Housing Associations
a legal handbook

FIFTH EDITION

Christopher Handy and John Alder

 Legal Action Group
2019

This edition published in Great Britain 2019
by LAG Education and Service Trust Limited
National Pro Bono Centre, 48 Chancery Lane, London WC2A 1JF
www.lag.org.uk

© Christopher Handy and John Alder 2018

First edition published 1987
Second edition 1991
Third edition 1997
Fourth edition 2003

Previous editions all published by Sweet & Maxwell

While every effort has been made to ensure that the details in this text are correct, readers must be aware that the law changes and that the accuracy of the material cannot be guaranteed and the author and the publisher accept no responsibility for any loss or damage sustained.

The rights of the authors to be identified as authors of this work have been asserted by them in accordance with the Copyright, Designs and Patents Act 1988.

All rights reserved. No part of this publication may be reproduced, stored in a retrieval system or transmitted in any form or by any means, without permission from the publisher.

British Library Cataloguing in Publication Data
a CIP catalogue record for this book is available from the British Library.

Crown copyright material is produced with the permission of the Controller of HMSO and the Queen's Printer for Scotland.

This book has been produced using Forest Stewardship Council (FSC) certified paper. The wood used to produce FSC certified products with a 'Mixed Sources' label comes from FSC certified well-managed forests, controlled sources and/or recycled material.

print ISBN   978 1 912273 15 7
eBook ISBN   978 1 912273 16 4

Typeset by Refinecatch Limited, Bungay, Suffolk
Printed in Great Britain by Hobbs the Printers, Totton, Hampshire

Preface

'The courts should be slow to find that tenants in social housing had given up their rights to object by not taking an objection to what their housing association landlord was doing ...'.
  White v Riverside Housing Association Ltd
  [2005] EWCA Civ 1385 per Peter Gibson LJ

Why a book on housing association law? One answer is that housing associations are increasingly important and are neglected in the legal literature. Housing association law is often treated as a marginal topic, buried in the footnotes and lacking distinctive principles. In fact, ever since local authority housing development was killed off late in the last century, housing associations have become the main providers of social housing in the UK with a corresponding growth in government regulation of the sector. They have been regarded as a bridge between the public and private sectors, a position that has become increasingly fuzzy.

This book aims to provide a framework for the housing practitioner and lawyer working in or with the sector. It also seeks to provide an introduction for students. For those already acquainted with social housing law we hope to provide perspectives and insights demonstrating how the law has evolved and developed in this rapidly changing sector. We try to identify the principles and rules peculiar to housing associations and to highlight other areas of law which have a distinctive application to the sector.

Housing associations house about six million people in need. For several decades the scale and range of their activities has continued to grow. The rate of growth in the last decade has been phenomenal. The private market can never meet the housing needs and demands of the population as a whole. Housing associations promote low-cost renting and also low-cost home ownership through various government part-funded projects. Over the last twenty or so years they have raised well in excess of £65bn of private finance. Their roles have diversified: not only do they provide housing but they are substantial providers of care as well as civic services such as running libraries and leisure facilities. They run factories manufacturing timber homes, own land development and construction companies as well as other private sector activities. They are both big and small in nature, with the largest owning some 120,000 plus properties, having an annual turnover into the billions and assets equalling the largest *Times* top 100 companies. The smallest manage just a few homes and work on a very local basis.

The story of housing associations is one of survival and mutability in the face of government capture, a fate which can often fall upon well organised voluntary endeavours. The government wants to control this sector because of the amount of grant invested in it, but not to go so far as to nationalise it, due to the impact on public sector borrowing. There is an almost 'treading the tightrope' like relationship with government, with the sector sometimes disliked in good times but tolerated and even seen as essential in times of economic downturn.

The variety and scale of housing association activity and the relationship with government both national and local has generated a substantial body of law. This has been piecemeal, context-specific and unstable responding to the short term concerns of successive governments and occasionally to policy lurches by a single government. The law is scattered amongst numerous statutory provisions. The promise of the largely obsolete Housing Associations Act 1985 has not been fulfilled by codification.

A common element in the law is an underlying tension between three dynamics, namely the private law of commercial relationships, the public law of social housing and to a lesser extent the charitable/voluntary sector movement, the latter providing the historical roots of the sector.

The nearest we have to a distinct housing association law is the regulatory system. Since October 2018 there has been an independent Social Housing Regulator responsible for a plethora of regulatory 'Standards' and 'Guidance' backed by powers of intervention and punishment. There is a growing body of case-law notably on the vexed question of the extent to which housing associations, spanning as they do both public and private sectors, are subject to public law and to the Human Rights Act 1998.

Layered onto this framework in almost bewildering complexity, are many kinds of housing association, their charitable and non-charitable status, their different legal structures, notably the relatively little known co-operative and community benefit societies, and whether they are mutual or non-mutual. Thus a flexible legal framework is required generating a demand for a range of legal disciplines, notably for public lawyers and charity lawyers, as well as housing lawyers of all kinds. Within this context we try to identify key areas of law. There are of course many relevant areas of general housing law, corporate law and charity law where there are no special rules for housing associations and which we do not discuss except occasionally to supply a context to help understanding.

The core role of housing provision in the context of severe housing shortage is discussed with emphasis on how far allocation decisions can be controlled by law. Distinctive tenures have been created some surviving from earlier regimes while others are the product of regulatory requirements. Over the years housing associations have attracted many different sponsors and funding regimes and we discuss their multiple funding arrangements. We also discuss the requirements of governance and accountability generated by responsibilities spanning the public and private domains.

Housing is a devolved area so that different statutory provisions and regulatory regimes apply to England and Wales. Indeed, Welsh housing law is becoming increasingly distinctive. We concentrate on English law and the law common to both regimes (which remain a single legal system) but try to identify the main ways in which Welsh law has begun to diverge especially in respect of regulation. We do not discuss the separate legal systems of Scotland and Northern Ireland.

The law is based on materials available to us at the end of September 2018.

Christopher Handy
John Alder
October 2018

Contents

Preface   v
Table of cases   xiii
Table of statutes   xxv
Table of statutory instruments   xxxvii
Table of European and international legislation   xli
Abbreviations   xliii

Part 1: General principles   1

1   Introduction: the scope of housing association law   3
Housing associations: background   4
Housing association law?   6
Historical development   8
Current policy trends   12
The meaning of 'social housing' and related concepts   21

2   The legal framework of a housing association   27
The definition of 'housing association'   28
English and Welsh housing associations   33
Different kinds of housing association   34
Local authority connections   43

3   Public or private sector: public or private law?   47
Introduction: the nature of the problem   48
Government accounts   50
Human Rights Act 1998   52
Public bodies and EU law   61

Part 2: Regulation   63

4   Regulation: general   65
Introduction: the regulators   66
Jurisdiction of the regulators   69

Registration: English bodies   70
Registration: Welsh bodies   73
Removal from the register   76
The framework of regulation   77
The objectives of social housing regulation   78
Standards   80
Guidance   81
General constraints on the powers of the English regulator   82
Consultation and information   84
Tenant involvement   85
Openness: disclosure of information – gradings   86
Regulation of accounts and audit   88
Financial assistance   89
The practice of the English regulator   89
Regulation of Welsh bodies   91

5 Particular regulatory powers   93
Introduction   94
Investigatory/monitoring powers   95
Powers to impose penalties   101
Powers over governance and management   104
Transfer of land and amalgamation   109
Relaxing regulation   110
Insolvency and winding up   114
Appeals   114
Powers of the Welsh regulator   116

6 Other regulatory bodies   119
Financial Conduct Authority   120
Registrar of Companies (Companies House)   122
Charity Commission   122
Care Quality Commission   125

Part 3: The provision of housing   127

7 Housing provision, allocation and management   129
Background   130
Who do housing associations house?   132
Specific housing duties   133
Selection of tenants   136
Human rights implications   144
Housing quality and safety   149

8 Tenants' rights: the different tenures 151
Introduction 153
Wales 155
The residual regime: secure and fair rent tenants 155
Fair rents 157
The contemporary regime: assured tenants 157
Assured shorthold tenancies 159
Fully mutual tenancies 162
Collision between the residual and contemporary regimes: special cases 163
Probationary/flexible tenancies 165
Punishment for unlawful subletting 169
Long tenancies 170
Shared ownership 172
Leaseholds for the elderly 182
Other ownership schemes 184

9 Particular rights 187
Introduction 188
Security of tenure/eviction 189
Rents 191
Succession 196
Transfer/exchange of tenancies 197
Shared ownership 200
The right to buy: secure tenants 201
Human rights 207
Judicial review 212

10 Supported housing problems 217
Introduction 218
Supported housing, residential and nursing care: costs in a time of austerity 218
Residential care: deprivation of liberty 225

Part 4: Governance and investment 229

11 Governance generally 231
Introduction 232
Current governance issues 232
Governance principles and practice 235
Governance and regulatory framework 237
The membership 239

12 The governing body   247
Introduction   248
Powers of the governing body   249
Composition of the governing body   251
Regulatory requirements   252
Liability of the governing body   256
Enforcing director's liability   262
Conflicts of interest: fiduciary duties   264

13 Accountability   273
Introduction   274
Accountability to the regulator   274
Accountability to local authorities   276
Accountability to tenants   281
Accountability to the community and general public   285
The Housing Ombudsman   288

14 Capital and revenue: investment, grants and income   291
Part 1: Housing development investments and grants   293
Part 2: Revenue, rents and service charges   306
Part 3: Taxation and fiscal privileges   318

15 Mergers, amalgamations, group structures and winding up   327
Trends and introduction   328
Mergers and merger methods   330
A note on group structures   333
Winding up and insolvency   341
Insolvency in Wales   344

Index   345

Table of cases

Adams v Cape Industries plc [1990] Ch 433, [1990] 2 WLR 657, [1991] 1 All ER 929, [1990] BCC 786, [1990] BCLC 479, CA   15.34

Adan v Newham LBC [2001] EWCA Civ 1916, [2002] 1 WLR 2120, [2002] 1 All ER 931, [2002] HRLR 17, [2002] UKHRR 229, [2002] HLR 28, 2002 Hous LR 11, (2002) 99(9) LSG 29, (2002) 146 SJLB 28, [2001] NPC 185, (2002) *Independent*, January 18   9.86

Ali and others v Birmingham City Council [2010] UKSC 8, [2010] 2 AC 39, [2010] 2 WLR 471, [2010] 2 All ER 175, [2010] PTSR 524, [2010] HRLR 18, [2010] UKHRR 417, [2010] HLR 22, [2010] BLGR 401, (2010) 154(7) SJLB 37, (2010) *Times*, February 19   7.51, 9.83

AMEC Capital Projects Ltd v Whitefriars City Estates Ltd [2004] EWCA Civ 1418, [2005] 1 All ER 723, [2005] BLR 1, 96 Con LR 142, (2005) 21 Const LJ 249, (2004) 154 NLJ 1690, (2004) 148 SJLB 1285, (2004) *Times*, November 8   5.19

Anufrijeva v Southwark LBC [2003] EWCA Civ 1406, [2004] QB 1124, [2004] 2 WLR 603, [2004] 1 All ER 833, [2004] 1 FLR 8, [2003] 3 FCR 673, [2004] HRLR 1, [2004] UKHRR 1, 15 BHRC 526, [2004] HLR 22, [2004] BLGR 184, (2003) 6 CCLR 415, [2004] Fam Law 12, (2003) 100(44) LSG 30, (2003) *Times*, October 17, (2003) *Independent*, October 23   9.82

Artingstoll v United Kingdom (App No 25517/94) (1995) 19 EHRR CD92, EComHR   9.78

Ashbury Railway Carriage & Iron Co Ltd v Riche (1874–75) LR 7 HL 653, HL   12.13

Ashby v Ebdon [1985] Ch 394, [1985] 2 WLR 279, [1984] 3 All ER 869, (1985) 17 HLR 1, (1984) 81 LSG 2935, (1984) 128 SJ 686, Ch D   5.21

Aston Cantlow and Wilmcote with Billesley Parochial Church Council v Wallbank [2003] UKHL 37, [2004] 1 AC 546, [2003] 3 WLR 283, [2003] 3 All ER 1213, [2003] HRLR 28, [2003] UKHRR 919, [2003] 27 EG 137 (CS), (2003) 100(33) LSG 28, (2003) 153 NLJ 1030, (2003) 147 SJLB 812, [2003] NPC 80, (2003) *Times*, June 27   3.17, 3.36

Attorney General v Charity Commission for England and
  Wales, *Independent* Schools Council [2011] UKUT 421
  (TCC), [2012] Ch 214, [2012] 2 WLR 100, [2012] 1 All
  ER 127, [2012] PTSR 99, [2011] ELR 529, [2012] WTLR
  41, 14 ITELR 396, (2011) *Times*, November 8   2.45
Auld v Glasgow Working Men's Building Society (1887) 12
  App Cas 197, (1887) 14 R (HL) 27, HL (Scotland)   15.11
Automatic Self Cleansing Filter Syndicate Co Ltd v
  Cuninghame [1906] 2 Ch 34, CA   11.34
Barings plc (No 5), Re [2000] 1 BCLC 523, CA   12.44
Bartlett v Barclays Bank Trust Co Ltd [1980] Ch 515, [1980]
  2 WLR 430, [1980] 2 All ER 92, (1980) 124 SJ 221, Ch D   12.45
Berrisford v Mexfield Housing Co-operative Ltd [2011]
  UKSC 52, [2012] 1 AC 955, [2011] 3 WLR 1091, [2012] 1
  All ER 1393, [2012] PTSR 69, [2012] HLR 15, [2012] 1 P
  & CR 8, [2012] L & TR 7, [2011] 3 EGLR 115, [2011] 46
  EG 105 (CS), (2011) 155(43) SJLB 35, [2011] NPC 115,
  [2012] 1 P & CR DG10, (2011) *Times*, November 21   8.24, 8.25, 8.37,
  8.40
Bhai v Black Roof Community Housing Association Ltd
  [2001] 2 All ER 865, (2001) 33 HLR 55, (2000) 97(45)
  LSG 41, [2000] NPC 117, (2001) 81 P & CR DG22,
  (2000) *Times*, November 14, CA   8.13, 8.15, 9.49
Boardman v Phipps [1967] 2 AC 46, [1966] 3 WLR 1009,
  [1966] 3 All ER 721, (1966) 110 SJ 853, HL   12.58
Brick Farm Management Ltd v Richmond Housing
  Partnership Ltd [2005] EWHC 1650 (QB), [2005] 1 WLR
  3934, [2006] HLR 3, [2005] 3 EGLR 57, [2005] 48 EG
  224, (2005) 155 NLJ 1483, [2005] NPC 108, [2006] 1 P &
  CR DG5, (2005) *Times*, August 30   2.40, 8.78
British Oxygen Co Ltd v Minister of Technology [1971] AC
  610, [1969] 2 WLR 892, [1970] 3 WLR 488, [1970] 3 All
  ER 165, HL   7.42, 9.87
Campbell v Mirror Group Newspapers Ltd [2004] UKHL
  22, [2004] 2 AC 457, [2004] 2 WLR 1232, [2004] 2 All ER
  995, [2004] EMLR 15, [2004] HRLR 24, [2004] UKHRR
  648, 16 BHRC 500, (2004) 101(21) LSG 36, (2004) 154
  NLJ 733, (2004) 148 SJLB 572, (2004) *Times*, May 7,
  (2004) *Independent*, May 11   3.33
Campbell v Paddington Corp [1911] 1 KB 869, KBD   12.53
Cardiff Savings Bank, Re [1892] 2 Ch 100, Ch D   13.36
Chapman v United Kingdom (App No 27238/95) (2001) 33
  EHRR 18, 10 BHRC 48, (2001) *Times*, January 30, ECtHR   7.52, 9.72
Charterbridge Corp v Lloyds Bank Ltd [1970] Ch 62, [1969]
  3 WLR 122, [1969] 2 All ER 1185, [1969] 2 Lloyd's Rep
  24, (1968) 113 SJ 465, Ch D   15.37
City Equitable Fire Insurance Co Ltd, Re [1925] Ch 407,
  [1924] All ER Rep 485, CA   13.34
Clays Lane Housing Cooperative Ltd v Patrick (1985) 17
  HLR 188, (1985) 49 P & CR 72, CA   8.33
Clemens v Clemens Bros Ltd [1976] 2 All ER 268, Ch D   11.44

Cocks v Thanet DC [1983] 2 AC 286, [1982] 3 WLR 1121,
    [1982] 3 All ER 1135, (1983) 6 HLR 15, 81 LGR 81,
    [1984] RVR 31, (1982) 126 SJ 820, HL   7.33
Commission v France (C-237/99) [2001] ECR I-939, ECJ   3.51
Construction Industry Training Board v Attorney General
    [1971] 1 WLR 1303, [1971] 3 All ER 449, 1 KIR 277,
    (1971) 115 SJ 505, Ch D   11.28
Cotter v National Union of Seamen [1929] 2 Ch 58, CA   11.33
Creasey v Breachwood Motors Ltd [1992] BCC 638, [1993]
    BCLC 480, (1992) *Times*, July 29, QBD   15.34
Credit Suisse v Allerdale BC [1997] QB 306, [1996] 3 WLR
    894, [1996] 4 All ER 129, [1996] 2 Lloyd's Rep 241, [1996]
    5 Bank LR 249, (1997) 161 JP Rep 88, (1996) *Times*, May
    20, (1996) *Independent*, June 7, CA   15.37
DHN Food Distributors v Tower Hamlets LBC [1976]
    1 WLR 852, [1976] 3 All ER 462, 74 LGR 506, (1976)
    32 P & CR 240, [1976] JPL 363, (1976) 120 SJ 215, CA   15.36
Dimes v Grand Junction Canal Proprietors 10 ER 301,
    (1852) 3 HL Cas 759, HL   4.1
Dingle v Turner [1972] AC 601, [1972] 2 WLR 523, [1972]
    1 All ER 878, (1972) 116 SJ 195, HL   2.45
Dixon v Wandsworth LBC [2008] EWCA Civ 595   7.51, 9.83
Dorchester Finance Co v Stebbing [1989] BCLC 498, Ch D   12.44
Eastlands Homes Partnership Ltd v Whyte [2010] EWHC
    695 (QB)   7.38, 7.39, 8.44,
                                                                        9.88, 9.93
FJM v United Kingdom Application No 76202/16,
    29 November 2018   3.35, 9.72
Foss v Harbottle 67 ER 189, (1843) 2 Hare 461   11.33
Foster v British Gas plc (C-188/89) [1991] 1 QB 405, [1991]
    2 WLR 258, [1990] 3 All ER 897, [1990] ECR I-3313,
    [1990] 2 CMLR 833, [1991] ICR 84, [1990] IRLR 353,
    [1990] Pens LR 189, (1990) *Times*, July 13, ECJ   3.48
Ghaidan v Godin-Mendoza [2004] UKHL 30, [2004] 2 AC
    557, [2004] 3 WLR 113, [2004] 3 All ER 411, [2004]
    2 FLR 600, [2004] 2 FCR 481, [2004] HRLR 31, [2004]
    UKHRR 827, 16 BHRC 671, [2004] HLR 46, [2005]
    1 P & CR 18, [2005] L & TR 3, [2004] 2 EGLR 132, [2004]
    Fam Law 641, [2004] 27 EG 128 (CS), (2004) 101(27)
    LSG 30, (2004) 154 NLJ 1013, (2004) 148 SJLB 792,
    [2004] NPC 100, [2004] 2 P & CR DG17, (2004) *Times*,
    June 24   3.33, 8.94, 9.83,
                                                                        9.84
Giacomelli v Italy (App No 59909/00) (2007) 45 EHRR 38,
    ECtHR   7.52
Gillies v Secretary of State for Work and Pensions [2006]
    UKHL 2, [2006] 1 WLR 781, [2006] 1 All ER 731, 2006 SC
    (HL) 71, 2006 SLT 77, 2006 SCLR 276, [2006] ICR 267,
    (2006) 9 CCLR 404, (2006) 103(9) LSG 33, (2006) 150
    SJLB 127, 2006 GWD 3-66, (2006) *Times*, January 30   5.19

Governors of the Peabody Donation Fund v Higgins [1983]
1 WLR 1091, [1983] 3 All ER 122, (1983) 10 HLR 82,
(1983) 127 SJ 596, CA   7.2
Guild and others v Inland Revenue Commissioners [1992]
2 AC 310, [1992] 2 WLR 397, [1992] 2 All ER 10, [1992]
STC 162, 1992 SC (HL) 71, 1992 SLT 438, [1992] STI
234, (1992) 89(17) LSG 49, (1992) 136 SJLB 88, (1992)
Times, March 2, HL (Scotland)   14.110
Halifax Building Society v Meridian Housing Association
Ltd and another [1994] 2 BCLC 540, (1995) 27 HLR 123,
[1994] EG 41 (CS), (1994) *Independent*, March 21, Ch D   2.5, 12.53
Harris v Microfusion 2000-3 LLP [2016] EWCA Civ 1212   12.52
Heathview Tenants Cooperative, Re (1980) 258 EG 645   9.16
Helena Partnerships Ltd (formerly Helena Housing Ltd) v
Revenue and Customs Commissioners [2012] EWCA
Civ 569, [2012] 4 All ER 111, [2012] PTSR 1409, [2012]
STC 1584, [2012] HLR 32, [2012] BTC 156, [2012]
WTLR 1519, [2012] STI 1659   2.30, 2.35
Hole v Garnsey [1930] AC 472, HL   15.11
Hounslow LBC v Hare (1992) 24 HLR 9, 89 LGR 714, Ch D   2.39, 2.40
Hounslow LBC v Powell [2011] UKSC 8, [2011] 2 AC 186,
[2011] 2 WLR 287, [2011] 2 All ER 129, [2011] PTSR
512, [2011] HRLR 18, [2011] UKHRR 548, [2011] HLR
23, [2011] BLGR 363, [2011] 1 P & CR 20, [2011] 9 EG
164 (CS), (2011) 155(8) SJLB 31, [2011] NPC 24, (2011)
Times, March 1   9.74, 9.75
Howard Smith Ltd v Ampol Petroleum Ltd [1974] AC 821,
[1974] 2 WLR 689, [1974] 1 All ER 1126, 118 SJLB 330,
(1974) 118 SJ 330, PC (Australia)   11.33
IR (Sri Lanka) v Secretary of State for the Home
Department [2011] EWCA Civ 704, [2012] 1 WLR 232,
[2011] 4 All ER 908, [2011] UKHRR 988, [2011] ACD
102, (2011) *Times*, August 26   7.53
Inland Revenue Commissioners v Church Commissioners
for England [1977] AC 329, [1976] 3 WLR 214, [1976] 2
All ER 1037, [1976] STC 339, 50 TC 516, [1976] TR 187,
(1976) 120 SJ 505, HL   14.93
Inland Revenue Commissioners v Helen Slater Charitable
Trust Ltd [1982] Ch 49, [1981] 3 WLR 377, [1981] 3
All ER 98, [1981] STC 471, 55 TC 230, [1982] TR 225,
(1981) 125 SJ 414, CA   14.107
Jones v Lipman [1962] 1 WLR 832, [1962] 1 All ER 442,
(1962) 106 SJ 531, Ch D   15.39
Joseph Rowntree Memorial Trust Housing Association Ltd v
Attorney General [1983] Ch 159, [1983] 2 WLR 284, [1983]
1 All ER 288, (1983) 133 NLJ 126, (1983) 127 SJ 137, Ch D   2.28, 2.31, 2.45,
                                                                        8.88
Lawal v Circle 33 Housing Trust [2014] EWCA Civ 1514,
[2015] HLR 9, [2015] 1 P & CR 12   9.75

Table of cases xvii

Lawal v Northern Spirit Ltd [2003] UKHL 35, [2004] 1 All ER
  187, [2003] ICR 856, [2003] IRLR 538, [2003] HRLR 29,
  [2003] UKHRR 1024, (2003) 100(28) LSG 30, (2003) 153
  NLJ 1005, (2003) 147 SJLB 783, (2003) *Times*, June 27   5.19, 8.45
Leeds Federated Housing Association, Re (1981) 260 EG 813 9.16
Liverpool and District Hospital for Diseases of the Heart
  v Attorney General [1981] Ch 193, [1981] 2 WLR 379,
  [1981] 1 All ER 994, (1981) 125 SJ 79, (1980) *Times*,
  November 4, Ch D   12.45
Locabail (UK) Ltd v Bayfield Properties Ltd [2000] QB 451,
  [2000] 2 WLR 870, [2000] 1 All ER 65, [2000] IRLR 96,
  [2000] HRLR 290, [2000] UKHRR 300, 7 BHRC 583,
  (1999) 149 NLJ 1793, [1999] NPC 143, (1999) *Times*,
  November 19, (1999) *Independent*, November 23, CA   5.19, 8.45
London Housing Society Ltd's Trust Deeds, Re [1940] Ch
  777, [1940] 3 All ER 665, Ch D   15.17
McDonald v McDonald [2016] UKSC 28, [2017] AC 273,
  [2016] 3 WLR 45, [2017] 1 All ER 961, [2016] HRLR
  18, [2017] BPIR 728, [2016] HLR 28, [2017] L & TR 9,
  [2016] 2 P & CR DG22, (2016) *Times*, June 29   3.35, 9.72
McDonald v United Kingdom (App No 4241/12) [2014]
  ECHR 412, (2015) 60 EHRR 1, 37 BHRC 130, (2014)
  17 CCLR 187, (2014) *Times*, June 13, ECtHR   9.88
Manchester City Council v Pinnock [2010] UKSC 45, [2011]
  2 AC 104, [2010] 3 WLR 1441, [2011] 1 All ER 285, [2011]
  PTSR 61, [2011] HRLR 3, [2010] UKHRR 1213, 31
  BHRC 670, [2011] HLR 7, [2010] BLGR 909, [2011] L &
  TR 2, [2010] 3 EGLR 113, [2010] 45 EG 93 (CS), (2010)
  107(44) LSG 16, (2011) 108(8) LSG 20, (2010) 154(42)
  SJLB 30, [2010] NPC 109, (2010) *Times*, November 4   3.35, 9.74, 9.75
Mary Clark Home's Trustees v Anderson [1904] 2 KB 645,
  KBD   2.36
Maxwell v Department of Trade and Industry [1974] QB
  523, [1974] 2 WLR 338, [1974] 2 All ER 122, (1974) 118
  SJ 203, CA   5.13
Medway Housing Society Ltd v Cook (Inspector of Taxes)
  [1997] STC 90, 69 TC 319, [1997] BTC 63, (1997) *Times*,
  January 1, Ch D   14.90
Mill v Hawker (1874–75) LR 10 Ex 92   12.53
Miller-Mead v Minister of Housing and Local Government
  [1963] 2 QB 196, [1963] 2 WLR 225, [1963] 1 All ER 459,
  (1963) 127 JP 122, 61 LGR 152, (1963) 14 P & CR 266,
  [1963] JPL 151, (1962) 106 SJ 1052, CA   5.34
Ormskirk Union v Chorlton Union [1903] 1 KB 19, KBD   2.32
Over Seventies Housing Association v Westminster LBC
  (1974) 230 EG 1593   2.45
Owners of Cargo Laden on Board the Albacruz v Owners of
  the Albazero [1977] AC 774, [1976] 3 WLR 419, [1976] 3 All
  ER 129, [1976] 2 Lloyd's Rep 467, (1976) 120 SJ 570, HL   13.34

P v Cheshire West and Chester Council and another; P and
Q v Surrey CC [2014] UKSC 19, [2014] AC 896, [2014] 2
WLR 642, [2014] 2 All ER 585, [2014] PTSR 460, [2014] 2
FCR 71, [2014] COPLR 313, [2014] HRLR 13, (2014) 17
CCLR 5, [2014] Med LR 321, (2014) 137 BMLR 56, [2014]
MHLR 394, (2014) 158(13) SJLB 37, (2014) *Times*, April 1   10.25–10.30, 10.32, 10.33

Palmer Birch (a partnership) v Lloyd [2018] EWHC 2316
(TCC)   12.53

Peabody Housing Association Ltd v Green and others
(1979) 38 P & CR 644, (1978) 122 SJ 862, CA   3.42, 7.35, 9.95

Poplar Housing & Regeneration Community Association
Ltd v Donoghue [2001] EWCA Civ 595, [2002] QB 48,
[2001] 3 WLR 183, [2001] 4 All ER 604, [2001] 2 FLR
284, [2001] 3 FCR 74, [2001] UKHRR 693, (2001) 33
HLR 73, (2001) 3 LGLR 41, [2001] BLGR 489, [2001]
ACD 76, [2001] Fam Law 588, [2001] 19 EG 141 (CS),
(2001) 98(19) LSG 38, (2001) 98(23) LSG 38, (2001) 145
SJLB 122, [2001] NPC 84, (2001) *Times*, June 21, (2001)
Independent, May 2, (2001) *Daily Telegraph*, May 8   3.20, 3.22, 3.30, 3.31, 3.39, 7.50, 8.3, 9.75

Porter v Magill [2001] UKHL 67, [2002] 2 AC 357, [2002] 2
WLR 37, [2002] 1 All ER 465, [2002] HRLR 16, [2002] HLR
16, [2002] BLGR 51, (2001) 151 NLJ 1886, [2001] NPC 184,
(2001) *Times*, December 14, (2002) *Independent*, February
4, (2001) *Daily Telegraph*, December 20   5.19, 9.26

R (A) v Croydon LBC [2009] UKSC 8, [2009] 1 WLR 2557,
[2010] 1 All ER 469, [2010] PTSR 106, [2010] 1 FLR
959, [2009] 3 FCR 607, [2010] HRLR 9, [2010] UKHRR
63, [2010] BLGR 183, (2009) 12 CCLR 552, [2010] Fam
Law 137, (2009) 159 NLJ 1701, (2009) 153(46) SJLB 34,
(2009) *Times*, November 30   7.51, 9.86

R (A (a child)) v Secretary of State for Health [2015] EWCA
Civ 771, [2016] 1 WLR 331, [2016] 2 FLR 502, (2015) 146
BMLR 107, [2015] Fam Law 1175, (2015) *Times*, July 28   9.84

R (Alconbury Developments Ltd) v Secretary of State for the
Environment, Transport and Regions, *see* R (Holding
& Barnes plc and others) v Secretary of State for the
Environment, Transport and the Regions—

R (Beale) v Camden LBC [2004] EWHC 6 (Admin), [2004]
HLR 48, [2004] BLGR 291, [2004] NPC 2   13.32

R (Committee of Care North East Newcastle) v Newcastle
City Council [2012] EWHC 2655 (Admin)   10.4

R (East Midlands Care Ltd) v Leicestershire CC [2011]
EWHC 3096 (Admin)   10.4

R (Gilboy) v Liverpool City Council [2008] EWCA Civ 751,
[2009] QB 699, [2009] 3 WLR 300, [2008] 4 All ER 127,
[2009] PTSR 987, [2009] HLR 11, [2008] BLGR 521,
[2008] 2 P & CR 25, [2008] ACD 90, [2008] 27 EG 116
(CS), (2008) 152(27) SJLB 30, [2008] NPC 79, (2008)
Times, August 20   9.81

R (Heather) v Leonard Cheshire Foundation [2002] EWCA Civ 366, [2002] 2 All ER 936, [2002] HRLR 30, [2002] UKHRR 883, [2002] HLR 49, (2002) 5 CCLR 317, (2003) 69 BMLR 22, [2002] ACD 43, (2002) *Times*, April 8; *Affirming* [2001] EWHC Admin 429, (2001) 4 CCLR 211, [2002] MHLR 185, [2001] ACD 75, (2001) *Daily Telegraph*, June 26	3.20, 11.28
R (Holding & Barnes plc and others) v Secretary of State for the Environment, Transport and the Regions [2001] UKHL 23, [2003] 2 AC 295, [2001] 2 WLR 1389, [2001] 2 All ER 929, [2002] Env LR 12, [2001] HRLR 45, [2001] UKHRR 728, (2001) 3 LGLR 38, (2001) 82 P & CR 40, [2001] 2 PLR 76, [2001] JPL 920, [2001] 20 EG 228 (CS), (2001) 98(24) LSG 45, (2001) 151 NLJ 727, (2001) 145 SJLB 140, [2001] NPC 90, (2001) *Times*, May 10, (2001) *Independent*, June 25, (2001) *Daily Telegraph*, May 15	4.11
R (JL) v Secretary of State for Defence [2013] EWCA Civ 449, [2013] PTSR 1014, [2013] CP Rep 34, [2013] HLR 27	9.75
R (JM and NT) v Isle of Wight Council [2011] EWHC 2911 (Admin), [2012] Eq LR 34, (2012) 15 CCLR 167	10.4, 10.10, 10.20, 10.21
R (Limbuela) v Secretary of State for the Home Department [2005] UKHL 66, [2006] 1 AC 396, [2005] 3 WLR 1014, [2007] 1 All ER 951, [2006] HRLR 4, [2006] HLR 10, (2006) 9 CCLR 30, (2005) 102(46) LSG 25, (2005) 149 SJLB 1354, (2005) *Times*, November 4	9.82
R (Loader) v Secretary of State for Communities and Local Government [2012] EWCA Civ 869, [2013] PTSR 406, [2012] 3 CMLR 29, [2013] Env LR 7, [2012] BLGR 862, [2012] JPL 1509	4.52
R (McDonald) v Kensington and Chelsea RLBC [2010] EWCA Civ 1109, [2011] BLGR 246, (2010) 13 CCLR 664, (2011) 118 BMLR 42, [2011] ACD 40	10.10
R (McIntyre) v Gentoo Group Ltd [2010] EWHC 5 (Admin), (2010) 154(2) SJLB 29, [2010] 2 P & CR DG6	1.12, 3.23, 3.29, 3.43, 7.36, 7.40, 7.50, 9.85, 9.88, 9.91
R (Macleod) v Governors of the Peabody Trust [2016] EWHC 737 (Admin), [2016] HLR 27	3.29, 3.44, 3.45, 7.32, 8.23, 9.92
R (McLellan) v Bracknell Forest BC [2001] EWCA Civ 1510, [2002] QB 1129, [2002] 2 WLR 1448, [2002] 1 All ER 899, [2002] HRLR 12, [2002] UKHRR 45, (2001) 33 HLR 86, [2002] BLGR 191, [2002] ACD 54, (2001) 98(46) LSG 35, (2001) 145 SJLB 258, [2001] NPC 149, (2001) *Times*, December 3, (2001) *Independent*, October 24	3.33, 9.80
R (Members of the Committee of Care North East Northumberland) v Northumberland CC [2013] EWHC 234 (Admin), [2013] PTSR 1130, [2013] BLGR 265, (2013) 16 CCLR 276	10.4

R (Moseley) v Haringey LBC [2014] UKSC 56, [2014] 1 WLR
3947, [2015] 1 All ER 495, [2014] PTSR 1317, [2014]
BLGR 823, [2015] RVR 93, (2014) *Times*, November 5   4.60
R (Savva) v Kensington and Chelsea RLBC [2010] EWCA
Civ 1209, [2011] PTSR 761, [2011] BLGR 150, (2011)
14 CCLR 75, (2010) *Times*, November 15   10.11
R (Sefton Care Association) v Sefton Council [2011] EWHC
2676 (Admin), [2012] PTSR D13   10.4, 10.15–10.19
R (South West Care Homes Ltd) v Devon CC [2012] EWHC
2967 (Admin), [2013] Eq LR 50   10.4
R (Spath Holme Ltd) v Secretary of State for the
Environment, Transport and the Regions [2000] 3 WLR
141, [2000] 1 All ER 884, (2000) 32 HLR 495, [2000] EG
10 (CS), (2000) 144 SJLB 100, [2000] NPC 4, (2000)
Times, February 15, CA   9.16
R (Trafford) v Blackpool BC [2014] EWHC 85 (Admin),
[2014] 2 All ER 947, [2014] PTSR 989, [2014] BLGR
180, [2014] 1 P & CR DG19   3.44, 7.42, 9.87,
    9.94
R (W, M and others) v Birmingham City Council [2011]
EWHC 1147 (Admin), [2011] Eq LR 721, [2012]
BLGR 1, (2011) 14 CCLR 516, (2011) 120 BMLR 134,
[2011] ACD 84   10.12
R (Weaver) v London & Quadrant Housing Trust [2009]
EWCA Civ 587, [2010] 1 WLR 363, [2009] 4 All ER 865,
[2010] PTSR 1, [2009] HRLR 29, [2009] UKHRR 1371,
[2009] HLR 40, [2009] BLGR 962, [2009] L & TR 26,
[2009] 25 EG 137 (CS), (2009) 153(25) SJLB 30, [2009]
NPC 81, (2009) *Times*, August 26; *Affirming* [2008]
EWHC 1377 (Admin), [2009] 1 All ER 17, (2008) 158
NLJ 969, [2008] NPC 74, (2008) *Times*, July 8   3.2, 3.16, 3.18,
    3.20, 3.22, 3.24,
    3.25, 3.27, 3.28,
    3.29, 3.31, 3.39,
    3.43, 3.46, 7.32,
    7.35, 7.36, 7.39,
    7.47, 7.48, 7.49,
    7.58, 9.12, 9.72,
    9.95
R v Army Board of Defence Council ex p Anderson [1992]
QB 169, [1991] 3 WLR 42, [1991] 3 All ER 375, [1991]
ICR 537, [1991] IRLR 425, (1991) 3 Admin LR 297,
[1991] COD 191, (1990) *Guardian*, November 13   5.48
R v Board of Visitors of the Maze Prison Ex p Hone [1988]
AC 379, [1988] 2 WLR 177, [1988] 1 All ER 321,
(1988) 132 SJ 158, (1988) *Times*, January 22, (1988)
Independent, January 22, (1988) *Guardian*, January 22,
HL   5.21
R v Brent LBC ex p Morris (1998) 30 HLR 324, (1997) 74 P
& CR D29, CA   13.32

R v Gateshead MBC ex p Smith (1999) 31 HLR 97, QBD	13.32
R v Gloucestershire CC ex p Barry [1997] AC 584, [1997] 2 WLR 459, [1997] 2 All ER 1, (1997) 9 Admin LR 209, (1997–98) 1 CCLR 40, (1997) 36 BMLR 92, (1997) *Times*, March 21, (1997) *Independent*, April 9, [1997] COD 304, (1997) 94(14) LSG 25, (1997) 147 NLJ 453, (1997) 141 SJLB 91, HL	10.10
R v Hillingdon LBC ex p Puhlhofer [1986] AC 484, [1986] 2 WLR 259, [1986] 1 All ER 467, [1986] 1 FLR 22, (1986) 18 HLR 158, [1986] Fam Law 218, (1986) 83 LSG 785, (1986) 136 NLJ 140, (1986) 130 SJ 143, HL	7.40, 9.88
R v Inland Revenue Commissioners ex p National Federation of Self Employed and Small Businesses Ltd [1982] AC 617, [1981] 2 WLR 722, [1981] 2 All ER 93, [1981] STC 260, 55 TC 133, (1981) 125 SJ 325, HL	7.33, 13.51
R v Kirklees MBC ex p Daykin (1997–98) 1 CCLR 512, QBD	10.10
R v Newham LBC ex p Miah (deferring accommodation: rent arrears) (1996) 28 HLR 279, QBD	7.22
R v North and East Devon HA ex p Coughlan [1999] EWCA Civ 1871, [2001] QB 213, [2000] 2 WLR 622, [2000] 3 All ER 850, (2000) 2 LGLR 1, [1999] BLGR 703, (1999) 2 CCLR 285, [1999] Lloyd's Rep Med 306, (2000) 51 BMLR 1, [1999] COD 340, (1999) 96(31) LSG 39, (1999) 143 SJLB 213, (1999) *Times*, July 20, (1999) *Independent*, July 20	7.34
R v Northavon DC ex p Smith [1994] 2 AC 402, [1994] 3 WLR 403, [1994] 3 All ER 313, [1994] 2 FLR 671, [1994] 2 FCR 859, (1994) 26 HLR 659, 92 LGR 643, [1994] COD 492, [1995] Fam Law 16, (1994) 158 JPN 651, (1994) 158 LG Rev 990, (1994) 91(38) LSG 42, (1994) 144 NLJ 1010, (1994) 138 SJLB 178, [1994] NPC 113, (1994) *Times*, July 18, (1994) *Independent*, July 21, HL	7.4, 7.13
R v Secretary of State for the Environment ex p Hillingdon LBC [1986] 1 WLR 192, [1986] 1 All ER 810, (1986) 52 P & CR 409, [1987] RVR 6, (1985) *Times*, November 20, [1986] JPL 363, (1986) 83 LSG 525, (1986) 136 NLJ 16, (1986) 130 SJ 89, QBD	12.6
R v Servite Houses ex p Goldsmith (2001) 33 HLR 35, (2000) 2 LGLR 997, [2001] BLGR 55, (2000) 3 CCLR 325, [2001] ACD 4, QBD	3.42
R v West Dorset DC, West Dorset Housing Association ex p Gerrard (1995) 27 HLR 150, QBD	7.13
Rae v Meek (1889) 14 App Cas 558, (1889) 16 R (HL) 31, HL	12.56
Redfearn v United Kingdom (App No 47335/06) [2012] ECHR 1878, [2013] 3 Costs LO 402, [2013] IRLR 51, (2013) 57 EHRR 2, 33 BHRC 713, (2012) 162 NLJ 1466, (2013) *Times*, January 10, ECtHR	3.33

Regal (Hastings) Ltd v Gulliver [1967] 2 AC 134, [1942] 1 All
ER 378, HL   12.57
Ridge v Baldwin [1964] AC 40, [1963] 2 WLR 935, [1963]
2 All ER 66, (1963) 127 JP 295, (1963) 127 JP 251, 61
LGR 369, 37 ALJ 140, 234 LT 423, 113 LJ 716, (1963)
107 SJ 313, HL   5.48
Riverside Group Ltd v Thomas [2012] EWHC 169 (QB)   9.75
Riverside Housing Association Ltd v White [2007] UKHL
20, [2007] 4 All ER 97, [2007] HLR 31, [2008] 1 P & CR
13, [2007] L & TR 22, [2007] 2 EGLR 69, [2007] 29 EG
144, [2007] 18 EG 152 (CS), (2007) 104(19) LSG 25,
(2007) 151 SJLB 574, [2007] NPC 46, (2007) *Times*,
May 7   1.11, 1.12, 8.5,
                                                                              9.18
Robinson v Torbay BC [1982] 1 All ER 726, QBD   7.12
Rolled Steel Products (Holdings) Ltd v British Steel Corp
[1986] Ch 246, [1985] 2 WLR 908, [1985] 3 All ER 52,
(1984) 1 BCC 99158, CA   15.38
Rosemary Simmons Memorial Housing Association Ltd v
United Dominions Trust Ltd [1986] 1 WLR 1440, [1987]
1 All ER 281, (1987) 3 BCC 65, (1987) 19 HLR 108,
(1987) 84 LSG 112, (1986) 130 SJ 923, Ch D   15.37
Royal British Legion Housing Association Ltd v East
Midlands Rent Assessment Panel (1989) 21 HLR 482,
[1989] 23 EG 84, [1989] EG 7 (CS), QBD   9.16
RSPCA v Attorney General [2002] 1 WLR 448, [2001] 3 All
ER 530, [2001] UKHRR 905, (2001) 98(11) LSG 43,
(2001) *Times*, February 13, Ch D   11.28
Runa Begum v Tower Hamlets LBC [2003] UKHL 5, [2003]
2 AC 430, [2003] 2 WLR 388, [2003] 1 All ER 731, [2003]
HRLR 16, [2003] UKHRR 419, 14 BHRC 400, [2003]
HLR 32, [2003] BLGR 205, 2003 Hous LR 20, [2003]
ACD 41, (2003) 100(13) LSG 28, (2003) 147 SJLB
232, [2003] NPC 21, (2003) *Times*, February 17, (2003)
Independent, February 18   5.76, 9.80
Salomon v Salomon & Co Ltd [1897] AC 22, HL   15.36
Sanctuary Housing Association v Baker (No 1) (1998) 30
HLR 809, [1998] 1 EGLR 42, [1998] 09 EG 150, CA   9.39
Scott-Malden v Auriol Housing Association (1980)
unreported, 7 July, QBD   5.21
Scottish Cooperative Wholesale Society Ltd v Meyer [1959]
AC 324, [1958] 3 WLR 404, [1958] 3 All ER 66, 1958
SC (HL) 40, 1958 SLT 241, (1958) 102 SJ 617, HL
(Scotland)   15.41
Secretary of State for Work and Pensions v M [2006] UKHL
11, [2006] 2 AC 91, [2006] 2 WLR 637, [2006] 4 All ER
929, [2006] 2 FLR 56, [2006] 1 FCR 497, [2006] HRLR
19, [2006] UKHRR 799, 21 BHRC 254, [2006] Fam Law
524, (2006) 150 SJLB 363, (2006) *Times*, March 14   9.83

Smith, Re, Barclays Bank Ltd v Mercantile Bank Ltd and others [1962] 1 WLR 763, [1962] 2 All ER 563, (1962) 106 SJ 389, CA	2.32
Southend-on-Sea BC v Armour [2014] EWCA Civ 231, [2014] HLR 23, [2014] 2 P & CR DG7	9.74, 9.75
Spath Holme Ltd v Greater Manchester and Lancashire Rent Assessment Committee (No 1) (1996) 28 HLR 107, [1995] 2 EGLR 80, [1995] 49 EG 128, [1995] NPC 138, (1996) 71 P & CR D8, (1995) *Times*, August 9, (1995) *Independent*, August 28, CA	9.16
Speight v Gaunt (1883) 9 App Cas 1, HL	12.45
Sun Permanent Benefit Building Society v Western Suburban and Harrow Road Permanent Building Society (No 2) [1921] 2 Ch 438, CA	15.12
Tesco Stores Ltd v Secretary of State for the Environment [1995] 1 WLR 759, [1995] 2 All ER 636, 93 LGR 403, (1995) 70 P & CR 184, [1995] 2 PLR 72, [1995] 2 EGLR 147, [1995] 27 EG 154, [1995] EG 82 (CS), (1995) 92(24) LSG 39, (1995) 145 NLJ 724, (1995) 139 SJLB 145, (1995) *Times*, May 1, HL	4.60
Thurrock BC v West [2012] EWCA Civ 1435, [2013] HLR 5, [2013] 1 P & CR 12, [2013] L & TR 11, [2013] 1 P & CR DG9	9.75
Tomlinson v Birmingham City Council, *see* Ali and others v Birmingham City Council—	
Tsfayo v United Kingdom (App No 60860/00) (2009) 48 EHRR 18, [2007] HLR 19, [2007] BLGR 1, (2006) *Times*, November 23	9.80
Turner v Enfield LBC [2018] EWHC 1431 (QB)	9.75
Udovicic v Croatia (App No 27310/09) [2014] ECHR 443, ECtHR	3.33
Wandsworth LBC v Michalak [2002] EWCA Civ 271, [2003] 1 WLR 617, [2002] 4 All ER 1136, [2003] 1 FCR 713, [2002] HLR 39, [2002] NPC 34	9.83
West Kent Housing Association Ltd v Haycraft [2012] EWCA Civ 276, [2013] PTSR 141, [2012] HLR 23, [2012] BLGR 493, [2012] 2 EGLR 38, [2012] 21 EG 100, [2012] 12 EG 92 (CS), [2012] 1 P & CR DG23	9.75
Westminster City Council v Clarke [1992] 2 AC 288, [1992] 2 WLR 229, [1992] 1 All ER 695, (1992) 24 HLR 360, 90 LGR 210, (1992) 156 LG Rev 681, [1992] EG 13 (CS), (1992) 142 NLJ 196, (1992) 136 SJLB 82, [1992] NPC 18, (1992) *Times*, February 13, (1992) *Independent*, February 7, (1992) *Guardian*, February 12, HL	8.16
Woolfson v Strathclyde RC 1978 SC (HL) 90, 1978 SLT 159, (1979) 38 P & CR 521, (1978) 248 EG 777, [1979] JPL 169, HL (Scotland)	15.36, 15.39
X v Federal Republic of Germany (1956) 1 YB 202	7.52

YL v Birmingham City Council [2007] UKHL 27, [2008]
1 AC 95, [2007] 3 WLR 112, [2007] 3 All ER 957, [2007]
HRLR 32, [2008] UKHRR 346, [2007] HLR 44, [2008]
BLGR 273, (2007) 10 CCLR 505, [2007] LS Law Medical
472, (2007) 96 BMLR 1, (2007) 104(27) LSG 29, (2007)
157 NLJ 938, (2007) 151 SJLB 860, [2007] NPC 75,
(2007) *Times*, June 21   3.4, 3.5, 3.20,
                                                     3.21, 3.23, 3.26,
                                                     3.34, 7.35, 7.50,
                                                     9.95
Zenati v Commissioner of Police of the Metropolis [2015]
EWCA Civ 80, [2015] QB 758, [2015] 2 WLR 1563,
[2015] 4 All ER 735   10.23

Table of statutes

Abolition of the Right to Buy and Associated Rights (Wales) Act 2018	1.41, 9.69, 9.70	s136	6.16
		ss144–147	6.16
		s156	6.17
		s157	6.17
Anti-social Behaviour Act 2003	8.48	s160	6.11
		s165(1)	6.11, 13.50
Care Act 2014	10.9, 10.12	s169	13.46
Charities Act 1993–		s170	6.11, 13.50
s53	15.19	s171	13.50
s64(1)	15.19	s172	13.50
Charities Act 2011	2.18, 5.47, 6.16, 6.17, 12.13, 13.7	s185	12.62
		s191	12.54
		s197	5.69, 11.42, 15.19, 15.47
s3	2.27	s198	11.43, 12.62, 15.98
s3(1)	2.28		
s4	2.27	s353(1)	12.45
s14	6.9	Sch 3	6.10, 6.12, 6.14
s15(1)	6.9	Chronically Sick and Disabled Persons Act 1970	10.10
s22	6.12, 6.14		
s25	6.12		
s26	6.13	s2(1)(a)	10.10
s28	6.13	Commonhold and Leasehold Reform Act 2002	8.79
s30(2)	6.10		
s37	6.10	s141	8.73
s46	6.13	Companies (Audit, Investigations and Community Enterprise) Act 2004	2.16
s48	6.13		
s52	6.11		
s53	6.11		
s58	6.13	Companies Acts	14.105
s69	6.15	Companies Act 2006	2.7, 2.10, 2.14, 2.15, 11.37, 11.40, 12.13, 12.37, 12.42, 12.44, 12.61, 12.78, 13.7, 13.48, 15.29
s70(2)	6.15		
s70(4)	6.15		
s70(5)	6.15		
ss76–85	6.13		
s76(2)	6.9		
s105	14.35		
s110	12.54	s21	11.43, 15.12
ss130–135	6.16	s22	11.43, 15.12

Companies Act 2006 continued		Co-operative and Community Benefit Societies Act (CCBSA) 2014 continued	
s23	15.26		13.49, 13.50, 14.87, 14.93, 14.95, 14.98, 14.105, 14.118, 15.11, 15.47, 15.48, 15.50
s31	2.15		
s114	13.48		
s116	6.8		
s154(1)	10.26		
s162	6.8		
ss170–173	12.37		
s174	12.38		
s175	12.37, 12.61	s2	2.9, 6.5
s177	12.61	s2(2)(b)	11.26
s178(2)	12.38	s2(2)(c)	11.26
s179	12.55	s3(1)	6.2
s181(4)	12.61	s3(1)(a)	11.26
ss182–185	12.61	s3(2)	2.9
s232	12.55	s5	2.9
s233	12.55	s5(3)(b)	11.26
s251	12.41	s11	14.35
Part 11	12.51	s14	11.26, 11.37, 12.6
s275	6.8		
s382	13.48	s15(2)	11.38
s384A	13.48	s16	6.3
s384B	13.48	s16(1)	11.38, 15.11
s465	13.48	s16(4)(a)	15.11
s994	11.44, 11.45, 12.51	s18	13.49
		s24(1)	15.26
s1085	6.8	s24(2)	2.13
s1086	6.8	s24(2)(a)	15.26
s1112	6.8	s24(2)(b)	2.55, 15.26
s1157	12.54	s24(2)(c)	2.55, 15.26
Company Directors Disqualification Act 1986	5.47, 12.16	s30(2)	11.38
		s30(7)	11.38
s22E	12.16	s32	15.26
Co-operative and Community Benefit Societies Act (CCBSA) 2014	2.7, 2.8, 2.9, 2.10, 2.12, 2.14, 2.16, 2.18, 2.22, 2.34, 2.35, 2.43, 2.55, 4.17, 4.18, 4.23, 4.29, 5.50, 5.52, 5.54, 5.58, 5.66, 5.68, 5.69, 5.70, 5.72, 6.2, 6.3, 6.10, 6.16, 6.17, 11.3, 11.38, 11.45, 12.6, 12.42–12.44, 12.75, 13.6, 13.7, 13.8, 13.15, 13.48,	s43	11.40
		s43(1)	12.10
		s43(2)	12.11
		s43(4)	12.11
		s43(5)	12.12
		s44	11.40, 12.12
		s45	12.6, 12.10
		s46	12.10
		s47	12.10
		s59(4)	13.49
		s75	11.38
		s81	11.38, 13.49
		s83	11.38
		s84	13.7
		s87	11.38
		s89	6.2
		s90	13.49
		s91	13.9

Table of statutes xxvii

Co-operative and Community Benefit Societies Act (CCBSA) 2014 *continued*	
s92	13.9
s103	11.38, 13.49
s105(1)–(6)	6.6
s106	6.6
s106(6)	6.6
s108	13.49
ss110–113	5.70
s111	11.34
s111(2)(a)	15.12
s111(2)(b)	15.12
s112	11.34, 15.17
s113	15.17
s115	15.13
s117	15.17
s118(3)	15.50
s119	11.34, 15.48
s119(4)(b)	15.48
s119(6)	15.48
s120(2)	15.48
s121	6.3
s122	6.3, 20.49
s123	15.47
s124(2)	15.47
s125(2)	15.50
s126	6.4, 20.49
s134	2.14
s135	2.14
s144	11.34
s223	12.44
Corporation Tax Act (CTA) 2010–	
s2	14.93
ss466–493	14.89
s478	14.93
s485	14.93
ss491A–496	14.93
ss642–657	14.90, 14.95
s642	14.95
s642(2)–(4)	14.96
s643	14.96, 14.112
s645	14.95
s651(1)	14.97
s652	14.97, 14.112
s657	14.98
s1284	14.102
Criminal Law Act 1977–	
s12A(6)	9.6
s12A(6)(a)	9.6
s12A(7)(d)	9.6

Data Protection Act 1998	4.72, 7.23
Deregulation Act 2015	8.26
s108	4.43
Disability Discrimination Act 1995–	
s49A	10.18
Equality Act (EA) 2010	7.55–7.61
s4	7.58
s32	7.58
s33(3)	7.58
s33(4)	7.58
s34	7.58
s35	7.58
Sch 19	7.56
Finance Act 1965	14.88, 14.114
s93	14.88
Finance Act 2000–	
s79(1)(b)	14.113
Finance Act 2003–	
Sch 9	1.58
Fraud Act 2006	8.55
Freedom of Information Act 2000	3.7, 4.73, 7.23, 13.47
s2	4.73
s44	4.73
Greater London Authority Act 1999–	
s333ZG	4.75
Health and Social Care Act 2008–	
s1	6.18
s3	6.18
s4(1)	6.19
Sch 1	6.18
Homelessness Act 2002	7.12
s16	6.18
Housing (Wales) Act 2014	2.21, 3.6, 9.4, 9.13
s4	9.4
s5	9.4
s6	9.4
s8	9.4
Pt 4 (ss111–130)	9.4
s137	8.36, 9.13
s138	8.36, 9.13
s267	4.83
Housing Act 1935–	
s26	2.2

Housing Act 1964	1.15, 12.64, 14.88	Housing Act 1985 *continued*	
		s143	9.51
Housing Act 1974	1.16, 12.64	s171(2)	3.6, 8.78
Housing Act 1980	1.17, 7.2, 8.39, 8.67	ss171A–171H	9.52
		s171A(3)	9.55
s140	8.92	s171B	9.53
Housing Act 1985	2.56, 7.2, 7.21, 8.12, 8.40, 8.48, 9.4, 9.9, 13.29, 13.40	s171B(6)	9.57
		s171B(7)	9.70
		s171D	9.56
		s171D(2ZA)	9.54
s6	2.37, 8.78	s171E	9.56
s8(1)	7.1	s171F	9.57
s9(5)	7.1	s172	8.62
s10	9.50	s174	8.58
s27B	8.40	s429A	3.6
s32	2.58	s554(2A)	8.40
s34	2.58	s622	8.21
s34A	2.58	Sch 1 para 1	8.58
Pt IV (ss79–117)	13.26	Sch 1 para 12	8.16
s79(1)	8.16	Sch 2	9.8
s80(2)	8.33, 8.34	Sch 2 Pt II ground 10	9.38
s85(3)	8.33		
s91	9.37	Sch 2 Pt II ground 10A	9.9
s92	9.37		
s104	13.35	Sch 2 Pt II ground 11	9.8
s105(1)–(7)	13.33		
s105(1)	13.26	Sch 2 Pt III ground 14	9.8
s105(2)	13.28, 13.30		
s105(3)	13.28, 13.31	Sch 2 Pt V para 6	9.9
s105(6)	13.39		
s106	7.21, 7.33, 7.45	Sch 3	9.38
		Sch 3A	2.58, 3.7
s106(1)	7.22, 8.67	Sch 4 paras 6–10	3.6
s106(2)	7.22	Sch 5 paras 1–3	9.52
s106(4)	7.22	Sch 5 para 2	8.33, 9.49
ss107A–107E	8.46	Sch 5 para 3	9.49
s107C	8.46	Sch 5 para 11	9.50
s107D	8.46	Housing Act 1988	1.20, 1.21, 8.4, 8.18, 8.19, 8.39, 8.41, 8.61, 9.4, 14.51
s107E	8.46		
s109	13.25		
s114(1)	7.21		
s115	8.58	s1	8.19
s115(2)	8.58, 8.89	s1(3)	8.39
s118	9.49	s1(5)	8.36, 8.39
s119(A1)	9.63	s6A	8.48
s119(1)	9.63	s13	9.17
s121ZA	9.70	s13(1)(b)	9.18
s121ZB	9.70	s14	9.17
s122A	9.63	s15(1)	9.39
s122B	9.63	s15A	8.56
s136	.9.57	s17(1A)–(1E)	9.32

Table of statutes   xxix

Housing Act 1988 continued	
s17(1E)(b)	9.32
s17(7)	9.33
s19A	8.26, 9.43
s20	9.43
s20B	8.48
s20C	8.48, 8.49
s21	8.26
s21(1A)	8.47
s21(1B)	8.26, 8.47
s21D	8.53
s22(4)	8.26
s35	8.13
s35(2)	8.19
s35(2)(b)	8.40
s35(4)	8.13, 8.19
s35(5)	2.25, 8.40
s36	8.18
s37(1)	8.39
s38	3.7, 8.13
s38(1)	8.39
s38(2)	8.39
s38(3)	8.39
s54	14.90
s91(2)	8.56
s93(2)	8.56
s127	9.52
s127(3)	9.52
Sch 1 para 3	8.20
Sch 1 para 3A	8.20, 8.59
Sch 1 para 3B	8.20, 8.59
Sch 1 para 12(1)(h)	8.36
Sch 1 para 12ZA	8.50
Sch 2	9.10
Sch 2 Pt I ground 2A	9.13
Sch 2 Pt I ground 6	9.10
Sch 2 Pt I ground 8	9.11, 9.12
Sch 2 Pt II ground 10	9.11
Sch 2 Pt II ground 11	9.11
Sch 2 Pt II ground 14A	9.10
Sch 2A	8.26
Sch 18 para 4(a)	8.13
Sch 18 para 4(c)	8.13
Housing Act 1996	1.22, 1.65, 2.21, 2.24, 4.14, 4.29,

Housing Act 1996 continued	
	4.30, 4.31, 4.36, 4.82, 5.71, 5.82, 8.27, 9.4, 9.59, 12.71, 12.79, 12.80, 12.81, 13.53, 13.59, 14.63
s1A	4.18, 4.29
s2(1)	4.29
s2(2)	4.29
s2(3)	4.29
s2(4)	4.29
s2(5)	4.30
s2(7)	4.31
s2A	4.29
s3(1)	4.28
s5	4.32
s6A	5.78
s8	5.57
s9	5.60
s9(2)	5.61
s16	9.58
s16(1)(a)	8.73
s16(2)	9.59
s17(1)(a)	9.60
s17(1)(b)	9.60
s22	2.55
s33A	4.47, 4.83, 9.4
s33B	4.49, 4.84
s33C	4.61
s34	4.83
s35(A1)	5.77
s35(1)	5.77
s35A	5.79
s35B	4.84
s36	4.84
s37	5.7
ss39–50	5.82, 15.61
s44(5)	15.62
s44(6)	15.62
s50A	5.80
s51	13.53
s57(2)	12.81
s60	2.21
s61	2.21
s61(1)	12.79
s62(2)	12.79
s63	4.29, 8.73
s96(1)	8.27
s124(1)	8.41

Housing Act 1996 continued	
s159	7.18
s159(2)–(4)	7.18
s166A	7.12
s167	7.12
s170	2.55, 3.5, 7.4, 7.12
Pt VII (ss175–218)	7.13
s213	2.55
s213(1)	7.13
s213(2)	2.24, 7.13
s219	9.21
s220	9.21
Sch 1	4.82, 12.64, 12.65, 12.77
Sch 1 Pt I	12.78
Sch 1 para 1(3)	12.77
Sch 1 para 2(4)	12.77
Sch 1 Pt III	4.83
Sch 1 Pt IIIA	5.80
Sch 1 Pt IV	5.15, 5.18
Sch 2	13.53
Sch 3 para 19	14.116
Sch 7	8.27
Housing Act 2004	1.23, 3.6
s181	9.50
Housing and Planning Act 1986	8.74, 8.93
s8	9.52
s9	13.18
Sch 4	8.72, 8.74
Sch 4 Pt 2	15.19
Housing and Planning Act 2016	1.36, 1.42, 1.51, 2.20, 2.59, 3.13, 3.46, 4.21, 4.39, 4.48, 4.50, 4.82, 5.5, 5.21, 5.71, 7.25, 8.6, 8.19, 8.32, 8.92, 9.44, 9.62, 14.35, 14.44, 14.103, 15.18, 15.47, 15.51
s17(4)	9.31
ss69–76	1.51
ss89–90	1.51
ss95–117	5.71
s95(1)(b)	15.51
s96	15.53
s99(1)	15.51

Housing and Planning Act 2016 continued	
s100(2)	15.52
s100(3)	15.52
s103	15.55
s104	15.58
s105	15.57
s106	15.58
s118	8.26, 8.30
s120	8.12
s199	5.7
Sch 1	9.54
Sch 4	5.55, 5.58, 8.93
Sch 4 paras 33–35	5.65
Sch 4 para 36	5.51
Sch 4 para 38	5.15
Sch 8	9.31
Housing and Regeneration Act (HRA) 2008	1.57, 2.20, 2.29, 2.30, 4.4, 4.7, 4.8, 4.9, 4.14, 4.22, 4.39, 4.41, 5.15, 5.28, 5.30, 5.31, 5.37, 7.61, 7.65, 8.74, 9.14, 9.19, 9.51, 12.67, 14.5
s19	7.3, 14.4–14.8, 14.9
s19(1)	14.4
s19(1A)	4.75
s19(2)	14.4
s19(3)	14.5
s19(4)	14.5
s31	14.5
s31(4)	7.4
s31(6)	7.4
s31(8)	7.4
s36A	4.9
s40	4.48
s40(5)	4.60
Pt 2 (ss59–278A)	7.63, 12.65
s60(3)	2.24
s61	4.14
ss68–76	4.17
ss68–77	1.58
s69	5.69
s70	8.64, 8.96
s70(4)	8.67
s71	14.61
s72	1.59

Housing and Regeneration Act (HRA) 2008 *continued*		Housing and Regeneration Act (HRA) 2008 *continued*	
s73	1.59	s160	5.67
s74	1.59	s161	5.67
s74A	1.59	s163	5.67
s76	1.59	s165	5.67
s77	4.17	s169A	5.67
s79	4.17	s169B	5.67
s79(1)(e)	4.34	s171(1)	5.57
s79(2)	2.50	s171(2)	8.14, 8.40
s80	4.22	s176	5.58
s80A	4.7	s179	2.24
s80B	4.8	ss180–191	9.58
s80C	4.8	s180(2)(a)	8.73
s80D	4.8	s181	9.59
s92K	4.42	s184	2.24, 9.60
s94(1)	11.25	s188	9.58
s96	4.60	s189	9.58
s98	4.64	s193	4.45
s100F	4.9	s193(3)	4.55
s107	5.8, 5.12	s194	4.45
s108	5.8, 5.12	s194(1A)	11.25
s109	4.72	s194(3)	4.55
s109(4)	5.30	s195	4.45
s110	5.70	s196	4.60
s111(2)	13.47	s197	4.58
s112	2.51, 4.16, 4.22	s198	5.69
s112(4)	4.24, 4.63	s198A	4.81, 7.63, 13.58
s113	2.56, 4.19	s198A(2)	4.52
s114	2.56, 4.19	s198A(5)	4.52
s115	2.26, 4.25	s198A(6)	4.60, 7.65
s115(8)	4.26	ss201–203	5.10
s116	4.22	s201	5.7
s117	4.27	s202	5.13
s118	4.35	s204	5.77
s119	4.35	s205	4.66, 5.77
s120	6.7	s206	5.7, 5.14, 5.18
s121	4.36	s207	5.22
s122	12.65, 12.66	s208	4.55, 5.21
s122(6)	12.67	s209	5.16
s122(7)	12.67	s210	5.14
s122(8)	12.67	s215	4.48
s124	2.24, 13.53	s216	4.60
s125	4.57	s216(4)	4.60
s126	2.55	s217	5.43
s128	4.74, 13.5	ss219–225	5.31
s131	13.9	s220(12)	5.31
s133	13.7	s223	5.34
s134	13.7	s224	5.33
s139	13.7	s225(1)	5.35
s141	13.8	s225(2)	5.31

Housing and Regeneration Act (HRA) 2008 continued		Housing and Regeneration Act (HRA) 2008 continued	
s225(3)	5.31	s278A	4.63
s226	5.69	s294	2.58
s227	5.36	s295	2.56
s228	5.37	s297(2)	8.50
s229	5.37	s297(4)	8.52
s230	5.38	s297(5)	8.52
s231	5.38	s297(7)	8.52
s233	5.37	s298	8.52
s234	5.37	s300	8.62
s235	5.37	s302	8.86
ss237–245	5.39	Housing Associations Act (HAA) 1985	4.29
s239	5.39, 13.58		
s241	5.39	s1	2.1, 2.43
s242	5.39, 13.8	s1(1)	14.95
s243	13.8	s1(2)	2.42, 12.66
s247	5.41	s1(3)	2.49, 14.97
s249	5.41	s9	4.21
s250(4)(c)	5.41	s35	2.41
s251	5.41	s36	2.41
s252	5.41	s42(1)	7.3
s253	5.52	s54	14.114, 14.115
s253(3)	5.53	s58	2.55
s253(4)	5.53	s59(2)	2.55
s254	5.52	Housing Corporation (Delegation) etc Act 2006	4.59
s255	5.54		
s256	5.26		
s257	5.44, 5.27	Housing Finance Act 1972	12.64
s258	5.28		
s260	5.45	Housing, Town Planning etc Act 1909	2.2
s260(5)	5.45		
s261	5.46	Human Rights Act (HRA) 1998	1.10, 3.8, 3.14–3.47, 5.28, 7.46–7.54, 8.55, 8.94, 9.12, 9.68, 9.71, 9.72, 9.75, 9.83
s262	5.46		
s262(5)	5.46		
s263	5.46		
s264	5.46		
s265	5.46		
s266	5.47		
s267	5.47	s3	3.33
s268	5.49	s6	3.39
s269	5.51	s6(1)	3.14, 3.34
s269(2)	5.51	s6(3)(b)	3.15
s269(6)	5.50	s6(5)	3.15
s270	5.44, 5.48, 13.8	s7	3.34
s271	2.48, 5.8, 15.24	s7(1)	3.14
s272	12.68	s7(1)(b)	3.34
s272(2)	12.69	s7(7)	3.34
s273	5.61	Immigration and Asylum Act 1999	3.5, 7.14
s274	5.16, 5.50		
s275	4.50, 5.15	s100(1)	7.14

Table of statutes xxxiii

Immigration and Asylum
  Act 1999 *continued*
  s100(2)   7.14
  s100(3)   7.14
  Sch 4 para 73   7.14
  Sch 4 para 88   7.14
Income and Corporation Taxes
  Act 1988–
  s505(3)   14.93
  s505(4)   14.93
Income Tax (Trading and Other
  Income) Act 2005–
  s5   14.93
Income Tax Act (ITA) 2007–
  ss521–536   14.89
  s524   14.93
  s528   14.93
  s531   14.93
  s536   14.93
  s644(6)   14.95
Industrial and Provident Societies
  Acts (IPSA)   2.7
Industrial and Provident Societies
  Act 1965–
  s1(2)   2.16
Inheritance Tax Act 1984–
  s24A   14.116
Insolvency Act 1986   12.44, 13.48,
                      15.52, 15.55
  s72G   15.50
  s214   12.40
  Sch 1B   15.55
  Sch 2   15.60
  Sch 5   15.55, 15.59
  Sch 6   15.59
Land Compensation
  Act 1973   7.15
  s29(d)   7.15
  s39   7.15
Land Registration Act 2002–
  s3   8.29
  s7   8.29
  s24   8.29
  s33   8.29
  s132   8.29
Landlord and Tenant (Covenants)
  Act 1995   9.47
  s28(1)   9.47
Landlord and Tenant Act
  1954   8.59, 8.61
  s2(1)   8.59

Landlord and Tenant
  Act 1987   8.79
  s8(1)   8.79
  s11(4)   8.79
  s25(5)(a)   8.79
Landlord and Tenant Act 1988–
  s1   9.39
Law of Property Act 1925–
  s52   8.29
  s149(6)   8.25, 9.35
Leasehold Reform Act
  (LRA) 1967   8.24, 8.62,
                  8.72, 8.73, 8.74,
                  8.75, 8.76, 8.77,
                  8.85, 8.86, 8.91,
                  8.92
  s1(3)   8.76
  s1(3A)   8.76
  s301   8.74
  s312   8.74
  Sch 4A   8.72, 8.74,
                  8.93
  Sch 4A para 2   8.75
  Sch 4A para 3A 8.74
  Sch 4A para 4A 8.74
Leasehold Reform, Housing
  and Urban Development
  Act (LRHUDA)
  1993   3.6, 8.62, 8.72,
                  8.74, 8.76, 8.77,
                  8.78, 8.85, 8.91,
                  9.51
  s2(5)   8.78
  s5(2)   8.78
  s7   8.78
  s38   8.78
  s67   8.76
  s107   8.76, 8.78
  Sch 9 para 2   8.78
  Sch 9 para 3   8.78
  Sch 10 para 2   8.78
Legislative and Regulatory Reform
  Act 2006   4.7, 4.38, 4.39
  s22   4.43
Local Authority Social Services Act
  1970–
  s7(1)   10.10
Local Democracy, Economic
  Development and
  Construction Act 2009–
  s26(2)   4.63

Local Government Act 1972–		National Health Service	
s101(1)	12.81	Act 2006	14.85
Local Government Act 1988–		National Health Service and Community Care	
s24	3.7		
Local Government Act 2000–		Act 1990	10.10
s2	2.55	s47	10.10
Local Government Act 2003–		Prevention of Social Housing Fraud	
s87(1)	9.67	Act 2013	8.54, 8.55
Local Government and Housing Act (LGHA) 1989–		Protection from Eviction Act 1977	7.14, 9.6
Pt V (ss67–73)	13.15	s3	9.6
s67	13.15	s3A	9.6
s68	13.16	s5(1B)	9.6
s68(1)(d)	13.16	Public Services Ombudsman (Wales)	
s68(6)	13.16	Act 2005	3.6, 5.79, 13.59
s69(5)	13.17		
s69(6)	13.17	Regulation of Registered Social Landlords (Wales)	
s69	13.16		
s70	13.15	Act 2018	1.36, 2.21, 2.59, 3.13, 4.14, 4.21, 4.50, 4.82, 5.5, 5.15, 5.56, 5.67, 5.82, 12.35, 13.18, 14.35, 14.44, 15.18
s72	13.15		
s186	8.60		
Sch 10	8.60, 8.61, 8.90		
Sch 11	8.13		
Localism Act 2011	1.65, 2.20, 4.5, 4.39, 4.42, 4.66, 4.82, 8.6, 8.19, 8.29, 8.49, 9.32, 9.33, 9.41, 9.43, 12.67, 14.14	ss6–12	5.15
		s10	4.50
		ss13–15	5.60
		Rent Act 1977	8.17, 8.34, 8.35, 8.74, 8.91, 9.15, 9.16, 14.63
ss1–7	2.55		
s154	8.46, 9.7		
s156	8.29	s5	8.59
s157	8.29	s5A	8.74
s158	9.41	s15	8.17, 9.15
s159	9.42	s15(3)(d)	8.34
s163	8.53	s16	2.43, 8.17, 9.15
s180	13.53, 13.54, 13.57	s18(2)	12.35
		s19	8.18
Sch 14	9.42	s86	8.17, 9.15
Sch 16 para 69	4.17	s86(2)	8.34
Sch 17	4.41	s86(3)	8.34
Sch 17 para 9	7.63	s86(3A)	2.52
Sch 17 para 12	5.77	s87	8.17, 8.59, 9.15
Sch 17 para 13	4.66, 5.77		
Sch 25 Pt 27	4.66	Renting Homes (Wales)	
Mental Capacity Act		Act 2016	2.21, 8.9, 8.10, 8.43, 9.4
2005	10.29	s2	8.10
National Assistance Act		Senior Courts Act 1981–	
1948	10.10		
s29	10.10	s31	13.51

Table of statutes   xxxv

Settled Land Act 1925–		Trustee Act 2000	12.47, 12.55
s71	14.35	s1	12.46, 12.47
Statistics and Registration Service		s2	12.47
|Act 2007	3.10	s11(3)	12.9
s9	3.10	s11(3)(c)	12.9
s17	3.10	s23	12.9
Taxation of Chargeable Gains		s24	12.13
Act (TCGA)		Sch 1	12.47
1992	14.105, 14.106	Welfare Reform and Work Act (WRWA)	
s1	14.105	2016	5.41, 9.19, 9.20, 14.47, 14.49, 14.50, 14.61
s145(2)	14.110		
s171	14.117		
s256	14.106	s23	1.28, 9.19, 14.59
s256(2)(b)	14.106	s23(1)	14.59, 14.60
s258(2)	14.110	s23(2)	14.60
s259	14.111	s23(3)	14.60
s259A	14.111	s23(6)	14.60
s486(8)	14.118	s23(6)(b)	14.49
Town and Country Planning Act		s24	9.19, 14.61
1990–		s24(2)–(4)	14.62
s106	15.55	s25(1)–(6)	14.67
Trustee Act 1925–		s28	9.19, 9.20
s25	12.9	s30	9.19
s61	12.54	s31	14.49

Table of statutory instruments

Charitable Incorporated Organisations
 (Consequential Amendments) Order 2017
 SI No 1231 — 2.18
Civil Procedure Rules 1998 SI No 3132—
 r54.1 — 3.41
Housing (Exclusion of Shared Ownership
 Tenancies from the Leasehold Reform Act
 1967) Regulations 1982 SI No 62—
 reg 2 — 8.92
Housing (Preservation of Right to Buy)
 (Amendment) Regulations 1999 SI No
 1213 — 9.52
Housing (Preservation of Right to Buy)
 Regulations 1993 SI No 2241 — 9.52, 9.63
Housing (Right to Acquire) Regulations 1997 SI
 No 619 — 9.63
 Sch 1 para 29 — 8.58
Housing (Right to Enfranchise) (Designated
 Protected Areas) (England) Order 2009 SI
 No 2098 — 8.86
Housing (Right to Manage) (England)
 Regulations 2012 SI No 1821 — 2.56
Housing (Shared Ownership Leases) (Exclusion
 from Leasehold Reform Act 1967)
 (England) Regulations 2009 SI No 2097—
 reg 8 — 8.86
 reg 9 — 8.86
 reg 10 — 8.86
 Sch 4A para 3A — 8.74
 Sch 4A para 4A — 8.74
Housing (Wales) Measure 2011 nawm 5 — 2.21, 4.14, 4.65, 4.82, 5.78, 5.81
 ss1–6 — 9.63
 s5(4) — 9.67
 s27 — 9.66
 s29 — 9.65
 s30 — 9.66
 s33 — 9.64

Housing (Wales) Measure 2011 nawm 5
    s33(2)   1.67
    s33(4)   1.67
    Pt 2 Ch 2 (s41)   5.78
Housing (Wales) Measure 2011 (Consequential Amendments to Subordinate Legislation) Order 2012 SI No 2090 (W 240)   9.63
Housing and Regeneration Act 2008 (Consequential Provisions) Order 2010 SI No 866—
    Sch 2 para 2(4)   7.13
Housing and Regeneration Act 2008 (Registration of Local Authorities) Order 2010 SI No 844   2.56, 4.19
Housing Association Shared Ownership Leases (Exclusion from Leasehold Reform Act 1967 and Rent Act 1977) Regulations 1987 SI No 1940—
    reg 2   8.74
    reg 3   8.74
    Sch 2   8.93
Insolvency of Registered Providers of Social Housing Regulations 2018 SI No 728   15.51
Large and Medium-sized Companies and Groups (Accounts and Reports) Regulations 2008 SI No 410—
    Sch 7 para 10   13.48
    Sch 7 para 11   13.48
Legislative Reform (Regulator of Social Housing) (England) Order 2018 SI No 1040   1.39, 4.75
    Sch para 49   4.8, 4.13
Local Authorities (Capital Finance) (Amendment) Regulations 1998 SI No 371   14.41
Public Contracts Regulations 2015 SI No 102   3.49, 3.51
Regulation of Social Housing (Influence of Local Authorities) (England) Regulations 2017 SI No 1102   2.59, 3.12, 13.19, 13.23
    reg 1(3)   13.19
    reg 2(c)   13.20
    reg 3(1)   13.20
    reg 3(2)   13.21
    reg 3(3)   13.21
    reg 3(4)   13.21
    reg 3(5)   13.20
    reg 4   13.21
    reg 5   13.22
    reg 6   13.23
Social Housing Rents (Exceptions and Miscellaneous Provisions) (Amendment) Regulations 2017 SI No 91   9.23, 14.65
    reg 4(1)   14.84

Social Housing Rents (Exceptions and Miscellaneous Provisions) Regulations 2016 SI No 390	14.63
reg 2	14.63, 14.77, 14.78, 14.85
reg 3(1)	14.63
reg 3(1)(a)	14.63
reg 3(2)	14.64
reg 19	9.24
Social Landlords (Additional Purposes or Objects) Order 1999 SI No 985	4.31
Social Landlords (Additional Purposes or Objects) (No 2) Order 1999 SI No 1206	4.31
Social Landlords (Permissible Additional Purposes or Objects) Order 1996 SI No 2256	4.31
Transfer of Tenancies and Right to Acquire (Exclusion) Regulations 2012 SI No 696	9.43
reg 2	1.62, 1.63
reg 3	9.43, 9.61

Table of European and international legislation

Directive 2009/101/EC of the European Parliament and of the Council of 16 September 2009 on coordination of safeguards which, for the protection of the interests of members and third parties, are required by Member States of companies within the meaning of the second paragraph of Article 48 of the Treaty, with a view to making such safeguards equivalent–
    Art 2   13.48

Directive 2013/34/EU of the European Parliament and of the Council of 26 June 2013 on the annual financial statements, consolidated financial statements and related reports of certain types of undertakings, amending Directive 2006/43/EC of the European Parliament and of the Council and repealing Council Directives 78/660/EEC and 83/349/EEC–
    Art 19(2)   13.48

Directive 2014/23/EU of the European Parliament and of the Council of 26 February 2014 on the award of concession contracts   3.49

Directive 2014/24/EU of the European Parliament and of the Council of 26 February 2014 on public procurement and repealing Directive 2004/18/EC   3.49

European Convention on the Protection of Human Rights and Fundamental Freedoms 1951 (ECHR)   3.14, 3.16, 3.33, 3.34, 3.39, 7.46, 7.53, 7.54, 9.78, 9.79, 9.82, 9.83, 10.30, 12.50

    Art 1   10.30
    Art 3   9.82
    Art 5   9.78, 10.23
    Art 5(1)   10.23

European Convention on the Protection of Human
   Rights and Fundamental Freedoms 1951
   (ECHR) Art 6   4.10, 4.11, 4.51,
                                                     5.21, 5.48, 5.75,
                                                     5.76, 7.51, 9.75,
                                                     9.79, 9.81, 9.83,
                                                     12.50
   Art 8   2.30, 3.33, 3.35,
                                                     7.52, 7.53, 9.12,
                                                     9.72, 9.73, 9.74,
                                                     9.75, 9.76, 9.77,
                                                     9.78, 9.82, 9.83
   Art 9   9.82
   Art 10   9.82
   Art 11   9.82
   Art 14   3.33, 7.53, 9.83
   Art 34   3.34
   Protocol 1 Art 1   9.82
   Protocol 1 Art 2   9.68, 9.82
Maastricht Treaty 1992 (Treaty on the European Union)   3.48
Treaty of Rome 1957 (Treaty establishing the European
   Economic Community, EEC Treaty)–
   Art 85   13.13

Abbreviations

AGM	annual general meeting
ALMO	arms-length management organisation
AHP	Affordable Housing Programme
BC	Borough Council
CBS	community benefit society
CCBS	co-operative and community benefit society
CCBSA 2014	Co-operative and Community Benefits Societies Act 2014
CCG	clinical commissioning group
CIO	charitable incorporated organisation
CLT	community land trust
CPI	Consumer Price Index
CPO	compulsory possession order
CQC	Care Quality Commission
CSPL	Committee on Standards in Public Life
CTA 2010	Corporation Tax Act 2010
DCLG	Department for Communities and Local Government
DOLS	deprivation of liberty safeguards
DPF	Disposal Proceeds Fund
DPP	Director of Public Prosecutions
EA 2010	Equality Act 2010
ECHR	European Convention on Human Rights
EHRC	Equality and Human Rights Commission
FCA	Financial Conduct Authority
FIT	family intervention tenancy
FOIA 2000	Freedom of Information Act 2000
GLA	Greater London Authority
HAA 1985	Housing Associations Act 1985
HAG	Housing Association Grant
HAO	housing administration order
HCA	Homes and Communities Agency
HIST	high income social tenant
HRA 1998	Human Rights Act 1998
HRA 2008	Housing and Regeneration Act 2008
HRP	household reference person
HSE	Health and Safety Executive
IDA	in-depth assessment

IPSA	Industrial and Provident Societies Act
ITA 2007	Income Tax Act 2007
LBC	London Borough Council
LGHA 1989	Local Government and Housing Act 1989
LHA	Local Housing Allowance
LRHUDA 1993	Leasehold Reform, Housing and Urban Development Act 1993
LRA 1967	Leasehold Reform Act 1967
LRA 2002	Leasehold Reform Act 2002
LSVT	Large Scale Voluntary Transfer
MBC	Metropolitan Borough Council
MHCLG	Ministry of Housing, Communities and Local Government
NHF	National Housing Federation
OBR	Office of Budgetary Responsibility
ONS	Office for National Statistics
OTSL	Office for Tenants and Social Landlords
PFI	private finance initiative
PRP	private registered provider
PSED	public sector equality duty
quango	quasi-autonomous non-governmental organisation
RCGF	Recycled Capital Grant Fund
RP	registered provider of social housing
RPI	Retail Price Index
RSH	Regulator of Social Housing
RSL	registered social landlord
RTB	right to buy
RTE	right to enfranchise
SHG	Social Housing Grant
SOAHP	Shared Ownership and Affordable Homes Programme
TAP	Tenant Advisory Panel
TCC	Technology and Construction Court
TCGA 1992	Taxation of Chargeable Gains Act 1992
TMO	tenant management organisation
TSA	Tenant Services Authority
WRWA 2016	Welfare Reform and Work Act 2016

PART 1

General principles

CHAPTER 1

Introduction: the scope of housing association law

1.1 Housing associations: background
1.8 Housing association law?
1.14 Historical development
1.27 Current policy trends
1.27 Austerity: rents and benefits
1.34 Public or private – classification and declassification as public bodies: a continuing merry-go-round
1.38 Regulation: renaming, then splitting, the Homes and Communities Agency – further musical chairs
1.40 The deepening housing crisis
1.43 Grenfell Tower disaster and housing standards
1.47 The housing green paper
1.52 Brexit

1.57 **The meaning of 'social housing' and related concepts**
1.57 'Social housing'
1.60 Related concepts
1.67 Social housing in Wales

Housing associations: background

1.1 The concept of a 'housing association' is very wide. Essentially it means any non-profit body that includes housing or housing-related services among its objects or powers. There are about 1,600 housing associations in England and Wales, of varying sizes, types and origins. Some date back to the medieval period. Many have Victorian beginnings as model dwelling societies, 'five per cent philanthropy' bodies and charities. Others were formed in the 1960s and 70s in the aftermath of the *Cathy come home* film about homelessness first shown by the BBC in 1966. More recent formations are the result of stock transfers of local authority housing ('Large Scale Voluntary Transfers' (LSVTs)) and the political movement of black, Asian and minority ethnic associations during the late 1980s and early 1990s. A further strand is that of housing co-operatives, which has developed on a small scale alongside the movement more generally.

1.2 The story of this sector as it has developed and evolved demonstrates that housing associations are great survivors: they are incredibly malleable, they have strong perseverance and staying power capable of weathering even the most damaging political and economic storms. They have changed their shape and size, but fundamentally they are still organisations which at their root meet housing need. They have developed and evolved commercially in order to direct resources – no matter how earned, whether through grant, private finance or profiteering – to that fundamental cause of meeting need. Hence, the housing association journey can be seen as an enduring success story.

1.3 The sector owns some three million homes, housing more than six million people (it supports many more bearing in mind its wider customer base providing care and other services beyond housing). It comprises some 65 per cent of social housing stock,[1] and employs some 300,000 people. Additionally, the sector contributes some £20bn to the UK economy annually, has over £143bn of assets and builds on average some 42,000 new homes each year,[2] although this dropped to below 30,000 during 2016/17. Against this, however, approximately 18,000 homes per year are sold off from the sector.

1.4 Housing associations rent at below market levels and at market levels, and sell homes outright and by way of various 'low-cost home

---

1 National Housing Federation (NHF), *Key statistics briefing*, 11 October 2016.
2 Homes and Communities Agency (HCA), 2016; *Global accounts of private registered providers*, February 2017.

ownership' schemes. The sector also provides residential, domiciliary care services and provides care homes and other forms of supported housing on a substantial scale, in some cases running into several thousands. It also delivers a wide range of 'added value' services, such as employment, welfare advice and support for enterprise formation. The range of those services and activities is wide and eclectic, including factories producing timber homes, library services, management and ownership of swimming pools and leisure centres, schools and hospitals. One substantial housing association, L&Q, recently purchased a private-sector land holding and development company, Gallagher's, for a substantial sum. There are strong partnership links with a range of organisations, including local authorities, voluntary and private sectors and financial institutions.

1.5 The flexibility of the housing association structure means that housing associations range from huge national or regional conglomerates managing many thousands of dwellings to local almshouses with half a dozen homes. In recent years there has been a trend towards larger associations and group structures. This has been fueled by government funding cuts and by the transfer of local authority stock to housing associations. In 2017, out of the total of about 1,500 housing associations in England, 319 associations with at least 1,000 homes owned 95 per cent of the stock.[3] Some associations have a turnover of over £1bn and manage over 100,000 homes. However, a majority have fewer than 250 homes each. Thus the influence of a minority with a culture distinct from that of the majority is disproportionate.

1.6 Some unity is given to the sector by government regulation. Since the early 1970s, almost all housing associations have chosen to register with government agencies and so to subject themselves to regulation in return for an increasingly meagre slice of government funding and, importantly, the confidence of private funders such as banks. Accordingly, the housing association sector has invariably followed the government policy of the day. Thus the sector is a political football favoured by governments for its malleability but distrusted by others, supporters of local government especially, as an interloper.

1.7 In England, the sector is heavily regulated primarily by the Regulator of Social Housing (RSH) who has close links with central government; the Care Quality Commission (CQC); and in some instances the Charity Commission and the Financial Conduct

3 See *Global accounts of private registered providers*, HCA, 2017.

Authority (FCA). In Wales, where housing is a devolved field, the Welsh Ministers are responsible, thus providing direct democratic accountability.

Housing association law?

1.8 Is there a body of law which can be termed 'housing association law'? There are many statutory provisions which are specific to the sector, and there is an extensive range of regulatory administrative law measures, deriving from statutory powers. An example of the latter is where the RSH issues standards and codes of practice which have binding elements within them. There is also a range of legal provisions relating to social housing which apply to the housing association sector, but not exclusively so. An example of this is 'financial assistance' by Homes and Communities Agency (HCA), now renamed Homes England (HE). If we turn the clock back to before 2008 when the HCA was created, the Housing Association Grant (HAG) and Social Housing Grant (SHG) provisions were exclusive to the sector, but piece by piece competition has been opened up. Moreover, the increasing involvement of housing associations in commercial activity has made housing association law less insulated than it was before 2008.

1.9 Nevertheless, housing association law is a distinctive, perhaps unique, albeit a patchwork, area of law. What holds the law together is not a distinct set of principles, far less a code, but by virtue of its pervasive underlying themes. The dominant theme is the problem of reconciling three dimensions – these are, first, the public law of social housing whereby the state has taken on the responsibility to contribute to housing provision; second, the commercial private law dimension whereby associations compete for scarce resources; and third, and perhaps eclipsed by the other two, is the philanthropic/charitable dimension from which the housing association concept emerged. The three dimensions clash, especially in connection with tenants' rights, and the duties owed by the governing bodies of a housing association. In crude terms, the sector is a volatile mix of well-meaning paternalism, state bureaucracy and what *The Times* has called 'aggressive commercial practices'.[4] It may be unkind to suggest that the sector is in a state of aporia.

4   17 July 2018, p14.

1.10   In the public law sphere, the principles of judicial review and the Human Rights Act (HRA) 1998 are the dominant concerns. The regulator has considerable discretionary power to fashion relationships with tenants, to impose penalties and to intervene in the affairs of an association. In England, questions arise concerning the independence of the RSH given its close relationship with the funding body, Homes England. The Charity Commission also has regulatory powers, and questions may arise concerning the relationship between the two regulators.

1.11   The private law sphere mainly comprises ad hoc modifications of landlord and tenant law, corporate governance, trusteeship and insolvency law. A unifying element is the approach that should be taken to the matter of interpretation. *Riverside Housing Association Ltd v White*,[5] concerned the interpretation of a rent review clause in a standard tenancy agreement. Lord Neuberger, with whom the other members of the panel agreed, said that that correct approach was not that of an ordinary commercial agreement but should take account of the fact that the agreement was made by a publicly funded charitable housing association with tenants most of whom would have little if any experience of interpreting legal documents. In particular, an interpretation of the agreement that might expose the landlord or the tenants to large risks should if possible be avoided.

1.12   In the voluntary sphere, there are issues concerning the boundaries of charitable objects; the standards of conduct to be expected from volunteer members of governing bodies; and the role, if any, of democratic involvement in governance. The different legal structures available to housing associations also come under scrutiny since these were originally designed as vehicles for voluntary endeavour but are now expected to fulfill wider and larger purposes akin to those of a commercial enterprise. Conflicts have increasingly surfaced in the courts, who have begun to recognise the distinctive nature of the sector. For example, apart from the *Riverside* case (above), in *R (Mcintyre) v Gentoo Group Ltd*[6] the High Court stressed that, in view of the not-for-profit nature of a housing association and of its experience and expertise, the court will give great respect to its decisions.

1.13   The structure of the book is primarily functional, based on the main bodies of law encountered by housing associations in their

---

5 [2007] UKHL 20.
6 [2010] EWHC 5 (Admin).

work. There are also broader and overlapping socio-economic themes which defy any attempt at legal classification, but which influence the content of the law. These are many and various. Prominent ones are summarised as follows:
1) Social housing as a poverty trap, or a safety-net/springboard?
2) Paternalism, empowerment or repression? Short-term temporary tenancies; encouraging people into work; government policy around affordable housing, which is in short supply only going to those who are deserving of it.
3) Shifts towards the 'squeezed middle' of families not in acute need, ownership v renting, social justice and generating social capital.
4) The stigma attached to social housing, diversified ownership and mixed developments.
5) Social engineering and placeshaping, troubled families, unequal societies and equality law.
6) Health, welfare and housing connections – such as homelessness and fuel poverty.
7) Financial institutions: commercialism and managerialism, financial short-termism, adequacy of security – impact on structures and governance.
8) Policies around local economies: wider role of housing associations and legal constraints, recirculation of local money, supporting local jobs, social enterprise formation, training initiatives, volunteering, engagement within new structures.

Historical development

1.14 Mediaeval almshouses created by private bodies such as churches were a prototype housing association, some of which have survived until today as housing trusts. The direct ancestors of modern housing associations developed from the mid nineteenth century through local voluntary initiatives of which the Peabody and Guinness Trusts are prominent survivors. After World War I, a number of state supported 'public utility societies' were formed, of which the Sutton Trust and Bournville Village Trust are surviving examples. These origins give the sector a distinctive character associated with the 'third sector', comprising charities and other self-governing bodies being neither part of government nor profit-seeking private enterprises and with a substantial commitment by unpaid volunteers. In recent years, however, the links between the housing association sector and the wider third sector have become tenuous. This is a result of the size of the sector and its extensive governmental regulation.[7]

1.15 After World War II, most social housing was provided by local authorities. The Housing Act 1964 created the Housing Corporation, as a regulatory and funding body for housing associations. This was a 'quango' (quasi-autonomous non-governmental organisation) controlled by the central government. Originally the Corporation sponsored only a limited number of 'co-ownership' societies funded by government loans and intended as a stepping stone to private ownership. However, from the late 1960s, public concerns about homelessness were raised by the BBC television drama, *Cathy come home* (see para 1.1 above). Following this, the activities of campaigning organisations such as Shelter led to a major expansion of the sector.

1.16 The Housing Act 1974 increased the powers of the Housing Corporation including responsibility for administering a new scheme of central government Housing Association Grant. This was originally up to 100 per cent of the cost of providing a dwelling. The Housing Act 1974 led to the formation of many housing associations to meet needs not met by local government. The Act transformed the sector from a loose collection of local interests into a servant of government policy, assiduously falling in with changing political ideologies and priorities as a textbook example of state capture.

1.17 Under the Housing Act 1980 the legal rights of housing association tenants became broadly similar to those of local authority tenants including security of tenure, rights to exchange dwellings, the right to buy for tenants of most non-charitable associations, and rights of succession for family members. There was a special fair rent scheme for housing association tenants. A residue of tenancies created under this regime survives today complicating the law for the foreseeable future.

1.18 However, this was reversed by fundamental political changes later in the 1980s. These produced the dominant ingredients of the present regime. First, the political hostility of central governments to local authorities led to drastic reductions in local government housing powers and finance. Local authorities were prevented from directly providing new housing and undertook housing activities mainly through housing associations. During the 1990s, housing associations stock was massively increased by wholesale transfers of local

---

7 See generally, Mullins, *Housing associations*, Third Sector Research Centre, 2010.

authority housing stock following a vote by tenants (LSVTs). Thus housing associations, previously having the role of niche providers supplementing local authorities, now became mass providers of social housing. Today, local authorities retain about 35 per cent of social housing stock.

1.19 Second, government policy, as is still the case, favoured the ideology of the market and the resulting adoption of private sector values and practices. This has been eagerly embraced by some housing professionals who, despite being government groupies envisage themselves as independent businesspeople. In particular the governing committees or boards of housing associations, have reinvented themselves from being public spirited volunteers to paid professionals.[8] Although there are often tenant board members, these are usually a small minority. As in the case of commercial companies, this has the potential to generate an incestuous network of senior housing managers and consultants and former officials, although no recent research is available.[9]

1.20 Under the Housing Act 1988, the law governing tenants' rights was now modelled on that of private landlord and tenant law. Thus, most housing association tenancies entered into after the Act are 'assured tenancies' with limited security and subject to market rents albeit these are limited by government influence. Any further protections were imposed by Housing Corporation regulation. Thus a regime of legal rights became one of administrative discretion.

1.21 Under the Housing Act 1988, grant finance became a fixed up-front payment rather than covering the residual cost of providing the dwelling thus transferring development risk to the individual association. Government funding for general rental housing was steadily reduced although there was special funding for supported housing. For example government funding was reduced from £11.4bn in 2009 to £5.3bn in 2015. Associations became dependent on their reserves and on private loans secured on their land serviced by rent income. Financial support for tenants now relied primarily on welfare benefits paid to individuals as with the private sector. Thus changes in welfare benefits are among the main risks faced

---

8 In the case of a charity, payment must be justified as of benefit to the charitable purposes of the body. There seems to no empirical evidence relating to these matters. See Housing Corporation, *Modernising governance: an enabling approach*, 2001; *Analysis of responses*, 2001; *Remuneration for board members*, 2002; Grant Thornton, *Housing governance review*, 2016, 2017.

9 See McDermont, *Governing independence and expertise: the business of housing associations*, Hart Publishing, 2010.

1.22 Further changes were made by the Housing Act 1996. This Act introduced the regulatory framework we have today. It also created the concept of a 'registered social landlord' (RSL) which cosmetically blurred the distinction between the public and private sectors although the term in fact covers only housing associations.[10] The Housing Act 1996 regime remains the basis of Welsh regulation.

1.23 An important development took place after the Housing Act 2004 which extended government regulation and finance to private profit-seeking providers of social housing. This could change the character of the housing association sector towards a private sector model even more. However, only about 38 such providers are currently registered.

1.24 Moreover, after the emergence of the Conservative/Liberal Democrat coalition government in 2010 there was a policy emphasis on ownership as opposed to renting so that people in the greatest housing need were disadvantaged. Many housing associations in competition with private developers rely on the sale of dwellings including 'low-cost home ownership' schemes and commercial non-social housing. This has been combined with changes to social housing tenure, away from principles of security and rights towards encouraging short term lettings coupled with discretionary control devices based on the conduct of tenants.

1.25 In the case of local authority tenants, there has been direct statutory intervention. In the case of housing associations, nominally voluntary bodies, intervention derives mainly from the financial muscle of the regulator. However, since 2017, in the context of increased poverty, severe housing shortage and limited private development, the pendulum has swung back towards the provision of grant funding for social renting. Problems of increased needs of the elderly and of regions outside the south east have also been highlighted.[11]

1.26 Since the early 2000s, falling in with market based political ideology and responding to recent drastic cuts in government funding, many larger housing associations have embarked on commercial ventures in order to subsidise their social housing. These may

---

10 Below, para 4.29.
11 See white paper, *Fixing our broken housing market*, Cm 9352 February 2017; *Building homes building trust*, Future Shape of the Sector Commission, June 2018 (Land Q, Clarion, Network Homes).

amount to about ten per cent of housing association activity. They include lettings at 'market rents'; student accommodation; key worker housing; and the sale of houses on the open market. Associations have also entered into partnerships with the private sector – for example, providing architectural and design services and repair services for private landlords. At least in theory, commercial activities could help to integrate social housing with other housing, thereby alleviating the stigma of 'ghettoisation' by combing social and market housing in the same development. On the other hand, commercial ventures increase the risk of insolvency. Indeed, there is a special insolvency regime for housing associations. Some larger associations have attracted criticism for excessive payments to their senior management.[12]

Current policy trends

Austerity: rents and benefits

1.27 The prevailing political and economic challenge for housing associations has been to thrive in a time of government-imposed austerity. Following the financial collapse of 2008, austerity has infected the work of the sector and individual associations in a number of ways. The virus can be positioned on a vicious cycle: the impact of welfare reform; the reduction in tenants' incomes; and the impact that has on the collection of rents.

1.28 Perhaps the most immediate impact of austerity was the volte face of the Conservative government in 2016 on the rent settlement for the sector in England by turning a policy of certainty around rent increases to a policy of one per cent rent reduction each year for a period of five years.[13] This in itself wiped billions off the house-building potential of the sector. There is no equivalent in Wales. The sector still performed, but enormous ground was lost. So much more could have been achieved to help tackle crippling housing shortages and lessen the impact of house price inflation on a generation of young aspiring house buyers who were left to rent. Tens of thousands more homes would have been built had this policy shift not applied. Various estimates suggest a reduction in building per year for the duration of the policy of anything between 10,000–50,000

---

12 See *Times*, 17 July 2018.
13 Welfare Reform and Work Act 2016 s23.

Introduction: the scope of housing association law   13

homes, thus between 50,000–250,000 homes for the whole of the period at a time when there is a significant and growing housing shortage.

1.29   The reduction of rents was part of a government policy of attempting to reduce the housing benefit bill and to reform benefits generally. Since a significant proportion of social housing tenants were dependent to some degree on benefits, the reduction of rent levels within the sector would inevitably cut the housing benefit bill and effectively pass the risk and cost of the impact onto individual housing associations. This was a similar policy approach to the introduction of the minimum wage, which effectively passed the cost of the increase to employers and reduced the burden to the benefit system. However, the current government has announced a new settlement in relation to rents, allowing rents to increase by Consumer Price Index (CPI) plus one per cent from April 2020 for a five-year period.

1.30   The application of the Local Housing Allowance (LHA) to benefit eligibility had a similar effect, particularly for under 35-year-olds who were presumed to share or remain with their parents, limiting the amount of housing benefit which could be received to £58 per week in parts of the Midlands, much below rent levels in the social housing and private sectors.

1.31   The reduction of rents policy met with much criticism from the sector and others, since it effectively reduced the capacity of the sector to build new homes by removing potential growth in business plans right across the housing association world. This measure, coupled with welfare reform on limiting rents for single people to the LHA, had the effect of attacking an entire generation. If in work, they could not afford to buy because of the income multipliers making access to mortgages unattainable; and, if on benefits, also pricing them out of the rental market unless they were prepared to share. And thereby alienation of the young!

1.32   The housing association sector is an easy sector to target, since it is not loved by all. Local authorities may distrust it as a competitor for scarce resources; the hard right see it as perpetuating poverty and creating dependency, with officials earning overblown salaries at the tax-payers expense; and the hard left see these organisations as undemocratic and thus outside the political sphere.

1.33   Nevertheless, historically – and illustrating its resilience – the sector has been counter-cyclical and has continued to build new homes during times of economic downturn, at least in part assisting in providing a degree of activity to the housing market. Indeed, it has avoided the phenomenon of 'fraudulent insolvency', a prime cause of the financial collapse whereby huge sums of money were borrowed so as to disguise the inability to pay. Very few housing associations have experienced insolvency, although a tailor-made insolvency regime has recently been introduced for the sector.

Public or private – classification and declassification as public bodies: a continuing merry-go-round

1.34 Because housing associations receive public funds – although considerably reduced in scale per property over the decades – successive governments have seen them as a legitimate target for public capture. During the Conservative/Liberal Democrat coalition government years (2010–2015), a particular kind of thinking emerged through a growing spat around housing associations and their receipt of public funds. Threats were made by key figures from the coalition government that the sector should become government-controlled. At the heart of these threats was the view that because the sector had effectively been created or at least significantly expanded with aid of grants from government and its receipts of substantial subsidies through housing benefit payments it should be made subject to government control. This focused on the sector's apparent lack of accountability on publishing expenses, the level of senior pay and the application of 'right to buy' (RTB), among other issues.

1.35 George Osborne as Chancellor threatened the sector with classification as public bodies, so taking away its independence as a sector. This was duly supported by Grant Shapps as Housing Minister and Eric Pickles as Secretary of State for the Environment. Following the election of the Conservative government in 2015, the temperature rose even further. The Office for National Statistics (ONS) immediately classified housing associations as part of the public sector – to be precise, 'public non-financial corporations', which meant that some £60bn of debt was added to the overall public debt.[14]

1.36 The government then seemed to have second thoughts. A voluntary deal was reached on RTB, taking away the threat of statutory

---

14 See ONS, Classification Announcement: 'Private registered providers of social housing in England', October 2015. See also Northern Ireland Federation of Housing Associations, *The classification of housing associations: final report*, 2016. See also, for example, P Aldrick, 'Housing associations are failing, says Osborne', *Times*, 9 September 2015.

imposition on the sector. Further measures were outlined which meant that the regulator, then the HCA, would reduce its control over housing associations. These measures included the removal of the power to consent to the disposal of homes and other land and to changes to the rules and constitutional structures of most housing associations. Importantly, local authority influence would also be reduced. The measures were implemented by the Housing and Planning Act 2016 in England and the Regulation of Registered Social Landlords (Wales) Act 2018. A Voluntary RTB scheme was also included in the 2016 Act but, although much anticipated, it had seemed to disappear from the policy agenda with its fixation on the withdrawal of the UK from the European Union ('Brexit'). However, a pilot scheme in the Midlands is currently in place.

1.37   In November 2017, the ONS declassified housing associations as public bodies, reclassifying them as 'private non-financial corporations', thus leading to the sector regaining its nominally independent status. Nevertheless, there is significant government control. Indeed, this independence may be largely cosmetic since although consent powers have been removed, the regulator still has to be notified of these matters and can exercise its general powers to intervene. Moreover, the ONS ignored the fact that the government had imposed one per cent rent reductions year-on-year for four years to 2020 (see above). Surely this amounts to a substantial degree of government control of the sector, and is perhaps the most significant intervention in the sector in its whole history.

Regulation: renaming, then splitting, the Homes and Communities Agency – further musical chairs

1.38   Related to the public/private issue (above), the system of regulating housing associations has proved unstable, riven by disagreement as whether the functions of funding and regulation should be exercised by the same body. The more that housing associations are considered to be part of the public sector, the stronger is the case for a single body, preferably a democratic one. This is the case in Wales, where the Welsh Ministers combine funding and regulation.

1.39   In England, the HCA seems to be a key player in the future of housing supply since most government funding programmes are to be delivered through the Agency. However, the Agency has been subject to change. It has been renamed Homes England, and the regulatory function has been hived off to a new regulatory agency.

This takes us back to the brief years from 2008 to 2012, when there was a separate regulator in the shape of the Tenant Services Authority. This was much disliked during the coalition government's period of office by Grant Shapps and Eric Pickles, the responsible ministers, apparently on the ground that it paid too much attention to tenants' interests as opposed to financial controls.

The deepening housing crisis

1.40 So far this century new building levels have been disappointingly low, although over 100,000 were built in the housing association and local authority sectors during 2016–2017, an artificially high figure because the Approved Development Programme had come to an end and everything had to be completed before a drop dead date for associations to claim grants. There is a need to build at least 250,000 homes a year for ten years in order to meet the current demand and need, with greater degrees of acuteness on housing shortage in different parts of the country. The Chancellor announced in the 2017 budget that the government wishes to oversee a building programme of 300,000 homes per year by the mid-2020s, and has outlined a number of new funding streams to assist in a step-change in production primarily funded through the HCA and various combined authorities across the country. This includes some £15.3bn of new capital, guarantee and loan based funding. Prime Minister Theresa May announced a further £2bn of funding for strategic partnerships at the National Housing Federation housing summit in September 2018.

1.41 RTB importantly affects the viability of the sector by threatening to remove many dwellings from the social housing pool. Assured tenants of non-charitable housing associations currently have a form of RTB ('right to acquire') and 'secure tenants' under the older regime have a similar right to buy to that enjoyed by local authority tenants. There is also a proposed 'voluntary right to buy' scheme which individual associations can implement in their discretion. In Wales, more radical steps have been taken to limit, and ultimately to abolish, the right to buy.[15]

1.42 As regards tenants' rights, the housing shortage, coupled with alleged problems of anti-social behaviour, has given rise to legislative developments both in England and Wales which have challenged the notion of a 'lifetime tenancy' by making it easier to evict a social housing tenant. However, provisions in the Housing and Planning

15 Abolition of the Right to Buy and Associated Rights (Wales) Act 2018.

Act 2016 which increase the rents payable by higher income tenants, have not been implemented.

Grenfell Tower disaster and housing standards

1.43 The devastating fire at Grenfell Tower in North Kensington, London on 14 June 2017 is a truly tragic event in literally every respect. The only possible good thing that can come from it is that the loss of life and damage to people's lives and homes is so catastrophic that the government, local authorities, fire authorities and social landlords must act to ensure such a tragedy never happens again. It is vital to learn quickly from this horrific event and to avoid any further loss of life for those people who are living in or near to premises which may not be compliant with adequate safety standards.

1.44 The social housing sector has responded to the event by rapidly testing, inspecting and evaluating not just aluminium composite claddings, but by looking at other potentially hazardous materials such as insulation and related issues such as fire stopping between floors. In addition, evacuation procedures or stay-put policies have been or are being reviewed comprehensively with the Fire Service. Residents are being informed, engaged and are participating to varying degrees across the country. The impact of the fire has huge immediate resonance and will have a continuing impact on social housing. Equally, the response has been huge, with social housing landlords undertaking significant physical and reassurance work for their tenants.

1.45 The government have carried out listening exercises with social tenants right across the country, with laudable leadership from Alok Sharma, then Housing Minister, with some of the findings being introduced into the social housing green paper (below). There has also been a review of building standards and fire safety by Dame Judith Hackett,[16] which has made a number of recommendations to government, stressing the need for a stronger regulatory framework; whole system testing; rigorous enforcement powers; a clear and transparent audit trail; and accountability in relation to costs saving decisions. More regulation will inevitably follow.

1.46 However, the process has not been without its problems, and a perceived or actual lack of response has been criticised. The housing stock of Kensington and Chelsea Council was managed by a tenant

16 See Cm 9607, *Building a safer future, independent review of building regulations and fire safety: final report*, May 2018.

management organisation (TMO), a form of housing association, and questions may arise about the relationship of TMOs with their sponsoring authority. One aspect of the declassification measures discussed above is the reduction of local authority influence over housing associations in which they have a stake.

The housing green paper

1.47 After waiting for more than a decade for a new housing green paper, the publication of *A new deal for social housing*[17] in August 2018 received a somewhat lukewarm reception by the housing world due to the apparent lack of measures to tackle the shortages of housing supply.[18] In some ways this was unfair criticism, bearing in mind the government had announced a wide range of measures to address housing supply, including new money just months before publication of the green paper. The green paper espoused five 'core principles':

1) a safe and decent home;
2) swift and effective resolution of complaints;
3) empowerment of residents;
4) tackling stigma and celebrating thriving communities; and
5) building the social homes that we need.

1.48 Examining the green paper, there are new measures in giving 'sharper teeth' to the regulator with more focus on consumer regulation with a remit for intervention over tenant services creating a more 'proactive approach to enforcement, like ... Ofsted'[19] to ensure homes are well managed and of decent quality, thus aligning enforcement on consumer issues to those of economic issues. This is seen as a response to the Grenfell Tower tragedy. The regulator's powers on consumer interventions are currently limited by statute to only cover issues of 'serious detriment'.

1.49 Strengthening consumer protection is also supported by the proposed introduction of league tables (with a link to the future decisions relating to the award of grants for social housing) and the

---

17 Cm 9671.
18 See, for example, *Inside housing*: Melanie Rees, 'The green paper: a golden opportunity missed'; John Bibby, 'Green paper measures are not enough to create May's "new generation" of council houses'; and for a round-up of comments Carl Brown, 'Social housing green papers one week on: the debate rages', 21 August 2018.
19 Green paper, para 99.

Introduction: the scope of housing association law 19

publication of key performance indicators.[20] There are proposals for greater resident involvement, tackling stigma in the social housing sector, along with a potential programme to see council housing stock transferred to community-based housing associations which has been widely welcomed.[21] There are also proposals to allow new buyers of shared ownership homes to staircase ownership by one per cent increments each year.

1.50 An important aspect of this is tackling stigma associated with social housing. This was a significant message that came out of the green paper. The importance of this was reinforced by Prime Minister Theresa May when she addressed the National Housing Federation's (NHF) Housing Summit in September 2018.

1.51 Particularly welcome were the volte face proposals which will drop the high value asset levy (on local authorities, which meant that these properties had to be sold to fund the 'voluntary right to buy' initiative), and higher rents for tenants in work who have high earnings both of which had been key measures in the Housing and Planning Act 2016.[22] In some ways these changes go further towards completing the picture of turn-around represented by the change of mind on capping rents for younger people in the LHA, and also recent announcements on supported housing.[23] This indicates a substantial move away from the period of hostility during the governments of 2009–15 led by David Cameron and George Osborne, instead creating a perhaps a more trusted partner relationship with government.

Brexit

1.52 An uncertain impact on the sector is that of Brexit (the UK's decision to leave the EU in March 2019). While there are no specific Brexit implications for housing association law as such, the sector has particular vulnerabilities which may raise regulatory issues. There are a number of 'ifs' at this stage, depending on the nature of the

---

20 Although these measures have been described as potentially counter-productive, see Gavriel Hollander, 'League tables could prove "blunt" and "counter-productive"', sector warns', *Inside housing*, 16 August 2018.
21 See, for example, Mark Smulian, 'Ministers consider new stock transfer programme to "community-led" associations', *Inside housing*, 14 August 2018.
22 Housing and Planning Act 2016 ss69–76 and 89–90.
23 See, for example, Peter Apps, 'Housing associations plan more supported housing following LHA cap U-turn', *Inside housing*, 17 August 2018.

deal or whether there is a deal at all with the European Union and our ability as a nation to enter into trade deals elsewhere.

1.53 It is well known that the housebuilding industry faces challenges around the availability of labour. This problem has been a reality for some years, with traditional tradespeople on the verge of retirement, with a significant further loss through additional retirement over the next five to ten years. There is also the problem of the exodus of Eastern European labour in particular which has helped in recent years to bolster the availability of building sector labour. There are some questions as to whether skilled building sector workers from abroad will be allowed to enter the UK. Labour shortages will drive building costs upwards. A move to off-site manufacturing will help bridge that shortage, but the slow take-up of modular and panelised systems in the UK means the pace of that shift will be glacial rather than a full solution to labour shortages and building quality deficits of the traditional construction industry.

1.54 Recent reductions in the value of the pound on international currency markets, has helped exporters, since foreign buyers can simply get more for their purchasing power. On the other hand imported good cost more. Housing associations do not export but they do import a range of building materials and if they purchase through the UK supply chain, they rely on other countries for the supply of such products as steel and wood. Although the UK is strong on manufacturing it does not produce a great deal of the raw materials. Therefore we are likely to see, at least in the short term, building price inflation on materials as well as labour.

1.55 On the positive side, EU requirements concerning public procurement may no longer impose costs on the sector. Demand to buy homes from people abroad may reduce (there is already some evidence of this in the South East housing market, and London in particular). The price of land therefore may reduce, especially during any transitional period as a result of uncertainty. Whether this would be sufficient to counteract the increase in labour and building supply chain inflation remains to be seen.

1.56 On the other hand, a further potential cause for concern in the sector linked to Brexit is general uncertainty which may impact strongly on consumer confidence in the housing market. Those associations who sell significant numbers of homes may well find a reduction in sales or timescales of sales stretching out beyond their business plan assumptions. The market downturn in 2008 saw a number of housing associations struggle which had predicated their business planning on strong sales. There is already some reduction in demand in London and the South East, This is often followed by a ripple effect across the country when economic conditions worsen.

The meaning of 'social housing' and related concepts

'Social housing'

1.57 Under previous legislation there was no need for a legal concept of 'social housing', since only housing associations could register with the government. This remains the case for Welsh bodies. Under the current regime in England, governed by the Housing and Regeneration Act (HRA) 2008, any provider of social housing can apply to register. Housing associations that are so registered (along with profit-making providers) are now called 'private registered providers' (PRPs). Thus 'social housing', previously only policy jargon with no consensus at to its meaning, is now a primary legal concept. Apart from being the gateway to registration, the concept of social housing is used in particular contexts to define the powers of the regulator and relates also to aspects of tenants' rights.

1.58 Under the English regime, social housing is of two kinds.[24] In both cases accommodation must be made available in accordance with rules designed to ensure that it is made available to people whose needs are not adequately served by the commercial housing market. The two kinds of social housing are as follows:

1) *Low-cost rental accommodation* which must be below the market rate.
2) *Low-cost home ownership accommodation*. This includes three kinds of arrangement:
   a) 'Shared ownership', where a tenant is granted a lease (which can be of any length) at a premium calculated by reference either to the value of the dwelling or the cost of providing it and where the tenant or his personal representatives are entitled to a payment by reference to the value of the dwelling. For example, the premium might be 25 per cent of the value, with the tenant also paying a top-up rent. On leaving, the lessee is entitled to 25 per cent of the market value at that date. Thus, the sums concerned are flexible. They includes the

24 HRA 2008 ss68–77.

common 'staircasing' arrangement, whereby a tenant can purchase by stages further slices of the value of the dwelling with a proportionate reduction of rent. After acquiring 100 per cent, the tenant may have an option to acquire the freehold without further payment. An arrangement which is both low-rent and low-cost home-ownership is treated as low-cost home-ownership.
b) 'Equity percentage arrangements' under which a buyer buys the dwelling outright but the seller defers a percentage of the price to be paid in stages which must be secured by a mortgage. The sale of housing at below market price does not in itself qualify as social housing.
c) 'Shared ownership trusts'. These are special shared ownership arrangements based on stamp duty legislation, where the amount of payment on leaving the dwelling is fixed at the beginning.[25] They also comprise cases of a similar kind where the dwelling is subject to a 'transferred right to buy', ie where the dwelling has been transferred to a housing association by a local authority from which its tenants had a statutory right to buy.

1.59 A dwelling ceases to be social housing in certain cases. These are where the dwelling is sold to the tenant (including under shared ownership or equity percentage arrangements); or sold to a non-registered provider or where the registered provider has a lease (other from a subsidiary or associate) which expires.[26] In addition, the secretary of state can make regulations removing or adding properties or kinds of property from the definition of social housing.[27] The regulator can direct that a specified dwelling is no longer social housing, but only on the application of the provider.[28]

Related concepts

1.60 Readers will know that the world of housing associations, in common with other professional spheres, is replete with jargon and acronyms where words might be used in Alice in Wonderland ways intended to exclude outsiders. Moreover, in the deferential world of public sector

---

25 Finance Act 2003 Sch 9.
26 HRA 2008 ss73, 74, 74A, see regulatory guidance, *De-classifying social housing*, 2018.
27 HRA 2008 s72.
28 HRA 2008 s76.

Introduction: the scope of housing association law 23

1.61 housing, distinctions between binding law, administrative discretion, professional usage, brand names and misconception may be blurred.
Most importantly for housing associations, government funding and the rights of tenants may be rationed and targeted according to categories of social housing such as 'affordable housing' or 'socially rented housing' based only on subordinate legislation or policy documents and therefore defined, if at all, by the executive according to its immediate political agenda. This applies in particular to rights relating to transfers of tenancies and the 'right to acquire'.[29]

1.62 The terms 'social rent' or 'socially rented housing' refer to the lowest rent levels. In England, a 'social rent' is a rent fixed by the regulator for certain types of tenancy originally under the 'national rent regime'.[30] This was introduced in 2011 under the coalition government's 'rent influencing policy' which coupled the legal freedom of a housing association to fix its own rent with government funding schemes. A social rent is intended to approximate to a local authority rent and is set according to a formula that takes into account regional variations of income etc. It is up to about 70 per cent of a market rent. Some 75 per cent of housing association provision comprises social rents, about half of this being dwellings transferred from local authorities.

1.63 The term 'affordable housing' is often used incorrectly to refer to all social housing. The coalition government introduced 'affordable' rents in 2011 primarily to cater for working people unable to buy a home. 'Affordable rent' means a rent for prescribed kinds of scheme above the social rent level but set by the RSH at not more than 80 per cent of market value.[31] The recent green paper[32] suggests that, as far as resources are concerned, the government's main interest for new provision is in affordable housing and other schemes such as 'low-cost home ownership' at the upper end of the social housing range. There is also 'intermediate rent'. This is a rent not set by the regulator but required by a specific funding condition (which can be varied with consequences for the stability of an association) also up to 80 per cent of the market level.[33]

---

29 Below para 9.42.
30 See Transfer of Tenancies and Right to Acquire (Exclusion) Regulations 2012 SI No 696 reg 2. (Below para 9.43.)
31 See Transfer of Tenancies and Right to Acquire (Exclusion) Regulations 2012 SI No 696 reg 2.
32 *A new deal for social housing* Cm 9671, 2018.
33 Above note 33.

1.64 Under the *National planning policy framework*,[34] affordable housing is tightly defined so as to target various specific government-favoured providers or schemes. These include rented homes and discounted sales of at least 20 per cent below local market values and other routes to home ownership such as shared ownership.

1.65 Sometimes (eg in the Localism Act 2011) the expression 'social tenancy' is used. In the absence of a specific definition, this probably means a tenant of social housing generally. The term 'housing association tenancy' is occasionally used to mean a tenancy subject to regimes dating from before the Housing Act 1996. The term 'registered housing association' is similarly used. This refers to associations previously registered with the Housing Corporation and is usually updated to include RSLs and PRPs.

1.66 Various labels have been attached to certain kinds of housing association connected with local authorities. These have no legal significance but are fashioned either by administrative practice or professional jargon – for example, the 'local housing company', 'large scale voluntary transfer association,' or the 'stock transfer association' (below). There are special provisions relating to local government involvement in any housing association but otherwise these associations are subject to the same law as other housing associations.

Social housing in Wales

1.67 In Wales, the statutory definition of social housing is looser and broader. However, this is not a general definition but was enacted in the particular context of legislation to restrict the right to buy. Social housing is 'any' housing provided by a 'social housing provider' which in turn means either a local authority or any other person which provides housing to or has functions relating to the allocation of housing to people whose needs are not adequately served by the commercial housing market.[35] Thus any housing provided by a housing association seems to be social housing if the association also provides sub-market housing even on a small scale. However, for statistical purposes, only housing at social rents and some supported housing schemes are treated as social housing. 'Non-social housing'

---

34 2018, Annex 2.
35 Housing (Wales) Measure 2011 s33(2), (4).

includes various low cost schemes all of which would be within both the English and Welsh statutory definitions of social housing.[36]

1.68 In Wales, the key statutory concept is the RSL. As we shall discuss in chapter 4, this includes only housing associations and with designated objectives and powers.

---

36 See Welsh Government, *Statistical first release*, SFR 91/2017, paras 2, 4.

CHAPTER 2

The legal framework of a housing association

2.1	**The definition of 'housing association'**
2.7	'Society, body of trustees or company'
2.19	'Non-profit'
2.20	**English and Welsh housing associations**
2.25	**Different kinds of housing association**
2.26	Charitable housing associations
2.37	Housing trusts
2.42	Fully mutual housing associations
2.54	**Local authority connections**

28 *Housing associations: a legal handbook* / chapter 2

The definition of 'housing association'

2.1 A 'housing association' is:

... a society, body of trustees or company,
a) which is established for the purpose of, or amongst whose objects or powers are included those of, providing, constructing, improving or managing, or facilitating or encouraging the construction or improvement of, housing accommodation and,
b) which does not trade for profit or whose constitution or rules prohibit the issue of capital with interest or dividend exceeding such rate as may be determined by the Treasury, whether with or without distinction between sand the flat falls within its charitable purposes and loan capital.[1]

2.2 This definition but with an additional limitation to 'the working classes' was introduced by Housing Act 1935 s26, replacing the concept of a ' public utility society' dating from the Housing, Town Planning etc Act 1909.

2.3 The definition does not require the body to be called a 'housing association' thus creating a risk of confusion, for example where a body calls itself a 'trust'. More importantly the definition does not limit the objects of the association to 'social housing' nor indeed requires it to provide social housing at all. However, only an association that includes the provision of social housing among its objects, is eligible for registration with the Regulator of Social Housing (RSH) as a private registered provider (PRP).

2.4 Provided that it has at least one of the listed housing-related objects or powers, a housing association's objects can include any other lawful purpose. Moreover, activities other than those expressly designated as objects are lawful provided that the activity in question is a 'reasonably incidental' means of achieving the association's permitted objects. This has been applied generously. The court will not examine the promotors' actual reasons for carrying out an activity. The test is whether what is done is *capable* of falling within the association's rules.

2.5 For example, in *Halifax Building Society v Meridian Housing Association Ltd*,[2] a housing association entered into an ill-advised leaseback scheme in partnership with a commercial developer to produce a mixed development of sheltered flats and offices the offices to be leased to the developer once completed. The association's

1 Housing Associations Act (HAA) 1985 s1.
2 (1995) 27 HLR 123.

objects were to carry out the 'industry, business or trade of providing housing or any associated amenities'. The development was never completed. Arden J held that the project was lawful even though the director's purposes were to make money, and were not related to housing. Since the provision of offices as such was capable of being incidental to the proper objects of the association, for example as an estate office, the actual purpose to which the offices would be put was irrelevant. (However, the Committee of Management might be liable for misusing their power.)

2.6 In the following paragraphs we shall outline some important features of the definition.

'Society, body of trustees or company'

2.7 This is wide enough to include every possible type of constitutional structure for a group of people recognised by the law. However, as result of their historical evolution, all housing associations now take one of three forms, namely: 1) (most commonly) registration with the Financial Conduct Authority (FCA) under the Co-operative and Community Benefits Societies Act (CCBSA) 2014; 2) incorporation as a company registered under the Companies Act 2006; or 3) structured as a charitable trust.[3] Both corporate forms can be charitable or non-charitable (below). In theory, a housing association could also be an unincorporated association, essentially a group of individuals linked by a common contract but sometimes recognised as having a group identity. An unincorporated association is not eligible for registration with the social housing regulator.

2.8 Of the 1529 English housing associations registered with the RSH in October 2018, 919 were incorporated under the CCBSA 2014.[4] (We will refer to these either as 'CCBSA societies' or 'CCBSs'). In all, there are about 7,000 bodies of various kinds so registered, ranging from social clubs and village halls to substantial trading enterprises. The CCBSA 2014 replaces a series of Industrial and Provident Societies Acts (IPSA). These originated in the Victorian co-operative movement and were designed to provide a structure for socially worthy or community-based enterprises. (Associations previously registered under the IPSA with the registrar of friendly

---

3 The Peabody Housing Association was incorporated by statute in 1948, but is now registered under the CCBSA 2014.
4 The equivalent Welsh register does not identify legal structures.

societies are automatically registered under the CCBSA 2014 as 'pre-commencement societies'.)

2.9 To be eligible for registration, a body must satisfy the FCA either that it is a 'bona fide co-operative society' or 'its business is being or is intended to be conducted for the benefit of the community'.[5] Neither of these requirements is defined in the Act. The FCA has provided general guidelines (below), although these are not exhaustive and the matter is considered on a case-by-case basis. The FCA can also cancel registration.[6]

2.10 Registration gives limited liability and requires a specific form of membership structure and objects involving equal participation of members. The constitution of a CCBSA society is embedded in its 'rules' which can be changed according to methods created by the rules themselves. These rules set out the objects and powers of the society thus playing essentially the same part as the articles of a company but without the safeguards contained in the Companies Act 2006. Unlike the case of a Companies Act company, a basic democratic structure is required.

2.11 Among housing associations registered with the RSH, 210 'fully mutual' housing associations (below) are registered as a 'bona fide co-operative society' under the CCBSA 2014. According to the FCA Guidance[7] a bona fide co-operative society must be an autonomous association of persons united voluntarily to meet their common economic social and cultural needs and aspirations through a jointly owned and democratically controlled enterprise (one member one vote). The main purpose of the society must not be to make money. Any agreement, such as with government or other organisations, for example where the co-op is part of a larger group of housing associations, must preserve its autonomy. A co-operative society should provide its members with education and training and should provide public information.

2.12 The other kind of body eligible for registration under the CCBSA 2014 is a community benefit society (CBS). 709 English housing associations, by far the largest group, are registered under this head. The purposes of a CBS must be wholly for the benefit of the community and benefits cannot be linked to membership. Its surpluses, if not ploughed back into the business, can be distributed only for other community benefit purposes. A CBS can be charitable

5 CCBSA 2014 s2.
6 CCBSA 2014 ss3(2), 5.
7 FCA, *Finalised guidance* 15/2, November 2015, paras 4.10–4.16, 5.2.

or non-charitable (below). If it is charitable, as an exempt charity it need not register with the Charity Commission.

2.13 A CBS must usually be controlled democratically. Any departure from the 'one member, one vote' principle must be justified as being in the interests of the community. The size of a member's shareholding therefore cannot affect the member's voting powers. A member can hold shares of up to £100,000, but these cannot be sold. Certain corporate members, including other CCBSs or local authorities, are exempt from these limits, thus allowing for groups or consortia of housing associations.[8] Individual membership of a housing association is often nominal, comprising mainly its governing board or committee members. As with a company, the members have limited liability.

2.14 It has sometimes been suggested that housing associations are at a disadvantage because of their 'nineteenth century' constitutions. Certainly the CCBSA 2014 seems more suited to small-scale voluntary enterprises where the leading participants know and trust each other rather than to the large conglomerates which dominate the housing association sector. In particular the provisions of the Companies Act 2006 concerning the regime of directors' responsibilities and liability are not reflected in the CCBSA 2014. However, the Act enables the Treasury to make 'such modifications' (including additions to the Act) 'as they consider appropriate' in order to assimilate the two regimes, but only where the Companies Act itself is altered.[9] Basic constitutional principles cannot be changed by these means. There is also power to apply company law to some regulatory matters.[10] No relevant changes or additions seem to have been made.

2.15 291 English housing associations are registered with the social housing regulator as Companies Act companies. A charitable company must also be registered with the Charity Commission. Incorporation is as a company registered by guarantee, since, having no shareholders and the members invariably guaranteeing a nominal amount, this kind of company is suited to a non-profit regime. Company law places little restriction on the objectives, mode of governance and membership of a company. Unless it specifically restricts them a company can have any object.[11] Unlike a CBS, there is no requirement of equal democratic participation or community benefit. Thus a company can

8 CCBSA 2014 s24(2).
9 CCBSA 2014 s134.
10 CCBSA 2014 s135.
11 Companies Act 2006 s31.

2.16 carry out a wider range of activities than can the other types, being limited only by the definition of a housing association.

A somewhat mysterious and apparently unused provision of the pre-CCBSA 2014 law relating to what are now CBSs has been removed. This required 'a special reason' to be shown that why the body could not be registered as a company.[12] A company can equally well have community benefit purposes. Indeed, the 'community benefit company' established by the Companies (Audit, Investigations and Community Enterprise) Act 2004 is designed for this purpose. There seems to be no housing association created under this Act. The CBS structure is favoured by housing associations partly for historical reasons, but maybe also because this structure is relatively simple and flexible.

2.17 Finally a housing association trust can be a charitable trust. 319 English housing associations are so registered with the social housing regulator. These were generally founded by private gifts or by institutions such as churches or schools or by local communities. Many are almshouses. Such a trust need not have democratic governance but must be for the benefit of the community (below). A charitable trust is constituted and governed by trustees appointed according to the instrument creating the trust. There can be any number of these. The trust instrument or the trustees themselves could also create a 'membership' to act in an advisory capacity. A charitable trust must be registered with the Charity Commission. In some cases, mainly concerned with winding up and restructuring, trusts are subject to less stringent regulation than are other forms of housing association. Unfortunately the term 'trust' is sometimes used indiscriminately as the name of a housing association that is not a trust at all.

2.18 There is also a special structure, a 'charitable incorporated organisation' (CIO), available to charities under the Charities Act 2011. This enables a charitable trust to be incorporated with limited liability by registering with the Charity Commission without the relatively cumbersome procedural rules applying to companies and CBSs. Thus a single corporate body owns the property and the trustees are protected by limited liability, albeit they remain liable for their personal defaults. A company and a CCBSA society can also convert to a CIO.[13]

---

12 Industrial and Provident Societies Act 1965 s1(2).
13 See *2010 to 2015 government policy: social enterprise* (Cabinet Office); Charitable Incorporated Organisations (Consequential Amendments) Order 2017 SI No 1231.

'Non-profit'

2.19 A housing association must not trade for profit, or if it does so, it must not pay interest or dividends above a rate prescribed by the Treasury (there seems to be no current instance of the latter). A body trades for profit if it uses surpluses for purposes other than its legitimate objects or purposes incidental to them such as paying its staff or directors or accumulating reserves (although in both cases there is a danger of abuse). An association can give surpluses to other bodies, provided that the recipient is also non-profit and its objects are consistent with the association's objects. A non-profit body can pay interest at commercial rates, but cannot pay dividends. This prevents housing associations from raising equity finance so that their private finance depends mainly on mortgage securities or bonds.

English and Welsh housing associations

2.20 Since Wales attained the power to enact primary legislation in 2011, English and Welsh housing association law has begun to diverge. The Housing and Regeneration Act (HRA) 2008, substantially modified by later statutes,[14] provides the legal framework in England. All 'English bodies' (defined in chapter 4) providing social housing are eligible for registration with the Regulator of Social Housing (RSH) as PRPs.

2.21 The registration and regulatory system under the Housing Act 1996, which previously applied to England and Wales, now applies only to 'Welsh bodies'.[15] In Wales, the Welsh ministers directly register, fund and regulate Welsh housing associations, thereby providing greater democratic accountability than is the case in England. Welsh housing associations are regulated under the Housing Act 1996 as modified considerably by internal Welsh legislation.[16]

2.22 The scope and terminology of the two regimes differ. In Wales regulation applies only to registered social landlords (RSL). An RSL is either a charitable housing association of any kind or a non-profit body incorporated as a company or under the CCBSA 2014. In the latter two cases, it must provide, construct, improve or manage

---

14 Localism Act 2011; Housing and Planning Act 2016.
15 Housing Act 1996 ss60, 61.
16 Principally the Housing (Wales) Measure 2011; Housing (Wales) Act 2014; Renting Homes (Wales) Act 2016 and the Deregulation of Registered Social Landlords (Wales) Act 2018.

dwellings 'kept available for letting' or co-operative dwellings, and can have certain prescribed additional objects (below chapter 4). Unlike an English body, therefore, an RSL need not provide social housing at all.

2.23 Unless the legislation creates a specific exception, RSLs exist only in relation to Welsh law. An RSL, although based in Wales, might also have stock in England although the powers of the Welsh regulator over such stock are severely limited. By contrast, it seems that the English regulator has full jurisdiction where a PRP provides stock in Wales.[17]

2.24 In a few cases, the Housing Act 1996 still applies to England.[18] The main overlapping areas are as follows. Others will be mentioned in context.

a) various 'right to buy' matters;[19]
b) the housing ombudsman scheme of the Housing Act 1996 applies only in England since there is a separate scheme for Wales;[20]
c) by virtue of HRA 2008 s184, the 'right to acquire' under the Housing Act 1996 which applies to many publicly funded housing association dwellings both in England and Wales is kept alive for PRPs in England;
d) Housing Act 1996 s213(2) defines RSLs to include PRPs in the duty to co-operate with local authorities in relation to homelessness.

Different kinds of housing association

2.25 There are various species of housing association which have evolved over many years and which have different consequences in specific contexts. These differences concern the constitutional structure of the body; its mode of regulation; its relationship with its tenants; and its purposes. They are outlined as follows. The classification here is of course based on legal categories, but other more socially based classification may also be useful, such as general and supported housing. Together with the various types of tenancy engineered under the regulatory regime, they enable the sector to be flexible and responsive to changing demands and needs. Indeed the generic

17 Below para 4.33.
18 HRA 2008 s60(3).
19 HRA 2008 s179.
20 HRA 2008 s124.

The legal framework of a housing association 35

concept of housing association is rarely applied alone. The main case where it does so concerns shared ownership leases.[21]

Charitable housing associations

2.26 About three-quarters of PRPs are charitable bodies. Charitable housing associations have taxation and certain other privileges under the general law and in certain cases are subject to special regulatory principles. A fundamental feature of a charity is that its assets are locked in, meaning that they cannot be used for a non-charitable purpose if the particular body no longer functions but must be applied to another similar purpose. The members of other kinds of housing association could convert their association into a profit-making body. Within the envelope of its charitable purposes, a charitable housing association registered with the social housing regulator can have any objectives. Under the registration requirements, a non-charitable association is more constrained in that its purposes must be to provide or manage housing and any other purposes must be connected with or incidental to the provision of housing.[22]

2.27 Under Charities Act 2011 s3, the objects of a charity must either fall exclusively within certain designated purposes or fall exclusively within categories established under earlier law as charitable or be 'within the spirit' of an existing category (ie analogous to it). As a separate requirement, under section 4 there must be an identifiable benefit to the community in the particular case, thereby overriding previous assumptions that the charitable categories in themselves carry sufficient public benefit.[23]

2.28 The law is therefore developed incrementally by the courts. Housing as such is not a charitable purpose, and whether a scheme is backed by government is irrelevant. The charitable purposes most relevant to housing associations are the following: relieving or preventing poverty; meeting the needs of the sick, disabled and elderly or of those in financial hardship, or other disadvantage;[24] providing accommodation for those in need, for example in areas of housing shortage and urban or rural regeneration. The advancement of education or health are charitable purposes that may be met by

---

21 See below, para 8.63.
22 HRA 2008 s115.
23 Charity Commission, *Charitable registered social landlords*, 2013.
24 Charities Act 2011 s3(1); see *Joseph Rowntree Memorial Trust Housing Association Ltd v Attorney General* [1983] Ch 159.

2.29 'key workers' housing schemes intended to meet labour shortages in teaching and other public services.

A body, the objects of which are limited to 'social housing' within the meaning of the HRA 2008, would be charitable under the 'poverty' head in view of the requirement of the Act to meet a need that cannot be met by the market. However, schemes at the more expensive end intended to encourage home ownership may not be charitable given that home ownership as such is arguably a political aspiration rather than a genuine need.[25] Shared ownership sales are borderline and may depend on the buyer having only a limited share of the equity and on provisions for the dwelling to remain in the social housing sector if it is disposed of. A sale at market value can be charitable only in special circumstances.

2.30 In *Helena Partnerships Ltd v Revenue and Customs Commissioners*[26] the Court of Appeal endorsed a restrictive approach. A housing association which had taken over local authority housing stock, had objects limited to those of an RSL (as under the pre HRA 2008 regime) 'for the benefit of the community'. The Court of Appeal held that *Helena's* objects were too wide to be charitable. Neither community benefit nor housing are in themselves charitable. The objects of an RSL are not charitable since they are not limited to social housing.[27] Similarly transferred local authority tenancies cannot be charitable unless every tenant is in need. More questionably, perhaps, the court held that the private benefit to the individual in being housed far outweighed any community benefit in there being a supply of decent housing. Lloyd LJ,[28] with whom the others agreed, referred to housing as falling with Article 8 (right to family life) of the European Convention on Human Rights (ECHR), as an individual right as opposed to a public right.

2.31 By contrast, where a person in need is housed, the individual benefit is treated as being incidental to the public charitable objective of caring for the disadvantaged. Thus, in the *Joseph Rowntree* case,[29] which concerned the provision of housing for the elderly, the fact that some residents were able to sell their properties at a market rate was held not to affect charitable status on the basis that this enhanced

---

25 Compare HM Revenue and Customs (HMRC), Charity Commission, HCA, *Affordable home ownership, charitable status and tax*, 2009.
26 [2012] EWCA Civ 569.
27 Below para 4.29.
28 At [109].
29 Above note 24.

the security which was especially needed in old age. To be charitable, therefore, a housing association must restrict its objects to meeting special kinds of need where there is a strong public interest.

2.32 There is well established case-law setting out trading activities and particular types of project which apart from housing schemes, are charitable in nature. These are not limited to the poor and so in theory could command market fees. In the context of hospitals, a number of homes established for supported housing fall into this definition including a home for epileptics[30] and a private nursing home.[31] Since many sheltered schemes for the frail and elderly or 'very sheltered schemes' or 'extra-care schemes' as they are known, are private nursing homes they would fall into this category as would, a supported housing project which provides nursing care, such as a communities care scheme where patients have been rehoused from hospital.

2.33 A non-charitable purpose can be valid if it is 'incidental' to another charitable purpose, for example intended to subsidise the latter. This applies especially to the trading and market sales activities carried out by many larger housing associations. However, there is a risk that the weight of the non-charitable activities cast doubt on the association's charitable status. The charity must not fund the non-charity other than on a commercial basis and shared services must be separately accounted for and charged at a commercial rate. The non-charitable element must not have any control over the charity's activities or the use of its funds.

2.34 A charitable housing association may have any of the basic three structures, namely, (by far the most common), a CBS under the CCBSA 2014 (above), a company or a trust. It can also have the special CIO structure mentioned above.[32] A company, trust or CIO must be registered with the Charity Commission, and is regulated both by the Commission and by the social housing regulator. Such a body is called a 'registered charity'. A CCBSA society is an 'exempt charity and, as such, is not subject to the full extent of Charity Commission regulation. In any given statutory context, therefore, it must be checked whether the matter concerns all charities (as is usually the case when considering tenants' rights), 'exempt charities' or 'registered charities'.

---

30 *Ormskirk Union v Chorlton Union* [1903] 1 KB 19.
31 *Re Smith, Barclays Bank Ltd v Mercantile Bank Ltd* [1962] 1 WLR 763.
32 Above para 2.18. In October 2018 two such bodies were registered with the RSH.

2.35 For the purpose of the CCBSA 2014, the notion of 'community benefit' differs from the 'public benefit' test for a charity in two respects. First, the notion of community benefit is free-standing and open-ended, not being limited by specific kinds of benefit; for example, *Helena* (above) could have qualified as a CBS. Second, charitable status does not require democratic control. Indeed, democratic control may be inconsistent with charitable status.

2.36 An 'almshouse charity' is a special category of housing association. An almshouse has been vaguely described as 'a house provided for the reception of poor persons', although they need not be destitute.[33] However, an almshouse charity must presumably be a trust proper. The residents of an almshouse are usually licensees without statutory security of tenure. An almshouse charity can register with the regulator although, out of some 1,600 almshouse charities, only about 200 have done so.[34] There are special taxation privileges and accounting provisions relating to registered almshouses, but otherwise they are in the same position as other charitable associations. A CBS often acts as a trustee on behalf of one or more almshouse charities.

Housing trusts

2.37 This somewhat archaic concept is not necessarily a trust in the legal sense and can apply to any legal structure. A housing trust is a housing association with more limited objectives. It is a body that is: a) required by its constitutive instrument to use the whole of its funds, including any surplus that may arise from its operations, for the purpose of providing housing accommodation; or b) required by the terms of its constituent instrument to devote the whole, or substantially the whole, of its funds to charitable purposes and in fact uses them for the purpose of providing housing accommodation.[35]

2.38 Therefore all housing trusts are non-profit-making and so fall within the definition of a housing association. However, many housing associations provide a range of services in addition to providing housing, such as personal care and support services, so that housing trusts as such form only a small part of the sector. (Unfortunately some housing associations are called housing trusts

---

33 *Mary Clark Home's Trustees v Anderson* [1904] 2 KB 645.
34 See HCA, *Registration for new entrants*, 2017, para 4.4.
35 Housing Act 1985 s6.

2.39 without being so in the strict sense, not helped by the apocryphal solicitor who told his client that 'as a housing association you are therefore a housing trust'.)

Whether a body is a housing trust depends on its purpose, not its structure. In *Hounslow LBC v Hare*[36] a testatrix left her home and garden to the local authority for the charitable purpose of providing flats for old people. The issue was whether the tenants had a statutory 'right to buy'. There was a conflict between a 'structural' approach based on the local authority as landlord under which the right to buy would exist, and a 'functional' approach based on the use of the flats. Knox J held that the latter approach prevailed, so that the identity of the landlord and the structure of the body were irrelevant. The will created a charitable housing trust which has a special exemption from the right to buy.

2.40 In *Richmond Housing Partnership Ltd v Brick Farm Management Ltd*[37] Stanley Burton J added the limitation that 'housing accommodation' in this context means only social housing. This seems questionable. If it is correct then the set-up in *Hare*, although charitable as serving the elderly, would not necessarily qualify as a housing trust since it would not necessarily be limited to social housing. Moreover, in a block of flats owned by a housing association, all the flats would have to be social housing. In *Richmond* itself, some of the flats were occupied by non social tenants.

2.41 In relation to its tenants, a *charitable* housing trust is usually treated the same as an RSL or PRP although, of course, unless registered as such, it is not subject to regulation except by the Charity Commission. A few special rules apply to housing trusts as such, mainly in connection with shared ownership leases. A housing trust, but not if it is a PRP or RSL, has statutory power to sell, lease or transfer management to the local housing authority.[38] The secretary of state has certain powers in relation to legal proceedings involving housing trust property.[39] Otherwise, a housing trust is in the same position as a private landlord.

---

36 (1992) 24 HLR 9.
37 [2005] EWHC 1650 (QB).
38 HAA 1985 s35.
39 HAA 1985 s36; see Law Commission No 4 (ii), Cmnd 9515.

Fully mutual housing associations

2.42 Fully mutual housing associations derive from the Victorian ideal of a self-governing co-operative society run on democratic principles. The criteria of full mutuality is that all the members of the association must be its tenants or prospective tenants and a tenancy cannot be granted or assigned to a person other than a member.[40] The term 'prospective' is undefined, but could mean a person who has an offer of a tenancy.[41] A fully mutual association is therefore formally a self-governing co-operative run by its tenants.

2.43 A fully mutual association can be registered under the CCBSA 2014, as a 'bona fide co-operative society' (above). If this is so, it is a 'co-operative housing association'.[42] Approximately 218 English co-operative housing associations are registered with the social housing regulator as PRPs. A fully mutual association could also be constituted as a company. There seems to be no fully-mutual company registered as a PRP.

2.44 A fully mutual association has certain privileges even if not registered as a PRP. The main privilege is that, unlike most other tenants, fully mutual tenants in England have no statutory security of tenure. It is important however when considering a fully mutual association to check in each case whether a particular privilege applies only to a co-operative housing association or to all fully mutual associations.

2.45 It has been suggested that a fully mutual association cannot be charitable because the mutuality of membership excludes the necessary public benefit element by limiting benefits to a closed group of members.[43] Most of the co-operatives registered with the social housing regulator are registered as non-charitable bodies.[44] This is questionable. It seems that for the purpose of relieving poverty, a charity can limit its benefits to a closed group perhaps on the basis that, even after the 2006 reforms, relieving poverty is in itself

---

40 HAA 1985 s1(2).
41 This creates a loophole which in earlier year enabled grasping professionals to form associations, reward themselves from fees and then not take up an offer of a tenancy. This is now combated by stringent controls over conflicts of interest (below chapter 10) and the powers of the regulators.
42 HAA 1985 s1, not to be confused with a 'housing co-operative' a term relating to certain obsolete local government bodies, see Rent Act 1977 s16.
43 *Joseph Rowntree* case (above), at 298.
44 There are six bodies described on the register as co-operatives and charitable. However, these may not be fully mutual bodies, although some originated as mutuals.

sufficient public benefit.⁴⁵ Therefore, if a fully mutual housing association limits membership to low-income people, it could be charitable. There is no decisive case-law. In *Over Seventies Housing Association Ltd v Westminster LBC*,⁴⁶ a fully mutual association claiming to cater for low-income people was denied charitable status, not because of mutuality but because its members did not have a genuine charitable need.

2.46 Sometimes housing owned by a local authority is managed by its tenants on mutual principles under a management agreement. Such a body is not fully mutual since it is not itself a landlord. Under earlier legislation, such bodies were confusingly called 'housing co-operatives', but are now called 'tenant management organisations' (TMOs). Finally, there are 'secondary co-operatives' which advise or assist other co-operatives. Unless they are themselves providers of housing, they cannot register with the social housing regulator.

2.47 Unlike the case in continental Europe, co-operatives have played a relatively small part in UK housing activity. They have been created by local authorities, by groups of individuals and by other housing associations; they have also been set up by banks as part of a mortgage rescue package. Indeed, it is unlikely that the original aspiration of a self-governing co-operative can be fully realised today, at least in the case of bodies subsidised by government. Stringent regulatory requirements concerning governance and finance are likely to require the delegation of management to professional managers. Indeed, many co-operative associations delegate management to another housing association.

2.48 However, a co-operative society cannot be a subsidiary of another housing association. Although there is no statutory requirement of autonomy, the FCA's conditions for registration as a bona fide co-operative (above) normally require autonomy. Thus member/tenants must retain formal control, for example through powers of veto or dismissal of the governing body. In the case of a subsidiary, the parent must either control the composition of the board of management or hold at least 50 per cent of the nominal equity.⁴⁷ The regulator requires that the parent be in 'unequivocal control' of its subsidiary.

---

45 *Dingle v Turner* [1972] AC 601; *Attorney General v Charity Commission for England and Wales* [2011] UKUT 421.
46 (1974) 230 EG 1593.
47 HRA 2008 s271.

2.49 Related to co-operatives are 'self-build housing associations'. A self-build housing association must have as its sole object the provision of dwelling houses for sale to or occupation by its members which must have been built or improved principally with the members' own labour.[48] Self-build schemes are eligible for government funding whether or not registered as RPs. There are also special tax provisions. Apart from that, self-build associations have no special regime. They are not necessarily fully mutual.

2.50 Broadly similar to a co-operative, is a 'community land trust' (CLT).[49] Introduced by the Labour government in 2008, a CLT is a corporate body (either a CBS or a company), established by a local community in order to further its own social, economic and environmental interests by acquiring land or other assets in order to provide a benefit to the local community (people who live and work in a specified area or wish to do so). There is no requirement of full mutuality, but a CLT must be controlled by its members and members of the local community must have the opportunity to become members.

2.51 If it owns land in England and provides social housing or intends to do so, a CLT can register with the regulator in its own right.[50] Out of some 225 CLTs, seven have done so mainly in rural areas. CLTs are not in any special position as regards housing association law, but public funding from a variety sources is available to them.[51] In order to provide social housing for the benefit of local people, a CLT may grant leases of land or buildings to other developers who may themselves be housing associations of any kind. Subject to the community benefit requirement, a CLT might distribute profits, in which case it would not be a housing association but could still register with the regulator as a PRP.

2.52 Finally, there are 'co-ownership housing associations'. In the case of the ordinary fully mutual association, a 'par value' co-operative, an individual tenant/member has no financial claim to the equity of the association other than his or her nominal share. By contrast, a co-ownership member/tenant who vacates his or her dwelling has the right, under the tenancy agreement, to a payment based on a formula loosely representing his or her proportion of the equity minus various expenses.[52] The term 'co-ownership' is therefore

48 HAA 1985 s1(3).
49 HRA 2008 s79(2).
50 HRA 2008 s112.
51 See HC Briefing Paper 2903, 14 June 2017.
52 Rent Act 1977 s86(3A).

misleading, since the relationship between the society which owns the dwelling and the individual occupier is at all times one of landlord and tenant. Co-ownerships of this kind may also fall within the current definition of 'shared ownership'.

2.53 Most co-ownerships were dissolved in the early 1980s under a non-statutory scheme which enabled their members to buy their dwellings at a price representing that dwelling's share of the association's debts mainly a government mortgage. A few co-ownerships remain. There appears to be no co-ownership society registered with the regulator in England and one registered with the Welsh ministers in Wales.

Local authority connections

2.54 There have always been strong relationships between local authorities and housing associations. Although local authority provision has recently been revived, most new building is still carried out by housing associations.[53] Housing associations have certain requirements to work with local authorities. In particular, an association registered with the social housing regulator must co-operate with local authorities 'to such extent as is reasonable in the circumstances' in offering accommodation to people with priority on the authority's housing register and must co-operate more generally if so requested. If invited to do so, it must co-operate with a local authority in preparing or modifying its 'sustainable community strategy.[54]

2.55 Local authorities have a range of powers to promote and influence housing association.[55] These include making loans or grants to housing associations and nominating tenants. Local authorities may directly participate in a housing association by acquiring shares in it. To this end a local authority is exempt from rules which limit the size of the shareholding of a member of a CCBSA society.[56]

2.56 There are several varieties of local authority participation. At one extreme, an 'arm's length management company' (ALMO) is wholly controlled by the authority and manages council owned stock. Its

---

53 See Morphet and Clifford, *Local authority direct provision of housing*, RTPA, 2017.
54 Housing Act 1996 ss170, 213; HRA 2008 s126.
55 See Local Government Act 2000 s2: promotion of well-being of the area; Localism Act 2011 ss1–7: general competence; HAA 1985 ss58, 59(2); Housing Act 1996 s22: promotion of and assistance to housing associations.
56 CCBSA 2014 s24(2)(b), (c).

membership usually comprises one-third tenants, the rest being a mix of councilors and 'independents', the latter chosen by the authority. The Housing Act 1985 provides for agreements with a TMO.[57] Under these provisions, where the tenants make a proposal, regulations made by the secretary of state require the authority to provide facilities to assist the proposal. The governing body of the TMO can include local authority members and, since a TMO is funded by the authority, its autonomy may be doubtful. Although they are housing associations, neither an ALMO nor a TMO can be registered with the social housing regulator, since they are not themselves providers. However, their parent local authority must be registered.[58]

2.57 A local authority can also create an ordinary housing association. Here there might be local authority representation on the board but not necessarily with control or financial responsibility. These are often called 'local housing companies.' There are about 50 established local housing companies used as vehicles for local authority housing developments.

2.58 Stock transfers either to specially created or existing associations are carried out under a local authority's general power to dispose of land with the consent of the secretary of state provided that, following a ballot, a majority of the tenants are not opposed.[59] Such transfers are sometimes required by the government as a condition of funding and may be without payment due to the bad repair of the dwellings. There have been about 100 'Large Scale Voluntary Transfers' (LSVTs) of council tenanted stock to housing associations comprising about 1.7m homes. The average size of a stock transfer association is 5,000 dwellings, much exceeding the average of traditional associations of 1,400. About 40 per cent of housing association stock was formerly owned by local authorities. This further complicates the identity of the sector, leaning as it does towards the public dimension.

2.59 However, as part of the government's aim of treating housing associations as part of the private sector, regulations made under the Housing and Planning Act 2016 limit local authority influence over housing associations of which they are members by reducing their

---

57 As modified by HRA 2008 s295. See Housing (Right to Manage) (England) Regulations 2012 SI No 1821.
58 HRA 2008 ss113, 114. Housing and Regeneration Act 2008 (Registration of Local Authorities) Order 2010 SI No 844.
59 Housing Act 1985 ss32, 34, 34A, Sch 3A; HRA 2008 s294.

voting and representation rights.[60] The Regulation of Registered Social Landlords (Wales) Act 2018 does the same. These measures prevent a local authority from blocking a decision of a PRP or RSL. These restrictions can be removed where an association (an ALMO, above), is wholly owned by a local authority. They are discussed in chapter 13.

60 Regulation of Social Housing (Influence of Local Authorities) (England) Regulations 2017 SI No 1102.

CHAPTER 3

Public or private sector: public or private law?

3.1 Introduction: the nature of the problem
3.9 Government accounts
3.14 **Human Rights Act 1998**
3.14 Overview
3.33 'Horizontal effect'
3.36 Can a housing association have human rights?
3.38 Judicial review
3.48 **Public bodies and EU law**

Introduction: the nature of the problem

3.1 It is sometimes necessary to decide whether a particular housing association is a public body or is exercising functions governed by public law. 'Public' in this context does not mean 'the public interest' or 'benefiting the public' – it is concerned with the relationship between the association and government bodies. English law is historically and conceptually orientated towards private law, but in recent years public law concepts have been grafted on in particular contexts. Unlike most European jurisdictions, English law has no general concept of the state or even of government. The Crown is undeniably a public body, but otherwise there is a spectrum of separate bodies created or adopted by particular statutes such as local authorities or recognised as public by the courts or adopted by the government itself.[1] There is therefore no general principle we can reach for.

3.2 Housing associations are in a conspicuously ambivalent position. On the one hand, they are structured and operate in the same way as any private business – building, renting or selling homes and providing care services. Indeed, most of their funding is private from rents, sales and bank loans.[2] They are not obliged to register with the government, although most of them do so. The relationship between a housing association and government is based on agreements and the statutory powers of the regulator. The position of their tenants is ambivalent, based on a cocktail of private and public sector rules. Housing associations claim the advantages of the private, most obviously access to money and also expertise, flexibility and the capacity for long-term planning.

3.3 On the other hand, their main activity is to deliver government social housing policy, and to this end they accept registration, government subsidy and government direction. These controls may neutralise some of the private sector advantages. However, no housing association is an agent of government in the full sense – for example, of the companies that run jails where government functions are delegated to a private body. At the operational level at least, housing associations have substantial autonomy.

---

1 See Cabinet Office, *Categories of public bodies: guidance for departments*, April 2016.
2 See the dissenting judgment of Rix LJ in *R (Weaver) v London & Quadrant Housing Trust* [2009] EWCA Civ 587.

3.4   As non-profit voluntary bodies, often charities, housing associations are historically part of what is sometimes called the 'third sector' for which the law has no pigeon hole. The predominant view of the courts is that charitable status does not make a body a public body and is at most a background factor.[3] Regulation by government is perhaps the most prominent 'public' aspect of a housing association. However, this is not conclusive since it applies to all charities and most private enterprises for reasons of public protection.[4] Similarly, government subsidy is not enough in itself, since many palpably private entities such as farms and theatres enjoy this, leaving aside the many indirect subsidies enjoyed by most of us.

3.5   The possession of special statutory powers is a more reliable indicator of a public function, but may be definitive only if these powers are 'relatively wide ranging and intrusive'.[5] In common with local authorities and other public agencies, housing associations registered with government have certain statutory powers to apply to the court for anti-social behaviour orders and parenting orders. They also have powers along with local authorities to apply to the court to create 'demoted tenancies' and 'family intervention tenancies'.[6] Their tenants are treated as public sector tenants as regards access to the Housing Ombudsman. Under Housing Act 1996 s170, a private registered provider (PRP) or registered social landlord (RSL) must co-operate with a local authority in offering accommodation to people with priority under the authority's allocation scheme. There is a similar duty to the central government under the Immigration and Asylum Act 1999.

3.6   It is not surprising, therefore, that a housing association is public for some purposes and private for others. The courts have usually been left to sort it out. Occasionally statute deals with the matter directly, with mixed results. For example, a non-profit PRP and an RSL are 'public sector landlords' for various purposes, notably in connection with the Leasehold Reform, Housing and Urban Development Act 1993.[7] A PRP or RSL tenancy is a 'public sector tenancy' for certain purposes related to the right to buy.[8] Under Housing Act 1985 s429A, the secretary of state can give financial assistance to any persons 'managing public sector or former public sector

---

3   *YL v Birmingham City Council* [2008] 1 AC 95.
4   *YL v Birmingham City Council* [2008] 1 AC 95 at [116], [134].
5   *YL v Birmingham City Council* [2008] 1 AC 95 at [101], [167].
6   Below paras 8.48 and 8.50.
7   Below para 8.78. Housing Act 1985 s171(2) as amended provides a general key.
8   Housing Act 1985 Sch 4 paras 6–10.

housing', including for this purpose PRPs and RSLs. An RSL is a public body under the Public Services Ombudsman (Wales) Act 2005 for the purposes of the Welsh Public Services Ombudsman service. Housing associations registered with the RSH are exempt from the licensing schemes applicable in England and Wales to private sector landlords under the Housing Act 2004. RSLs and fully mutual associations are similarly exempt under the Housing (Wales) Act 2014.

3.7 On the other hand, the power of a local authority under Local Government Act 1988 s24 to give assistance to a 'private body' for housing purposes treats a housing association as a private body. The same applies to the transfer of local authority housing to the private sector.[9] Most importantly the Freedom of Information Act 2000, which, subject to many exceptions, requires a 'public authority' to disclose information, deals with the meaning of 'public authority' by listing the bodies that qualify and empowering the secretary of state to add to the list. Housing associations are not on the list.

3.8 The most important general contexts in which the question whether a housing association is public or private are as follows. Different criteria apply in each context, albeit the second and fourth are closely related.

1) Are housing associations part of the public sector for the purposes of the government's financial accounts and therefore subject to oversight by parliament and to public spending disciplines?
2) Is a housing association subject to the Human Rights Act (HRA) 1998?
3) Can a housing association have human rights?
4) Is a housing association subject to judicial review so that its actions can be challenged in the Administrative Court?
5) Is a housing association a public body for the purpose of EU law, especially in relation to procurement and competition law?

Government accounts

3.9 Characteristic of the unwritten UK constitution, the question whether a body is deemed to be a public or private sector body for this purpose is decided by the government itself. There are no legal criteria, and the matter seems to be one of convention depending only on general acceptance by officials and politicians. The ultimate arbiter of the government accounts is the House of Commons, which

9 See Housing Act 1985 Sch 3A; Housing Act 1988 s38.

3.10 The decision is formally made by the Office for National Statistics (ONS) which, as part of the Statistics Board, a non-ministerial central government department, provides independent statistical information and advice on behalf of the Crown.[10] This includes classifications, but no statutory criteria is provided.[11] The ONS is not required to give reasons for a particular classification. However, it is required to publish the principles and procedures which it uses.[12]

3.11 Following the political events discussed in chapter 1, the ONS has for now classified housing associations in England and Wales as private bodies.[13] This does not directly affect the position of a housing association under the general law, since only statute or the courts can do this but is of great importance for a housing association's dealing with government notably the removal of public sector borrowing limits and accounting rules.

3.12 The ONS criterion appears to be the extent to which government can control the constitution and assets of the body in question. The matter is one of overall impression, and as such highly political. The current classification that of 'private non-financial corporation' was triggered by new regulations intended to weaken the influence of local government over housing associations.[14] This meets the problem of the emergence of a 'two-track' sector comprising housing associations developed by local authorities which, in terms of size, are a majority and others less favoured.

3.13 In addition, the Housing and Planning Act 2016 removed certain regulatory powers to consent to the disposal of land and constitutional changes and reduced the regulator's powers of intervention. These powers were replaced by requirements to notify the regulator who therefore retains considerable influence (see para 5.55). However, a factor that does not seem to have been treated as significant was the increasing control exercised by government over rents and the conditions housing association endure. In Wales, similar measures were introduced by the Regulation of Registered Social Landlords (Wales) Act 2018.

---

10 Statistics and Registration Services Act 2007.
11 Statistics and Registration Services Act 2007 s9.
12 Statistics and Registration Services Act 2007 s17.
13 See letter from ONS to the Treasury, 17 November 2017; letter from ONS to Welsh Ministers, 27 June 2018.
14 Regulation of Social Housing (Influence of Local Authorities) (England) Regulations 2017 SI No 1102. See letter from ONS to the Treasury, 17 November 2017.

52 *Housing associations: a legal handbook / chapter 3*

Human Rights Act 1998

Overview

3.14 Many aspects of social housing may fall within the HRA 1998. The HRA 1998 requires that 'Convention rights' under the European Convention on Human Rights (ECHR) be enforceable in domestic courts. HRA 1998 s6(1) makes it unlawful for a 'public authority' to act in a way which is incompatible with a Convention right. Section 7(1) enables a 'victim' to bring proceedings against a public authority.

3.15 'Public authority' includes anybody 'certain of whose functions are functions of a public nature' (section 6(3(b)). Crucially, under this head, 'if the nature of the act' is private it will not be deemed to be exercising a public function in respect of that act' (section 6(5)).

3.16 Thus the Act does not provide a comprehensive definition of public authority, but has left the matter to the courts. The cases display substantial disagreement, and the judgments are diffuse and unco-ordinated. There is a need for a definitive Supreme Court decision, but so far no suitable case has emerged. The current leading case, namely *R (Weaver) v London and Quadrant Housing Trust*,[15] reached the Court of Appeal only after the claimant had withdrawn and perhaps for that reason the Supreme Court refused leave to appeal. Given the uncertainty involved, the Equality and Human Rights Commission suggests that, if an organisation is not sure whether it is likely to be subject to the HRA 1998, it should carry out its business in a way which complies with the Convention rights.[16]

3.17 It is common ground that there are two kinds of public authority. First, there are bodies, such as central and local government and the police, which are inherently public. These are known as 'core' or 'paradigm' public authorities. As a statutory public body, the regulator is of course a core public authority, as are the Welsh Ministers and local authorities. Apparently a core authority cannot act privately, since all the activities of core public authorities fall within the HRA 1998.[17]

3.18 Second, there are 'functional' or 'hybrid' public authorities. These are bodies which perform some public functions, but also perform private functions. A clear case is that of a security company transporting prisoners for the government, but which is also doing work

---

15 [2009] EWCA Civ 587.
16 Equality and Human Rights Commission, *Human rights at home: Guidance for social housing providers*, 2011.
17 *Aston Cantlow and Wilmcote with Billesley Parochial Church Council v Wallbank* [2004] 1 AC 546.

unconnected with government. It was conceded in *Weaver* that housing associations are hybrid public authorities.

3.19 Thus the inquiry is a two-stage one. First, it must be established that the body in question is exercising a public *function*. Second, it must be established that the particular *act* is not of a private character. For example, housing social tenants is plausibly a public function, but is evicting an individual tenant a public act?

3.20 The courts have concluded that some functions of a housing association can be public functions. The Court of Appeal has suggested that a 'generous' approach should be taken.[18] Nevertheless, attempts to fashion a single overarching test have failed. These include government subsidy and regulation, charitable status or acting in the public interest;[19] acting on behalf of government as where a local authority provides care through a private agency;[20] and historic connection with local government as where a tenancy is transferred from a local authority or the association was created by a local authority.[21] However, these matters may re-emerge as background matters, reinforcing conclusions reached on other grounds.

3.21 The courts take what has been called a 'factor-based' approach.[22] A housing association exercises a public function because of an accumulation of factors concerning connections with government, none of which is enough in itself, and which outweigh any private ingredients. Thus the matter depends on subjective impression – 'a sufficient public flavour' – in all the circumstances of the particular case. There is therefore no sharp dividing line hence the problem.

3.22 The particular activities in issue must be looked at separately from the rest of the association's activities. The earliest formulation was that the more closely that an act is 'enmeshed' in the activities of a public body, the more likely it is to be public.[23] *R (Weaver) v London and Quadrant Housing Trust*,[24] is the leading case. It concerned the eviction of an assured tenant of a publicly funded social housing

---

18 *Poplar HARCA Ltd v Donoghue* [2001] 4 All ER 604 at [58], [65].
19 *YL v Birmingham City Council* [2008] 1 AC 95; *R (Heathers) v Leonard Cheshire Foundation* [2002] 2 All ER 936 at [53].
20 *YL v Birmingham City Council* [2008] 1 AC 95, Lord Bingham at [17]–[20], Baroness Hale [62]–[68]: it should not matter through whom the government carries out its duties.
21 *R (Weaver) v London and Quadrant Housing Trust* [2009] EWCA Civ 587 at [97]; *YL v Birmingham City Council* [2008] 1 AC 95 at [61], [105].
22 Per Lord Mance in *YL v Birmingham City Council* [2008] 1 AC 95 at [91].
23 *Poplar HARCA Ltd v Donoghue* [2001] 4 All ER 604 at 621 (Lord Woolf CJ).
24 [2009] EWCA Civ 587 at [35].

scheme for non-payment of rent. Thus it concerned the core function of a social landlord. Elias LJ suggested that the broad approach is to ask whether the particular body is 'governmental', but warned that this can be only a rough guide since the phrase in the Act is *public*.

3.23 Indeed, apart from defence, public order and foreign affairs, it is doubtful whether any function is inherently governmental. What is 'governmental' is a matter of political choice as to what functions particular governments take on. According to Baroness Hale in *YL v Birmingham City Council*,[25] caring for the elderly is such a function. In *R (McIntyre) v Gentoo Group Ltd*[26] the High Court suggested that managing and allocating social housing were inherently public functions. What Elias LJ seems to mean is that there must be specific links between the function in question and the activities of central or local government. These may include public funding, co-operating with a government body, exercising statutory powers, 'taking the place of' government proper or 'providing a public service' although the meaning of the latter two is obscure.[27]

3.24 In *Weaver* the majority (Elias and Lawrence Collins LLJ) held that the trust's management of the scheme was a public function. This was primarily because the scheme in question had a 'significant reliance' on public finance and the trust was regulated as to policy matters beyond securing good behaviour.[28] The regulator controlled such matters as tenure, rent levels, allocation policies and governance.

3.25 The other main factor was that the association worked closely with the local authority by virtue of its statutory duty to co-operate. Indeed, although it did not arise in *Weaver*, some local authorities exercise influence over housing associations through voting rights on their boards (a practice which central government has intervened to weaken). Elias LJ also said that charitable status was a background factor (although in the other cases it did not seem to be relevant at all). However, since all housing associations are non-profit bodies, it is unlikely that a non-charitable association would have fared differently.

3.26 Crucially, it was held that an 'act' done in direct pursuance of a public function, such as a tenancy termination, is a public act irrespective of its source in the private law of contract since the way in which a function is performed is inseparable from the function itself. This endorses the approach of Baroness Hale dissenting in the *YL*

---

25 *YL v Birmingham City Council* [2008] 1 AC 95.
26 [2010] EWHC 5 (Admin).
27 See *YL v Birmingham City Council* [2008] 1 AC 95 at [105], [135].
28 At [68]–[71].

3.27 case (above) that an act in relation to the person for whom the public function is being provided cannot be a private act.

Thus all the circumstances of each case must be examined which, given the range and mix of housing association activity, is not conducive to legal certainty. In particular, the relative importance of individual elements of the mix is unclear. However it appears from *Weaver* that the mainstream activity of a PRP and RSL to provide publicly subsidised social rented or shared ownership housing will normally be a public function.

3.28 Rix LJ strongly dissented, holding that the management of social housing is not a public function. He approached the matter through a commercial prism, namely the practical perspective that 'a housing association's finance structure and operations are essentially in the private and business world rather than in the world of government' and that there is nothing special about the various government interventions. It may that the disagreement arises because Rix LJ was concentrating on the operational level while the majority focused on broader policy issues. This exemplifies the schizophrenic nature of the housing association sector, doomed by its Faustian pact to lurch between the commercial and the governmental worlds. Controversially, Rix LJ also asserted that, in delivering public objectives on a large scale, private sector management expertise may be best. He thought that the private law contractual basis of an association's relationship with its tenants spoke against a public relationship, since neither the HRA 1998 nor judicial review should override a contract.

3.29 *Weaver* was followed in a judicial review case, *R (McIntyre) v Gentoo Group Ltd*.[29] The association in question was charitable and was created by a local authority in 2001. The High Court did not emphasise the local connection, but suggested that the functions of managing and allocating social housing were inherently public functions. In *R (MacLeod) v Governors of the Peabody Trust*, also a judicial review case,[30] *Weaver* was distinguished on its facts. The High Court held that the association was exercising a private function in relation to a relatively high rent 'key-worker' scheme which, although promoted by government, was neither funded nor regulated by it. These cases are discussed further in the next section.

3.30 In summary, therefore, a scheme-by-scheme approach must be taken. A housing association exercises a public function in respect of the allocation and management of social housing where there is a

---

29 [2010] EWHC 5 (Admin).
30 [2016] EWHC 737 (Admin). See para 3.45.

substantial enmeshing with government in the form of policy direction or a substantial relationship with a local authority. The exercise of statutory powers is likely to be conclusive. At the other extreme, unsubsidised schemes are likely to be governed by private law. Otherwise, the range of uncertainty includes actions which are neutral in the sense that they may contribute towards a public function but are not inherently connected with it, such as raising private funding or carrying out repairs. These are unlikely to be public acts.[31]

3.31 The extent to which a relationship with a local authority is required is also obscure. It is unclear whether the outcome of *Weaver* would have been different in the absence of a local authority connection. The decision of the Court of Appeal in *Poplar HARCA v Donoghue* was criticised on the ground that it gave too much weight to the fact that the tenancy in question had been transferred from a local authority but this is not the same thing. We suggest that a local authority connection is a major factor where the association is directly collaborating with the authority but is otherwise only a background factor.

3.32 More difficult is the range of projects that are not funded or closely regulated by government but which contribute indirectly to its mainstream activities such as lettings at the higher rent ranges not closely controlled by government ('affordable', 'intermediate') and market sales. These are unlikely to be held public, but here the line is particularly blurred. Moreover, from the point of view of an association it may be artificial to separate its different projects in this way. From the point of view of a tenant, neighbours may be subject to different levels of protection depending on the nature of the particular tenancy, lower rents being more likely to attract the HRA 1998.

'Horizontal effect'

3.33 On the face of it, the HRA 1998 is enforceable only against a person exercising a public function. However, the Act may sometimes have a 'horizontal effect' in the sense that a private person may also be liable. Unfortunately, the courts have not ruled on the question. There are arguments both for and against horizontality. Arguments in favour are as follows.

1) The court itself is a public authority subject to the HRA 1998, especially where its discretionary powers to give a remedy apply as in the case of a possession order.[32]

31 *Poplar HARCA v Donoghue* [2001] 4 All ER 604 at [66].
32 *R (McLellan) v Bracknell Forest BC* [2002] 1 All ER 899 at [42]; *Campbell v MGN Ltd* [2004] 2 All ER 995 at [133].

2) At least in the case of a serious breach, the state has a duty to protect the individual against a failure by a private landlord. The European Court applied this to Article 8 of the ECHR (respect for privacy and family life) in *Udovicic v Croatia*[33] where a private landlord had persistently failed to deal with noisy neighbours.
3) HRA 1998 s3 requires that all legislation must be interpreted according to the Convention. In *Ghaidan v Godin-Mendoza*[34] the House of Lords applied this in the context of Articles 8 and 14 (discrimination) to a private tenancy.

3.34 The main arguments against a horizontal effect are, first, that section 6(1) seems to impose a duty only on a public authority and secondly that, according to section 7, a claim under the Act can be made only by a person who would be a 'victim' if proceedings were brought in Strasbourg (section 7(1)(b), (7)). Under Article 34 of the ECHR, a claim in Strasbourg can be made only against a party to the Convention, usually a state. Therefore, since the purpose of the HRA 1998 is no more than to give effect to the ECHR, a person can perhaps be a victim only against the state. However, in *YL v Birmingham City Council* (above) Baroness Hale suggested that the best way to enforce a duty against the state may be to take action against the private body concerned.

3.35 Even if the HRA 1998 might otherwise apply, in the private context, a power exercised by a private body derived primarily from the private law of contract, such as the termination of a tenancy agreement, is not subject at least to Article 8. *McDonald v McDonald*[35] concerned the eviction by a private landlord, under the terms of a mortgage agreement, of a tenant with a personality disorder. The Supreme Court held that, while Article 8 is not excluded altogether, it cannot be used to justify a different outcome than that required by the contractual relationship, at least where there is a statutory safeguard. By contrast, in *Manchester City Council v Pinnock*,[36] (eviction of a local authority tenant) the Supreme Court held that the court should examine all the circumstances of an eviction including contractual matters of a *public sector* tenant to ensure compliance with Article 8. Thus *Pinnock* would apply to the public functions of a housing association but *McDonald* to its private functions.

---

33 [2014] ECHR 443. See also *Redfearn v UK* [2012] ECHR 1878.
34 [2004] 3 All ER 411.
35 [2016] UKSC 28: decision upheld by ECtHR in *FJM v UK*, Application No 76202/16, 29 November 2018.
36 [2010] 3 WLR 1441.

Can a housing association have human rights?

3.36 There is a widespread assumption that a public body cannot claim a human right of its own.[37] If this is so, then a housing association, where it is exercising a public function, may not claim the protection of the HRA 1998 but can do so in its private capacity. For example in respect, of a decision by the regulator to take over its land or management the matter would depend on whether the issue concerned its publicly funded activities. An individual member or employee of a housing association can of course always invoke a human right against the regulator.

3.37 However, the assumption in question seems to derive from the European legal concept of the 'state' as a single entity and so may not apply to the common law framework of the UK which does not recognise the state as an entity but envisages the public sector as comprising many distinct bodies.[38] If this is so, then, just as a public body such as a local authority can bring ordinary legal proceedings against another public authority such as a minister, so it should be able to invoke the HRA 1998.

Judicial review

3.38 Judicial review is concerned with ensuring that a public body acts in accordance with basic principles of legality, fairness and rationality. It therefore overlaps to some extent with human rights issues. The HRA 1998 and the common law of judicial review overlap since the scope of the latter also depends on a public function.

3.39 It has been stressed, however, that the purpose of the two regimes is not the same, the HRA 1998 having the more limited purpose of following the ECHR. Therefore, it cannot be assumed that a body is public in both contexts.[39] However, in all the cases the courts have taken the same approach. Indeed, in *Poplar HARCA v Donoghue*[40] the Court of Appeal suggested that HRA 1998 s6 was 'inspired' by the approach of the courts to judicial review.

3.40 From a housing association point of view, important judicial review issues focus on compliance with an association's rules and

---

37 *Aston Cantlow and Wilmcote with Billesley Parochial Church Council v Wallbank* [2004] 1 AC 546 at [8], [11].
38 See Cabinet Office, *Categories of public bodies: guidance for departments*, April 2016.
39 See *R (Weaver) v London and Quadrant Housing Trust* [2009] EWCA Civ 587 at [35], [37].
40 At [65].

polices and whether a tenant or an applicant has a legitimate expectation that the association will treat him or her fairly. This is discussed further in later chapters in the context of individual rights.

3.41 The High Court process for judicial review depends on the matter in question being concerned with a 'public function'.[41] Unlike the human rights context, there is no distinction between 'core' and 'hybrid' bodies, nor between 'function' and ' act'. If a 'function' is public, 'acts in pursuance' of that function are also public even if carried out under a private law power. Within an overall public law framework, an individual element should not therefore be insulated from review.

3.42 Earlier cases had taken a simplistic approach, namely whether the particular function was based on a private law mechanism such as contract or was derived from statute. Thus in *R v Servite Houses ex p Goldsmith*,[42] a case about the closure of a care home, Moses J held that a housing association was not a public body for judicial review purposes. However, he reached this conclusion reluctantly, on the basis of precedent[43] rather than principle, taking the view that in current conditions of privatised public services a more liberal approach might be preferable. *Servite* is therefore probably no longer good law.

3.43 Indeed in *Weaver* (above), the Court of Appeal held that judicial review would be available as well as the HRA 1998, although the matter was not fully argued.[44] The matter arose next in *R (McIntyre) v Gentoo Group Ltd*,[45] which concerned a decision under a mutual exchange scheme. It was held that that the matter was one of public law, since public law principles apply whether or not there's a contractual relationship. The court also held that the matter does not depend on whether a statutory function is involved. Indeed the High Court expressed the matter broadly by suggesting that the functions of managing and allocating social housing were inherently public functions.

3.44 And in *R (Trafford) v Blackpool BC*,[46] the eviction of a solicitor from a council owned 'Enterprise Centre' providing accommodation and support for developing small businesses, was held to be subject to judicial review. Despite its contractual and commercial nature, the tenancy was sufficiently related to the council's public functions. This was, first, because lettings were subject to policies relating to the

---

41 Civil Procedure Rules 1998 r54.1.
42 [2001] BLGR 55.
43 *Peabody Housing Association Ltd v Greene* (1979) 38 P & CR 644.
44 At [83].
45 [2010] EWHC 5 (Admin).
46 [2014] EWHC 85 (Admin).

welfare of the area; and second, because the relationship was not 'a purely arm's-length' one since the centre had been built with public money and contained support agencies for its tenants. On the other hand, in *R (MacLeod) v Governors of the Peabody Trust*[47] the High Court held that the trust was exercising a private function. *MacLeod* concerned a refusal to permit a tenancy exchange of what was described as 'a social tenancy lite'. The claimant's tenancy had been transferred to Peabody by the Crown Estates Commission (CEC) as part of a large scale transfer. This was under a government-promoted 'key-worker' scheme which provided housing at an 'intermediate' rent slightly below market level but above social levels to persons nominated by public employers to meet housing shortages in London.

3.45 Despite having initially supported it, Peabody had refused the claimant's application for an exchange of his flat, a right available under its policies to ordinary social housing tenants, because under the arrangement with CEC which was part of the tenant's contract, the flat could be re-let only to another key worker in the same scheme. The High Court held that factors pointing to the private side of the line were, first, that the flat was unsubsidised being bought with private funds. Second, unlike Peabody's ordinary stock, the flat was not 'socially rented' since the rent was not subject to the same level of government regulation. Third, Peabody was not assisting a local authority. On the other side of the equation, the fact that the tenancy was part of a government scheme was a public element. Overall, however, there was insufficient 'public flavour' or 'enmeshing' with government. This was perhaps an easy case, not being truly borderline.

3.46 The recent relaxation of the regulatory regime (above) raises further doubts. However, it is suggested that the Housing and Planning Act 2016's loosening of control over assets do not affect the main factor in *Weaver*, namely that the particular scheme was carried out with government subsidy and control. On the other hand, the reduction of local authority influence may in some circumstances be relevant. The ONS classification of housing associations as private bodies (above) is at most a background factor.

3.47 In our common law system, public law and private law are not ring-fenced. Where a matter is held to be one of public law, it does not follow that contractual matters are irrelevant. A contract may provide the framework against which the fairness or reasonableness of a public law act is assessed. However, where a contract is inconsistent with a public law principle the latter prevails. This is discussed in chapter 9.

---

47 [2016] EWHC 737 (Admin).

Table of tests of public law function for judicial review and human rights purposes

Tests apply to specific schemes. No single test is either necessary or sufficient, and most are questions of degree. Those under 'minor' do not qualify in themselves, but might assist in a borderline case.
'?' indicates judicial disagreement.
'*' means unlikely.

	Major	Minor	Neutral	Contra-indication
Statutory powers:	Y			
Government directed scheme:	Y			
Regulation in itself:			Y	
Government subsidy:	Y			
Working with local government:	Y			
Function also or previously carried out by government:		Y		
Provision of social housing:	Y			
Local government history:		Y?*	Y	
Private law origins of power:				Y?*
Charitable status:		Y?		Y?

Public bodies and EU law

3.48 While the EU Treaty and EU regulations are capable of binding individuals or corporations directly in their national courts ('horizontal effect' – see above), EU directives do not have direct effect except against the state and its agencies ('vertical effect'). According to *Foster v British Gas plc*,[48] a body is part of the state if it has been made responsible

---

48 [1990] ECR I-3313.

pursuant to a measure adopted by the state for providing a public service under the control of the state and which has for that purpose *special powers* beyond those which result from the normal rules applicable in relations between individuals. Therefore, a housing association may not be part of the state except in connection with the limited special powers it possesses.

3.49 The main context where European law affects housing associations is that of public procurement of services, supplies and works. A series of directives regulates public procurement procedures in the interests of fair and open competition.[49] These seem to apply to housing associations. There are financial thresholds below which the directives do not apply.

3.50 For the purpose of the procurement regulations a contracting authority includes as far as relevant 'the state, regional or local authorities, bodies governed by public law or associations formed by one or more such authorities or one or more such bodies governed by public law'. To be governed by public law a body must 'be established for the specific purposes of meeting needs in the general interest, not having an individual or commercial character', must be financed 'for the most part by the state, regional or local authorities or other bodies governed by public law' *or* 'subject to management or supervision by such bodies' *or* 'more than half' of the board is appointed by such bodies'.

3.51 In view of the extent of regulation, housing associations seem to fall within this definition at least when carrying out government sponsored schemes.[50] Despite the range of their activities, it is doubtful whether housing associations could be regarded as 'industrial or commercial in character', particularly in view of the public interest and the non-profit basis of their constitutions. In many cases, of course, housing association contracts will be below the threshold values, and for that reason alone would fall outside the public procurement regime.

---

49 Directives 2014/23/EU, 2014/24/EU, Public Contracts Regulations 2015 SI No 102.
50 See Public Contract Regulations 2015 reg 2 and *Commission v France* C-237/99.

PART 2

Regulation

CHAPTER 4

Regulation: general

4.1	Introduction: the regulators
4.15	Jurisdiction of the regulators
4.20	Registration: English bodies
4.22	Eligibility for registration
4.28	Registration: Welsh bodies
4.35	Removal from the register
4.37	The framework of regulation
4.40	The objectives of social housing regulation
4.44	Standards
4.48	Guidance
4.50	General constraints on the powers of the English regulator
4.60	Consultation and information
4.62	Tenant involvement
4.66	Openness: disclosure of information – gradings
4.74	Regulation of accounts and audit
4.75	Financial assistance
4.76	The practice of the English regulator
4.82	Regulation of Welsh bodies

Introduction: the regulators

4.1 The regulation of housing associations has been subject to considerable instability arising mainly because of an unending and repetitive debate as to whether the functions of funding and regulating housing associations should be exercised by separate bodies. Until 2008 the same body, namely the Housing Corporation, carried out both functions, albeit its funding power was on behalf of the secretary of state. There is an established legal principle of 'natural justice', not always acknowledged in government circles, that the appearance of justice is as important as justice itself.[1] On this basis, regulation should be genuinely independent both of the funder and of government.

4.2 Moreover, where the same legal entity exercises both functions, its investment activities are exposed to legal liability for regulatory failure. On the other hand, it was sometimes maintained by Housing Corporation officials that efficiency, co-operation, and expertise make it desirable to combine the two functions in a single body and that voluntary measures ('Chinese walls') to prevent the untoward exchange of information ensure sufficient independence since officials who know each other personally think each other trustworthy. There was also an element of cronyism between Housing Corporation officials and managers of the larger housing associations.

4.3 In 2007, the 'Cave review' of social housing regulation[2] recommended that there should be comprehensive regulation of housing associations by an independent body exclusively focused on regulation. Cave identified the following weaknesses in the Housing Corporation: concern for financial matters at the expense of tenants' interests; overregulation and bureaucratic rigidity; inadequate separation of regulation from housing policy; and lack of incentives for efficiency and for expanding the social housing sector.

4.4 Cave was partly implemented by the Housing and Regeneration Act (HRA) 2008 which still provides the basic principles of the regulatory system. The Act broke new ground by creating a 'Regulator of Social Housing' (RSH) as an institution. It initially set up a separate regulator, namely the Office for Tenants and Social Landlords (OTSL) known as the Tenant Services Authority (TSA). It also created the Homes and Communities Agency (HCA) as a non-departmental

---

1 *Dimes v Grand Junction Canal Proprietors* (1852) 3 HL Cas 759.
2 *Every tenant matters: a review of social housing regulation*, Department for Communities and Local Government (DCLG), June 2007.

public body ('quango' – quasi-autonomous non-governmental organisation) responsible for, among other things, funding social housing.

4.5 After apparent government dissatisfaction with the independent line the regulator was taking and with its tenant orientated focus,[3] the Localism Act 2011 put both functions into the hands of the HCA. The regulatory powers were exercised by a special statutory committee with an external majority albeit appointed by the government. (In an attempt to make regulation appear independent, the HCA began to call itself Homes England in its funding capacity.) However, the obvious conflict of interest affects both public confidence and legal liability. Indeed, as a direct investor, the HCA is akin to a creditor of an association.

4.6 In a further U-turn, in November 2016 the then Department for Communities and Local Government's (DCLG) *Tailored review of the Homes and Communities Agency* concluded that the HCA should be formally presented as concentrating on the delivery of housing, to drive up supply and promote home ownership. Although some consultees hankered after the old tribalism, the review recommended that an independent regulator should be restored, albeit with close collaboration with the HCA and sharing administrative services.

4.7 Accordingly, in England a separate statutory regulator, also a non-departmental government body, was created by a Legislative Reform Order under the Legislative and Regulatory Reform Act 2006.[4] The Order, which took effect on 1 October 2018, transfers the powers and functions of the Regulation Committee of the HCA to a new non-departmental public body, the RSH.

4.8 The regulatory framework and powers remain the same as before. There is a Chair and between six and ten members appointed and removed with wide powers to do so by the secretary of state.[5] The secretary of state appoints the first Chief Executive, and subsequent appointments requires the approval of the secretary of state.[6]

---

3 See *Regulating social housing*, DCLG, October 2010; OTSL Final Report 2011–2.
4 See Legislative Reform (Regulator of Social Housing) (England) Order 2018 SI No 1040 Sch para 14, which amends the HRA 2008 by inserting s80A. The new body came into being as a corporate entity on 1 October 2018.
5 HRA 2008 ss80B, 80C.
6 HRA 2008 s80D; Legislative Reform (Regulator of Social Housing) (England) Order 2018 SI No 1040.

4.9 Relationships with the HCA (Homes England) are maintained by means of many amendments to the HRA 2008. There are general provisions requiring the HCA to co-operate with and consult the regulator when exercising its powers and vice versa,[7] and specific consultation or notification requirements in relation to most of the regulator's powers.

4.10 The need for an independent regulator is reinforced by Article 6 of the European Convention on Human Rights (ECHR) which requires there to be a hearing by an independent body with 'full jurisdiction' where 'civil rights and obligations' are in issue. The regulator has power to remove rights belonging to housing associations, their officers and staff and so seem to fall within Article 6.

4.11 It is questionable whether the new RSH is sufficiently independent to satisfy Article 6. On the one hand, where a matter is bound up with government policy, the test of independence is relaxed, enabling, for example, government ministers to take a prominent role. In this context, independence may be sufficiently secured by the judicial review powers of the court.[8]

4.12 On the other hand, the regulator's powers are not directly concerned with policy matters. They are judicial in nature, focused on ensuring that a housing association has adequate standards of governance, management, finance and tenant services. The RSH has powers to adjudicate on whether a housing association is behaving lawfully. It may therefore be desirable that the appointment of the members of the regulator be supervised by the Judicial Appointments Commission.

4.13 The mutual requirements between the HCA (Homes England) and the regulator to co-operate and consult the HCA do not seem conducive to independence. Nor do the secretary of state's wide powers to appoint and remove members of the regulator which include, for instance, the possibility of fixed-term renewable appointments. Indeed, in a provision characteristic of the UK government's insensitivity to the concept of independence, the existing members of the previous HCA regulation committee must be reappointed as the first members of the new body.[9] There seem to be no safeguards.

---

7 HRA 2008 ss36A, 100F.
8 See *R (Alconbury Developments Ltd) v Secretary of State for the Environment, Transport and the Regions* [2001] 2 All ER 929.
9 Legislative Reform (Regulator of Social Housing) (England) Order 2018 SI No 1040 Sch para 49.

4.14　　　In Wales, both funding and regulation are the responsibility of the Welsh Ministers.[10] Thus, unlike the case in England, there is direct democratic accountability thus recognising the political basis of social housing. There is also an independent advisory Regulatory Board for Wales. In Wales, the registered social landlord (RSL) system of the Housing Act 1996 applies, which was abolished in England by the 2008 Act. However, subsequent Welsh legislation has made changes to the Housing Act 1996 bringing the law more closely into alignment with the new English regime.[11] To some extent, the Welsh regime gives the regulator broader discretionary powers. In particular, it does not require a lower level of intervention in the sphere of services to tenants.

Jurisdiction of the regulators

4.15　In both England and Wales, registration is voluntary. The English regime applies to housing associations, with-profit bodies and local authorities, with specific differences in each case. The Welsh regime applies only to RSLs, all of which are by definition housing associations.[12] In the case of an 'English body' the regulation of a housing association depends on registration with the regulator as a 'private registered provider' (PRP) and in the case of a 'Welsh body' on registration with the Welsh Ministers.

4.16　　　Under HRA 2008 s112, an 'English body' providing or intending to provide social housing in England (but not necessarily exclusively so) is eligible to apply for registration. Thus profit-making private bodies such as property developers can apply, as well as housing associations of all kinds. A subsidiary[13] of a housing association must apply for and be registered in its own right.

4.17　　　An 'English body' means a registered charity the address of which is in England, a company or body registered under the Co-operative and Community Benefit Societies Act (CCBSA) 2014, the registered office of which is in England, a community land trust (CLT) owning

---

10　HRA 2008 s61.
11　Housing (Wales) Measure 2011; Regulation of Registered Social Landlords (Wales) Act 2018.
12　Below para 4.29.
13　Above para 2.48.

land in England and 'any other person who makes available accommodation in England or intends to do so other than a Welsh Body'.[14] Apart from certain special cases,[15] English bodies registered with the Housing Corporation under the previous regime are automatically registered with the RSH as PRPs, whether or not they comply with the current definition.[16] Similarly their dwellings are considered to be social housing.[17]

4.18 A 'Welsh body' means a registered charity, the address of which is in Wales, or a non-profit-making company or body registered under the CCBSA 2014, the registered office of which is in Wales.[18]

4.19 English local housing authorities and bodies controlled by them are *required* to register separately with the RSH under rules made by the secretary of state thus, as the Cave report suggested, creating a unified regime of social housing regulation albeit with some specific variations.[19] In Wales, local housing authorities are also regulated by the Welsh Ministers. Regulation and finance of with-profit bodies and local authorities are outside the scope of this book.

Registration: English bodies

4.20 Regulation is triggered by the association registering with the RSH. Registration is voluntary, but an unregistered housing association is unlikely to receive public funding and is also unlikely to be attractive to a private funder. An unregistered housing association is generally in the same legal position as a private landlord. However, unregistered co-operative housing associations and charitable housing trusts sometimes have the same privileges as registered bodies and a few privileges apply to all housing associations mainly in connection with shared ownership. The number of unregistered associations is unknown, but probably less than 1,500 (mainly almshouses with a few co-operatives).

4.21 A few unregistered housing associations may have received government money under regimes existing before the registration

---

14 HRA 2008 s79.
15 Open market lettings, student accommodation, care homes, asylum-seekers.
16 HRA 2008 ss68–76; Localism Act 2011 Sch 16 para 69.
17 HRA 2008 s77.
18 Housing Act 1996 s1A.
19 HRA 2008 ss113, 114; Housing and Regeneration Act 2008 (Registration of Local Authorities) Order 2010 SI No 844.

system was created in 1975. Under Housing Associations Act 1985 s9, subject to certain exceptions,[20] such a 'grant aided' association both in England and Wales requires the regulator's consent to dispose of land. This does not seem to be affected by the removal of consent requirements in the Housing and Planning Act 2016 and the Regulation of Registered Social Landlords (Wales) Act 2018 (below). However, general consents are in place to deal with this historic issue so that individual applications are usually unnecessary.[21]

Eligibility for registration

4.22 An English body has a right to be registered as a registered provider (RP) of social housing if the following two 'conditions of eligibility' are fulfilled (HRA 2008 s112). (Under the previous law, the Housing Corporation had a discretion whether or not to register a body.) The body is not required to have any particular corporate form so that all bodies qualifying as housing associations are eligible.

1) The body must provide or intend to provide 'social housing'[22] in England although not exclusively so. Thus an RP can carry out any activities permitted under its own constitution, reflecting the wide scope of contemporary housing association activity. However, specialist housing associations that provide only supported housing involving personal care may not be eligible for registration since rents may be at market level or above thus not qualifying as social housing.

   A 'provider' is either the landlord or seller as the case may be.[23] Thus a parent body might operate through subsidiaries while being itself unregistered. Indeed unless it is itself a landlord or seller of social housing it cannot register.

2) The body must satisfy 'criteria' set by the regulator as to its a) financial situation, b) constitution and c) other arrangements for its management. Thus by making subordinate legislation, the regulator can ration entry to the social housing system. The Act does not restrict the regulator's discretion in setting criteria.

---

20 Disposals by charitable associations where Charity Commission consent needed (below) and lettings of secure or assured tenancies.
21 Unregistered Housing Associations General Consent 2010 (General Consent) (Wales) Order 2009.
22 Above para 1.27.
23 HRA 2008 ss80, 116.

4.23 The current criteria[24] largely comprise basic requirements of competence, financial viability, and provision for accountability to tenants, the regulator and taxpayer and accessibility:
- Every applicant must show that it meets the 'Governance and Financial Viability Standard' at the point of registration and demonstrate that it can 'sustain its financial viability on an ongoing basis' and that it has management arrangements in place that have the capacity to meet the other regulatory standards.
- A charitable body must specifically include social housing in its constitution, and if it is a subsidiary 'must state as much and ensure that the parent and its controls are clearly identified'.
- A non-charitable body must have the provision of social housing 'embedded' among its objects (presumably in its Rules if it is a society under the CCBSA 2014, its articles of association if it is a company).
- A 'restructured body' must also include these requirements in its constitution. This is a body that changes its corporate status from a company to a CCBSA society or vice versa or carries out an amalgamation or 'transfers of engagements' between CCBSA 2014 societies. This requirement reflects the fact that regulatory consent is no longer needed for restructuring.
- Additional requirements to provide information about changes of status, including winding up or voluntary insolvency arrangements, apply to the specialised kind of charitable trust, the charitable incorporated organisation (CIO).[25]

4.24 Before setting criteria, the regulator must consult the following: one or bodies representing RPs; the Greater London Authority (GLA), on or more bodies nominated by the secretary of state as representing the interests of tenants and also one or more other bodies which appear to the regulator to represent the interests of tenants.[26]

4.25 Registration of PRPs requires designation either as a non-profit or a profit-making organisation (HRA 2008 s115). (Some regulation rules differ accordingly.) The definitions here echo the old Housing Corporation registration requirements. A non-profit body must either be a charity, in which case it can have any objects; or, the purposes of the body must be to provide or manage housing and any other purposes must be connected with or incidental to the provision

---

24 *Decision statement: consultation on registration criteria and use of powers*, HCA, 2017, Annex 3.
25 Above para 2.18.
26 HRA 2008 s112(4).

4.26　All other bodies are deemed to be profit-making organisations (HRA 2008 s115(8)). 44 'with-profit' bodies are currently registered. These develop schemes which are then managed by a housing association. If the regulator thinks that what was a profit-making organisation has become a non-profit making one or vice versa, it must change the designation accordingly.

4.27　A fee can be charged for registration, and there are provisions intended to ensure that this is reasonable, proportionate to the association's expenditure and transparent.[28] The regulator must maintain a register open to public inspection and must notify other relevant regulators (Charity Commissioners, Financial Conduct Authority (FCA) and Registrar of Companies) of every registration or de-registration.

Registration: Welsh bodies

4.28　Unlike the English regime, there is no right to be registered as an RSL – the Welsh ministers have a discretion to do so.[29] Again, unlike the English regime which makes a fresh start, the requirements for registration as an RSL are based on those which applied in England and Wales under the previous regime.

4.29　Despite the label, the Housing Act 1996 does not require the body in question to provide 'social housing'. Instead the requirements to be an RSL include a list of eligible activities which are the accumulation of legislative interventions over many years. Simplification and rationalisation is overdue. The Welsh requirements are more restrictive than those in England. The statutory requirements are as follows.[30]
1) The body must be a Welsh body as defined above.
2) It must be either a registered charity (ie registered with the Charity Commission), which is a housing association; or a CCBSA society, or a company.

27　HRA 2008 s115. The secretary of state can make regulations providing that a specific purpose does or does not qualify.
28　HRA 2008 s117. See *Social housing regulation fees guidance*, Regulator of Social Housing, 2018.
29　Housing Act 1996 s3(1).
30　Housing Act 1996 ss1A, 2(1).

3) A registered charity can have any charitable object and can provide housing anywhere. In both the other cases, whether or not they are charitable, there are further restrictions as follows.[31]
   a) The body must be 'principally concerned with Welsh housing'. This means that the Welsh Ministers think that it owns housing only or mainly in Wales or that its activities are carried out principally in Wales.[32] However, if a registered body is no longer principally concerned with Welsh housing, it does not cease to be eligible.
   b) The body must be non-profit-making (including the case of a body paying dividends or interest within Treasury limits under the Housing Associations Act 1995 (above)).[33]
   c) Its objects must include at least one specified 'permitted object'. These are: 'the provision, construction, improvement or management of dwellings: to be kept available for letting (including a licence), or of dwellings where the rules of the association restrict membership to occupiers or prospective occupiers[34] or of 'hostels'. (A hostel is shared accommodation providing board or cooking facilities or both).[35] Thus there is no requirement that the body must provide social housing as such. An RSL is a social housing provider only if its activities include provision at below market rents.[36]
   d) Any additional purposes or objects must be limited to those specified, all of which are housing-related.[37] The purpose of this seems to prevent wholly non-housing activities being undertaken, although this is possible under the English regime which does not exclude any object. These objects are as follows:
      – providing land, amenities or services, or providing, constructing, repairing or improving buildings, for the benefit of its residents, either exclusively or together with other persons;
      – acquiring, repairing, improving or converting dwellings to be disposed of on sale or lease or on shared ownership terms;

---

31 Housing Act 1996 s2(2). It is difficult to see why all charitable associations could not be in the same category for this purpose.
32 Housing Act 1996 s.2A.
33 Housing Act 1996 s2(3).
34 This includes a co-operative association but does not require full mutuality since not all occupiers need be members.
35 Housing Act 1996 s63.
36 Above para 1.67.
37 Housing Act 1996 s2(4).

- constructing houses to be disposed of on shared ownership terms. 'Shared ownership' means in Wales that the lease must be sold at a percentage of its market value or of the historic cost or that the tenant is entitled to a payment on leaving calculated by reference to its market value). An RSL cannot therefore build new dwellings for outright sale;
- managing rented or leased houses blocks of flats;
- providing services of any description for owners or occupiers of houses in arranging or carrying out works of maintenance, repair or improvement, or encouraging or facilitating the carrying out of such work;
- encouraging and giving advice on the formation of other housing associations or providing services for, and giving advice on the running of such associations and other voluntary organisations concerned with housing, or matters connected with housing.

4.30 The Housing Act 1996 provides a limited degree of flexibility in respect of commercial activities used as an incidental means of achieving the permitted housing objects. Thus a landlord is not ineligible for registration by reason only that its powers (as opposed to its objects), include the following: to acquire commercial premises or businesses incidentally to projects authorised under its other powers; to repair improve or convert such premises or to carry on the business for a limited time; to repair or improve housing or buildings in which houses are situated after a disposal of houses by the body.[38]

4.31 Finally, the Act empowers the Welsh Ministers to add to the lists of additional objects or powers and to make provision for the priority of mortgages.[39] This power originally exercised by the secretary of state has responded to the expansion of housing association activity by permitting various forms of shared ownership arrangement, discounted sales, mortgage assistance and resident related neighbourhood projects.[40] It may be that these cumbersome arrangements should be replaced by the more streamlined provisions applying to English bodies.

4.32 The Welsh Ministers can establish and must publish criteria for registration and removal from the register.[41] However, at the time of writing none have been published.

38 Housing Act 1996 s2(5).
39 Housing Act 1996 s2(7).
40 See SI 1996 No 2256; SI 1999 No 985; SI 1999 No 1206.
41 Housing Act 1996 s5.

4.33 A Welsh body, as long as it is principally concerned with housing in Wales, can also provide housing in England. However, as we shall see, many of the regulatory powers of the Welsh Ministers do not apply to property in England but there seems to be no restriction on the English regulator's powers over housing in Wales provided by an English body. However the English regulator cannot register housing anywhere provided by a Welsh body (HRA 2008 s79(1)(e)). The two regimes are therefore lop-sided creating a gap outside both regimes. The subordinate nature of Welsh law underlies this problem.

4.34 Thus in the case of land owned by a Welsh body and situated in England, there may be no regulation. Furthermore, a Welsh body principally providing housing in England, cannot register under either regime whereas an English body providing some social housing in England can also provide housing in Wales. Any practical problems caused by this apparent lop-sidedness cannot adequately be dealt with by the familiar British contrivance of a 'memorandum of understanding' or the like between the two regulators, since, in the absence of a statutory power of delegation this could amount to an unlawful fettering of discretion.

Removal from the register

4.35 Responding to historic problems where inactive associations remained on the register, the regulator has power to remove an association from the register where it thinks that it is no longer eligible or is inactive.[42] An RP can request deregistration on these grounds or on the ground that it is adequately regulated by another body (eg in the case of a small trust by the Charity Commission), or in accordance with published de-registration criteria set by the regulator.[43] The current criteria are that 'satisfactory arrangements are in place to ensure the continued protection of tenants and that there is no misuse of public funds.[44]

4.36 Even if these conditions are satisfied the regulator has a discretion whether or not to de-register. Before complying with an application the regulator must consult relevant local authorities and cannot de- register a non-profit provider if it thinks that the provider wants

42 HRA 2008 s118.
43 HRA 2008 s119.
44 *De-registration requirements*, HCA, April 2015.

to distribute assets to its members. In all cases, there are provisions for notice and representations and a right of appeal to the courts.[45] Similar provisions apply to Welsh bodies under the Housing Act 1996. However, in the case of a request for removal from the register the matter depends on criteria published by the Welsh Ministers.

The framework of regulation

4.37 The background to the current system of regulation is, first, the Hampton report, *Reducing administrative burdens: effective inspection and enforcement*;[46] and second, the Cave report (above). Hampton concluded that there were too many regulators, that their powers overlapped unnecessarily and were insufficiently flexible and too burdensome. It recommended that there should be a reduced number of regulators operating on a more systematic basis with tougher penalties at their disposal. Key principles should include accountability; 'proportionate and meaningful sanctions for persistent defaulters'; intervention only in clear cases based on risk; easy and cheap access to advice; and avoiding duplication.

4.38 This led to the Legislative and Regulatory Reform Act 2006, which gave ministers wide powers to alter or repeal statutes for the purposes of reorganising or abolishing individual regulators to create criminal offences subject to limits. These abnormally wide powers are subject to the special form of parliamentary scrutiny known as the 'super affirmative procedure'. The McRory report, *Regulatory justice, making sanctions effective*,[47] endorsed long-standing proposals for a standardised system of flexible administrative sanctions which regulators could apply on a sliding scale of increasing stringency. The sanctions include persuasion, warnings, enforcement notices requiring action to be taken, fixed or variable civil financial penalties and finally criminal sanctions in the ordinary courts.

4.39 The notion of administrative penalties is contrary to traditional ideas of the rule of law according to which no one should be punished except for a breach of the law established in the ordinary courts. Safeguards under the Legislative and Regulatory Reform Act 2006 include appeals to the ordinary courts and compliance with 'regulatory principles'. These require any person exercising a regulatory

---

45 HRA 2008 s121.
46 HM Treasury, 2005.
47 2006.

function to be 'transparent, accountable, proportionate, consistent' and to 'target cases only in which action is needed'. Regulators must publish reports of what enforcement action has been taken. The regulatory regime for social housing draws on these principles in the HRA 2008 as substantially modified by the Localism Act 2011 and the Housing and Planning Act 2016.

The objectives of social housing regulation

4.40 The 2007 Cave report proposed that the objectives of social housing regulation should be made explicit, namely continued provision of high quality housing, empowering and protecting tenants and expanding the choice of provider The same approach should apply to all providers of social housing, namely housing associations, private profit bodies and local authorities. There should be an overriding statutory duty to minimise interference in accordance with the principle of proportionality. Somewhat inconsistently, Cave suggested that the role of the regulator should be primarily economic to protect the taxpayer. It should intervene only in serious cases. There should be 'co-regulation' meaning that, within general 'outcome-focused' standards set by the regulator, the landlord should be responsible for regulating itself. In 2010 the coalition government recommended changes in the emphasis of regulation in favour primarily of encouraging private funding of social housing by providing reassurance to private funders that providers are well-run, solvent and stable.[48] Proactive and more intensive regulation should apply primarily to economic/financial matters while regulation of services to tenants should be enforced only where serious problems arise. In particular, tenants' complaints should be the responsibility of the Social Housing Ombudsman, not the regulator.

4.41 Localism Act 2011 Sch 17 implements this by modifying the HRA 2008. It provides in some detail the principles which the regulator is required to apply. A problem with such regulation is that it favours large organisations and is a barrier to new entrants, so inhibiting the development of social housing. For their part, associations, regarding themselves as private enterprises, may seek carry out new activities in ways beyond the detailed scrutiny of the regulator.

---

48 See *Regulating social housing*, DCLG, October 2010.

4.42 The above aspirations are codified by the Localism Act 2011 as 'fundamental objectives'[49] under the heads of 'economic regulation' and 'consumer regulation'. These objectives are primarily concerned with saving public money and protecting private funders and with modest aspirations towards the provision of housing and tenants' interests.

1) Economic objectives:
   a) to ensure that providers are financially viable, and properly managed and perform their functions efficiently and economically;
   b) to support the provision of social housing sufficiently to meet 'reasonable' needs, including encouraging and promoting private investment;
   c) to ensure that value for money is obtained from public investment (requiring the balancing of sustainability against cost);[50]
   d) to ensure that unreasonable burdens are not placed on public funds;
   e) to guard against the misuse of public funds.
2) Consumer objectives:
   a) to support the provision of social housing that is well managed and of 'appropriate' quality (an unambitious goal);
   b) to ensure that actual or potential tenants have an 'appropriate' degree of choice and protection;
   c) to ensure that tenants have the opportunity to be involved in management and to hold the landlord to account;
   d) to encourage RPs to contribute to the environmental, social, and economic well-being of the area in which the housing is situated.

4.43 There is also a somewhat tenuous 'growth' duty which applies to all regulators, namely to 'have regard to the desirability of promoting economic growth',[51] and a general government Regulators Code.[52] The latter concerns regulatory policies and procedures but not individual decisions.

---

49 Adding section 92K to the HRA 2008.
50 See 'Value for Money Standard', HCA, 2015.
51 Deregulation Act 2015 s108.
52 Legislative and Regulatory Reform Act 2006 s22.

Standards

4.44 Within the above objectives the regulator can set 'standards' relating to the conduct of a RP's business as regards social housing. These structure the specific powers of the regulator, which will be discussed in the next chapter. There are separate provisions covering consumer and economic standards. In both cases the standards can include requirements to comply with detailed rules. For example, associations may be subject to detailed requirements regarding the rights of tenants thus replacing the legal codes of former regimes with administrative discretion. A new set of standards is expected to appear soon.

4.45 'Standards' in respect of 'consumer matters' are as follows:
- allocations of tenancies;
- the terms of tenancies;
- maintenance;
- complaints;
- tenants' 'participation';
- exchanges;
- anti-social behavior policies;
- landlords contribution to the environmental, social and economic well-being of the area; and
- estate management.[53]

Standards in respect of 'economic' matters concern:
- rent levels; and
- the association's management and efficiency of its 'finances and other affairs'.[54]

The regulator can also issue a code of practice amplifying the standards, but only as regards the economic standards. While not binding, this can be taken into account in assessing an association's compliance.[55]

4.46 Failure to meet a standard is not in itself unlawful but is one among several grounds for triggering powers of investigation or intervention (below chapter 5). The *risk* of a breach if either the regulator or the provider fail to take action triggers the investigatory powers but not the intervention powers. The regulator also has power

---

53 HRA 2008 s193.
54 HRA 2008 s194. The economic standards do not apply to the non-social housing of with-profit bodies.
55 HRA 2008 s195 as amended.

to make binding rules in relation to particular matters as follows. We have already discussed 'criteria' for registration. The regulator can also give 'directions' under specific provisions. These concern accounts and audit processes, management functions following intervention by the regulator (below) and notifications in relation the disposal of assets and constitutional or structural changes (below). Failure to comply with these is an offence. In the absence of specific power to make binding rules the regulator must not 'fetter its discretion' by applying general principles so rigidly as to ignore exceptional circumstances.[56]

4.47 In the Welsh system there are similar provisions for standards but couched in the broader terms of 'functions relating to the provision of housing and matters relating to governance and financial management'.[57]

Guidance

4.48 The regulator is required to give and to publish 'guidance' as to the information to be provided by a RP and how it intends to use its enforcement powers.[58] The regulator also has a general power to give guidance concerning any of its objects. It does not have to publish this, but must draw it to the attention of those affected.[59] Guidance is not strictly binding, but may give rise to a 'legitimate expectation', enforceable by judicial review, that the regulator will act consistently with its current guidance unless it can show a strong reason not to do so.

4.49 There are also powers to give guidance in the Welsh system. This can relate to and amplify any matter addressed by a standard. Failing to comply can be taken into account in deciding whether to intervene.[60]

---

56 See McHarg, 'Administrative discretion, administrative rule-making and judicial review' (2017) 70 *Current Legal Problems* 267–303.
57 Housing Act 1996 s33A.
58 HRA 2008 s215. See particularly, HCA, *Regulating the standards*, 2017; and *Guidance on the Regulator's approach to intervention, enforcement and the use of powers*, 2017. These do not cater for various changes made by the Housing and Planning Act 2016.
59 HRA 2008 s40.
60 Housing Act 1996 s33B.

General constraints on the powers of the English regulator

4.50 Before the Housing and Planning Act 2016 came into force, the regulator's more drastic sanctions could be triggered by mismanagement including misconduct in a general sense. As part of the government's policy of weakening regulation, mismanagement now means only 'managed in breach of any legal requirements (imposed by or under an Act or otherwise).[61] This includes a breach of the regulator's binding requirements namely 'directions', and 'criteria' but not standards, guidance or codes of practice since these are not directly enforceable in law. The Regulation of Registered Social Landlords (Wales) Act 2018 s10 is narrower but clearer. It triggers these powers only in the case of a breach of a 'requirement imposed by or under an enactment'. This excludes breaches of common law and equitable duties.

4.51 This legally orientated definition of mismanagement may be uncomfortable since it casts the regulator in judicial mode, essentially as a court of law, and so attracts Article 6 of the ECHR (right to a fair trial). As we saw above, this calls into question the close relationship of co-operation between the regulator and the HCA which is part of the executive. This might also trample over the principles of natural justice. In particular, the nature and content of communications between the two bodies, in so far as they are adverse to the association concerned, must be fully disclosed. The regulator's powers are often limited to the social housing aspects of a provider's business and some powers to intervene do not apply to with-profit bodies.

4.52 In the case of the consumer standards, the regulator is currently more restrained than with the economic standards. There is a higher threshold for intervention. In most cases (the removal of staff is an exception) the regulator can intervene only if it thinks that there are reasonable grounds to suspect that there is serious detriment or a significant risk of serious detriment to tenants or potential tenants.[62] The term 'significant' depends on the particular context but requires a threshold higher than merely a non-negligible risk.[63]

---

61 HRA 2008 (as amended) s275.
62 HRA 2008 s198A(2), (5).
63 See *R (Loader) v Secretary of State for Communities and Local Government* [2012] EWCA Civ 869 (environmental assessment).

4.53 The regulator has pointed out in its guidance[64] that the higher threshold for intervention in consumer matters means that urgent situations are more likely to arise than is the case with economic matters, so that the regulator's favoured 'graduated' approach may not be appropriate and drastic action may be needed. Moreover, breach of economic standards and consumer matters may sometimes be inextricably mixed.

4.54 The recent social housing green paper[65] has proposed that the regulation of the consumer standards be more proactive, including, for example, the publication of performance indicators while avoiding dealing with individual complaints for which the Housing Ombudsman is appropriate. The 'serious detriment' test which currently applies to intervention might also be relaxed and a binding code of practice for consumer standards be introduced.[66]

4.55 The regulator's powers are biased towards restraint. Thus in exercising its powers to intervene the regulator must: 'have regard to' the desirability of RPs being free to choose how to provide services and conduct their business.[67] However, no particular weight need be attached to this.

4.56 A stronger provision is that in the exercise of its functions the regulator must a) minimise interference and b) 'so far as is possible' be proportionate, consistent, transparent and accountable. (However, transparency and accountability may not be fully possible when dealing with matters of commercial confidentiality or personal privacy. On the other hand, lack of proportionality and inconsistency are arguably never justifiable.)

4.57 There are provisions designed to encourage negotiation in the shape of a 'voluntary undertaking' as an alternative to enforcement proceedings. In considering whether to exercise any of its powers, the regulator must have regard to whether such an undertaking has been offered or given and can found a decision wholly or in part on the extent to which a voluntary undertaking has been honoured.[68]

4.58 The secretary of state has powers to give directions to the regulator including making exemptions from the consultation requirements (below). These powers apply to quality of accommodation,

---

64 HCA, *Guidance on the Regulator's approach to enforcement, intervention and use of powers*, 2017, para 10.
65 MHCLG, *A new deal for social housing*, Cm 9671, August 2018.
66 MHCLG, *A new deal for social housing*, Cm 9671, August 2018, paras 61, 94, 95, 99.
67 HRA 2008 ss193(3), 194(3), 208.
68 HRA 2008 s125.

tenure, rent, tenant involvement in management, and methods of assisting tenants to change tenancies.[69] These directions are a major influence on the regulator's guidance.

4.59 As a public body, the regulator is subject to judicial review. Our sampling, albeit limited, indicates that there have to date been no judicial review claims against the regulator. However, retrospective legislation has been required to correct unlawful delegation by the Housing Corporation.[70] It may be that the regulator's decision-making is excellent or that housing association boards and staff are conditioned to be deferential.

Consultation and information

4.60 There is a range of powers and obligations requiring the regulator to take account of the views of interested parties. These relate to specific contexts, and extend from consultation proper to notification with a discretion to have regard to the views of the person notified. Consultation is a two-way process, requiring clear provision of information to the person consulted including options, a genuine opportunity for consideration and time to respond. Evidence that a regulator has already made up its mind invalidates a consultation.[71] There are the following general provisions.
1) In considering whether to exercise any of its powers, the regulator 'may have regard to' information from any source including in particular tenants and bodies representing them, local housing authorities or the local government or social housing ombudsman.[72] This is only a discretionary requirement. It is passive, reactive and does not require consultation. Nor does it require any weight to be given to any such material.[73]
2) By contrast *in relation to the consumer standards*, in considering whether to exercise its powers the regulator *must* have regard to information or opinions from the following mainly official bodies: the local government and social housing ombudsman, any body 'appearing to the regulator' to represent the interests of tenants (thus the influence of tenants is limited), local authorities or their

---

69 HRA 2008 s197.
70 Housing Corporation (Delegation) etc Act 2006.
71 See *R (Moseley) v Haringey LBC* [2014] UKSC 56.
72 HRA 2008 s96.
73 See *Tesco Stores Ltd v Secretary of State for the Environment* [1995] 2 All ER 636.

members, the GLA, an MP, fire and rescue authorities, the Health and Safety Executive and the secretary of state.[74]
3) There are some positive consultation requirements. We have already mentioned those concerning registration criteria. Before specifying standards or issuing a code of practice or giving guidance concerning its powers of intervention, the English regulator must consult the following, or ensure that they have been consulted: one or more bodies representative respectively of providers, secured creditors and tenants (below); local housing authorities; the GLA (where the association is in London); the secretary of state; and the Charity Commission.[75] In the case of guidance, the regulator must also consult a body nominated by the secretary of state as representing tenants' interests.[76] In the case of the regulator's general powers to give guidance it must consult 'such persons as it considers appropriate'.[77]

4.61 The Welsh Ministers must consult one or more bodies appearing to them to represent the interests of RSLs, tenants and local housing authorities.[78]

Tenant involvement

4.62 The terminology, used in this area – tenant participation, tenant empowerment, tenant involvement – does not have prescriptive legal meanings. It might include a range of levels, from merely being informed of decisions through influencing them by being consulted to participation by voting membership of decision making bodies. It also ranges from accountability of the landlord in relation to its functions as such to wider community issues. The law gives few specific rights of involvement to tenants collectively and none to individuals the matter being primarily one of administrative discretion.

4.63 Under the English regime, the regulator must consult one or more bodies it regards as representative of tenants in specified cases (above)[79] and the secretary of state can nominate a body to represent

---

74 HRA 2008 s198A(6).
75 HRA 2008 ss196, 216.
76 HRA 2008 s216(4) (below).
77 HRA 2008 s40(5).
78 Housing Act 1996 s33C.
79 And see HRA 2008 s112(4): registration criteria.

86 *Housing associations: a legal handbook / chapter 4*

tenants for these purposes.[80] In February 2010, following the Cave report, the then Labour government set up such a body namely *The national tenants' voice*. This was abolished later in 2010 by the incoming Conservative/Liberal Democrat coalition government. At present there is no representative body for social housing tenants as such in England.

4.64 In addition the regulator is required to promote 'awareness' of its functions among social housing tenants and 'where the regulator thinks appropriate' consult tenants '(for example by holding meetings)' and involve them in the exercise of its functions '(for example by appointments to committee or sub committees).' The regulator must publish a statement from time to time about how it proposes to comply.[81] The *Tenant involvement and empowerment standard* issued by the regulator requires providers to make provision for informing and consulting tenants about specified significant acts and decisions including changing landlords and management arrangements.

4.65 The Housing (Wales) Measure 2011 makes similar provision for consultation. There is some tenant representation in Wales in the form of the Tenant Advisory Panel (TAP). Created in 2010, this consults with the Welsh Regulatory Board (itself only an advisory body). The Welsh government's *Regulatory framework* (2017) requires effective tenant involvement as a performance standard but without further specification.

Openness: disclosure of information – gradings

4.66 HRA 2008 s205 originally required the regulator to publish information about the performance of each housing association. This was repealed by the Localism Act 2011.[82] However, the recent green paper[83] proposes to reintroduce provision for publishing such information.

4.67 There is a non-statutory sanction of publicity especially as regards investor confidence. This takes the form of a grading system which applies to all PRPs with at least 1,000 social housing units. The

---

80 HRA 2008 s278A inserted by Local Democracy, Economic Development and Construction Act 2009 s26(2).
81 HRA 2008 s98.
82 Sch 17 para 13; Sch 25 Part 27.
83 MHCLG, *A new deal for social housing*, Cm 9671, August 2018.

grading system, although having no specific statutory basis, seems to be within the general powers of the regulator as incidental to its statutory functions. However, it would be unlawful for the regulator to disclose to anyone other than another public body the underlying evidence for its gradings (below).

4.68 The regulator publishes a list of grades awarded to each provider following its periodic review of the economic standards (below).[84] These are divided into 'governance' (G) and 'viability' (V) grades each comprising four levels. G1 (which is the normal benchmark) and G2 are 'compliant', but in the case of G2 with particular defects that should be addressed. G3 is non-compliant with serious regulatory concerns which are being dealt with by voluntary action. G4 is non-compliant where the association is subject to regulatory intervention or enforcement. V1 and V2 are 'compliant' – V1 means that the association 'has the financial capacity to deal with a wide range of adverse situations'. V2 means that it can meet a 'reasonable range' of such situations but needs to manage material risks. V3 and V4 are non-compliant on the same basis as with G3 and G4 (above).

4.69 Individual grades are announced in the form of a press release and the regulator publishes its grades and regulatory judgments on its website. The regulator also publishes 'regulatory notices' where particular issues arise. These can also apply to bodies with 1,000 social dwellings or fewer where there is a finding of non-compliance with a standard.

4.70 The Welsh Ministers apply a similar system. Its gradings are categorised as 'increased', 'standard' and 'intervention' and published on its register under the heads of 'governance and service delivery' and 'financial viability'. Thus the Welsh system gives greater prominence to the interests of tenants.

4.71 The grading system depends on subjective judgments and has the potential seriously to harm the interests of an individual housing association in terms of its reputation and investor confidence. Indeed that is its purpose. In particular, in current conditions of financial instability, there is obviously a heightened risk of a body being rated as V2. Given the extent to which housing associations are involved in private funding and other commercial activities it is clear that a rating below the highest has serious adverse consequences. Some protection against an unfair rating is provided by the common law principles of fairness (natural justice). These give a body a right to be informed in advance of the grounds for a downgrade and to give

---

84 *Regulating the standards*, HCA, 2017, paras 4 and 5.

a response. However the common principles do not require any particular procedure, only the substance of fairness, and it is likely that the matters in question will previously have been raised as part of the regulator's routine monitoring process or a statutory inquiry.

4.72 Subject to restrictions on disclosure in other statutes such as the Data Protection Act 1998, the regulator can disclose information to another 'public authority' in connection with its functions or those of the other body and vice versa.[85] It can impose restrictions on further disclosure breach of which is an offence. For this purpose a public authority means any person 'having functions of a public nature' and so may include a housing association (above chapter 3).

4.73 This provision seems by implication to forbid the regulator from disclosing information to anyone else If this is so, then any public right to obtain information under the Freedom of Information Act 2000 is also excluded since information prohibited by statute from disclosure is 'exempt information' under that Act.[86] Housing associations themselves are not public bodies under the Act. However, as we have seen, under the common law principles of natural justice, the regulator must disclose relevant information when it exercises its enforcement powers.

Regulation of accounts and audit

4.74 The regulator can give directions to all RPs concerning the way in which their accounts must be presented for the purpose of ensuring 'a true and fair view' of the association's social housing activities and the use of assets relating thereto. Annual accounts must be submitted to the regulator together with an auditor's report or, where there is no statutory audit requirement, any other report required by statute.[87] These requirements are on top of any requirement imposed by other legislation to give information to the regulator concerned. These provisions are discussed more fully in chapter 13 on accountability.

---

85 HRA 2008 s109.
86 FOI 2000 ss2, 44.
87 HRA 2008 s128.

Financial assistance

4.75 The regulator can direct the GLA, which is the main funder of social housing in London, *not* to give financial assistance to a specified RP. This power applies when the regulator is holding an inquiry into mismanagement or where insolvency proceedings are involved or where the regulator has intervened by appointing a manager.[88] The power is a constitutional anomaly of an unelected body being empowered to give orders to an elected one. According to statutory guidance[89] this power would be exercised only exceptionally, such as where regulatory action is being taken against the provider because of a risk to public finances. A similar power applies (but without constitutional implications) in relation to the power of the HCA to give financial assistance to a private registered provider.[90] However, this does not apply to grants in respect of discounts on sales of dwellings to tenants.

The practice of the English regulator

4.76 Within these legal requirements, the regulator can determine its own operating processes. Apart from the statutory requirements, the regulator consults interested bodies or requires providers to do so. The regulator's guidance adopts the Cave report's notion of co-regulation. Thus the governing bodies of a provider must monitor its performance, and a provider must support tenants to 'shape and scrutinise' service delivery and to hold governing bodies to account. The onus is on the provider to provide assurance of compliance with standards.[91] The regulator places emphasis on a professional proactive governing body in contrast to the older tradition of volunteer boards.[92]

4.77 Regulation of the economic standards is continuous and proactive and requires the association to provide copious information. However there is a different approach between large and small providers (those with fewer than 1000 social housing units). Economic

---

88 Greater London Authority Act 1999 s333ZG.
89 Guidance note 2, 2017.
90 HRA 2008 s19(1A) added by the Legislative Reform (Regulation of Social Housing) (England) Order 2018 SI No 1040.
91 See *Regulating the standards*, 2017, para 1. In the case of a group, overall assessment is at group level.
92 *Regulating the standards*, paras 2.10–2.12.

monitoring of small providers is mainly through annual accounts and statistical returns except where a body is regarded as a high financial risk in which case business plans and other narrative documents may be required. In the case of large providers a range of documents is examined. This includes quarterly surveys and annual accounts, business plans, risk management policies and financial forecasts.[93]

4.78 There is also an 'in-depth' assessment (IDA). This takes place roughly every three or four years, but may be more frequent in the case of especial risks. In particular, an assessment might be provoked by a statutory notification to the regulator of a disposal of property or a constitutional change. An IDA is based on the submission of comprehensive documentary evidence and can focus on any aspect of the provider's business.[94]

4.79 IDAs are risk-based assessments, where a 'deep dive' is undertaken on key issues within individual associations. They are used to change gradings if problems are found or where issues have not been addressed. They are mechanisms used, therefore, to examine individual associations in detail and focus on regulatory compliance. There are numerous examples (to be found on the RSH website) where, following an IDA, gradings have been changed and therefore in practice it is a mechanism which is in wide scale use.

4.80 Economic matters are investigated even further where either they affect the viability of the provider, or affect the regulator's overall 'regulatory judgment' (below), or 'could have' a 'significant reputational risk' for the sector.[95] In the case of small providers, investigation is triggered only if, in addition to the above, there is a failure to comply with a standard or mismanagement.[96]

4.81 By contrast, the regulation of the consumer standards is reactive and the regulator does not regularly monitor performance.[97] As we saw above, intervention is based on the concepts of serious detriment or a significant risk of serious detriment to tenants or potential tenants.[98] Information of a breach that qualifies for intervention is referred to the regulator's non-statutory Consumer Regulation Panel. However, in the wake of the Grenfell Tower tragedy in June 2017, in

---

93 *Regulating the standards*, para 2.9 and Annex A. In the case of a group, overall assessment is at group level.
94 *Regulating the standards*, paras 2.21–2.29.
95 *Regulating the standards*, paras 2.32.
96 *Regulating the standards*, paras 2.33.
97 *Regulating the standards*, paras 2.37.
98 Section 198A.

which a council-owned tower block in London managed by a TMO was destroyed, the recent green paper (para 1.47) proposes to increase the level of regulation over consumer matters.

Regulation of Welsh bodies

4.82 Welsh RSLs are subject to regulation by the Welsh Ministers under the Housing Act 1996[99] as modified by the Housing (Wales) Measure 2011. Unlike English bodies, Welsh housing associations have a self-contained system of regulation which is directly accountable democratically to the Welsh National Assembly. The 2011 Measure revised the Housing Act 1996 to correspond to the powers which the Localism Act 2011 introduced in England. The Regulation of Registered Social Landlords (Wales) Act 2018 removed some regulatory powers in the wake of the English Housing and Planning Act 2016[100] in order to justify the government treating RSLs as private sector bodies.

4.83 The investigation, enforcement and intervention powers of the Welsh regulator are similar to those in England. There are also broadly similar provisions concerning standards and rules made under them albeit without the distinction between consumer and economic matters that is prominent in English regulation. Standards about housing provision can apply generally but governance and financial management standards cannot apply to the provision of housing in England.[101] This may be a difficult distinction to apply. As is the case in England the Welsh government can also make determinations concerning accounting standards.[102]

4.84 There is no statutory requirement of fundamental objectives as such, nor is there a statutory distinction between consumer standards and economic standards as such. The Welsh Ministers' published regulatory judgments distinguish between 'governance (including service provision)' and 'financial viability'.[103] As regards Welsh housing, the Welsh Ministers' power to issue and publish guidance seems to be wider than that of the English regulator in that guidance can relate to any matter addressed by a standard and can

---

99 Sch 1.
100 See below para 5.80.
101 Housing Act 1996 ss33A, 34 (as amended); Housing (Wales) Act 2014 s267.
102 Sch 1 Part 3; Accounting Requirements for Registered Social Landlords General Determination (Wales) 2015.
103 Welsh Government, *The regulatory framework for housing associations registered in Wales*, 2017, p6.

explicitly be taken into account in deciding whether a standard has been met.[104] However, in respect of housing in England, the Welsh Ministers can issue guidance concerning only housing provision.[105] Representatives of RSL tenants and local housing authorities must be consulted in relation to standards and guidance.[106]

---

104 Housing Act 1996 s33B.
105 Housing Act 1996 s36 as amended.
106 Housing Act 1996 s35B.

CHAPTER 5
Particular regulatory powers

5.1	Introduction
5.7	**Investigatory/monitoring powers**
5.8	Acquiring information
5.10	Inspections
5.14	Inquiries and audit
5.25	Freezing transactions
5.29	**Powers to impose penalties**
5.29	Introduction
5.31	Enforcement notice
5.36	Penalty notice
5.39	Compensation notice
5.40	**Powers over governance and management**
5.41	Management
5.44	Suspending or removing individuals
5.50	Appointing officers
5.52	**Transfer of land and amalgamation**
5.55	**Relaxing regulation**
5.57	The disposal of land
5.66	Constitutional changes and restructuring
5.71	**Insolvency and winding up**
5.73	**Appeals**
5.77	**Powers of the Welsh regulator**

Introduction

5.1 Both the English and Welsh regulators have a range of powers that can be used in a flexible way. They include;
- inspections;
- inquiries and audits;
- warning notices;
- penalties and compensation;
- the appointment of managers or officers;

and, only as a result of an inquiry or audit:
- transfers of land;
- transfers of management;
- amalgamations;
- removal of board members and other officers; and
- freezing assets or transactions.

5.2 The powers are backed by criminal penalties and, in the case of powers to obtain information, by a High Court Order. The level of regulation differs in particular contexts according to whether the body is profit or non-profit, charitable or non-charitable and whether social housing is involved. In particular, some finance-related powers do not apply to with-profit bodies.

5.3 We saw in the previous chapter that the powers must be exercised with minimum interference, there must be provision for voluntary remedies and that the regulator uses its powers more rigorously and more proactively in relation to the economic standards than the consumer standards.

5.4 The Welsh regulator has a similar range of powers, but these apply only to housing associations. The Welsh regulator's powers are more flexible, without a formal distinction between economic and consumer standards and with a broader concept of social housing.

5.5 The powers of the English regulator were relaxed in certain areas by the Housing and Planning Act 2016, mainly concerning control over constitutional changes and assets. This is intended to enable the government under Treasury internal rules to treat housing associations as part of the private sector and so remove them from the public debt.[1] There is similar legislation in Wales.[2]

---

1 See above para 3.9.
2 Regulation of Registered Social Landlords (Wales) Act 2018.

5.6 The English regulator has the following powers over private registered providers (PRPs).[3] Unless we state otherwise, the Welsh powers are similar.

Investigatory/monitoring powers

5.7 Investigatory/monitoring powers are as follows:

1) In relation to the *consumer standards*, to enter property at any reasonable time in order to carry out a survey of its condition on suspicion of a breach by the landlord. The landlord must be given 28 days' notice and the occupier seven days' notice.[4] In the Welsh regime, without reference to standards there is a similar power of entry on the ground of a failure to maintain or repair in accordance with published guidance.[5]
2) In all cases, to require information and to carry out an inspection of the association's activities (below).[6]
3) In all cases, to hold an inquiry by an independent person if the regulator suspects 'mismanagement' together with an extraordinary audit (below).[7]

Acquiring information

5.8 The regulator has a wide power to require documents or information concerning the 'affairs or activities' of a registered provider or of a person applying to be one for a purpose relating to any of its functions.[8] This applies any person, but to someone other than the provider itself only where the provider has failed to provide the information or if the regulator thinks that it is unable to do so. However, legal professional privilege applies, as does a banker's duty of confidentiality to persons other than the association itself, a subsidiary or an associate.[9] An 'associate' means a fellow subsidiary or a parent body.[10]

---

3 See generally, Homes and Communities Agency (HCA), *Guidance on the regulator's approach to intervention, enforcement and use of powers* and associated guidance notes, 2017.
4 Housing and Planning Act 2016 s199.
5 Housing Act 1996 s37.
6 Housing and Regeneration Act (HRA) 2008 s201.
7 HRA 2008 s206.
8 HRA 2008 s107.
9 HRA 2008 s108.
10 HRA 2008 s271.

5.9   Apart from the usual criminal penalties for disobedience, the power can be enforced by the High Court with the sanction of imprisonment for contempt. This power is used to check whether the 'standards' are being complied with but only with notice and as a last resort where information is not provided voluntarily.[11]

Inspections

5.10   The regulator can 'arrange for a person' to carry out an inspection relating to an association's performance of its social housing functions or to its 'financial and other affairs'.[12] This can take place without notice and without any particular grounds or allegations being shown. However, the regulator states that it would use it only where there is evidence including that of a whistleblower, of a serious failure or malpractice. It would normally discuss the matter in advance but may intervene speedily where it considers there to be is a risk to tenants or the taxpayer.[13]

5.11   Apparently the inspector can be anyone, but, if a member of the regulator's staff only with the consent of the secretary of state. The inspector can enter premises at any reasonable time and inspect, copy or take away documents or electronic data and require information and co-operation but not apparently search premises. Thus there can be spot checks.

5.12   The inspector, by notice in this case, can require specific documents or information. This power applies only to documents or information falling within the regulator's general power to collect information under sections 107 and 108 of the HRA 2008.

5.13   A written report must be made to the regulator. Both the regulator and the inspector have a discretion whether or not to publish the report.[14] However, under the common law, anyone criticised in the report must before publication be given an outline of any accusations and a chance to answer them. Known as 'Maxwellisation',[15] this can be satisfied, for example, by the regulator after receiving the report or an interim report, writing to those criticised, outlining the criticisms, and asking for their comments on specific matters. The objection here of course is that the regulator having read the report may no

---

11 Guidance note 3.
12 HRA 2008 ss201–203.
13 Guidance note 7.
14 HRA 2008 s202.
15 *Maxwell v Department of Trade and Industry* [1974] 2 All ER 122.

longer be open-minded. The regulator's guidance[16] states that a copy of the report is given to the provider together with the regulator's 'own assessment of the outcome'. This may not suffice to comply with the common law.

Inquiries and audit

5.14 The regulator can direct an inquiry into the affairs of a registered provider including a subsidiary or associate (see para 15.24 below) even if not itself registered.[17] It can also direct an extraordinary audit, but only while or after an inquiry is held. These powers apply if the regulator believes that the affairs of a registered provider may have been 'mismanaged'. The regulator's belief need not be on reasonable grounds other than the normal legal standard that it must have a rational basis.

5.15 In this and other contexts under the HRA 2008, 'mismanagement' has a narrow and artificial meaning, namely, breach of any legal requirement[18] (an example of the recent relaxation of regulation). This supersedes the much broader concept of mismanagement, covering most serious failures, misconduct and 'inappropriate' conduct, contained in the regulator's guidance.[19] It is not clear what purpose is served by this limited approach since ultimately only the courts can decide whether there has been a breach of the law. The Welsh regulator's powers to hold an inquiry under Housing Act 1996 Sch 1 Part 4 were originally based on wider concepts of mismanagement or misconduct . However, under the Regulation of Registered Social Landlords (Wales) Act 2018 the threshold for intervention is even more limited, applying only to 'a breach of an obligation imposed by or under an enactment'.[20]

5.16 In the case of a charity registered with the Charity Commission (company, charitable incorporated organisation or trust), the regulator's power to hold an inquiry applies only where the association has received 'public assistance' meaning that the charity has received grants or loans from government or property from a local authority under various housing related provisions and then only in relation to its housing activities. The Charity Commission must be notified.[21]

---

16 Guidance note 7 para 13.
17 HRA 2008 ss206, 210.
18 Housing and Planning Act 2016 Sch 4 para 38 modifying HRA 2008 s275.
19 Guidance note 8 para 7.
20 See Regulation of Registered Social Landlords (Wales) Act 2018 ss6–12.
21 HRA 2008 ss209, 274.

However, the Charity Commission itself has regulatory powers including mismanagement in a wider sense (see chapter 6).

5.17 Certain enforcement powers can be exercised only after an inquiry or extraordinary audit. These include the transfer of management functions to another person or body, the transfer of land, amalgamating associations and removing board members and other officers (below). Other powers, mainly financial penalties and internal management changes are nominally freestanding. However, in these cases the common law requires that a person subject to a penalty has a right to a fair hearing.

5.18 Unlike the case with an inspection, and reflecting the more judicial character of an inquiry, the regulator must appoint one or more independent individuals to hold the inquiry. However, the requirement of independence is not stringent. A current member, employee or consultant (which includes any service provider) cannot be appointed, nor can a member or employee within the last five years.[22] Thus the regulator apparently can appoint someone who has finished working for it as a consultant, however recently.[23] As regards Welsh bodies, the Welsh Ministers can employ an existing consultant to hold the inquiry and can appoint two or more persons, one of which can be a member or employee.[24]

5.19 However, the common law of bias may be relevant here. An appointment can be challenged on the ground that a hypothetical reasonable outsider, knowing all the circumstances, might believe that there is a real risk of bias. While previous experience is not in itself a disqualification, recent direct involvement with the regulator, especially if the person in question is eligible for reappointment, might fall on the other side of the line. On the other hand the law is sufficiently pragmatic not to apply a threshold so high as to make it unrealistic to find suitable candidates. It also takes account of accepted professional standards. The fact that the person to be appointed is a member of a firm that is working for the regulator is not a disqualification in itself.[25] Nevertheless, is preferable if an appointment to an inquiry was required be made independently – for example, by the secretary of state.

22 HRA 2008 s206.
23 See guidance note 8 para 11.
24 Housing Act 1996 Sch 1 Part IV.
25 See eg *Porter v McGill* [2002] 1 All ER 465; *AMEC Capital Projects Ltd v Whitefriars City Estates Ltd* [2005] 1 All ER 723; *Gillies v Secretary of State for Work and Pensions* [2006] 1 All ER 731; *Locabail (UK) Ltd v Bayfield Properties Ltd* [2000] QB 451; compare *Lawal v Northern Spirit Ltd* [2004] 1 All ER 187.

Particular regulatory powers 99

5.20 There is no statutory provision for publicity for an inquiry or for notifying persons affected. However, the regulator's guidance[26] commits to notifying relevant public bodies and the association's secured creditors and issuing a press notice. In any case, the common law principles of 'procedural propriety/fairness', or 'natural justice',[27] a term which has fallen into disuse in the courts, require that advance notice of any allegations be given to anyone who is likely to be criticised in the inquiry.

5.21 Subject to the common law principles of fairness and relevance, the inquiry can decide its own procedure. It need not, therefore, hold a formal hearing and can decide what evidence to consider.[28] The inquiry can order the production of documents which are within the regulator's general powers to require (above).[29] It can also require evidence on oath.[30] The regulator's guidance[31] permits representation but does not make it clear whether this includes legal representation. Under the common law there is a right to representation only where this is necessary to do justice.[32] However, the narrow definition of 'mismanagement' introduced by the Housing and Planning Act 2016[33] means that there may be a criminal aspect to the matter. Under Article 6 of the European Convention on Human Rights (ECHR), this includes a right to legal representation, and rights to call and cross-examine witnesses.

5.22 The inspector can make an interim report and must make a final report.[34] The regulator has a discretion to publish all or part of the report in both cases. It will normally publish both in full except on public interest grounds concerning in particular safety or inhibiting people from coming forward.[35]

5.23 Similar, and indeed stronger, considerations about fairness apply as in the case of an inspection (above). Anyone criticised in the report must be given an opportunity to comment before the final report is issued. The same applies to an interim report where the regulator

26 Guidance note 8 paras 28, 29.
27 Guidance note 8 para 32.
28 See *Scott-Malden v Auriol HA* (unreported, QBD, 7 July 1980).
29 See above para 5.8.
30 HRA 2008 s208. Thus removing the absence of an enforcement power revealed by *Ashby v Ebdon* [1985] Ch 394.
31 Guidance note 8 para 32.
32 *R v Maze Board of Prison Visitors ex p Hone* [1988] 1 All ER 321.
33 Above para 4.50.
34 HRA 2008 s207.
35 Guidance note 8 para 50.

decides to take action on its basis. In respect of the regulator's final decision on the report, its guidance states that representations will be heard only as a matter of discretion.[36] However, the common law would require a right to make further representations if new evidence is taken into account or new issues were raised.

5.24 The regulator is not bound by the report. Its guidance[37] indicates that there will be an opportunity for further representations both while it is considering the report and after it has made its decision when reasons will be given and notification of any further action to be taken.

Freezing transactions

5.25 During or following an inquiry, the regulator can make orders freezing an association's assets and imposing restrictions on its transactions and those of banks and other persons holding money or securities on its behalf. This power applies to a registered charity (company, trust or charitable incorporated organisation (CIO)) only if it has received 'public assistance'.[38] It does not apply to with-profit providers.

5.26 The regulator can make a temporary order while a statutory inquiry is pending if it is satisfied either that there has been mismanagement or that the interests of the association's tenants or its assets require protection. After the regulator receives an interim report of the inquiry, the power applies only in case of mismanagement.[39] The measures can last for up to six months after the regulator receives the final report of the inquiry.

5.27 Following an inquiry or extraordinary audit, the regulator can impose an indefinite freeze on the assets of an association and impose restrictions on its transactions including a consent requirement. This applies only if the regulator is satisfied that there has been mismanagement.[40]

5.28 Before making any freezing or restriction order, the regulator must 'take all reasonable steps to give notice to the registered provider and to any bank or other person subject to the restriction holding the provider's money or securities.[41] Since a power of this kind affects property rights, the Human Rights Act 1998 may apply so that the

36 Guidance note 8, para 43.
37 Guidance note 8, paras 38–47.
38 See above, para 5.16.
39 HRA 2008 s256.
40 HRA 2008 s257.
41 HRA 2008 s258.

regulator must ensure that its actions are proportionate and based on public interest grounds.

Powers to impose penalties

Introduction

5.29 The regulator has a range of powers to intervene in the affairs of a housing association However, these are subject to specific limitations in favour of the independence of the association. For example, as we have seen in the case of an inquiry, 'mismanagement' is defined narrowly to mean only breaches of the law. The regulator's statutory guidance (above) states that these powers will usually be used in a graduated way in favour of the least intrusion and subject to advance notice, dialogue and reasons, with a presumption that the first resort is self-improvement by means of a voluntary undertaking. As we have seen, there is a higher threshold for enforcing the consumer standards than for the economic standards.

5.30 Apart from compensation orders, which are civil debts, the regulator's powers are ultimately enforceable by criminal sanctions. A prosecution for an offence under the HRA 2008 can usually be brought only by or with the consent of the regulator itself or the Director of Public Prosecutions (DPP).[42]

Enforcement notice

5.31 The core of the enforcement process is the power to 'give' an 'enforcement notice' to a registered provider.[43] This is essentially a notice laying the ground for further action and encouraging voluntary remedies. It requires the regulator to be 'satisfied' under any of the following ten heads that an enforcement notice is 'appropriate' either in itself or as a prelude to further action. The main heads are:

1) failure to meet a statutory standard;
2) mismanagement;
3) failure to comply with an earlier enforcement notice;
4) failure to publish information as required by a previous 'penalty notice' or 'compensation order' (below);

---

42 The single exception, HRA 2008 s109(4), is the disclosure of information by or to another public authority in breach of a restriction.
43 HRA 2008 ss219–225.

5) the interests of tenants require protection;
6) the association's assets require protection;
7) the association has failed to comply with a voluntary undertaking;
8) failure to pay registration fees;
9) commission of an offence under the social housing regulation provisions of the HRA 2008. Here the association cannot be prosecuted for that offence unless the enforcement notice is disobeyed.[44] Where the regulator is satisfied that such an offence was committed by another person such as a member, agent or employee of the association, it can give the notice to that person.[45] It can then either issue a penalty notice (below) or prosecute that person;[46]
10) failure to comply with an order of the Housing Ombudsman (below).

5.32 Before giving an enforcement notice, the regulator will seek the possibility of voluntary action.[47]

5.33 An enforcement notice must specify, first, the grounds on which it is given; second the action required by the regulator in response; third, when the action must be taken, which can be immediately; and fourth, the notice must explain the provisions for appeal, for withdrawing the notice and for the penalties for disobedience. An enforcement notice can be withdrawn by giving notice to the registered provider.[48]

5.34 In the light of experience with similar notices such as those required under town and country planning legislation, these requirements may be a recipe for problems relating to the validity of a notice which contains errors or is unclear. In particular, it may be necessary to distinguish between serious omissions, uncertainties or fundamental misconceptions making a notice a complete nullity, and legal or factual errors that do not affect the validity of the notice as such but may be a ground of appeal to the High Court.[49] Fortunately, the factual matters on which the social housing notice depends are unlikely to raise the uncertainties and complexities that arise in the planning context. Moreover the technicalities of communication of a

---

44 HRA 2008 s225(3).
45 HRA 2008 s220(12).
46 HRA 2008 s225(2).
47 See guidance note 9.
48 HRA 2008 s224.
49 Under HRA 2008 s223, see *Miller-Mead v Minister of Housing and Local Government* [1963] 2 QB 196 which remains the seminal authority.

notice may be avoided by the requirement that it is to be 'given' rather than served albeit the meaning of 'give' is itself obscure.

5.35 There is no specific sanction for disobeying an enforcement notice as such although this is one of several grounds for taking further steps to impose a penalty or award compensation. Under HRA 2008 s225(1), if an enforcement notice is not obeyed, the regulator 'shall consider' exercising another of its powers, including its monitoring powers (above). It is not clear whether these powers can be exercised independently without first giving an enforcement notice, or whether section 225(1) impliedly excludes this. It is arguable that the policy of the Act in favour of restrained regulation indicates the latter. On the other hand, the powers to hold an inspection, inquiry or extraordinary audit are clearly independent of the enforcement notice procedure.

Penalty notice[50]

5.36 The regulator can impose a financial penalty under HRA 2008 s227. This can be on any of the grounds listed above other than the protection of tenants or of the association's assets (grounds 5 and 6 above). In the case of the commission of an offence, the normal criminal standard of proof beyond reasonable doubt applies.

5.37 The penalty is triggered by the giving of a penalty notice similar in form and content to an enforcement notice and specifying a period for payment.[51] The penalty is a civil debt only. The regulator cannot prosecute the association for any offence in respect of which the penalty notice is given.[52] The size of the penalty is limited to £5,000 or, in the case of an offence, to the applicable level of fine.[53] After deducting the regulator's costs, the penalty money must be used by the Homes and Communities Agency (HCA) for social housing purposes.[54] There is a right of appeal to the High Court against a penalty notice.[55]

5.38 Before giving a penalty notice, the regulator must give a pre-penalty 'warning notice' to the association, allowing it at least 28 days from when it receives the notice to make representations.[56] The

50 See guidance note 10.
51 HRA 2008 s228.
52 HRA 2008 s234 (the notice must explain this). Under Treasury regulations, interest and additional penalties can be charged for late payment.
53 HRA 2008 s229 (the limit can be altered by the secretary of state).
54 HRA 2008 s233.
55 HRA 2008 s235.
56 HRA 2008 ss230, 231.

warning notice must refer to the possibility of the association giving a voluntary undertaking to remedy the matter and the terms on which the regulator would accept this.

Compensation notice

5.39 Independently of the penalty process, the regulator can require an association to pay compensation to a tenant, a class of its tenants or the whole class of its tenants who has suffered as a result of a failure to meet a regulatory standard or comply with a voluntary undertaking.[57] The process requires a notice and a warning notice, a right to make representations and an appeal similar to those in penalty cases.[58] There is a bias in favour of low compensation in that the regulator must take into account the association's financial situation and the likely impact of the compensation on its ability to provide services. It must aim to avoid jeopardising the financial viability of the association, or its ability to meet its commitments or to remedy the matters in respect of which the compensation is paid.[59]

Powers over governance and management

5.40 The regulator has a range of more drastic powers subject to somewhat vague consultation requirements.

Management

5.41 First, there are powers in respect of the management of the association. These are as follows.

1) To require the association to tender for a manager under requirements specified by the regulator relating to social housing.[60] The regulator must be satisfied that there has been a breach of a standard or mismanagement in relation to social housing or a failure to comply with certain rent limits requirements under the Welfare Reform and Work Act 2016 (see para 14.59). This power depends

---

57 HRA 2008 ss237–245.
58 In the case of a warning notice, the ombudsman must be consulted: HRA 2008 s242.
59 HRA 2008 s241. Compensation cannot be awarded where the ombudsman, who is not so constrained, has already awarded compensation (HRA 2008 s239).
60 HRA 2008 s247.

on all the circumstances and is likely to be triggered where there is a persistent poor performance.[61] Similar provisions for advance notice, opportunity for a voluntary undertaking and appeal apply as in the case of a penalty notice. The notice can be combined with a penalty or compensation warning notice or both (above).

Copies of the notice must be sent to the Greater London Authority (GLA) as funder where the association owns land in London, and any other person who the regulator thinks 'appropriate'.[62] The regulator is required to take into account the views of tenants, the association itself, and the GLA, but the views of local housing authorities only if it thinks 'appropriate' and those of the other 'appropriate' persons not at all. The regulator's guidance states that it will not take into account the views of the association's employees, agents or contractors but unspecified 'relevant' persons might be more favourably regarded.[63]

2) The regulator can also appoint an individual as a manager or require the association to do so in relation to the association's social housing or specified aspects of it.[64] This applies where the regulator is satisfied that the association has failed to reach a standard or there has been mismanagement or where the provider has violated statutory requirements concerning rent levels. It will do so in cases where there is a need for urgent action because of 'critical financial viability problem's or where the interests of tenants are seriously at risk'.[65]

There is no specific requirement for an inquiry or audit but arguably an inquiry would be necessary under the common law where there are allegations of mismanagement (above). Similar provisions for a warning notice, sending copies, voluntary undertaking and appeal apply as in 1) above.[66] There are no statutory consultation requirements. However, the regulator's guidance promises to send copies of the warning notice to the GLA where the property is in London and to 'any other person the regulator thinks appropriate' in particular to a whistleblower.[67]

---

61 Guidance note 18.
62 Once the regulator becomes fully independent, presumably this will apply also to the HCA.
63 Guidance note 18 para 21.
64 HRA 2008 s251.
65 Guidance note 12.
66 HRA 2008 s252.
67 Guidance note 12 para 9.

3) More drastically the regulator can require the transfer of all or any of the management functions relating to social housing or specified aspects of it to a person specified by the regulator. This could be, for example, another housing association or a contractor. This power requires the consent of the secretary of state and can be used only following an inquiry or extraordinary audit (above).[68] The regulator must be satisfied either that there has been mismanagement or that management of some or all of its social housing would be improved by exercising these powers. Similar provisions for notice, voluntary undertaking, and appeal apply as in 1) above. There are also limited consultation requirements similar to those in 1). However, the requirement to send a copy of the warning notice to other 'appropriate persons' specifically emphasises whistleblowers.[69] The regulator would also 'possibly' seek the views of other regulators and of secured creditors.[70]

5.42 These powers are likely to be used either alone or in combination with other powers, where there has been persistent mismanagement or serious detriment or a risk of it to tenants or where the management of housing needs improvement or previous requirements have not been complied with.

5.43 The regulator also has power to operate a scheme, or to approve a scheme operated by someone else such as a trade organisation, for the purpose of accrediting persons who provide management services for social housing.[71]

Suspending or removing individuals

5.44 While a statutory inquiry is in process the regulator may suspend for up to six months, an officer (which term includes a board member or trustee), employee or agent of a non-profit private registered provider who it thinks has contributed to' the failure or mismanagement'.[72] This power is subject to the same limits as the freezing or restriction power (above). However, it is not clear what is meant by 'failure' in this context, since the grounds for triggering this power or the freezing power do not include 'failure'. Presumably what is meant is a failure to protect the interests of the tenants or the assets.

68 HRA 2008 s249; guidance note 19.
69 HRA 2008 s250(4)(c).
70 Guidance note 19 paras 18, 19, 20.
71 HRA 2008 s217.
72 HRA 2008 ss257, 270.

Particular regulatory powers 107

5.45 Following an inquiry or extraordinary audit, the regulator can make an order permanently removing an officer employee or agent again on the same basis as in the case of a freezing or restriction order. Pending a decision the regulator can suspend the person for up to six months.[73] In the case of indefinite removal, the regulator must take 'all reasonable steps' to give the person concerned and the association at least 14 days' notice.[74]

5.46 Following a suspension, the regulator can give directions about the functions in question and appoint a replacement.[75] Following removal, the person concerned is disqualified permanently from acting as an officer of any registered provider (including therefore a local authority). The regulator can waive a disqualification but only on the application of the disqualified person.[76] The regulator must keep a public register of disqualified persons.[77] Acting while disqualified is an offence and any payments or benefits to such a person can be recovered.[78] However, people dealing with the association are protected in that the acts of a disqualified person are not invalid on that ground alone.[79]

5.47 The regulator has a further power to remove office holders of non-profit bodies but without disqualification. This applies to cases where there is lesser or no fault. They include bankruptcy and other insolvency arrangements, disqualifications of directors under the Company Directors Disqualification Act 1986 or of charity trustees under the Charities Act 2011, mental health and absence or failure to act.[80] As with the other power of removal, 14 days' notice is required and the power applies to a charity only if it has received public assistance as defined above.[81] This power is likely to be exercised in cases where there is a financial risk or where the conduct of an officer is impeding the work of the association, for example securing attendance at meetings.[82]

5.48 At common law where there is an allegation of wrongdoing there is a right to be heard before a sanction such as suspension or removal

73 HRA 2008 s260.
74 HRA 2008 s260(5).
75 HRA 2008 s261.
76 HRA 2008 s262.
77 HRA 2008 s263.
78 HRA 2008 ss264, 265.
79 HRA 2008 s262 (5).
80 HRA 2008 s266.
81 HRA 2008 s267.
82 Guidance note 15 para 7.

for office is imposed, in the form of an opportunity to answer any allegations and, at least in the case of permanent removal, a right to cross examine relevant witnesses.[83] It is probably not sufficient that the inquiry itself may have covered the same ground since the focus of the powers are not identical and the courts are reluctant to deny a person a hearing on the ground that it is redundant.[84] However, the regulator's guidance in fact provides for a further opportunity to make representations.[85] The right to be heard is reinforced, in the case of an' officer' such as a board member,[86] by the right to a fair trial under Article 6 of the ECHR. An 'office', but not an ordinary job, is arguably a 'civil right' for the purpose of Article 6.

5.49 In all cases of removal or suspension, there is a right of appeal to the High Court.[87] This in itself will not satisfy the common law right to a fair hearing on the facts.

Appointing officers

5.50 The regulator can appoint a new officer of a non-profit registered provider. This applies mainly to board members and trustees and to all members and employees in the case of a Co-operative and Community Benefits Societies Act (CCBSA) society.[88] The power applies to a charity only where it has received grants or loans or a transfer of housing from a local authority under specified housing legislation and where the regulator has consulted the Charity Commission.[89]

5.51 The appointment can be as a replacement for a person removed under the above provision or where there are no officers, or as an additional appointment to the governing body where the regulator thinks this is necessary to ensure that the registered provider's affairs are managed in accordance with legal requirements.[90] For example,

---

83 See eg *R v Army Board of Defence Council ex p Anderson* [1992] QB 169; *Ridge v Baldwin* [1964] AC 40.
84 *Ridge v Baldwin* [1964] AC 40.
85 Guidance note 16 para 11.
86 HRA 2008 s270.
87 HRA 2008 s268.
88 HRA 2008 ss269(6), 274.
89 HRA 2008 s274. It is not clear why, unlike other contexts, this is not called 'public assistance'.
90 HRA 2008 s269; Housing and Planning Act 2016 Sch 4 para 36 replaced the earlier 'proper management of affairs' reflecting the more limited notion of 'mismanagement' now in force.

the regulator would use this power where it thinks that the board needs additional skills.[91] The appointment can override any restriction on eligibility and on the number of board members in the association's constitution. The regulator can appoint more than one additional officer, but cannot appoint more than a minority unless the association has fewer officers than its constitution requires and its constitution does not specify a minimum number of officers.[92]

Transfer of land and amalgamation

5.52 The regulator can require an association to transfer specified land to a specified PRP or (exceptionally) to the regulator itself.[93] The power does not apply to a registered charity (a company, trust or CIO) thus applying only to a CCBSA society. A statutory inquiry or extraordinary audit must first be held. The prior consent of the secretary of state is required. The power can be exercised only on the grounds either of mismanagement of social housing or where the regulator is satisfied that such a transfer is likely to improve the management of the land. The price must be at least market value, as valued by the District Valuer, and must take account of the association's existing liabilities. There are no statutory consultation requirements. However, the consent of secured creditors under the general law would probably be necessary and the regulator has indicted that it will in practice consult interested parties including other regulators.[94]

5.53 A non-profit body cannot be required to transfer land to a profit-making body. Reflecting the general law, a charitable association can be required to transfer land only to another charity the objects of which the regulator thinks are similar. This can include a registered charity. The power to require a transfer also applies to profit-making bodies but only applies to land used for social housing or 'associated land'.[95]

---

91 Guidance note 16 paras 5, 6.
92 HRA 2008 s269(2).
93 HRA 2008 ss253, 254; guidance note 13. The regulator can sell on only to another non-profit registered provider.
94 Guidance note 13 paras 12, 14.
95 HRA 2008 s253(3), (4). 'Associated land' is land which the regulator thinks is used in connection with the social housing or its management such as shared facilities.

5.54 The regulator also has the power on a similar basis to execute an instrument amalgamating a CCBSA society with another such society.[96] The new society so created must be registered as a non-profit body prior to the amalgamation the second body will normally take the lead in terms of business and operational planning.[97] There are no statutory consultation requirements. However, the regulator's guidance undertakes to consult as widely as possible and specifically tenants, the association itself, funders, secured creditors, other regulators and local and central government.[98]

Relaxing regulation

5.55 Two groups of regulatory powers were removed in England by Housing and Planning Act 2016 Sch 4. The removal of these powers, which gave control akin to that of an owner, was a response to a ruling by the Office for National Statistics (ONS) in 2015, unwelcome to the Treasury, that housing associations are public bodies for the purposes of government finances. The first group of powers was to consent to the disposal of land, and to the use of money obtained from the sale of publicly funded property (the Disposal Proceeds Fund). The second group concerned constitutional changes, restructuring and dissolution and the power to bring a petition for winding up.

5.56 In addition, the threshold for regulatory intervention, namely 'mismanagement', has been raised to breaches of the law as opposed to misconduct. As a result, the ONS has revised its opinion and now classifies housing associations as private bodies.[99] The same applies in Wales, where the threshold for intervention is even more limited, being confined to breaches of an 'enactment'.[100]

The disposal of land

5.57 HRA 2008 s171(1) states that a registered provider may dispose of land. However, this is likely to be the case anyway under the provider's own rules. The previous version of this power (Housing Act 1996 s8) which still applies to registered social landlords (RSLs) in Wales

---

96 HRA 2008 s255.
97 Guidance note 14.
98 Guidance note 14 para 14.
99 Above para 3.11.
100 Regulation of Registered Social Landlords (Wales) Act 2018.

added the words, 'and not otherwise'. In England, the statutory power of disposal may perhaps be overridden by specific restrictions on disposal in association's constitution.

5.58 Housing and Planning Act 2016 Sch 4 has removed the requirement of the CCBSA 2014 that the regulator must consent to disposals. It also abolishes requirements of consent by the regulator or the secretary of state in other legislation including disposals of former right to buy property. Consent is replaced by a requirement to notify the regulator if a PRP disposes of a dwelling that is social housing, or if a non-profit PRP (ie a housing association) disposes of land that is not a dwelling.[101]

5.59 This opens the door to housing associations selling off dwellings in high-value areas, especially in London, thereby increasing the problem of shortage of social housing. At the extreme, it enables the effective privatisation of social housing. The regulator may police this by the use of its general regulatory powers especially financial pressures. However, in the case of a registered charity, ie a charitable trust or charitable company, there is in certain cases an additional requirement of consent by the Charity Commission.[102]

5.60 Regulation of Registered Social Landlords (Wales) Act 2018 ss13–15 enacts similar provisions in relation to RSLs, replacing consent powers with a duty to notify the Welsh Ministers. This seems to apply to all land owned by an RSL, not only to social housing.[103]

5.61 'Disposal' is widely defined, meaning selling leasing, mortgaging, charging or 'disposing of it or part of it in any other way'.[104] Notification can be after the event, the regulator specifying the period required. The regulator or the Welsh Ministers, as the case may be, can dispense by means of a direction with a notification requirement or permit general notifications.

5.62 Under the current English direction,[105] notification has been dispensed with in all cases except in the case of a 'relevant disposal' of a dwelling that is social housing. The underlying policy is to protect the social housing stock. Relevant disposals are of three kinds: first,

---

101 HRA 2008 s176 as amended.
102 Charities Act 2011 s117. However this does not apply where the disposal, which includes a tenancy is taken with prescribed advice and so has limited importance to a housing association.
103 Housing Act 1996 s9 (as substituted).
104 HRA 2008 s273; Housing Act 1996 s9(2).
105 See HCA, *Direction of the social housing regulator about notifications of disposal of social housing dwellings and of land other than a dwelling 2017* and associated guidance.

'landlord disposals', 'where the association ceases to be the landlord of the residential occupier;[106] second, 'finance disposals', where the disposal is to obtain finance such as a mortgage loan; and third, where the disposal is to support a guarantee, for example of the debts of an associate body.

5.63 Under the direction, notification is required for a 'landlord disposal' of a dwelling outside the sector (meaning to an unregistered body including a subsidiary or parent), whether occupied or not, and of an *occupied* dwelling within the sector. There is an exception for disposal to a sitting tenant so that the final transfer of ownership under 'staircasing' arrangements to a shared ownership tenant does not require notification. In all cases, however, the disposal of a provider's last social dwelling must be notified as must a disposal to a profit making registered provider. Any disposal in a single transaction by a 'small provider' (one having less than 1,000 social housing dwellings), of more than five per cent of its stock must also be notified.

5.64 Financial and guarantee disposals of social dwellings concern the association's debt risk. Small providers must notify the regulator of all financial disposals, large providers only of 'non-standard' methods of raising finance, ie those other than ordinary bank loans or bonds, such as sales and leasebacks or other new and novel arrangements'.[107] Guarantee disposals must be notified, other than those relating to public grant funding or for the purpose of securing finance since these are covered by the previous head.

5.65 Housing associations previously had to set up a separate 'disposal proceeds fund' for the proceeds of sales of dwellings to tenants under the 'right to acquire' (the housing association version of the public sector right to buy) and for the proceeds of sale of other publicly funded property. This fund which was subject to restrictions on its use has been abolished.[108]

Constitutional changes and restructuring

5.66 The other notification powers relate to constitutional changes and restructuring affecting assets which previously required regulatory consent. They include changes to the articles of a company and changes of rules of a CCBSA society; conversions of a company into

---

106 Or where it remains the landlord under a lease for less than seven years.
107 *Guidance for private registered providers on how to notify the regulator about the disposal of social housing dwellings* (March 2017) para 5.4.
108 Housing and Planning Act 2016 Sch 4 paras 33–35. Regulations can preserve controls over the fund as it stood immediately before the date of abolition.

a CCBSA society and vice versa; transfer of engagements and undertakings (meaning transfers of property and contractual rights and liabilities to another body), amalgamations and voluntary dissolution. Finally, they included changes in the objects of registered charities. There are special provisions about winding-up in insolvency, which are discussed below at para 15.44.

5.67 These consent powers have been replaced by duties to notify the regulator of these events. Where authorisation by other regulators is required, then, unless the association certifies that the regulator has duly been notified, the other regulator cannot authorise the changes.[109] The Regulation of Registered Social Landlords (Wales) Act 2018 has introduced similar measures.

5.68 The regulator can dispense with the notification requirements. It has done so completely in the case of charitable trusts. In the case of 2014 societies and companies, notification is required for article or rule changes only if they affect charitable or non-profit status, becoming or ceasing to be a subsidiary or change of name or address. Otherwise, there are no exemptions except that, in the case of a group restructuring of CCBSA societies such as an amalgamation, a single notification by the lead organisation on behalf of the others is required.[110]

5.69 A housing association can therefore in principle alter its constitution so as to become a profit-making body. If it does so, it can remain a registered provider of social housing in that capacity, but would of course cease to be a housing association. However, this does not apply to a charitable body. Neither a charitable company nor a charitable CCBSA society can alter its objects as to affect its existing assets.[111] In the case of a trust, either the court or the Charity Commission must approve a scheme to alter the terms of the trust unless the trust itself authorises the alteration.[112] In addition, in the case of a charitable company, 'regulated alterations' to its constitution require the consent of the Charity Commission.[113] These include changing its objects, directing its property or benefiting its directors,

---

109 HRA 2008 ss160, 161, 163, 165, 169A, 169B.
110 See HCA, *Directions of the social housing regulator about notifications of registered society restructuring, company arrangements and reconstruction, registered society dissolution, and constitutional changes*, 6 April 2017.
111 Charities Act 2011 s197.
112 HRA 2008 s69.
113 HRA 2008 s198.

members and their families and business associates. Similar restrictions apply to a CIO.[114]

5.70 In the case of a CCBSA society there is greater flexibility to change status so as to become a company or CIO and vice versa, or to transfer assets between societies or to a company or CIO. Other than the rule outlined above relating to existing assets, such constitutional changes do not require consent but require special resolutions varying with the context involving two successive meetings of members.[115] Thus a charitable society can become non-charitable after transferring its existing assets to another charity.[116]

Insolvency and winding up

5.71 The general law concerning insolvency and winding up applies to housing associations but is modified by a special regime for social housing. Superimposed on the general law in England is the special device of a housing administration order (HAO) created by the Housing and Planning Act 2016.[117] Before this Act, there was a scheme which still applies to Welsh bodies under the Housing Act 1996 (see para 15.61).

5.72 The new provisions are designed to balance the interests of creditors against those of keeping a PRP's assets in the social housing stock. They initially covered only companies (about 14 per cent of the total) but have since been extended to CCBSA 2014 societies and charitable incorporated organisations. Charitable trusts remain subject to the general law of charities, and so to the powers of the Charity Commission and the courts to transfer their assets to other charitable bodies 'cy pres'.

Appeals

5.73 There are rights of appeal to the High Court against individual registration, de-registration and enforcement decisions. These are not limited as to grounds, and are therefore wider than judicial review. An appeal can therefore include issues of fact.

---

114 HRA 2008 s226.
115 CCBSA 2014 ss110–113, see para 15.10 below.
116 HRA 2008 s110 under 'transfer of engagement' powers.
117 Sections 95–117 (see para 15.44).

Particular regulatory powers 115

5.74 In addition, the regulator has an internal non-statutory appeal system.[118] The main decisions subject to this are the following:
- registration and de registration;
- directions that a dwelling is not social housing;
- extraordinary audit;
- other monitoring powers, enforcement notices, suspension or removal of board members or officers; and
- decisions concerning exceptions or exemptions under the rent regime.

It does not apply to decisions that do not impose direct sanctions or costs nor to the power to hold an inquiry, nor to powers related to insolvency since the latter are directly under the control of the courts. It must normally be invoked within the short time-limit of ten working days from when the regulator notifies the body concerned that it has decided to use one of these powers. It does not affect access to the High Court. There is also an internal complaints procedure.

5.75 Internal appeals raise questions relating to the right to a fair trial under Article 6 of the ECHR. The issue is that they may lack sufficient independence and procedural safeguards. The appeal panel consists entirely of the regulators own staff, and the procedure is normally in writing, with special permission required for an oral hearing and with no specific right to cross examine or legal representation. Although an appeal body can adopt its own procedure the minimum common law requirements of a fair hearing apply.

5.76 Article 6 applies to administrative processes that affect 'civil right and obligations' as is undoubtedly the case with the social housing regulator. Moreover, 'mismanagement' as a trigger for regulatory intervention depends on a breach of a legal duty. However, Article 6 is applied flexibly in the context of the decision-making process as a whole. It requires an independent element with 'full jurisdiction to deal with the case as the nature of the case requires'. In some cases, this may be satisfied by the separate right of appeal to the High Court. This applies to most of the powers subject to the internal appeal but not to a direction that a dwelling is not social housing, nor to an extraordinary audit nor to the powers concerning rent. The court's judicial review powers are more limited in that they apply to errors of fact only where the error is clear and undisputed.[119]

---

118 See HCA, *Regulator of Social Housing, Appeals Scheme*, May 2018.
119 *Runa Begum v Towers Hamlets LBC* [2003] 1 All ER 731 at 736. See below para 9.86.

Powers of the Welsh regulator

5.77 Unlike the English regulator,[120] the Welsh regulator has power to collect and publish information about the performance levels of an association in respect of the provision of housing, governance and financial management.[121] However, in relation to housing provided by an RSL in England, this applies only to housing provision.[122] RSLs are required to provide an annual statement of compliance with performance standards.

5.78 There are similar constraints on regulation under both regimes. Thus the desirability of RSLs being free to choose how to provide services and conduct business must be taken into account and there is provision for voluntary undertakings.[123] The regulatory framework published by the Welsh Government stresses similar requirements to those of the English regime. These include self-assessment, and 'co-regulation', proportionality, transparency and openness and the independence of associations.[124] The Welsh requirements also include the promotion of learning and development, values missing from the English regime.

5.79 There is provision for complaints to the Welsh Ministers about the performance of RSLs in Wales.[125] The procedure and criteria for investigation are left to guidance published by the Welsh Ministers. At the time of writing no such guidance is available. This contrasts with the English regime where the Social Housing Ombudsman is primarily responsible for complaints.[126] In Wales the Public Services Ombudsman also deals with complaints against RSLs.[127]

5.80 As with the complaints procedure, the enforcement powers of the Welsh regulator do not apply in relation to the provision of housing in England.[128] The powers to carry out an inspection and to hold an inquiry or extraordinary audit do not apply to affairs relating only to

---

120 HRA 2008 ss204, 205 which required the regulator to publish performance information were repealed by the Localism Act 2011 Sch 17 paras 12, 13.
121 HA 1996.
122 HA 1996 as amended.
123 Housing (Wales) Measure 2011 Part 2 chapter 2; Housing Act 1996 s6A.
124 Housing (Wales) Measure 2011; and Welsh Government, *Self assessment – guiding principles for housing association in Wales*, RSL 33/09.
125 HA 1996.
126 See below, chapter 6.
127 Public Services Ombudsman (Wales) Act 2005.
128 Housing Act 1996 s50A.

housing in England.[129] The same applies to the powers relating to the appointment of a manager. There seems, therefore, to be a regulatory gap in that a Welsh body cannot be registered with the English regulator so that neither regulator has jurisdiction. On the other hand, housing in Wales provided by an English body can apparently be regulated by the English regulator. Thus devolution is not symmetrical.

5.81 As befits a regulator which is effectively a primary democratic body, the framework of regulation is broader and more flexible than is the English regime. In particular Welsh regulatory powers apply to all property owned by an RSL since 'social housing' includes any housing provided by an RSL.[130]

5.82 In Wales the insolvency regime of the Housing Act 1996 still applies to RSLs including charitable trusts.[131] It is in the hands of the Welsh Ministers and lacks the relatively independent balancing mechanism of the new English scheme. However, the Welsh Ministers power to petition for winding up has been removed by the Regulation of Registered Social Landlords (Wales) Act 2018.

---

129 HA 1996 Sch 1 Part 3A.
130 Housing (Wales) Measure 2011 s33.
131 Housing Act 1996 ss39–50.

CHAPTER 6
Other regulatory bodies

6.2	Financial Conduct Authority
6.8	Registrar of Companies (Companies House)
6.9	Charity Commission
6.9	Objectives and powers
6.16	Charity accounts and audit
6.18	Care Quality Commission

6.1   Every housing association has at least two layers of registration, each with its regulatory requirements. These are:

1) registration with the Regulator of Social Housing (RSH) (optional); and
2) registration either with the Financial Conduct Authority (FCA) or, the Companies Registry or, in the case of a trust, the Charity Commission.

A charitable body has a third layer in the form of the Charity Commission.

Financial Conduct Authority

6.2   The FCA has certain limited powers of supervision in relation to the many housing associations registered under the Co-operative and Community Benefit Societies Act (CCBSA) 2014, all of which must be registered. The FCA's primary functions are to ensure that their rules and objects comply with the co-operative or community benefit principle which underlies the CCBSA 2014 and to prevent financial irregularities. Its main duties concern registration, cancellation of registration and the submission of accounts and returns. An association has a right to be registered if it satisfies these principles.[1] As regards accounts, each registered society must send an annual return to the FCA including copies of their revenue accounts, auditor's reports and balance sheets.[2] Unlike the Registrar of Companies and the Charity Commission (below), the FCA has no duty to make these publicly available. Also unlike a company, a society does not have to inform the FCA of the appointment of new directors although the names of the directors will appear in the annual accounts.

6.3   The FCA has certain largely formal functions in relation to constitutional changes. Resolutions to amalgamate societies, to transfer engagements (assets and liabilities), to convert to a company or charitable incorporated organisation (CIO) or vice versa must be registered with the FCA in order to take effect, but there is no power to refuse consent. The FCA must consent to changes in the rules of a society registered with it, but only to ensure that the society still qualifies under the CCBSA 2014.[3] A resolution of voluntary dissolu-

1 CCBSA 2014 s3(1).
2 CCBSA 2014 s89.
3 CCBSA 2014 s16.

Other regulatory bodies 121

tion must be notified to the FCA, who must arrange for the resolution to be advertised.[4]

6.4 In all these cases, the change does not take effect until the liquidator or an officer approved by the FCA lodges a certificate with the FCA that all property has been duly transferred.[5] As discussed below in chapter 15, special winding-up arrangements apply to private registered providers (PRPs and RSLs) which overlay the rules governing other regulators.

6.5 The FCA has certain powers of intervention. These are mainly reactive depending on requests by members. However, there are provisions to discourage activity by disaffected members. This is unlikely in the case of a housing association, since the membership often comprises only its committee of management. A society must comprise at least three members or at least two other registered societies.[6]

6.6 These powers include the following:

1) Power to appoint an accountant or actuary to inspect the society's books and report back. Application by at least ten members of a year's standing is required. The members must bear the costs of the process.[7]
2) On the application of at least ten per cent of the membership, or 100 members if less, the FCA can appoint one or more inspectors to examine and report on the society's affairs or alternatively can call a special meeting of the society.[8] The applicant members must show evidence that they have good reasons without malicious motives. The costs of this inspection may be met by the applicants, the society's funds or by the society's members and officers or former members and officer in such proportions directed by the FCA.[9]

6.7 There are no statutory requirements for the RSH to consult with the FCA. However, in practice the regulator does consult in relation to relevant powers such as the transfer of land, amalgamations and appointment of officers. There seems to be no requirement to inform

---

4 CCBSA 2014 ss121, 122. Members, former members and other with a financial interest can apply to the court within 3 months for the dissolution to be set aside
5 CCBSA 2014 s126.
6 CCBSA 2014 s2.
7 CCBSA 2014 s105(1)–(6).
8 CCBSA 2014 s106.
9 CCBSA 2014 s106(6).

122 Housing associations: a legal handbook / chapter 6

the RSH when the FCA cancels a registration. However, the RSH[10] must inform the FCA of registrations or removal from its own register. Where the RSH's right to be notified of a constitutional change applies,[11] the FCA cannot register the change unless the association confirms to it that the regulator has been duly notified.

Registrar of Companies (Companies House)

6.8 All housing associations structured as companies must be registered with the Registrar of Companies. Companies House, as it is often called, does not have regulatory power. Its main functions are to incorporate and dissolve companies that comply with the required formalities and to maintain basic information about each company: address; directors; officers; and members, accounts and audit report and directors' report. An important responsibility of the Registrar is to ensure that basic information is available to the public. Accordingly, the register kept by Companies House must be available to the public for inspection and copying.[12] In addition, company registers of members, directors and secretaries must be available for inspection, but non-members may be charged.[13]

Charity Commission

Objectives and powers

6.9 The Charity Commission's objectives are to:
- increase public trust and confidence in charities;
- promote awareness of the public benefit requirement;
- ensure trustees comply with their legal obligations;
- promote effectiveness of public resources; and
- enhance accountability to donor, beneficiaries and the general public.[14]

---

10 Housing and Regeneration Act 2008 s120.
11 Above para 5.66.
12 Companies Act 2006 ss1085, 1086. The registry is not generally required to check whether the information is accurate: Companies Act 2006 s1112.
13 Companies Act 2006 ss116, 162, 275.
14 Charites Act 2011 s14.

The Commission's functions thus overlap with those of the social housing regulator and its regulatory powers are broadly similar although wider.

In particular, the Commission has powers to investigate, remedy and prevent misconduct or mismanagement.[15] These include:

- suspending and removing trustees, directors, officers, employees and agents;
- appointing an interim manager;
- freezing transactions; and
- directing action to be taken or property to be transferred.

As with the RSH, some of these powers can be exercised only following an inquiry. There is no definition of 'mismanagement', which can thus be much wider than that available to the social housing regulators (acting unlawfully). However, paying managers and employees too much is specifically included.[16] The Charity Commission also has various powers to consent to matters such as constitutional changes by charitable companies and some property transactions. These will be mentioned in their contexts.

6.10 A charitable company and a trust must be registered with the Charity Commission. However, most housing associations are 'exempt' charities.[17] An exempt charity includes all PRPs registered as co-operative or community benefit societies under the CCBSA 2014.[18] An exempt charity is not 'required' to register with the Charity Commission[19] with the implication that it can voluntarily register. However, the Charity Commission, without providing statutory authority, has stated that an exempt charity cannot be registered.[20] An advantage of registration for an exempt charity would be that registration is conclusive evidence that the body is a charity.[21]

6.11 An exempt charity is not subject to routine monitoring by the Charity Commission. It is not required to submit accounts and audits to the Commission.[22] The Commission can, however, require information relating to any charity from any person and can inspect and

---

15 Charites Act 2011 s15(1).
16 Charities Act 2011 s76(2).
17 See CC 23, *Exempt charities*, 2013.
18 Charities Act 2011 Sch 3.
19 Charities Act 2011 s30(2) merely excludes it from a requirement to register.
20 *Exempt charities and principal regulators*, CC 717-01 (2013).
21 Charities Act 2011 s37.
22 Charities Act 2011 s160.

copy the records of any charity including an exempt charity.[23] Annual reports and related documents kept by the Commission must be available for public inspection at all reasonable times.[24]

6.12 The rationale behind the exempt charity device is that such bodies – which include, for example, colleges and museums – usually have another regulator.[25] However, reforms made in 2006 attempted to deal with any regulatory gap by empowering the secretary of state formally to designate a 'principal regulator' for each type of exempt charity responsible for ensuring that the body complies with the law.[26] At time of writing (October 2018), no principal regulator has been formally designated for social housing.

6.13 Many of the Commission's powers require collaboration with the principal regulator and so seem to be in abeyance.[27] In particular, its main regulatory powers are triggered by holding an inquiry into the affairs of the charity but it can do so only if so requested by the principal regulator.[28] An inquiry can be generally or for particular purposes and is therefore a wider power than that of the social housing regulator the power of which is limited to mismanagement in the sense of a breach of the law.[29] The Charity Commission's power to hold an inquiry is also backed by stronger powers than those of the RSH in that, unlike the regulator, the Charity Commission can obtain a search warrant.[30] Provisions entitling the Charity Commission to disclose information to HM Revenue and Customs (HMRC) and other public authorities apply instead to the principal regulator.[31]

6.14 Where there is no designated principal regulator, the secretary of state can remove a body from the list of exempt charities thus bringing it within the full regulatory jurisdiction of the Charity Commission.[32] Social housing providers have not been removed from the list. In practice the Charity Commission apparently liaises with the RSH and appears to rely on the latter as the prime mover. However, any agreement or undertaking between the two bodies which effectively

---

23 Charities Act 2011 ss52, 53.
24 Charities Act 2011 ss165(1), 170.
25 Charities Act 2011 s22, Sch 3.
26 Charities Act 2011 s25.
27 Charities Act 2011 ss26, 28.
28 Charities Act 2011 s46.
29 Charities Act 2011 ss76–85. See CC 46, *Statutory inquiries into charities*, 2013.
30 Charities Act 2011 s48.
31 Charities Act 2011 s58.
32 Charities Act 2011 s22, Sch 3.

6.15 delegates a decision-making power or a veto to the other would be unlawful as a fettering of discretion.

There is a concurrent jurisdiction with the High Court to make schemes altering the rules of a charity and 'cy pres' arrangements where the charity is wound up or where its charitable objectives are not being fulfilled. In the case of an exempt charity, this is only on the application of the charity itself or under a court order or by the Attorney-General.[33]

Charity accounts and audit

6.16 As registered charities, a charitable trust and a charitable incorporated organisation must prepare annual accounts and reports, as required by the Charities Act 2011 and regulations made under it.[34] An exempt charity must keep proper accounts and preserve them for six years.[35] The level of audit requirements depends on the size of the body in question in terms of its gross income.[36]

6.17 An exempt charity must have an independent audit under the CCBSA 2014 and if such an auditor has reasonable cause to suspect misconduct or mismanagement by the charity or a subsidiary or parent, it must immediately make a written report to the 'principal regulator' designated under the Charities Act 2011. In other cases within the principal regulator's jurisdiction it may make a report.[37] As we have seen, no principal regulator has been designated.

Care Quality Commission

6.18 The Care Quality Commission (CQC), replacing separate bodies for physical and mental health services, regulates all providers of health and social care in England and Wales.[38] All providers of such services, including housing associations providing assisted housing of all

---

33 Charities Act 2011 ss69, 70(2), (4), (5).
34 Charities Act 2011 ss130–135. The requirements are simplified for small bodies, ie with gross income not more than £250,000. See generally, Charity Commission, *Charity reporting and accounting; the essentials*, March 2015.
35 Charities Act 2011 s136. (Accounts of CCBSA 2014 societies are regulated by the FCA under that Act.)
36 Charities Act 2011 ss144–147.
37 Charities Act 2011 s156, 157.
38 Health and Social Care Act 2008 s1 and Sch 1.

kinds, must register with the CQC. The CQC's objectives include encouraging:
1) the improvement of health and social care services;
2) the provision of health and social care services in a way that focuses on the needs and experiences of people who use those services; and
3) the efficient and effective use of resources in the provision of health and social care services.[39]

6.19 The CQC must take into account the views of service users, their families and friends and local Healthwatch organisations. It should balance the rights of those who use health and social care services in a way which is proportionate to risks and safeguards.[40] In practice, services are rated following inspection under five domains with an overall rating. The five domains cover whether services are: safe, caring, responsive, effective and well-led. Each of those domains is rated as to whether it is outstanding, good, requires improvement or is poor. In addition, an overall rating for the service is given. This enables service or care users to see the performance of the service. There are no special provisions for housing associations.

---

39 Health and Social Care Act 2008 s3.
40 Health and Social Care Act 2008 s4(1).

PART 3

The provision of housing

CHAPTER 7

Housing provision, allocation and management

7.1	Background
7.8	Who do housing associations house?
7.12	Specific housing duties
7.12	Requirement to co-operate with local authorities if requested
7.14	Duty co-operate: Immigration and Asylum Act 1999
7.15	Land Compensation Act 1973
7.16	Nomination agreements with local authorities
7.21	**Selection of tenants**
7.32	Legitimate expectation
7.46	**Human rights implications**
7.46	Human Rights Act 1998
7.55	Equality Act 2010
7.62	**Housing quality and safety**

Background

7.1 Perhaps the single key unifying or common aim of housing associations is to meet need through the provision of affordable housing to people on low incomes. Activities undertaken by the sector have diversified considerably since the 'housing plus' debate in the 1990s.[1] However, this key objective of meeting housing need remains at the heart of each individual housing association. Housing associations are not creatures of the state, (although there is an argument that some of their activities have been captured by the state), and as such are not under any statutory duty to provide housing, unlike their local authority counterparts who are required to undertake a periodical review of housing conditions and needs of their districts with respect to the provision of further housing accommodation.[2]

7.2 Tellingly, up to the introduction of the Housing Act 1980 (its provisions now incorporated into the Housing Act 1985) it was felt politically unnecessary to regulate the activities of housing associations as they were 'motivated by an interest to provide housing for the poorer classes', and 'could be trusted to exercise their discretion ... in a social and humanitarian manner'.[3] Legal protection was minimal, since they would select and evict tenants in a fair and just manner. With increasing public subsidy, this discretionary – perhaps even arbitrary – position was seen to be untenable. The housing association journey from that point has been subject to growing control and intervention.

7.3 Contractual obligations may arise to provide housing under nomination agreements with local housing authorities and also through grant agreements with Homes England. There is no statutory requirement under Housing and Regeneration Act (HRA) 2008 s19 requiring the provision of housing when the Homes and Communities Agency (HCA) (now named Homes England) gives financial assistance. This is a departure from the historical position relating to social housing grant where if a grant was awarded, then it

---

1 See, for example, David Page, *Building communities*, Joseph Rowntree Foundation, 1994; Anne Power with Liz Richardson, *Housing Plus*, LSE Housing, 1996.
2 See Housing Act 1985 s8(1). There is no duty to provide the accommodation directly: s9(5).
3 Per Cumming-Bruce LJ *Governors of the Peabody Donation Fund v Higgins* [1983] 1 WLR 1091.

must be used for the provision of dwellings for letting or provide a building for use as a hostel.[4]

7.4 However, where financial assistance is given to create social housing, conditions must be attached to the award to ensure that social housing does not pass to the private sector. Thus where any accommodation provided is for rent the landlord must be a relevant provider of social housing.[5] Housing associations must 'co-operate' to such an 'extent as is reasonable in the circumstances' in accommodating people from the local authority's allocation scheme if so requested.[6] However, the obligation to co-operate does not pass a local authority's duty onto a housing association.[7] Under specific initiatives such as redevelopment schemes, duties can pass from a local authority to a housing association for example where acquisition and duties to rehouse are vested in a housing association as part of a compulsory possession order (CPO).

7.5 Where housing associations borrow money (or raise funds through the bond markets, which as a method has grown considerably in recent years) the finance raised is to be applied largely in the provision of housing. A failure to provide housing within the terms of the finance agreement will amount to a breach of covenant or requirement. Most funding agreements will have a covenant which states that a breach of one agreement is a breach across all agreements. A breach will invariably mean the funds can be called back with obvious cash-flow consequences. Failure to adhere to covenants is therefore a major risk to housing associations.

7.6 Relevant constitutional objectives may create obligations for a housing association to provide housing. Arguably an interested shareholder or member or other interested party could legally challenge a housing association, which has among its objects the provision of housing, if that association has appropriate resources, for failure to use those resources in the provision of housing.

7.7 There are some specific requirements relating to relocation for example where a duty may arise to rehouse or provide suitable alternative accommodation, although such a provision need not be through the particular housing association directly. There are also some duties to co-operate as is reasonable in the circumstances with local housing authorities in the discharge of their duties to meet need and

---

4 Housing Associations Act 1985 s42(1).
5 HRA 2008 s31(4), (6), (8).
6 Housing Act 1996 s170.
7 See *R v Northavon DC ex p Smith* [1994] 2 AC 402, (1994) 26 HLR 659, HL.

also with the Home Secretary's duty to provide accommodation for asylum-seekers and their families.

Who do housing associations house?

7.8 The latest information published in the English Housing Survey[8] (2016/17) for the social rented sector says that social housing is the smallest tenure sector, accounting for 17 per cent of households in England, with housing associations, when excluding local authorities, accounting for ten per cent of the total, presenting some 2.4m households. The sector houses more vulnerable groups than any other sector, with 50 per cent of households having at least one member with a long-term illness or disability. There are more lone parents (some 24 per cent of all social rent households) and three-quarters of social renters were in the two lowest income quartiles.

7.9 Social renters in work have increased over the last decade, with 43 per cent in work compared to 31 per cent a decade ago. Despite this increase, the employment rate for social renters is substantially lower than other tenures – 74 per cent for private renters and 61 per cent owner-occupiers. Average (mean) gross weekly income of social renters was £403, compared to £696 for private renters and £884 for owner-occupiers.

7.10 Social renters tend to be older than tenants in the private rented sector, and some 58 per cent of renters had a female head of household ('household reference person' (HRP)). This is unsurprising since housing associations let on the basis of need, lone parents (the vast majority of whom are women) are more likely to be housed. The biggest group housed by the sector are single-person households (38 per cent – housing associations house a considerable number of older people in specialist accommodation of one kind or another), followed by couples with children and lone parents. 85 per cent of head of households were white. Almost half of all housing association social renters were living in neighbourhoods considered to be in 'urban adversity'.

7.11 Some 81 per cent of social renters were either very satisfied or fairly satisfied with their accommodation, although only 66 per cent were satisfied with the repairs and maintenance service.

---

8 See Ministry of Housing, Communities and Local Government (MHCLG), *English Housing Survey: social rented sector 2016–17*, July 2018.

Specific housing duties

Requirement to co-operate with local authorities if requested

7.12 This duty arises under Housing Act 1996 s170: where a local housing authority so request, a private registered provider (PRP) of social housing or registered social landlord (in the case of Wales) shall co-operate to such an extent as is reasonable in the circumstances in offering accommodation to people with priority under the authority's allocation scheme. This change of wording was introduced by the Homelessness Act 2002 which introduced new requirements on allocation schemes for local housing authorities relating to the homeless.[9] In fact the changes broadened the application of the principle of co-operation to 'people with priority' rather than purely to the homeless as was the case previously. It is unclear as to the extent of the duty to co-operate. Must a registered provider of social housing actually house, simply give advice or consider a person for housing by placing them on their waiting list, is not clear. If a housing association is to evict a tenant who would become homeless, it may well be reasonable to co-operate so as not to evict the tenant.[10] On the ground, there is much co-operation between housing associations and local housing authorities, especially in the provision of accommodation in local areas or through the provision of specialist accommodation.

7.13 There is an additional duty for housing associations in England and Wales to co-operate – and oddly enough, in England for this purpose the Welsh term 'registered social landlord' (RSL) (along with 'housing trust') is still used extended to include non-profit registered providers. This duty to co-operate applies to a local authority's duties relating to the homeless under Part VII of the Housing Act 1996. The wording is similar to the general duty to co-operate: where a local housing authority requests another relevant housing authority or body in assistance with the discharge of their functions relating to homelessness, the authority or body shall co-operate in rendering such assistance as is reasonable in the circumstances.[11] A 'relevant housing authority or body' means a local housing authority, a new town corporation, a registered social landlord (and a non-profit

---

9 See Homelessness Act 2002 s16 and Housing Act 1996 s166A (England) and s167 (Wales).
10 See *Robinson v Torbay BC* [1982] 1 All ER 726.
11 Housing Act 1996 s213(1).

registered provider)[12] or a housing trust[13]). A local housing authority cannot pass on their substantive duty to 'inquire'.[14] (Although housing authorities and other bodies are required to co-operate if no solution is forthcoming, the responsibility remains with the authority making the request.[15])

Duty co-operate: Immigration and Asylum Act 1999

7.14 A PRP (or a RSL in Wales) if requested by the secretary of state (the Home Secretary in relation to England, the appropriate Minister in relation to Wales), to assist in the discharge of his or her duty to provide or arrange accommodation provision for asylum-seekers or relatives of asylum-seekers who are destitute or likely to become destitute, must give reasonable assistance in the exercise of that duty as is reasonable in the circumstances.[16] It is not expected that a PRP should act ultra vires in giving assistance.[17] Any occupancy agreements entered into with asylum-seekers cannot be assured tenancies and do not have protection under the Protection from Eviction Act 1977, and are thus excluded tenancies.[18]

Land Compensation Act 1973

7.15 Oddly, where a housing association displaces a 'residential occupier' due to redevelopment, a duty to award home loss and disturbance payments arises but not apparently the provision of alternative accommodation.[19] However, the court can only grant an order in the case of a secure or assured tenant if certain conditions are met regarding redevelopment and the provision of suitable alternative accommodation. Hence in practice, a duty to rehouse will arise, or else possession of the property cannot be gained.

---

12 See Housing and Regeneration Act 2008 (Consequential Provisions) Order 2010 SI No 866 Sch 2 para 2(4).
13 Housing Act 1996 s213(2).
14 *R v West Dorset DC, West Dorset HA ex p Gerrard* (1995) 27 HLR 150.
15 *R v Northavon DC ex p Smith* [1994] 2 AC 402, (1994) 26 HLR 659, HL.
16 Immigration and Asylum Act 1999 s100(1), (2).
17 Immigration and Asylum Act 1999 s100(3).
18 Immigration and Asylum Act 1999 Sch 4 paras 73, 88.
19 Land Compensation Act 1973 ss29(d), 39.

Nomination agreements with local authorities

7.16 There is no statutory obligation as such to enter into a nomination agreement with a local housing authority. A nomination agreement confers a right to a local housing authority to nominate people in need usually from its waiting list for housing by a housing association. The Regulator of Social Housing (RSH) *Tenancy standard*[20] states that registered provider shall co-operate with local authorities relating to their strategic function and also their duties to meet housing need 'and through meeting obligations in nominations agreements'. This does not, as such, require that a nomination agreement be in place, simply that registered providers should meet their obligations if there is one. Thus nomination agreements are usually voluntary in nature.

7.17 Whether a nomination agreement has legal force may depend whether there is consideration which establishes such an agreement as a valid contract. Nomination agreements sometimes arise as the result of the sale of land to a housing association for market value, at a discount or at nil cost. Clearly in each of these cases there is consideration, although in the case of a sale at market value this is arguable. However, in many other instances nomination agreements can be in place without any particular consideration. These would seem to be voluntary arrangements to house people off a local housing authority's waiting list. Perhaps a strong argument in support of such agreements is that they demonstrate that particular housing associations are meeting their duty to cooperate in meeting priority housing needs.

7.18 Housing Act 1996 s159 identifies nomination arrangements as a means by which a local authority can allocate accommodation. So the nomination of a person to be a secure or introductory tenant or an assured tenant to another agency such as a housing trust, registered social landlord (in Wales) or a PRP of social housing amounts to an allocation whether or not the nomination arrangements are legally enforceable.[21] There are some difficulties with this approach, which has been criticised as 'oxymoronic'. First, the word 'require' is used, but how can a requirement arise if the arrangements may not be enforceable? Second, surely a nomination must be successfully accepted by the other agency for it to amount to an allocation of housing accommodation. There may not be a requirement that a housing association should accept a nomination, although this will

---

20 See para 2.1.1.
21 See Housing Act 1996 ss159(2)–(4).

depend upon the wording of any nomination agreement. Admittedly, a local authority could make a request for a particular housing association to co-operate. However, even then that does not amount to a specific obligation to accept the nomination which would lead to an actual allocation of accommodation. An allocation of accommodation would have to be reasonable in the circumstances. The wording of the section perhaps relies upon what is perceived as a long-standing right for local housing authorities to be able to nominate people from their waiting lists to housing association accommodation or a proportion of its accommodation.

7.19 The tenancy standard is not that strong, having a required outcome which states that registered providers should 'contribute to local authorities' strategic housing function'. The specific expectations section of the standard is much clearer, but does not amount to a requirement, although interestingly uses wording which suggests obligations under nomination agreements:[22]

> Registered providers shall co-operate with local authorities' strategic housing function, and their duties to meet identified local housing needs. This includes assistance with local authorities' homelessness duties, and through meeting obligations in nominations agreements.

7.20 Housing associations have been reluctant to enter into enforceable nomination arrangements since this may well fetter the value of properties in question, either creating a restrictive covenant on resale or the value for security purposes. This is very important when raising private sector debt as part of the mixed funding approach (a mixture of private finance and subsidy) for developing new projects.

Selection of tenants

7.21 Under Housing Act 1985 s106, housing associations are considered as a landlord authority for the purpose of providing information on housing allocations for secure tenants since it is a section enacted under a chapter of the Act specifically relating to secure tenants and their rights.[23] As such, a landlord authority shall publish a summary of its rules:

a) for determining priority as between applicants in the allocation of its housing accommodation; and

---

22 See RSH, 'Tenancy Standard', April 2012, paras 1.1.1, 2.1.1.
23 Housing Act 1985 s106, 114(1).

b) governing cases where secure tenants wish to move (whether or not by way of exchange of dwelling-houses) to other dwelling-houses let under secure tenancies by that authority or another body.

7.22 Under section 106(2), a landlord authority shall maintain a set of rules for determining priority between applicants and also rules governing the procedure to be followed, and send those rules to the Regulator of Social Housing and the relevant council in whose area the housing is to be let. A copy of the summary published under section 106(1) shall be given without charge and a set of the rules published under section 106(2) shall we given for a reasonable fee, to any member of the public who asks for one (section 106(4)). A failure by a local authority, for example, to publish its rules was not deemed ultra vires.[24] (It was also mentioned obiter interestingly that it was 'not unreasonable to prefer good tenants to bad tenants').

7.23 There is also a requirement to provide an applicant a copy of information provided by them in relation to their application, although this has been somewhat superseded by the requirements of the Data Protection Act 1998. The Freedom of Information Act 2000 does not apply to housing associations.

7.24 Despite the law restricting these provisions to secure tenants, housing associations interpret the provisions as if they apply to all tenants. The RSH 'Tenancy Standard' has a required outcome that:

> ... registered providers shall let their homes in a fair, transparent and efficient way. They shall take into account the housing needs and aspirations of tenants and potential tenants.

The standard goes on to say that registered providers shall demonstrate how their lettings:

c) make the best use of available housing;
d) are compatible with the purpose of the housing;
e) contribute to local authorities' strategic housing function and sustainable communities.

7.25 In addition, there should be clear application, decision-making and appeal processes. Except these overarching principles, there are not detailed requirements on who should be housed, and as such this possibly represents one of the greatest areas of operational freedom a housing association has bearing in mind the high degree of regulatory oversight that exists even following the declassification measures which were rolled out under the Housing and Planning Act 2016.

24 *R v Newham LBC ex p Miah* (1996) 28 HLR 279, QBD.

7.26 Oddly, there is no mention of published rules in the required outcomes section of the standard, but there is reference to the need to include how housing associations have made use of common registers, common allocation policies and local lettings policies in any of their published policies.[25] Registered providers in the specific expectations paragraph of the standard shall also clearly set out, and be able to give reasons for, the criteria they use for excluding actual or potential tenants from consideration for allocations, mobility or mutual exchange schemes. There are other expectations on online mutual exchange schemes, giving reasonable support to those who do not have access to the internet, relevant advice on housing options, minimising the time properties are empty and ensuring that allocations processes support the full range of tenants and potential tenants including those with support needs, those who do not speak English as a first language and others who have difficulties with written English.[26]

7.27 The rules of a particular housing association may well limit or prescribe who can be housed and what services can be provided. Fundamentally, a housing association must follow its constitutional objects. The constitution may well contain provisions which may be quite exact as to the type or group of people the association should assist by way of housing and services. Particularly in the case of charities the constitution may well specify people 'in necessitous circumstance', the 'old', the 'infirm' or use similar terms instead of referring more generally to people in need. Indeed, some will limit the purpose even further to such groups as 'the poor of this parish' or widows of ex-seamen, for example. Assisting people outside those constitutional boundaries or permissible purposes, whether or not charitable, would be ultra vires.

7.28 Similar to a local housing authority, a housing association, although giving a proportion of nomination rights to a local authority or, due to the area of operation, a number of local authorities, invariably keep a waiting list of people seeking accommodation. In some areas, common waiting lists of the local authority and those housing associations operating in its area are kept. Very often, where a local authority has transferred its stock to a large-scale voluntary transfer association, it is that association which keeps the waiting list since the local authority no longer retains any housing stock.

---

25 RSH, 'Tenancy Standard', para 2.1.3.
26 RSH, 'Tenancy Standard', paras 2.1.3–2.1.11.

Housing provision, allocation and management 139

7.29 Despite the diversification of activities, housing associations still primarily let on the basis of housing need, sometimes keeping separate waiting lists for people who want to buy (whether by virtue of shared ownership sales or outright sales) or market rent. Bearing in mind housing associations have limited stock availability, particularly in certain areas, they often have entry criteria for their waiting lists providing threshold assessment of whether someone is accepted. Over the last couple of decades, there has been concern that assessing the greatest housing need has supplanted the equally important need to create 'balanced communities'. By this is meant creating a community which does not comprise tenants all of whom have complex needs – it is important to create sustainable communities. Therefore in some cases applicants are not accepted onto a waiting list.

7.30 In other cases, which are especially relevant to supported housing, registered care or nursing care applicants will need to be referred by a statutory or voluntary body. In the latter case, the person will still need to be accepted for funding by the relevant statutory authority. This is because such spaces usually comprise a package of housing or bed-space and rental funding. Usually with nursing care it is the relevant clinical commissioning group (CCG) of the NHS which will meet the funding costs. Such projects are often built in partnership with adult services teams of local authorities of clinical teams within the NHS. Some associations do admit private payers into these schemes if the arrangements with the relevant funding authority or authorities allow. This can happen where the association takes some of the 'demand risk' relating to a project.

7.31 With fully mutual associations there are further issues to consider. As well as housing need the prospective tenant will be assessed as to whether they will make a good 'co-operator' in order to ensure the co-operative will have active members. If people do not actively participate this damages the fundamental idea of the co-operative. 'Prospective tenants' as well as actual tenants are eligible to be members of the co-operative. Does a person placed on the waiting list amount to a prospective tenant and does this give them the right to membership? This may well depend on the exact terms applied to entry onto the waiting list. On the face of it, someone accepted potentially to become a tenant would seem to fit that phrase. It is important to get this right since prospective tenants do have a right to be members of the co-operative but prospective tenants should not be given the dominant position within the membership of the co-operative. Perhaps the definitive position is determined if the association in question gives membership to a particular prospective tenant. But this does seem to be an area for potential dispute.

Legitimate expectation

7.32 Whether an applicant on a waiting list of a housing association who fulfils the lettings criteria would have a 'legitimate (or "reasonable") expectation' to be housed, is open to conjecture. A legitimate expectation is an aspect of the wider public law principle of fairness. A person claiming it must overcome several hurdles. First, although housing associations receive public funding and sometimes undertake activities which are public in nature, this does not necessarily turn a landlord and tenant relationship or an applicant and housing provider relationship into one of public law. As we saw in chapter 3, the particular housing scheme must be government promoted or otherwise enmeshed in the work of government.[27] Second, a legitimate expectation arises only where a clear and unequivocal promise or undertaking has been given on which it is reasonable to rely albeit this can take the form of a general policy publication. Third, it is possible, but not settled, that the claimant must incur detriment in reliance on the undertaking in question. Fourth, even where a legitimate expectation exists its main consequence is only that there is a right to a fair hearing if the benefit claimed is refused. Exceptionally, where a clear promise has been made, the claimant may be entitled to the benefit itself, in this case housing, but this can be overridden on public interest grounds.

7.33 Does a legal relationship exist between an applicant on a waiting list and a housing association? The letting in question must have sufficient public flavour in order for the matter to be considered by way of judicial review. So does the obligation under Housing Act 1985 s106 to follow tenant selection rules amount to a public law duty? An applicant for accommodation would have sufficient locus standi being within the range of the beneficiaries of the statute.[28] If such a statutory obligation can be established, it is unlikely that it confers a private right of action for damages and therefore the judicial review procedure is likely to be the only course of action, thus denying access to the county court.[29]

---

27 *R (Weaver) v London and Quadrant Housing Trust* [2009] EWCA Civ 587; *R (MacLeod) v Governors of the Peabody Trust* [2016] EWHC 737 (Admin).
28 See *R v IRC ex p National Federation of Self-employed and Small Businesses Ltd* [1982] AC 617.
29 See *Cocks v Thanet DC* [1983] 2 AC 286.

7.34   On the other hand, for every applicant on a waiting list to have a legitimate expectation to be housed is a difficult thing to achieve in practice due to the huge housing shortage across the country. In the famous 1999 *Coughlan* case[30] it was held that a severely disabled woman who was promised a home for life in clear unequivocal language had the right to such a home. In that case the claimant was already living in the home and had done so in reliance on a clear personal undertaking. However, in rationing scarce resources such as homes where there exists a housing shortage, the eligibility criteria may not be so unequivocal as to create an obligation even if it can be argued that the letting in question is public in nature.

7.35   Moreover, the power to let property is a private law power under a housing association's own constitution and the law of contract. Does this block the application of judicial review, despite the fact the scheme of letting is required by statute? On this basis the allocation of tenancies would be a private law matter and it is unlikely that a disappointed applicant would have a remedy in the courts since there is no contractual relationship and a refusal to house, or a failure to offer accommodation would not affect their legal rights.[31]

7.36   Recent cases, however, clearly suggest that this is an over formalistic approach, although there is no Supreme Court guidance. As we saw in chapter 3, in *R (Weaver) v London and Quadrant Housing Trust*[32] the Court of Appeal held that it is artificial to separate tenancy decisions from their public context and that applications and terminations are inseparable aspects of public housing policy. (Indeed, even Rix LJ dissenting conceded that an application as opposed to the termination of a tenancy agreement might be a public law matter.) In *R (McIntyre) v Gentoo Group Ltd*[33] which concerned a tenancy exchange, the High Court expressed the matter broadly by suggesting that the functions of managing and allocating social housing are inherently public functions. Moreover, as we also saw in chapter 3, a private law underpinning does not prevent a relationship from being subject to judicial review if there is also a strong public law element.

---

30 *R v North and East Devon Health Authority ex p Coughlan* [1999] EWCA Civ 1871, [2001] QB 213.
31 See *Peabody HA Ltd v Green and others* (1978) P & CR 644. Lord Scott in *YL v Birmingham City Council* [2008] 1 AC 95 at [34] took a similar approach, as did Rix LJ (dissenting) in *Weaver* (below).
32 [2009] EWCA Civ 587.
33 [2010] EWHC 5 (Admin).

7.37   If this is so, in the context of government sponsored housing schemes, once a lettings policy has been published, it is arguable that it creates a legitimate expectation that the policy will be followed. Whether making an application and being accepted onto a waiting list amounts in law to a contractual relationship is unclear, since there would seem to be a lack of consideration on the part of the applicant. Despite this, there does seem to be a possibility that a departure from a published lettings policy could be subject to review by the High Court.

7.38   In *Eastlands Home Partnership v Whyte*[34] a tenant faced with eviction established a legitimate expectation that a housing association would adhere to its published rules in connection with its appeals procedure relating to a refusal to convert a starter tenancy into an ordinary assured tenancy. The association had begun possession proceedings, but took short-cuts including premature action and failing to give the tenant adequate information. The High Court held that, in addition to breach of the legitimate expectation, the association's actions were unfair and unreasonable. However, it was emphasised that a procedural failure, such as in the respect of the giving of reasons, would justify the court interfering only if the claimant suffered substantial prejudice. It was also held that there could be no general legitimate expectation of a new tenancy following a starter tenancy since an applicant has no legal rights after a starter tenancy ended.

7.39   Moreover a legitimate expectation can be established only from a clear and unambiguous undertaking. In *R (Weaver) v London and Quadrant Housing Trust* (above) an assured tenant claimed to have a legitimate expectation based on Housing Corporation guidance that the tenancy would be determined only as a last resort. The first instance court held the guidance was too tenuous and ambiguous to create a legitimate expectation a finding that was not appealed.[35] Indeed, Richards LJ warned against treating guidance documents as if they created binding rules or promises. The same applies to a suggestion that guidance can form part of a contract.[36]

7.40   These decisions therefore fall short of supporting a legitimate expectation in a pure application case. Moreover, in the context of the huge housing shortage across the country, in cases involving rationing scarce resources such as homes the courts are reluctant to interfere with the discretion of a housing authority on the ground

---

34 [2010] EWHC 695 (QB).
35 [2010] EWHC 695 (QB) at [104]–[106], [108].
36 *R (Weaver) v London and Quadrant Housing Trust* [2008] EWHC 1377 (Admin) at [85]–[89].

that the latter is more aware of the local circumstances.[37] In *R (McIntyre) v Gentoo Group Ltd*[38] the High Court stressed that, in view of the non-profit nature of a housing association and its experience, the court will give great respect to its decisions.

7.41 For an applicant on a waiting list to have a legitimate expectation to be housed is therefore unlikely, unless perhaps an officer was unwise enough to make an unambiguous promise that the application would succeed. If properly drafted, allocation rules provide criteria for the grant a tenancy but where demand outstrips supply, are unlikely to guarantee one.

7.42 On the other hand, in a public law context, irrespective of any legitimate expectation, a landlord that refuses to consider an application on its merits and treats its policy as absolutely binding acts unlawfully by fettering its discretion. It can of course have a policy, but must be prepared to consider exceptional cases.[39] In *R (Trafford) v Blackpool BC*[40] the council refused to renew a tenancy held by a solicitor in its Enterprise Centre. It was held that the council's decision was invalid in public law since, among other things, it had consistently refused to consider applications for a new tenancy and so fettered its discretion. Thus a landlord must keep to its policy but not with Lutheresque rigidity.

7.43 Would the RSH take any regulatory action if a housing association has a published policy on lettings but did not sufficiently follow it for there to be 'serious detriment' to applicants? In theory this is a possibility, but no such action has yet been taken by the RSH in this regard. Certainly a disgruntled applicant could complain to the Housing Ombudsman about the failure to house or unfair treatment. The Housing Ombudsman scheme is open to applicants of properties owned or managed by members of the scheme.[41] Interestingly only three per cent of cases considered by the ombudsman are of this nature to do with lettings.[42]

7.44 With the increased diversification of activities by housing associations, there has in recent years been a move away from purely meeting the greatest housing needs. Very often housing associations build and let mixed tenure schemes in order to create 'balanced

---

37 See *R v Hillingdon LBC ex p Puhlhofer* [1986] AC 484.
38 Above note 33.
39 *British Oxygen Co Ltd v Minister of Technology* [1971] AC 610.
40 [2014] EWHC 85 (Admin).
41 See Housing Ombudsman Service, *The scheme*, May 2018, para 19(b).
42 See Housing Ombudsman, *Annual report and accounts 2017–18*, p8.

communities'. Indeed, the slavish adherence to meeting the highest housing needs do yield potentially problematic schemes to manage. Very often people with the highest needs have multiple problems, and housing purely on this basis can lead to concentrations of poverty. New schemes are often developed so there is housing for sale, including shared ownership as well as housing for rent. Even with housing co-operatives, news ways have been found which can tie in owners to the co-operative approach.[43]

7.45 There has thus been a shift away to address both need and demand. The requirements under Housing Act 1985 s106 do, though, require a scheme for determining the priority between applicants. Thus whatever approaches are adopted must be designed to ensure the statutory obligations are properly met. There may also be specific issues which charities must address in ensuring they still are meeting the needs of the poor, the infirm and the elderly or other charitable needs specific in their objects.

Human rights implications

Human Rights Act 1998

7.46 As we have seen in chapter 3, housing association for some purposes are considered as 'functional public authorities' and therefore it follows that for those purposes, especially where there is a close relationship between the housing association and a local authority, some of their work may be subject to the Human Rights Act (HRA) 1998. Thus where the work of a housing association is closely assimilated or enmeshed in the state, the HRA 1998 and the rights under the European Convention on Human Rights (ECHR) could apply to applications for housing.

7.47 Based on this, the Equality and Human Rights Commission (EHRC) advise housing associations to act in such a way as to assume the application of the HRA 1998 applies to their work. Its primary argument relies upon the Court of Appeal judgment in *Weaver* discussed in chapter 3, where it was held that a particular housing association was performing public functions when evicting a social tenant. The EHRC say that the court's decision was based on the following factors:

---

43 For example, Accord in the West Midlands have developed a very interesting multi-tenure approach to the housing co-operatives they have helped establish in the Redditch area.

- The housing association's work was subsidised by the state.
- The housing association was granted special intrusive powers by law, such as the power to apply for an anti-social behaviour order.
- The housing association was working closely with local government to help the local authority achieve its duties under the law.
- The housing association was providing a public service of a type which government would normally provide, that is, providing housing at below market rent.

7.48 The EHRC acknowledged that the decision in *Weaver* was highly specific, and only applies to London and Quadrant in the particular circumstances. In fact, the case related to possession proceedings and in addition applied to property which had been taken over from a local authority as former local authority housing stock. Nonetheless, the EHRC argued that 'other housing associations which operate in similar circumstances are also likely to be subject to the' HRA 1998.[44] This interpretation, therefore, is a substantial leap. Certainly lessons can be drawn from the case and the operating context of decisions made by other housing associations. The Court of Appeal did though state that terminating a tenancy is 'so bound up with the idea and principles of social housing that such acts must be seen as public functions'. The same could be said about applications.

7.49 Possibly it could be inferred that the HRA 1998 applies only to accommodation managed by a housing association where there is a close connection with a local authority. Working with a local authority was one of the key factors taken into account by the Court of Appeal. Thus if the housing association in question is a Large Scale Voluntary Transfer (LSVT) association where its stock has been transferred to a new body, or where an existing association, takes over previously owned local authority stock then the HRA 1998 as well as judicial review probably applies since the two lines of action have been largely interpreted by the courts to apply alongside one another (see *Weaver*).

7.50 However, this would create precisely the kind of two-track system which many in the sector are anxious to avoid. Moreover it would surely depend on the range of factors at play in a particular instance. Indeed the 'historic connection' approach in *Donoghue* (see para 3.31 above) has been criticised by the House of Lords.[45] *R (McIntyre) v*

---

44 See Equality and Human Rights Commission, *Human rights at home: Guidance for social housing providers*, 2011, p8.
45 *YL v Birmingham City Council* [2003] UKHL 27 at [61], [81], [105]; see also Collins LJ in *Weaver*.

Gentoo Group Ltd (above, para 7.36) involved a local authority stock transfer but this was not a crucial factor and the court suggested that the allocation and management of social housing was inherently public. The court also referred to the impact on human rights.

7.51 The question whether the HRA 1998 applies to an application for a tenancy is also doubtful. Article 6 of the ECHR concerning fair procedure applies only to 'a civil right or obligation'. Within the local authority sphere it has been held that until an applicant actually signs a tenancy agreement there is no civil right to accommodation (see *Dixon v Wandsworth LBC*[46]). Thus a letting has a different status to a termination event which clearly affects a civil right. However, under the homelessness legislation, where an applicant can show that the authority has a concrete duty without discretion towards him or her, this may count as a civil right and so trigger Article 6.[47]

7.52 Under the HRA 1998 there is no right to a home as such. Article 8 states that everyone 'has the right to respect for his private and family life, his home and his correspondence'. This does not go as far as creating an absolutely right to a home, it only protects a person from state interference for a home ('the place, the physically defined area where private and family life develops'[48]) they already have, no matter how temporary that home might be.[49]

7.53 These factors do seem to suggest that applications fall outside the HRA 1998. Conceivably, it could be argued that a departure from a published lettings scheme, possibly amounting to an unfair procedure, infringes Article 8, as showing lack of 'respect' since Article 8 requires a fair procedure but without the need to establish that a 'civil right' is affected.[50] Moreover, Article 14 (discrimination) might apply since, although not freestanding, Article 14 is triggered where the matter is connected ('within the ambit of') another right under the ECHR such as Article 8. The other right need not directly apply.[51]

7.54 Given the uncertainty involved, the EHRC suggests extending the application of the HRA 1998 further on a kind of jeopardy basis ('it is advisable to avoid the risk of a claim') by saying that if a particular organisation is not sure whether it is likely to be subject to the

---

46 [2008] EWCA Civ 595.
47 *Ali v Birmingham City Council* [2010] 1 All ER 175; *R (A) v Croydon LBC* [2009] 1 WLR 2557.
48 See *Giacomelli v Italy* (2006) 45 EHRR 38.
49 See *X v Federal Republic of Germany* (1956) 1 YB 202; and *Chapman v UK* (2001) 10 BHRC 48, ECtHR, paras 71–74.
50 *IR (Sri Lanka) v Secretary of State for the Home Department* [2011] 4 All ER 908.
51 See paras 7.56 and 9.83.

HRA 1998, it should carry out its business in a way which complies with the ECHR rights.

Equality Act 2010

7.55 The Equality Act (EA) 2010 brought together various strands of anti-discrimination law to protect service users against nine 'protected characteristics':
- age;
- disability;
- gender reassignment;
- marriage and civil partnerships;
- pregnancy and maternity;
- race;
- religion or belief;
- sex; and
- sexual orientation.

7.56 Housing associations are not listed in Schedule 19 to the Act as a public authority, so are not directly subject to the public sector equality duty (PSED), although if they are carrying out a public function or a public function on behalf of a public authority then the duty applies to that function.

7.57 The RSH and Homes England, as with other public authorities in England, in the exercise of their functions must have due regard to the need to:
- eliminate unlawful discrimination, harassment and victimisation and any other unlawful conduct in the EA 2010;
- advance equality of opportunity; and
- foster good relations.

7.58 More specifically, a person who has the authority to dispose of premises[52] must not unlawfully discriminate on the basis of a protected characteristic on any terms of disposal.[53] Harassment and victimisation are also prohibited.[54] Similar obligations apply to a manager of premises, including any terms relating to the use of any benefit or facility.[55] Following the argument of the EHRC in *Weaver* it could

---

52 EA 2010 s34.
53 EA 2010 ss4 and 32.
54 EA 2010 s33(3) and (4).
55 EA 2010 s35.

well mean that the PSED directly applies to housing associations as functional public authorities.

7.59 The key means by which the HCA can meet its obligation is to ensure it is pursued by registered providers and it incorporates clauses in development or partnership agreements to that effect. Since becoming the HCA it has not been vocal in relation to these obligations, although it does have an Equality and Diversity Board Advisory Group on meeting its obligations under the Act and also has an Equality and Diversity Strategy 2012–2015, although this is now seriously out of date. An internet search cannot find any equality impact assessments in relation to HCA activities. However, the HCA does have a range of programmes which do address the needs of specific vulnerable groups and in its various guises as the Housing Corporation, the HCA, the Tenant Services Authority (TSA) and now, at least for the moment in name only the RSH and Homes England, has taken its anti-discriminatory obligations seriously over the years.

7.60 The tenancy standard is silent on the duties of the EA 2010. It does not, for example, have a required outcome or a specific expectation on the requirements of the Act. This is odd, bearing in mind the key ways a housing association would meet its obligations are through its primary activity of allocating and managing tenancies. The 'governance and financial viability standard' does, in its required outcomes section,[56] state that governance arrangements shall ensure that registered providers adhere to the relevant law, but there is no specific mention to obligations under the EA 2010 or indeed not to discriminate.

7.61 In its *Regulating the standards*,[57] the RSH refers to unlawful discrimination when considering whether to exercise any of its powers if a registered provider has failed to meet a consumer standard to such an extent the failure has resulted (or likely to result) in a serious detriment to the provider's or prospective tenants. It is true that the HRA 2008 placed a significant restriction on the regulator in policing the consumer standards). The 'tenant involvement and empowerment standard'[58] does have a 'required outcome' which states that:

> . . . registered providers shall treat all tenants with fairness and respect and demonstrate they understand the different needs of their tenants, including in relation to the equality strand and tenant support needs.

56 Section 1.1.
57 April 2018.
58 Para 1.3.1.

Housing quality and safety

7.62 Gone are the days of regulatory non-intervention on consumer issues. The human tragedy of the Grenfell Tower fire in June 2017 has changed all of that. After the Grenfell Tower tragedy, regulatory interest in consumer matters is likely to alter significantly. Julian Ashby, previously the chair of the HCA's regulatory committee, stated that 'with hindsight' the RSH could have been 'more aggressive' over health and safety. He felt the RSH's actions were 'constrained' by legislation which limited its power to intervene in consumer affairs, after the winding up of the TSA, amid the so called 'bonfire of the quangos' in 2010.[59]

7.63 The government now wants the RSH to have sharper teeth. At present, the RSH can intervene in consumer matters only if there is serious detriment or the likelihood serious detriment to a PRP's tenants.[60] It is beyond the scope of this work to explore housing standards, environmental health standards and obligations around safety which apply to all landlords. However, it is worth highlighting the regulatory obligations which apply and exploring, in the light of the green paper on social housing,[61] how those obligations are likely to develop.

7.64 Up until now, following the merger of the TSA into the HCA, the focus on serious detriment has been on gas safety and the harm or potential harm that can arise with tenants and their families if gas appliances have not been properly maintained and serviced. However, as we saw in chapter 4, there is now an independent regulator of social housing.

7.65 Under the 'home standard'[62] issued under the RSH's consumer standards, registered providers shall meet 'all applicable statutory requirements that provide for the health and safety of the occupiers of their homes'. Individual housing associations have received governance downgrading if their gas servicing is lacking on the basis serious harm or serious detriment to tenants.[63] It is an area of work which is audited as part of the 'deep dive' 'in-depth assessment' (IDA) process.[64] It can

---

59 See above para 1.38. See also 'Social housing regulator "constrained" by government before Grenfell, says former chair', Inside Housing, 15 July 2018.
60 See Localism Act 2011 Sch 17 para 9, adding HRA 2008 s198A in Part 2.
61 MHCLG, 'A New Deal for Social Housing' Cm 9671 (2018).
62 Para 1.2(b).
63 See HCA, *Consumer regulation review 2013/2014*, September 2014, para.8.
64 For a more detailed discussion on this gas safety regulations as they apply to housing associations and this aspect of the regulator's work see CR Handy, 'Gas Safety and the implications for housing associations', *Journal of Housing Law*.

clearly be seen that the breach of fire regulations would be as serious to the breach of gas safety regulations. There is a duty under the HRA 2008 for the RSH to have regard to information received from a number of authorities, which includes specifically the fire and rescue authorities and the Health and Safety Executive (HSE).[65]

7.66 The establishment of the RSH provides an opportunity review its regulatory powers:

> ... the Secretary of State recognises the importance of social housing regulation ... particularly in light of the terrible tragedy of the Grenfell Tower fire. It will be for the Public Enquiry, and the Social Housing Green Paper more broadly, to consider the role and function of the Regulator.[66]

7.67 The green paper on social housing (see above note 61) emphasises the need for a fairer deal for social housing residents, which include 'ensuring homes are safe and decent' and 'strengthening the regulator'. Possible changes posited by the green paper include reviewing the decent homes standard, question whether 'serious detriment' is the appropriate test of intervention and the development of a code of practice on consumer regulation similar to the two codes of practice which apply to economic regulation.

7.68 There is also a question about whether the intervention powers and enforcement powers currently held by the regulator are sufficiently strong. However, bearing in mind that the Grenfell Tower tragedy related to council housing, some of these issues are particular to that sector. Nonetheless, lessons should be learned right across the two arms of the social housing sector.[67] Alongside these changes we are likely to see significant reform in the use of building materials, fire management and safety arrangements which will flow from the current public inquiry into the Grenfell Tower fire, and also from the Hackett review.[68]

---

65 HRA 2008 s198A(6).
66 See Legislative Reform (Regulator of Social Housing) (England) Order 2018: Explanatory Document by the MHCLG, para.3.12
67 See the green paper on social housing: *A new deal for social housing*, Cm 9671, August 2018, particularly chapters 1 and 3.
68 Dame Judith Hackett, MHCLG, *Independent review of building regulations and fire safety*, 17 May 2018.

CHAPTER 8

Tenants' rights: the different tenures

8.1	Introduction
8.9	Wales
8.12	The residual regime: secure and fair rent tenants
8.17	Fair rents
8.19	The contemporary regime: assured tenants
8.26	Assured shorthold tenancies
8.33	Fully mutual tenancies
8.38	Collision between the residual and contemporary regimes: special cases
8.39	Residual secure tenancies becoming contemporary regime assured tenancies
8.40	Contemporary era tenancies as residual regime secure tenancies
8.41	**Probationary/flexible tenancies**
8.41	Introduction
8.44	Starter tenancy
8.46	Flexible tenancy
8.48	Demoted tenancy
8.50	Family intervention tenancy (FIT)
8.54	Punishment for unlawful subletting

continued

8.57	**Long tenancies**	
8.58	Residual regime	
8.60	Contemporary regime	
8.63	**Shared ownership**	
8.63	Overview	
8.77	Flats	
8.80	Publicly funded shared ownership schemes: regulatory requirements in England	
8.86	Shared ownership schemes in shortage areas	
8.88	**Leaseholds for the elderly**	
8.96	**Other ownership schemes**	

Introduction

8.1 Unfortunately the law relating to housing association tenure is fragmented, frequently amended and lacks general principles. Special rules are tacked on to the general law of landlord and tenant. The basic law governing housing association tenancies is today that of private sector landlords. However, tenancies surviving from previous regimes have certain public sector rights. Also, special rules often apply to housing associations registered with the Regulator of Social Housing (RSH) (private registered providers (PRPs)) or with the Welsh Ministers (registered social landlords (RSLs)). Regulatory requirements have created a substantial body of 'quasi-law'.

8.2 Some kinds of unregistered association attract special rules. These are charitable housing trusts in the special sense explained in chapter 2, almshouses and fully mutual tenancies. Other special rules concern the interface between housing association tenancies and local authority tenancies. These cater for transfers of tenancies, rights of succession and especially the right to buy. Occasionally, notably in connection with shared ownership, special rules apply to all housing associations.

8.3 The vacillation of housing associations between the public and private sectors is especially significant. Ever since the state began to control housing associations in 1974, housing association tenancies have been vehicles for changing policy initiatives, sometimes not directly housing-related and to do with other political battles. Housing associations have lurched between the public and private sectors, adopting rules from both, the 'right to buy' being especially troublesome. During the early 2000s, the courts and commentators criticised this confused state of affairs.[1] We are left with geological layers kept alive from earlier regimes.

8.4 The main surviving older regime (others apply to shared ownership), which we shall call 'the residual regime', is geared to the public sector and places tenants in a position akin to those of local authorities. The residual regime governs tenancies created before the Housing Act 1988 came into force (15 January 1989) and some special cases created later. Subsequent changes have swung housing associations towards the private sector, so that the position of contemporary regime housing association tenants and local

---

1 See *Poplar HRCA Ltd v Donoghue* [2001] 4 All ER 604, at 614; Malpass (2000) 15(2) *Housing Studies* (March), Law Commission Consultation Paper 182 (2002) 39–42.

authority tenants substantially differs. The aspiration of a unified social housing regime, favoured for example by the Law Commission, has not been met.[2]

8.5 On the other hand, local authorities and housing associations are regulated by the same RSH and the space between the two regimes is to some extent occupied by rules imposed by the regulator in the form of binding 'standards' or 'guidance' and implemented in the case of housing associations by tenancy agreements. Thus tenants are protected largely by an administrative regime rather than by legal rights. Apart from the private law of contract (in the light of *Riverside Housing Association Ltd v White*[3] to be interpreted sympathetically to social tenants), judicial review or recourse to the Housing Ombudsman are therefore the main remedies.

8.6 Recent policies underpinned initially by the Localism Act 2011, and continued in England by the (not fully in force) Housing and Planning Act 2016, attempt to make social housing tenure more restrictive, ostensibly to encourage social mobility and save money. This is implemented by enabling different forms of tenure, especially fixed terms, making eviction easier, and varying rent levels. Measures to combat anti-social behaviour are also involved. Thus an element of paternalism has been introduced which, although based on different legal tools (statute and contract), brings the sectors closer together. However, these policies may now be relaxed (below).

8.7 Again in the interests of social mobility, for many years governments have encouraged access to home ownership. In the housing association sphere, this has produced various forms of shared ownership tenancy and also provisions for discounted purchases by sitting tenants akin to the public sector right to buy. The recent housing green paper[4] continues the policy of encouraging ownership schemes, but also suggests a return to encouraging more stable and longer social tenancies.

8.8 We cannot discuss the general law of landlord and tenant in detail. Our aim is to identify special legal rules applying to housing association tenancies and leases and, we hope, with sufficient context drawn from the general law and from the local authority regime to make sense of them. Apart from fully mutual associations, almshouses and charitable housing trusts, unregistered housing associations are subject to the general law.

2 See Law Commission no 297, *Renting homes: the final report*, 2006, Law Commission no 337, *Renting homes in Wales*, 2013.
3 [2007] UKHL 20.
4 *A new deal for social housing* Cm 9671, August 2018, paras 5.4, 5.5.

Wales

8.9 Comprehensive reforms were introduced by the Renting Homes (Wales) Act 2016, (not yet in force). This Act is intended to create a single clear framework for tenants' rights, placing tenants of RSLs and local authorities under a common regime shared to a limited extent with private landlords. It is based on Law Commission proposals rejected by the UK government, which currently has a strong ideological commitment to the private sector.[5]

8.10 Under this Act, tenancies and licences become 'occupation contracts'. RSLs, along with other public sector landlords will be known as 'community landlords' and their default tenancies will be subject to a higher level of security, namely 'secure contracts', than is the case with a private landlord. Secure contracts are modelled on the current local authority secure tenancy thus, more clearly than in England, treating housing associations as public sector landlords. For private landlords, the default contract is a fixed-term or periodic 'standard contract' modelled on the current 'assured tenancy'.[6] In certain cases, housing associations too can use different versions of the periodic standard contract. These are similar to the various kinds of probationary tenancy now used in England (below) and can also be used for supported housing.

8.11 Under these provisions, 'fundamental provisions' dealing with basic rights and duties prescribed by statute must be included in all contracts of a given kind, while supplementary terms, intended to deal with incidental matters can be prescribed by the Welsh Ministers as voluntary terms but subject to safeguards.[7]

The residual regime: secure and fair rent tenants

8.12 The residual regime gives tenants statutory rights. The main residual regime tenancy is the 'secure tenancy' under the Housing Act 1985. Housing association secure tenants are mainly subject to the same regime as local authority tenants, including a right of

---

5 See Law Commission no 337, *Renting homes in Wales*, 2013.
6 Renting Homes (Wales) Act 2016 s2.
7 See Renting Homes (Supplementary Provisions) (Wales) Regulations 2018 (draft), Renting Homes (Supported Standard Contracts) (Supplementary Provisions) (Wales) Regulations 2018 (draft).

156 *Housing associations: a legal handbook / chapter 8*

succession to spouses or family members,[8] security of tenure, rights to repair exchange, be consulted and to buy their dwelling at a discount. However, tenants of charitable associations do not have the statutory right to buy.

8.13 With some exceptions, a tenancy or licence created by a housing association on or after 15 January 1989 cannot be a secure tenancy.[9] Subject to exceptions (below) and by tortuous drafting, the secure tenancy regime is kept alive for tenancies commencing before that date and in certain special cases for tenancies commencing later.[10] The secure tenancy regime applies to PRPs other than co-operative housing associations, RSLs and charitable housing trusts in the special sense explained in chapter 2. (Co-operative associations are in a special position (below).) Given the rights of succession available to secure tenants, there may still be a substantial number of secure tenancies amounting to about 20 per cent of PRP tenancies. (The secure tenancy regime as much altered remains, at least for the time being, for local authority tenants.)

8.14 A non-profit PRP can dispose of the landlord's interest in a secure tenancy only to another non-profit PRP or to a local authority registered provider, thus ensuring that the secure tenancy continues (unless the new landlord is a co-operative housing association).[11] It seems, therefore, that there cannot be a disposal to an RSL.

8.15 Since the rules are ambulatory, it does not matter whether the tenancy was actually a secure tenancy on 15 January 1989, but only on whether he or she would qualify now under the residual regime. For example, in *Bhai v Black Roof Community Housing Association*[12] the tenant was previously a tenant of a co-operative association and as such could not be a secure tenant (below). However, the Court of Appeal held that when the landlord ceased to be a co-operative in 1991 the tenancy then became a secure tenancy.

8.16 The secure tenancy regime also applies to licences provided that the licensee has exclusive possession in the same way as a tenant

---

8 Although these will be limited for local authority tenants under Housing and Planning 2016 s120 (not yet tin force) to a fixed term of five years.
9 HA 1988 s35(4).
10 Housing Act 1988 ss35, 38 (amended by Local Government and Housing Act (LGHA) 1989 Sch 11), Sch 18 para 4(a), (c). See *Bhai v Black Roof Community Housing Association* [2001] 2 All ER 865–871: 'even on the most generous view it is difficult to describe para 4(a) as paradigm of clarity in statutory drafting', per Jonathan Parker LJ.
11 Housing and Regeneration Act (HRA) 2008 s171(2).
12 Above note 10.

proper.[13] Thus, supported housing which involves the provision of personal care within the dwelling did not usually attract secure tenancy status. Moreover, an occupier of an almshouse charity cannot be a secure tenant where the constitution of the landlord prohibits the grant of a tenancy.[14] It is unlikely that any residual licences remain.

Fair rents

8.17 Tenancies created before 11 April 1989 by PRPs, RSLs, charitable housing trusts in the special sense explained in chapter 2 and co-operative housing associations are excluded from the private sector Rent Act 1977 regime and subject to a special housing association fair rent regime, labelled 'housing association tenancies'.[15] Subject to certain procedural differences, this is substantially the same as the private sector protected tenancy regime. A residual regime tenancy is sometimes misleadingly described as a secure / fair rent tenancy. However, although the two usually happen to coincide, this is not necessarily the case. In particular, unlike secure tenancy status, the fair rent regime includes most co-operatives (below). An unregistered housing association is subject to the private sector fair rent regime.

8.18 There is another but probably obsolete status applicable under the residual regime to some supported housing, namely that of a 'restricted contract'. This gives limited security of tenure and rent control where there is payment for furniture or services but without substantial board. No new restricted contracts can be created after the Housing Act 1988 came into force.[16]

The contemporary regime: assured tenants

8.19 Contemporary regime tenancies are governed primarily by the Housing Act 1988 as amended especially by the Localism Act 2011 and, when finally implemented, by the Housing and Planning Act

---

13 Housing Act 1985 s79(1); *Westminster City Council v Clarke* [1992] 2 AC 288.
14 Housing Act 1985 Sch 1 para 12.
15 Rent Act 1977 ss15, 16, 86, 87. This label and definition is often the key to other applications eg in relation to shared ownership.
16 Rent Act 1977 s19; Housing Act 1988 s36.

2016 (although much of the latter applies directly only to local authority tenants). Subject to certain exceptions (below), this regime applies only to tenancies created on or after 15 January 1989. Thus, apart from certain exceptions (below) a tenancy created on or after that date cannot be a secure or fair rent tenancy.[17] The aim of the Housing Act 1988 was to treat housing association tenancies primarily as private sector tenancies.

8.20 Accordingly, most contemporary regime tenants have 'assured tenancy' status which also applies to a private sector tenant. Exceptions are long tenancies at a nil or low rent[18] and most fully mutual tenancies (below). About 80 per cent of housing association tenancies are assured tenancies. An assured tenant has security of tenure and other statutory rights but the rent can be a market rent thus enabling different kinds of social housing to be engineered.

8.21 A licence cannot be an assured tenancy. The rights of the resident therefore depend on the particular licence agreement. Many licences are within the definition of a 'hostel' which occasionally attracts special rules. A hostel is a building which provides shared accommodation and either board or facilities for preparing meals.[19] It thus includes several kinds of supported housing including some care homes. About 50 per cent of supported housing residents are licencees.

8.22 Housing association tenancies have diverged in some respects from the private sector model. Rights selectively corresponding to those of a public sector secure tenant and also rent controls have been created by standards imposed by the regulator (aka government) and either incorporated into tenancy agreements or encouraged as a funding requirement.

8.23 These are policed through uncertain public law principles ensuring that any requirement falls with the statutory objects of the regulator and that no irrelevant factors are taken into account. There is also the duty of fairness in the form of the 'legitimate expectation' according to which the regulator is bound by a clear promise or undertaking that has been given either to a person personally or in the form of a published policy. A published policy is binding unless and until it is formally withdrawn. A further complication is the need to show that the landlord is exercising a 'public function' in the particular context so as to engage the judicial review process.[20]

---

17 Housing Act 1988 ss1, 35(2), (4).
18 Housing Act 1988 Sch 1 paras 3, 3A, 3B.
19 Housing Act 1985 s622.
20 See *R (Macleod) v Governors of the Peabody Trust* [2016] EWHC 737 (Admin).

8.24 Where a landlord, perhaps required to do so by the regulator, puts special housing association provisions into a tenancy agreement, these may fit badly with established legal principles. For example, in the Supreme Court case of *Berrisford v Mexfield Housing Co-operative Ltd*[21] a periodic tenancy accidently became a 'long tenancy' with the possible result that the tenant could acquire the freehold under the Leasehold Reform Act (LRA) 1967 (below). A fully mutual co-operative housing association had been created by a bank as part of a mortgage rescue scheme. Fully mutual tenancies have no statutory security of tenure. Mexfield's standard form tenancy agreement provided that the tenancy was from 'month-to-month' but could be determined by the landlord only if the tenant fell into rent arrears or otherwise broke the agreement or ceased to be a member of the association or the association ceased to exist. The landlord served notice to quit for rent arrears.

8.25 However, under an ancient common law rule, a tenancy which can be determined on an uncertain event, meaning one that may never happen, is void unless a maximum certain limit is specified. It was reluctantly held that, in the light of established authority, such a tenancy held by an individual must be treated as a tenancy for life. Accordingly, by virtue of the Law of Property Act 1925 s149(6) the tenancy becomes a 90-year term determinable on an earlier death or under its other terms. Thus the landlord could not determine the tenancy by notice to quit. The tenant is also denied the repairing rights applicable to a periodic tenancy. The Supreme Court declined to overturn the uncertainty rule even though it had been much criticised as pointless on the ground that it was well established. Lord Neuberger mentioned that Housing Corporation guidance may have been involved, but unfortunately this aspect was not explored.

Assured shorthold tenancies

8.26 Housing associations have traditionally used ordinary periodic assured tenancies. Since the arrival of the Conservative led government in 2010, these have fallen into political disfavour, being disparagingly described even in legislation as 'tenancies for life'[22] since a tenant who complies with the tenancy agreement cannot be

---

21 [2011] UKSC 52; see also C Hunter and D Cowan, 'The future of housing co-operatives: Mexfield and beyond' (2012) 15 JHL 26.
22 Eg Housing and Planning Act 2016 s118.

evicted. Recent policies have favoured increasing flexibility by reducing tenants' rights.[23] In particular, fixed-term tenancies of two to five years have been favoured for general needs housing. (Almost all supported housing is for less than two years). An assured shorthold tenancy can relatively easily be terminated. Thus, in addition to the general grounds for possession, an assured shorthold tenancy can be terminated without reasons being given.[24] Where the initial tenancy is a fixed term, the landlord must give at least two months' notice. In the case of a PRP or RSL, where the tenancy is for a fixed term of two years or more, a possession order cannot take effect unless the landlord gives the tenant at least six months' notice before the end of the term that it does not intend to grant another tenancy. The landlord must inform the tenant how to obtain help or advice about the notice.[25] The English regulator also requires the landlord to provide advice and also to provide an independent review of its decision.[26] Where the tenancy is a periodic tenancy, the notice cannot be given within four months of the commencement of the tenancy.[27]

8.27 While there is no direct statutory requirement, under the influence of the regulator many new housing association lettings are fixed-term assured shortholds although some have bucked the trend. Indeed, for tenancies created after the Housing Act 1996 came into force (1 April 1997), shorthold is the default tenancy in that, subject to certain exceptions, an assured tenancy, whether periodic or fixed-term, is automatically an assured shorthold unless the landlord serves notice either before or during the tenancy that it is to not to be an assured shorthold.[28] Moreover, the periodic assured tenancy that arises following the end of a fixed term of any length is an assured shorthold. At present, most housing associations offer fixed-terms only as assured shortholds.

8.28 In relation to a housing association, the relevant exceptions are, first, that the tenancy has ceased to be a 'secure tenancy' (ie it has been transferred from a local authority), in which case the tenancy

23 See Parkin, Wilson, *Social housing: the end of 'lifetime tenancies' in England?* House of Commons Briefing Paper no 07173, 27 May 2016.
24 Housing Act 1988 s21, as modified in England for tenancies commencing on or after 1 October 2018 by the Deregulation Act 2015.
25 Housing Act 1988 s21(1B).
26 See HCA, 'Tenancy Standards', 2015.
27 Housing Act 1988 s22(4).
28 Housing Act 1988 s19A and Sch 2A, inserted by Housing Act 1996 s96 (1) and Sch 7. Previously an assured shorthold had to be expressly created and was limited to short fixed periods.

must be an ordinary assured tenancy; and second, a new tenancy granted to an existing assured tenant and thirdly following a 'demoted tenancy' (below)). A tenancy created before the Housing Act 1996 came into force is an assured shorthold only if it was a fixed-term for at least six months and before it began the landlord gave advance notice that it was to be an assured shorthold.

8.29 The Localism Act 2011 encourages the use of fixed terms by making it easier and cheaper to create them Thus, the long-standing rule that a lease for more than three years must be by deed does not apply to assured tenancies in England granted by a PRP other than 'long tenancies' (21 years or more) or shared ownership leases.[29] With the same exceptions, assured tenancies granted by a PRP do not have to be registered with the Land Registry.[30]

8.30 Turning the screw further, Housing and Planning Act 2016 s118, headed 'phasing out of tenancies for life', imposed a radical regime similar to the fixed-term assured shorthold for secure tenancies in England.[31] Housing association assured tenancies may have been required to follow suit. However, the 2018 green paper now indicates that these provisions may not be implemented and that the length of tenure should be decided at local level.[32]

8.31 The English regulator requires that PRPs have specific policies in place dealing with the grant of assured shortholds, and also transfers and terminations of tenancies and the circumstances in which they will not be renewed. General needs tenancies should normally be either periodic tenancies or for fixed terms of at least five years. Shorter terms can be given in particular circumstances (below). These are primarily concerned with combating anti-social behaviour.[33] In 2015/16, the most recent figures available to us, most new general needs tenancies were for between three and five years and supported housing for two years or less.[34] (By that year 82 per cent of social rent lettings by PRPs were still 'lifetime' periodic tenancies, while 18 per cent were shortholds.) Furthermore, it is noteworthy that housing association assured shortholds are usually renewed.

---

29 Localism Act 2011 s156 modifying Law of Property Act 1925 s52.
30 Localism Act 2011 s157 modifying Leasehold Reform Act 2002 ss3, 7, 24, 33, 132.
31 See Wilson, etc, *Implementation of the Housing and Planning Act 2016*, House of Commons Briefing Paper 8229, March 2018, Ch 4.6.
32 *A new deal for social housing*, Cm 9761, para 5.2.
33 *A new deal for social housing*, Cm 9761, para 5.2.
34 See *Social housing lettings in England and Wales*, DCLG, 2016.

8.32 However, the most recent policy indications suggest that the security of a tenant in their home is being treated more sympathetically.[35] We suggested above that hostile provisions in the Housing and Planning Act 2016 will not be implemented. Indeed, at least one large housing association has already abandoned the general use of fixed-term assured shorthold tenancies. Irrespective of the merits of the matter, this perhaps illustrates the responsiveness of the sector to government influence.

Fully mutual tenancies

8.33 Tenancies of a residual regime fully mutual housing association are anomalous, although there may be few surviving. A tenant of a co-operative housing association cannot be a secure tenant while the association is a PRP or RSL (see para 2.43 above), but can be a secure tenant if this is not the case.[36] This was enacted presumably as an incentive to register. If an association ceases to be a PRP or RSL it must notify relevant tenants within 21 days that they have become secure tenants. However, the right to buy does not apply.[37] The termination of a co-operative PRP or RSL therefore depends on the tenancy agreement.[38]

8.34 Most residual regime co-operatives are subject to the Rent Act housing association fair rent regime.[39] However, a special type of co-operative – the co-ownership housing association – is excluded from this regime, presumably because its members have an equity stake. [40] (In other contexts co-ownerships are not distinguished from other fully mutual tenancies.) Thus a co-ownership which is a PRP or RSL seems to fall outside all protective regimes.

8.35 A tenancy of a residual regime mutual association which is a PRP or RSL but not a co-operative, namely one structured as a company, is treated as an ordinary non- mutual tenancy and can therefore be a secure tenancy.[41] If it is not a PRP or RSL, it falls within the Rent Act private sector regime.[42]

35 Green paper, para 5.2.
36 Housing Act 1985 ss80(2), 85(3).
37 Housing Act 1985 Sch 5 para 2.
38 See *Clays Lane Housing Co-operative Ltd v Patrick* (1985) 49 P & CR 72.
39 Rent Act 1977 s86(2) as amended.
40 Rent Act 1977 s86(3); and above para 2.52.
41 Housing Act 1985 s80(2).
42 Rent Act 1977 s15(3)(d).

8.36 A contemporary regime tenancy of a dwelling in England granted by a fully mutual housing association (whether or not a co-operative housing association) cannot generally be an assured tenancy of either kind, and so has no statutory protection.[43] However, in Wales a fully mutual housing association can opt to make a specific tenancy of a dwelling house in Wales an assured tenancy.[44]

8.37 There is a pitfall if a co-operative tenancy agreement attempts to link the termination of a tenancy agreement to membership of the association by providing that the landlord can terminate the agreement only in specified circumstances including the tenant ceasing to be a member. As we have seen, such a provision falls foul of the common law principle of uncertainty.[45] A correct form of agreement would be a periodic tenancy where the landlord has an additional right to terminate the agreement if membership issues arise but without restricting the normal power to give notice. Alternatively, where the tenancy is a fixed-term tenancy with a definite maximum duration, the question of uncertainty does not arise.

Collision between the residual and contemporary regimes: special cases

8.38 There is further complexity in that the residual and contemporary regimes do not fully dovetail, and tortuous statutory language is required to deal with the interaction between the two regimes. The tenant must be informed of any change of status.

Residual secure tenancies becoming contemporary regime assured tenancies

8.39 Under special provisions, some residual secure and fair rent tenants can become contemporary regime assured tenants:

---

43 Housing Act 1988 Sch 1 para 12(1)(h). There is a specialised exception where the landlord is a body 'approved under an earlier regime': Housing Act 1988 s1(5).
44 Housing (Wales) Act 2014 s137. Moreover, there is a mandatory ground of possession in Wales to enable a fully mutual association to repay a mortgage: s138.
45 *Berrisford v Mexfield Housing Co-operative Ltd* [2011] UKSC 52 above para 8.24.

1) Where ownership of the dwelling is transferred more than two years after the Housing Act 1988 came into effect by a local authority or other public sector landlord to a housing association (treated as a private landlord in this context).[46] This is often under large-scale stock transfer arrangements. However, the tenant retains any right to buy previously available. Where an individual local authority tenant moves to a housing association landlord, there will be a new tenancy which, under general principles, will be an assured tenancy.

2) A housing association fair rent tenancy (thus including a cooperative as well as a secure tenancy), transferred *to* a private landlord including an unregistered housing association.[47]

3) Any remaining 'old style' assured tenancies. These have no connection with contemporary assured tenancies nor housing associations but were introduced under a short lived regime by the Housing Act 1980 intended to stimulate the rental market. Under this regime the secretary of state could exempt certain institutional landlords from rent controls. There were few takers and no new assured tenancies of this kind can be created. Existing tenancies whenever created become ordinary assured tenancies, even those of fully mutual bodies provided the landlord remain the same.[48]

Contemporary era tenancies as residual regime secure tenancies

8.40 As far as housing associations are concerned, these mainly concern new tenancies granted to people who were previously residual regime secure tenants:[49]

1) Where a new tenancy or licence is granted *by the same landlord* not necessarily in the same premises to a tenant who immediately beforehand was a residual regime secure or fair rent tenant of that landlord.[50] For example, a person in supported or specialist housing might move to ordinary accommodation or there might be an exchange arrangement. However, in some cases an exchange takes the form of an assignment of an existing tenancy in which

---

46 Housing Act 1988 s38(1), (3).
47 Housing Act 1988 s38(2), (3).
48 Housing Act 1988 ss1(3), (5), 37(1).
49 *Social housing lettings in England and Wales*, DCLG, 2016.
50 Housing Act 1988 s35(2)(b).

the tenancy itself remains the same. The tenant's position depends on the circumstances at the time of the new tenancy under the residual regime rules. For example, a tenant of a PRP whose landlord was a co-operative but has now becomes a non mutual association will become a secure tenant, and will retain fair rent status.[51]

2) Where a dwelling which was subject to a private sector protected or fair rent tenancy is acquired by a housing association, the tenant can be a secure tenant.[52] This is one of the rare contexts in which the generic concept of a housing association is used. There is some protection for a housing association secure tenant against a change of landlord, since a non-profit PRP can dispose of the landlord's interest under a secure tenancy only to another non-profit PRP.[53]

3) By a court order where the tenant is rehoused under the 'suitable alternative accommodation' grounds for possession of the Housing Act 1985. The previous tenancy must have been a secure tenancy.

4) Certain tenancies granted by public sector authorities, including PRPs and RSLs, to the previous tenant or to his or her family members, of defective dwellings which had previously been sold to sitting tenants and subsequently repurchased and repaired.[54]

5) Tenancies granted under now obsolete 'co-operative agreements' with a local authority.[55]

Probationary/flexible tenancies

Introduction

8.41 Statutory forms of probationary or temporary tenancy have become available primarily to local authority landlords based on fixed-term tenancies.[56] The main one is the 'introductory tenancy'.[57] They do not usually apply directly to housing associations. However, in the light of government policy, many housing associations have mimicked these

51 See *Bhai v Black Roof Community Housing Association* [2001] 2 All ER 865–871.
52 Housing Act 1988 s35(5).
53 HRA 2008 s171(2).
54 See Housing Act 1985 s554(2A).
55 Housing Act 1985 s27B.
56 See *Local decisions: a fair future for social housing: consultation*, DCLG, 2010.
57 Housing Act 1996 s124(1).

provisions by means of non-statutory arrangements. The mechanism for so doing is the assured shorthold tenancy of the Housing Act 1988 with embellishments incorporated into the tenancy agreement. There are also the statutory 'demoted tenancy' and the 'family intervention tenancy' which do apply to PRPs and RSLs (below). There is also the 'flexible tenancy'. This enables a landlord to grant a series of fixed-term tenancies and to terminate each one at its discretion.

8.42 Thus social housing ceases to be a right but becomes a tool of executive policy. The justifications claimed for these kinds of tenancy range from the need to ration scarce resources to encouraging self-help and social mobility and combatting anti-social behaviour. The basic aim of providing security in a decent home becomes secondary. However the recent green paper (August 2018) suggests a swing of the pendulum back to greater security of tenure.[58]

8.43 There are similar provisions for Wales under the Renting Homes (Wales) Act 2016 (above). These involve non secure ('standard') periodic tenancies known as 'introductory standard contracts' (for the first 12 months), and 'prohibited conduct standard contracts'. There are also 'supported standard contracts' for use with supported housing.

Starter tenancy

8.44 A 'starter tenancy' is a non-statutory equivalent of the local authority 'introductory tenancy'. This is a fixed-term tenancy with limited rights that can be converted into an ordinary assured tenancy. A starter tenancy is primarily used for tenants who are new to the social housing sector or whose previous social tenancy was not secure or assured. About 70 per cent of new 'social rented' tenancies are starter tenancies whereas the higher rented 'affordable tenancies' are not usually let as starter tenancies. The tenancy has an initial fixed term, usually of one year, after which it can become an ordinary assured tenancy either automatically if the agreement so provides or by means of the landlord serving notice to this effect. Alternatively, a further starter tenancy can be granted. However, a tenant has no right or even a public law legitimate expectation to a new tenancy, only that a fair procedure will be used.[59] During the starter period, there is no right to sublet or take in lodgers, nor to improve the property, nor to acquire the dwelling. Succession and assignment rights

---

58 See above para 1.47.
59 *Eastlands Homes Partnership Ltd v Whyte* [2010] EWHC 695 (QB).

are limited to a spouse or civil partner. Regular reviews which include visits to the dwelling are held.

8.45 During the starter period, the normal grounds for terminating an assured tenancy apply. In practice the published policies of most PRPs restrict termination of starter tenancies to breaches of the tenancy agreement especially non-payment of rent or anti-social behaviour. Reasons are given and an internal right of appeal is provided to an officer who is independent in the sense of not knowing the tenant. This may be sufficient to pass the common law 'bias' test, namely would a fair-minded and informed observer consider there to be a real possibility of bias.[60] It is unusual not to renew a starter tenancy.

Flexible tenancy

8.46 'Flexible tenancies' are now the norm for public sector tenancies. They may become so for publicly funded housing association tenancies. A statutory flexible tenancy applies to a secure tenancy and is a fixed-term secure tenancy for not less than two years.[61] The tenant can give notice to terminate at any time. The court must give the landlord possession at the end of the period if the landlord has served notice that it does not intend to grant a new secure tenancy.[62] The tenant can require a review of the landlord's proposals albeit only one by the landlord itself.[63]

8.47 The statutory provisions of course apply to a housing association only in the special cases where it can create a secure tenancy (above). However, a tenancy agreement may copy them by using a fixed-term assured shorthold tenancy which can be determined without giving reasons at the end of the fixed term. Where a fixed term is for at least two years, a PRP or RSL must give the tenant at least six months' prior notice of termination (including information where to get help or advice) that it does not propose to grant another tenancy at the end of the fixed term.[64] The English regulator also requires the landlord to provide advice and to review its decision.[65]

---

60 See *Locobail (UK) Ltd v Bayfield Properties Ltd* [2000] QB 451. But arguably institutional pressures for collegiality point the other way, see *Lawal v Northern Spirit* [2003] UKHL 35 at [22].
61 Localism Act 2011 s154 inserting Housing Act 1985 ss107A–107E.
62 Housing Act 1985 ss107C, 107D.
63 Housing Act 1985 s107E.
64 Housing Act 1988 s21(1A), (1B).
65 HCA, 'Tenancy Standards', 2015.

Demoted tenancy

8.48 The statutory 'demoted tenancy' applies to PRPs and RSLs as well as to local authority landlords. Housing association demoted tenancies are governed by Housing Act 1988 ss6A, 20B and 20C (local authority demoted tenancies are governed by the Housing Act 1985 as amended). Statute is, of course, required because, unlike the other probationary tenancies, existing rights are removed. Originating in the Anti-social Behaviour Act 2003, a demoted tenancy is intended to provide a halfway-house short of eviction. Following notice and a court order, an assured tenancy can be 'demoted' to the status of an assured shorthold periodic tenancy.[66] The landlord can apply for an order on the ground of behaviour which involves using or threatening to use for an unlawful purpose housing accommodation owned or managed by a PRP or RSL. After a period of one year, unless the landlord previously gives notice of an intention to take proceedings for possession, the tenancy again becomes an ordinary assured tenancy. If this notice is given, the assured shorthold is extended until the notice is withdrawn or is successfully challenged or no proceedings have been taken for six months.[67]

8.49 If the original tenancy was itself an assured shorthold tenancy for a term of two years or more, granted after the Localism Act 2011 came into force special provisions apply.[68] Here, if the landlord serves an appropriate notice on the tenant, the tenancy becomes a fixed-term assured shorthold tenancy for at least two years on terms set out in the notice. Thus a further probationary period is imposed.

Family intervention tenancy (FIT)

8.50 A 'family intervention tenancy' (FIT) is a statutory device available to PRPs, RSLs and local authorities to offer to tenants or other residents with anti-social behaviour problems as a means of avoiding loss of their home.[69] It might, for example, include specialist accommodation and support. A FIT is not an assured tenancy.[70] It can therefore be terminated by serving a notice to quit.

---

66 See Housing Act 1988 s6A.
67 Housing Act 1988 s20B.
68 Housing Act 1988 s20C.
69 HRA 2008 s297(2); Housing Act 1988 Sch 1 Part 1 para 12ZA; see *Guidance on the use of family intervention tenancies*, DCLG, 2009.
70 Housing Act 1988 Sch 1 Part 1 para 12ZA.

8.51 A landlord can offer a FIT where a possession order, on the ground of anti-social behaviour, has been made against a person in relation to an assured tenancy of another dwelling or in the landlord's opinion could have been made or could have been made if that person had such a tenancy. It must be for the purposes of the provision by any person of 'behavioural support services' to the tenant or to any person residing with the tenant. This requires a written 'behavioural support agreement' between the tenant the landlord and the local housing authority. A FIT usually lasts between six and 12 months.

8.52 The landlord must first serve a notice on the prospective tenant giving information as to the reasons for the tenancy, its terms, the fact that the tenant is not obliged to take up the offer and any likely action by the landlord if the tenant does not do so. Unlike a local authority, a PRP or RSL does not have to serve a prior notice of intent and hold a review before serving the notice but the regulator normally requires a similar process.[71] The notice must include advice as to how to get assistance (characteristic of the buck-passing practices favoured by contemporary government).[72] Thus, depending on one's prejudices, a FIT might be seen as a punitive authoritarian intrusion into private life, or as an attempt to break the cycle of deprivation.[73]

8.53 A landlord can by notice convert the FIT into an assured tenancy. In the case of a dwelling-house in England, if the tenant's previous tenancy was an assured shorthold tenancy this can be an assured shorthold where the notice so states.[74]

Punishment for unlawful subletting

8.54 The Prevention of Social Housing Fraud Act 2013 applies to secure tenants and assured tenants of PRPs and RSLs other than shared ownership tenants. It makes unlawful sub-letting a criminal offence, and dishonestly doing so a more serious offence, where the tenant ceases to occupy the dwelling as his or her only or principal home. The non-dishonest version does not apply where the tenant is fleeing from violence from a co-resident or neighbour, nor where the new

---

71 HRA 2008 s298, see above note 56, para 49.
72 HRA 2008 s297(4), (5), (7).
73 See Jill Morgan, *Family intervention tenancies: the de (marginalisation) [sic] of social tenants*, Taylor and Francis, 2010.
74 Localism Act 2011 s163; Housing Act 1988 s21D.

resident is entitled to apply to the court for a right of occupation. In the criminal proceedings the court can order any profits to be paid to the landlord. The landlord can also apply to the court for an order enforced as a civil order to the same effect.

8.55 The secretary of state or the Welsh ministers can make regulations setting up investigation processes relating to this Act and other offences under the Fraud Act 2006 including allocation of housing, and 'right to buy' and 'right to acquire'. The regulations can confer wide powers on unspecified persons to require information. They can also create offences relating to failure to provide information. Such powers are unusually wide in subordinate legislation. In a Human Rights Act 1998 challenge they would have to be defended as necessary and proportionate presumably to safeguard public money.

8.56 Irrespective of the above offences, if a tenant unlawfully parts with possession or sublets the whole of the dwelling the tenancy automatically and permanently ceases to be an assured tenancy.[75] The same applies to a secure tenant under the general law.[76]

Long tenancies

8.57 A long tenancy, is generally defined as a tenancy granted for over 21 years and sometimes includes a tenancy of any length or granted under the 'right to buy' or the 'right to acquire'.

Residual regime

8.58 Under the residual regime, a long tenancy, including a tenancy granted under the 'right to buy' or the 'right to acquire', cannot be a secure tenancy.[77] A tenancy which can be terminated by notice upon death or marriage[78] does not generally count as a long tenancy for this purpose. However, there are special housing association exceptions under which a shared ownership tenancy or a 'leasehold for the elderly', can retain long tenancy status. These rules are discussed below.

---

75 Housing Act 1988 s15A.
76 Housing Act 1988 ss91(2), 93(2).
77 Housing Act 1985 s115, Sch 1 para 1; Housing Act 1985 s174; SI 1997 No 619 Sch 1 para 29.
78 Housing Act 1985 s115(2).

8.59 A long tenancy is also excluded from the housing association fair rent regime if the rent is a 'low rent'.[79] Moreover, the special security of tenure regime for long residential tenancies at a low rent under the Landlord and Tenant Act 1954 (under which the tenancy continues indefinitely unless terminated on certain grounds or a new tenancy is granted), does not apply to PRPs, RSLs, charitable housing trusts in the special sense explained in chapter 2 and co-operative housing associations. This is because that regime applies only if the tenancy would fall within *private sector* Rent Act protection were it not at a low rent.[80] Thus residual regime long tenancies have no statutory protection.

Contemporary regime

8.60 A long tenancy can be an assured tenancy unless it is at a low or nil rent. For PRPs, RSLs, charitable housing trusts in the special sense explained in chapter 2 and co-operative housing associations a long tenancy at a low rent may fall within a special regime for long tenancies under Local Government and Housing Act (LGHA) 1989 s186 and Sch 10. This regime applies to a tenancy created on or after 1 April 1990, which, were it not at a low rent, would be an assured tenancy. It also applies to a tenancy created before that date if it was in existence on 15 January 1999.

8.61 Under this regime, at the end of the term, the tenancy continues until the landlord serves notice to terminate it. Unless the tenancy is renewed or terminated on prescribed grounds, it becomes an assured periodic tenancy. Schedule 10 was introduced to plug a gap in the Housing Act 1988 concerning private sector long tenancies under the Landlord and Tenant Act 1954. It therefore seems anomalous that PRPs etc are included since they were never within the Landlord and Tenant Act 1954. However, there seems to no housing association exclusion.

8.62 A long tenancy which is not a shared ownership lease (below) is subject to the tenant's right to acquire the freehold or to extend the lease under the Leasehold Reform Act 1967 (house) or the Leasehold Reform Housing and Urban Development Act 1993 (flat).

---

79 Rent Act 1977 ss5, 87. A tenancy granted before 1 April 1990 is at a low rent if the rent is less than two-thirds rateable value on 31 March 1990. In other cases it is £1,000 or less per annum in Greater London or £250 elsewhere: Housing Act 1988 Sch 1 paras 3A, 3B (subject to revision).
80 Landlord and Tenant Act 1954 s2(1).

There is no longer a requirement that the tenancy be at a low rent.[81] A housing association landlord has a limited exemption. This applies only to long leases of houses granted to secure tenants under the statutory right to buy and then only where the freeholder is a charity.[82]

Shared ownership

Overview

8.63 Shared ownership is the most important part of the sector's low cost home ownership activity. Most long tenancies created by housing associations are shared ownership leases, or, more correctly, let under shared ownership 'arrangements', since they are not shared ownership in the legal sense (ie a trust). The law relating to shared ownership is complex and technical mainly in order to exclude provisions which apply to ordinary leases which would frustrate the purpose of shared ownership.

8.64 Although it is defined as social housing in its own right,[83] shared ownership is not a distinctive tenure but is essentially a long lease. The 'shared' aspect comprises contractual financial arrangements entitling the leaseholder on leaving the property to a payment representing a proportion of the market value of the property. Apart from the lease, the leaseholder has no interest in the property itself. Thus if the lease is forfeited for breach of its terms the leaseholder may lose everything.

8.65 The basis of the financial arrangements is that the leaseholder pays a premium to acquire the lease which is less than its market value, typically about 25 per cent. This is the basis on which the leasholder's 'share' is calculated. In addition, the leaseholder pays a service charge and an ordinary 'affordable' rent (up to 80 per cent of the 75 per cent market value retained by the landlord. There is therefore an element of subsidy). Thus, not being at a low rent, a contemporary shared ownership lease is an assured tenancy.

8.66 Shared ownership is therefore a hybrid between leasehold ownership and ordinary renting and as such a recipe for confusion. It has not proved popular comprising only about 0.8 per cent of English

---

81 HRA 2008 s300.
82 Housing Act 1985 s172 introduced by LRHUDA 1993.
83 HRA 2008 s70.

housing stock. It exposes once again the public/private, commercial/ social fault lines of the housing association sector. For example, its hybrid nature raises problems in relation to service charges, responsibility for repairs and improvements and may lead to conflicts over relationships with managing agents of flats especially where there is a private sector element. Leaseholders may also be unclear as to their status. Moreover, the terminology may be a barrier to understanding. [84]

8.67 In its current form, shared ownership dates from the Housing Act 1980 superseding the limited fully mutual 'co-ownership' tenancy which we discussed in chapter 2. The usual statutory definition of a shared ownership lease is a lease granted at a premium calculated by reference either to the value of the accommodation or the cost of providing it and which provides that the tenant (or his or her personal representatives) will or may be entitled on termination of the tenancy to a payment calculated on the same basis.[85]

8.68 Most shared ownership arrangements involve a long tenancy, often for 99 years. Shared ownership leases usually include 'staircasing' provisions whereby a tenant can purchase by stages further percentages of the value of the dwelling with a proportionate reduction of rent. A tenant who has staircased up to 100 per cent has a right to acquire the landlord's interest or to an extended lease. These rights can be triggered automatically by a provision in the lease or can take the form of an option.

8.69 There can also be provision for 'downward staircasing' whereby a tenant who runs into problems can sell percentages back to the landlord.[86] The rent level changes accordingly. Thus the arrangements are flexible, and shared ownership can be targeted at particular groups under changing government policies. However, the overwhelming majority of shared ownership tenants retain the same share they started with.

8.70 If the fixed term ends without the tenant staircasing to 100 per cent, the general rules relating to long tenancies apply (above) so that the tenant becomes an ordinary assured tenant. The tenant is liable to eviction in the same way as any other tenant. There is non-statutory

---

84 See generally Cowan, Wallace, Carr, *Exploring Experiences of Shared Ownership Housing: Reconciling Ownership and Renting*, University of Bristol, Leverhulme Trust, University of Kent, Centre for Housing Policy (2015). See also (2018) *Sunday Times*, 30 September.
85 Eg HRA 2008 s70(4); Housing Act 1985 s106(1).
86 HCA, *Shared ownership: joint guidance for England*, October 2016, pp28–32.

guidance concerning the termination of a shared ownership lease in the event of a breach by the tenant.[87]

8.71 Under the regulator's model leases, the shared ownership payment provisions form a schedule to the lease which is made 'subject to' the schedule. The tenant does not have a charge on the land. On this basis, the shared ownership arrangements seem to be frail being only contractual in nature. Thus, if the landlord becomes insolvent, the tenant's claim may only be that of an ordinary creditor. Arguably though, the Schedule constitutes a condition of the lease and, as such, a fully-fledged property right. In any case, the right to acquire the freehold is a separate property right (see also para 9.47). If the tenant wishes to sell the property before fully staircasing, there are contractual provisions preventing transfer except as nominated by the landlord association or giving the landlord a right of pre-emption or requiring payment to the landlord association of its notional share of the equity.

8.72 The law relating to shared ownership is bedevilled by geological layers surviving from previous regimes. The main concern has been to preserve shared ownership as social housing by avoiding the various statutory rights to buy, acquire enfranchise (acquire the freehold) or to an extended lease under the LRA 1967 in the case of houses[88] and under the LRHUDA 1993 in the case of flats. The relevant provisions have been amended many times over the years, with a resulting multiplication of regimes depending on when the particular tenancy commenced. Unfortunately the dates of the changing regimes do not co-ordinate with the general dates of the contemporary and residual regimes for ordinary tenancies.

8.73 Unusually, many of these shared ownership principles apply to all housing associations whether or not registered.

1) As a long tenancy, a residual regime shared ownership tenancy cannot be a secure tenancy and so does not attract the public sector 'right to buy'. Similarly, the 'right to acquire' which applies to some contemporary regime tenants of non-charitable housing associations does not apply to a long tenancy.[89]

---

87 Council of Mortgage Lenders, NFH, HCA, Building Societies Association, *Guidance for handling arrears and possession sales of shared ownership properties*, 2014.
88 See LRA 1967 Sch 4A inserted by Housing and Planning Act 1986 Sch 4.
89 HRA 2008 s180(2)(a); Housing Act 1996 ss16(1)(a), 63.

2) A residual regime shared ownership tenancy might be subject to the housing association fair rent regime. However, there is a statutory exclusion affecting those with staircasing provisions (below).
3) In the case of houses, both residual regime and contemporary regime shared ownership tenancies would attract the LRA 1967. This gives qualifying tenants various rights to acquire the freehold or to an extended lease. Originally the LRA 1967 was excluded in many shared ownership cases because the rent was not a low rent. However, the low rent requirement has in most cases been abolished.[90] Special housing association exclusions (below) must therefore be relied on.

8.74 The overall effect of various unco-ordinated provisions seems to be that all shared ownership tenancies held by housing associations are outside the right to buy and right to acquire and most shared ownership tenancies of houses with staircasing provisions are exempt from the enfranchisement regime of the LRA 1967. The main provisions are outlined in the box below. However, the rights available to tenants of flats under LRHUDA 1993 have greater application (below).

Shared ownership houses

1) Older leases (created before the Housing and Planning Act 1986 came into effect). A shared ownership tenancy created by a 'registered housing association' (now a PRP or RSL) is exempt from the LRA 1967 subject to compliance with regulations made by the secretary of state. These older regulations are relatively simple and broad. They require either that the tenant has the right under the lease to acquire the landlord's interest or that the lease is a lease for the elderly within a special scheme (below).
2) Under the Housing and Planning Act 1986, as amended, a shared ownership tenancy created by a housing association *of any kind* on or after 11 December 1987 may be excluded from the LRA 1967 and also from the fair rent regime of the Rent Act 1977. The main feature of these later rules is that the lease must have staircasing provisions. This regime is the basic model for contemporary shared ownership schemes. It applies even if the association no longer owns the dwelling. The statutory requirements are as follows.[91]

---

90 Commonhold and Leasehold Reform Act 2002 s141.
91 LRA 1967 Sch 4A, inserted by Housing and Planning Act 1986 Sch 4; Rent Act 1977 s5A (in any case, a low rent will also exclude the Rent Act).

a) The term must be 99 years or more terminable only by re-entry or forfeiture, that is for breach of the agreement.
b) The premium must be not less than 25 per cent.
c) The tenant must be enabled to acquire additional shares as prescribed by regulations made by the secretary of state.[92] These regulations entitle but do not require the tenant to staircase up to 100 per cent in instalments of 25 per cent, or a lesser amount specified in the lease, and at times of the tenant's choosing.
d) If the lease enables the landlord to charge for further shares it must do so only where prescribed by regulations. These limit the landlords power to charge to the percentage outstanding and then only if the tenant disposes of his or her interest on the market.[93]
e) The tenant's power to mortgage or charge the house must not be restricted.
f) The lease must provide for the tenant to acquire the landlord's interest.
g) The lease must state the landlord's opinion that it complies with these requirements.

(In an attempt to make shared ownership attractive to the private sector, similar rules were introduced for non housing association landlords by the Housing and Regeneration Act 2008.[94] There are only a few private sector shared ownership schemes.)

8.75 The remaining exemptions of housing associations from the LRA 1967 are more restricted. A shared ownership tenancy of social housing created by a local authority and certain other public bodies on or after 11 December 1987 is excluded from the operation of the LRA 1967 at any time when the where the landlord's interest belongs to a designated body including a PRP or RSL.[95] This provision is therefore geared to stock transfers from the public sector. The lease need not have staircasing provisions but must enable the tenant to

---

92 Housing Association Shared Ownership Leases (Exclusion from Leasehold Reform Act 1967 and Rent Act 1977) Regulations 1987 SI No 1940 reg 2.
93 Housing Association Shared Ownership Leases (Exclusion from Leasehold Reform Act 1967 and Rent Act 1977) Regulations 1987 reg 3.
94 LRA 1967 ss301, 312, Sch 4A paras 3A, 4A; Housing (Shared Ownership Leases) (Exclusion from Leasehold Reform Act 1967) (England) Regulations 2009 SI No 2097.
95 LRA 1967 Sch 4A para 2.

acquire the freehold at a reasonable price. It is for the landlord to establish this.

8.76 A 'charitable housing trust'[96] has an additional exclusion from the LRA 1967. This applies to any tenancy, so not only to shared ownership, at any time where the housing trust is the immediate landlord and where 'the house forms part of the accommodation provided by it in pursuit of its charitable purposes'.[97] The exemption applies to the acquisition of the freehold but not to the right to an extended lease. Originally shared ownership tenancies could be granted under right to buy provisions. This right was abolished by LRHUDA 1993, but such tenancies that still exist are excluded from the LRA 1967.[98]

Flats

8.77 Flats are not subject to the LRA 1967. Instead, LRHUDA 1993 confers a right to acquire the landlord's interest on qualifying tenants collectively through a 'right to enfranchise' company (RTE) and a right to a new 90-year lease on an individual tenant.

8.78 For the purpose of the RTE and to an extension of the lease, LRHUDA 1993 applies to a shared ownership lease only where the tenant has staircased up to 100 per cent.[99] Thus the Act has limited application. Is main importance is where a housing association is itself a leaseholder in a mixed block of flats and with its tenants holding sub-tenancies. The following exemptions apply. The underlying objective seems to be to insulate public sector flats, defined to include housing associations, within mixed blocks.

1) A 'charitable housing trust' where the trust is the immediate landlord and 'the flat forms part of the accommodation provided by it in pursuit of its charitable purposes'.[100]

   This exemption has been construed narrowly. In *Brick Farm Management Ltd v Richmond Housing Partnership Ltd*[101] a local authority sold two blocks of flats to a charitable housing

---

96 Above para 2.37.
97 LRA 1967 s1(3), (3A), introduced by LRHUDA 1993 s67. Where the tenancy began before LRHUDA 1993 came into force (1 November 1993) this applies only in special cases concerning rent levels and valuation, leases determinable on death or marriage geared to various changes to the LRA 1967.
98 LRHUDA 1993 s107.
99 LRHUDA 1993 s7.
100 LRHUDA 1993 s5(2).
101 [2005] EWHC 1650 (QB).

trust. Most of the tenants had previously acquired long leases of 125 years under right to buy provisions and claimed rights under the Act. There were also some periodic assured tenants remaining. Using the traditional approach of strictly construing confiscatory legislation, the trust claimed that all its flats formed part of housing provided for its charitable purposes so that it was exempt from claims by the leaseholders. Stanley Burnton J held that the trust was not exempt. This was because his lordship read into the exemption a requirement that it applied only to flats specifically let as social housing and did not apply merely because the block included social housing. The long leases were neither social housing, nor were they created in pursuance of the trust's charitable objects. This approach avoids the anomaly of a single social tenant in a block being in a position to prevent enfranchisement of the non-social tenants.

More questionably, Stanley Burnton J seemed to suggest[102] that the definition of 'housing trust' itself applies only to social housing.[103] If this is correct, then the exemption applies only where all the flats in a block are social housing provided by the trust. Given the broad contemporary meaning of social housing his lordship's view that the exemption has little or no practical application may be questionable. However, it is not clear why in this and other contexts the archaic notion of a housing trust is used at all.

2) This exemption covers a case where a housing association is holds a tenancy in a block owned by someone else. Normally under LRHUDA 1993 the RTE company can acquire all tenancies between that of the qualifying tenant and the ultimate freehold. The tenancy of a 'public sector landlord' is exempt from collective enfranchisement where the flat is occupied by a secure tenant.[104] For this purpose, a *non-profit* PRP and an RSL are public sector landlords.[105] Any superior tenancies must also be held by a public sector landlord and are also exempt.

3) This exemption and the following one apply where tenants exercise the right to collective enfranchisement. Where a 'public sector landlord' is the freeholder and the flat is let to a secure tenant, then, provided that any intermediate landlords are also

---

102 At [19].
103 Above para 2.37; Housing Act 1985 s6.
104 LRHUDA 1993 s2(5).
105 LRHUDA 1993 s38; Housing Act 1985 s171(2).

public sector landlords, the RTE company must give the landlord a leaseback of the flat.[106] There is no break in continuity so as to adversely affect the secure tenant and any succession rights are preserved.[107] (These provisions are curious in that, contrary to the common law, they seem to force a person to accept a legal estate.)

4) This exemption applies to all housing associations. Where a housing association is the freeholder of a flat which is let to a tenant who: a) is not a secure tenant; and b) does not qualify under the collective enfranchisement provisions (ie an ordinary assured or assured shorthold tenant), the association is similarly required to take a leaseback of the flat.[108]

8.79 Housing association leaseholders have the collective 'right to manage' under the Commonhold and Leasehold Reform Act 2002 on the same basis as private leaseholders. However the tenant's right of first refusal under the Landlord and Tenant Act 1987 and the powers of the court under that Act to require a bad landlord to transfer its interest to tenants do not apply to PRPs, RSLs, charitable housing trusts or fully mutual housing associations.[109]

Publicly funded shared ownership schemes: regulatory requirements in England[110]

8.80 The Homes and Communities Agency (HCA) channels grant funding into shared ownership schemes. The policy is to help people to get onto the property ladder and to encourage social mobility. Such schemes are promoted under brand names including 'Help to buy', and 'Social Homebuy'. Housing association shared ownership tenancies are usually of 99 years for a house and 125 years for a flat. To qualify for grant funding, the lease must be 25 years longer than the tenant's mortgage and the initial share of equity must be between 25 and 75 per cent. The tenant must normally have a right under the lease to staircase up to 100 per cent and with an option to acquire the landlord's interest at that point.

8.81 In earlier leases, the regulator required that, for 21 years after the tenant had staircased to 100 per cent, the housing association landlord must have a right of preemption (first refusal) and that, before

---

106 LRHUDA 1993 Sch 9 para. 2.
107 LRHUDA 1993 Sch 10 para 2.
108 LRHUDA 1993 Sch 9 para 3.
109 Landlord and Tenant Act 1987 ss11(4), 25(5)(a), 8(1).
110 See *HCA Shared Ownership: Joint Guidance for England* (2016).

the final staircasing, the landlord must also have a right of preemption. Apart from certain special cases (below) these restrictions do not apply to leases created on or after 30 April 2015.[111]

8.82 In earlier regimes under the Housing Corporation, detailed 'model' shared ownership leases were required. The present regime is more liberal and leaves it to individual landlords to devise their leases within a general framework. However, model leases are available.[112] As a condition of a grant, the English regulator requires that certain fundamental clauses in the model leases be included *in unaltered form*. These clauses can be varied only with the regulator's consent. These requirements, (with variations for older leases), are as follows:

1) Assignment of the tenancy must conform to detailed procedures and the tenant must be prohibited from subletting or parting with possession of part of the property. Thus transfers of the lease can be limited to people eligible for social housing.
2) The amount which a mortgagee or chargee can claim is controlled.
3) There must be an 'upward only' rent review clause based on a formula. The initial rent must be limited to three per cent of the unsold capital value and rent increases limited to RPI plus 0.5 per cent.
4) There are detailed staircasing requirements and the model leases must be followed. In particular, the staircase steps must be at least ten per cent including the final instalment. The government's social housing green paper suggests that the permissible steps be reduced to one per cent together with measures to lower the incidental costs.[113]
5) There must be a clause concerning any protected area restrictions (below).
6) Older leases may contain 'key worker clawback' provisions which allow the landlord to take back the property if the worker ceases to qualify. These no longer apply and the leases in question can be varied if purchaser objects.[114]
7) A service charge provision is not a fundamental clause for leases entered into after 22 October 2010 but remains a condition of agency funding 'where appropriate'.

---

111 Homes England, *Capital funding guide*, March 2018, p11.
112 See HCA, *Capital funding guide*, 2015.
113 *A new deal for social housing*, Cm 9671, August 2018, para 192.
114 *A new deal for social housing*, Cm 9671, pp12, 21.

8.83 In addition, the landlord housing association must consent in writing to the mortgage before the lease is entered into.[115] Under the standard mortgage protection clause, the landlord underwrites part of the lender's loss in the event of a default. If consent is not obtained, the association is not liable under the mortgagee protection clause.

8.84 In the case of leases granted under the Housing Corporation regime – that is, before 1 October 2008 – there was a somewhat obsessive requirement of consent to any variation of a lease which was protected by an entry on the Land Register. In the minority of cases, where an entry still exists the regulator will normally give its consent.[116]

8.85 Although there are no statutory rights to extend a shared ownership lease under the LRA 1967 or LRHUDA 1993 (above), a lease can be extended with the consent of the regulator.[117]

Shared ownership schemes in shortage areas

8.86 The secretary of state or the Welsh ministers can designate by order an area as a 'protected area' if they consider it appropriate to support the provision of shared ownership housing in the area.[118] This applies to all providers of shared ownership. In a protected area, regulations exclude the LRA 1967 even where there is no right to staircase up to 100 per cent. A lease of a house must either give the tenant a right to staircase only up to 80 per cent, or it must require a tenant who has staircased above 80 per cent to give a right of first refusal to the landlord or to a housing association or RSL nominated by the landlord.[119] Grant funding is available for the landlord to repurchase the property and resell it on shared ownership terms. These rules do not apply to flats but the regulator applies a similar policy in relation to flats.

8.87 There is also an HCA 'rural repurchase scheme' under which grant funding is provided to enable a provider to buy back a shared ownership property at market value in other rural areas (defined as having a population of less than 3,000), where the leaseholder wishes to sell. This does not apply to leaseholds for the elderly. An option to

---

115 *A new deal for social housing*, Cm 9671, p14.
116 *A new deal for social housing*, Cm 9671, pp16, 17.
117 *A new deal for social housing*, Cm 9671, p19, 20.
118 HRA 2008 s302; Housing (Right to Enfranchise) (Designated Protection Areas) (England) Order 2009 SI No 2098. Regulatory guidance states that the house must 'by law' remain as shared ownership 'in perpetuity': above note 111, para 6 and pp23–25. However this is questionable.
119 Housing (Shared Ownership Leases) (Exclusion from Leasehold Reform Act 1967) (England) Regulations 2009 SI 2009 No 2097 regs 8, 9, 10.

purchase must be included in leases which have restricted staircasing.[120] The property must be marketed locally and resold on shared ownership terms.

Leaseholds for the elderly

8.88   Housing associations provide long leases at a premium designed for elderly people, usually defined as being over 55. They need not be shared ownership leases at all, or may be shared ownership leases but without staircasing. They are not necessarily social housing, and under the terms of the lease can usually be assigned to other qualifying elderly people. They are charitable in that they meet the special needs of a charitable class.[121]

8.89   Some older leases may be made terminable by notice on the death of the tenant and in certain other circumstances. As we have seen, under the residual regime, normally a lease terminable by notice on death is excluded from the definition of a long tenancy.[122] However, where the tenancy is a shared ownership tenancy granted by a PRP or RSL and complies with regulations made by the secretary of state, (below), it still qualifies as a long tenancy.[123] (Going back over the years to leases made before any regulations came into force (ie before 1982), the lease must comply with the first set of regulations to come into force.) Those which do not comply and contain a provision for notice after death can be secure tenancies under the residual regime.

8.90   Under the contemporary regime, there is no special exclusion from assured tenancy status. Therefore a long tenancy for the elderly is an assured tenancy unless it is at a low rent at the time the issue arises. If it is at a low rent and was created on or after 1 April 1990, it may fall within the protection of LGHA 1989 Sch 10 (above) under which, if the landlord serves notice to terminate, the tenancy becomes an assured periodic tenancy.

8.91   There are, however, special leasehold for the elderly provisions excluding the right to enfranchise under the LRA 1967 (houses). In the case of the residual regime, there are exemptions from the fair rent

---

120 HCA, *Shared ownership: joint guidance for England*, October 2016, pp22–23.
121 *Joseph Rowntree Memorial Trust Housing Association Ltd v Attorney General* [1983] Ch 159.
122 Eg Housing Act 1985 s115(2) as amended.
123 Housing Act 1985 s115(2) above.

provisions of the Rent Act 1977 (above note 8.74) and as charitable bodies they are outside from the right to buy.[124] In the case of flats, there are no special exemptions from LRHUDA 1993.

8.92 In the case of a tenancy created before 11 December 1987, when the Housing and Planning Act 1986, came into force, a leasehold for the elderly was exempt from the LRA 1967 only if it satisfied restrictive conditions.[125] In particular, it must be the practice of the association to let to persons of 'pensionable age' in a complex where dedicated support services are provided. The tenancy cannot be assigned or sublet, and can be terminated if the leaseholder becomes subject to the Court of Protection. It must *not* enable the tenant to acquire the landlord's interest, although staircasing up to a lower percentage seems permissible.

8.93 A more liberal regime under the Housing and Planning Act 1986[126] applies to a lease for the elderly created on or after 11 December 1987. For this purpose, a lease for the elderly is a lease entered into by a person of at least 55. The landlord must be a PRP or RSL. The tenancy must be a shared ownership tenancy complying with requirements prescribed by regulations. The lease must state that the landlord believes that it complies with the relevant requirements. Unlike the general shared ownership exclusion for staircasing arrangements this exclusion applies only while the association remains the landlord.

8.94 The regulations are less restrictive than the earlier regime so preserving the marketability of the lease. They require that a warden service be provided, that the dwelling shall not be sublet, that it can assigned or parted with only to a person over 55 or on death either to a resident spouse (of any age) or to a person over 55 'residing with the tenant'.[127] A mortgagee or charge can exercise a power of sale. However, unlike normal shared ownership, the lessee must not have a right to purchase the landlord's entire interest.

8.95 Under regulatory guidance, a leasehold for the elderly supported by public funds ('older persons' shared ownership') must limit staircasing to 75 per cent and must not charge rent for the remaining shares.[128]

124 Below para 9.50.
125 Housing Act 1980 s140: SI 1982 No 62 reg 2.
126 LRA 1967 Sch 4A, inserted by Housing and Planning Act 1986 Sch 4: see Housing Association Shared Ownership Leases (Exclusion from Leasehold Reform Act 1967 and Rent Act 1977) Regulations 1987 SI No 1940 Sch 2.
127 This provision is susceptible to a Human Rights Act 1998 challenge for discrimination: see *Ghaidan v Godin-Mendoza* [2004] 2 AC 557.
128 Above note 111, para 12.

Other ownership schemes

8.96 Apart from continuing right to buy provisions, other methods of promoting access to home ownership, such as 'Homebuy', have been introduced and abandoned over the years. These comprise financial assistance of various kinds for the purchase of properties without special kinds of tenure. Current schemes include:

1) The 'Rent to Buy' scheme promoted by the UK government uses ordinary tenancies at 80 per cent market rent to enable the tenant to save for a deposit on an ordinary purchase.
2) The 'Rent to Own' scheme still promoted by the Welsh government involves an assured shorthold tenancy at a market rent for five years coupled with an option to purchase or to acquire a shared ownership tenancy after two years. On exercising the option, the tenant receives a payment towards the deposit of 25 per cent of the rent paid plus 50 per cent of any increase in the value of the property during the rental period.

There is also the possibility of an 'equity percentage' arrangement under which the purchaser makes an initial payment (which could be funded by an ordinary mortgage) followed by regular rent- like payments to the association until the debt is repaid. The association has a charge on the property.[129]

---

129 HRA 2008 s70.

Summary: Tenures (England)

1) Secure tenancies
   a) PRP or RSL tenancy or licence created before 15 January 1989. Not co-operative housing associations, nor long tenancies.
   b) Unregistered co-operative housing associations created before 15 January 1989.
   c) Tenancy or licence from the same landlord to a tenant who immediately beforehand was a secure tenant.
   d) Rent Act tenancy transferred from a private landlord.

2) Housing association fair rent regime
   a) Tenancy created before 15 January 1989 or by the same landlord after that date. Not co-ownership tenancy nor shared ownership tenancy complying with regulations.
   b) Tenancy as in c) and d) above.

3) Assured tenancies and assured shorthold tenancies
   a) Tenancies created on or after 15 January 1989 other than fully mutual tenancies.
   b) Tenancies transferred from local authorities and certain other public bodies.

4) Long tenancy regime (LGHA 1989): tenancies for over 21 years at a low rent created on or after 1 April 1990.

5) No statutory regime
   a) Fully mutual tenancies created on or after 15 January 1989 (other than in Wales).
   b) Long tenancies created before 1 April 1990.
   c) Family intervention tenancies.
   d) Licences created on or after 15 January 1989.
   e) Co-ownership tenancies.

CHAPTER 9

Particular rights

9.1	Introduction
9.5	Security of tenure/eviction
9.14	**Rents**
9.14	Introduction
9.19	Statutory limits: the rent reduction regime
9.22	Regulatory rent controls
9.28	Rents in Wales
9.31	Succession
9.36	Transfer/exchange of tenancies
9.46	Shared ownership
9.48	**The right to buy: secure tenants**
9.48	Overview
9.52	The preserved right to buy: change of landlord
9.58	The right to acquire: assured tenants
9.62	The 'voluntary' right to buy
9.63	Wales
9.71	Human rights
9.85	Judicial review

Introduction

9.1   In this chapter we shall discuss special housing association rules relating to tenants' rights. The special rules for housing association tenants do not amount to a distinctive regime but take the form of pragmatic additions to or exceptions from more general rules. Housing association tenures occupy a twilight world between public and private sector tenures.

9.2   With a few minor exceptions,[1] there are no rules applying to housing associations across the board. Particular kinds of housing association are singled out for special treatment, usually private registered providers (PRPs) and registered social landlords (RSLs) (ie those registered with the Regulator of Social Housing (RSH) or the Welsh Ministers). These are sometimes coupled with charitable housing trusts in the special sense explained in chapter 2. Fully mutual tenancies are also singled out, usually to the disadvantage of individual tenants but for the collective good of the membership.

9.3   Apart from the legal rules, the regulator requires that particular provisions be included in tenancy agreements sometimes approximating to public sector rights. The English regulator's tenancy standard (2012) requires that clear and accessible policies be published with written reasons given for decisions and with provision for appeals or review of decisions and for advice and assistance. Tenants must sometimes be consulted. Given the very large numbers of housing association tenants, there is a particular risk that, where standardised tenancy agreements are used or where associations copy each other's provisions, drafting mistakes may have serious financial consequences.

9.4   After the Welsh Assembly acquired power to make primary legislation from 2011, Welsh law has begun to develop its own regime. Accordingly, the main UK legislation – Housing Acts 1985, 1988 and 1996 – has been amended. Under the Housing (Wales) Act 2014 private domestic landlords are required to be registered and licenced with a licencing authority. However, this does not apply to RSLs nor to fully mutual housing associations.[2] Under Part 4 of the same Act, special standards for social housing apply to local authority tenancies. The Welsh Ministers can impose standards on housing associations registered with them.[3] There is a distinctive rent regime. As

---

1 See paras 8.74, 9.8 and 9.38.
2 Housing (Wales) Act 2014 ss4, 5, 6, 8.
3 Housing Act 1996 s33A.

we saw in the previous chapter, the Renting Homes (Wales) Act 2016 will introduce more fundamental changes. The following areas feature special housing association rules.

Security of tenure/eviction

9.5 The ground of eviction depends on whether the tenant is a residual secure tenant or an assured tenant. As we saw in the previous chapter, an assured shorthold tenancy can be terminated without reasons being given and there are special provisions for certain type of probationary tenancy. We also saw that fully mutual tenancies both residuary and contemporary are without security of tenure in England. In Wales, a landlord can opt to confer assured tenancy status on a fully mutual tenant.

9.6 The general protection against eviction without a court order provided by the Protection from Eviction Act 1977 applies to housing associations as it does to private tenants. Certain kinds of tenant or licencee ('excluded' tenancy or licence) can be evicted without a court order.[4] Most of these cases (such as provision for asylum-seekers and 'short-life' arrangements for squatters) apply equally to other landlords. However, a hostel provided by a PRP, RSL or a charitable housing trust in the special sense defined in chapter 2, is an excluded licence. Where the dwelling is occupied by a trespasser including a person whose tenancy or licence has expired, the defence of 'intending residential occupier', to the offence of violent entry applies to a person who has a tenancy or licence granted by a PRP or RSL. There must be a certificate from the landlord and no more than reasonable force must be used.[5]

9.7 The English regulator's tenancy standard requires that general needs tenants be given either a periodic secure or assured tenancy or a fixed term of at least five years or, exceptionally, a fixed term for at least two years following a probationary tenancy. However, someone who was a social housing tenant when Localism Act 2011 s154 came into force (15 January 2012) and who has remained so ever since must be given security of tenure as good as it was before that date unless he or she chooses to move to an ' affordable rent' tenancy (below).

---

4 See Protection from Eviction Act 1977 ss3, 3A, 5(1B).
5 Criminal Law Act 1977 s12A(6), (7)(d). The drafting of section 12A(6)(a) seems obscure, perhaps circular, and the right may not apply to a tenant with less than two years still to run.

(Section 154 introduced the concept of a two-year 'flexible tenancy'.) In the light of recent changes in government policy in favour of fixed terms, it may be that this standard is subject to revision.

9.8 As regards the statutory grounds for eviction under the Housing Act 1985, in the case of a secure tenancy there are two grounds peculiar to housing associations.[6] These are: mandatory Ground 11: tenant's occupation conflicts with objects of a charity; and discretionary ground 14: any housing association or housing trust letting only for occupation by people with special housing needs and, either there is no longer such a person in occupation or the occupant has been offered a secure tenancy by a local authority, and the landlord requires the dwelling for occupation by another such person. Under both grounds, suitable alternative accommodation must be available. Other grounds relating to supported housing apply also to local authority landlords.

9.9 Ground 10A (mandatory subject to suitable alternative accommodation) applies where the landlord requires the dwelling as part of a redevelopment scheme. In the case of a PRP, this must be approved by the RSH.[7] The Housing Act 1985 seems unclear in respect of Wales, but presumably the approval of the Welsh Ministers is required.

9.10 As regards assured tenancies, there are two special housing association grounds for possession in England. These apply to a PRP and a charitable housing trust in the special sense defined in chapter 2. Ground 6 is a mandatory ground where a superior landlord intends to demolish the dwelling or carry out works, thus facilitating short life schemes.[8] Either the tenant does not agree to alternative arrangements or these would not be practicable. Ground 14A (domestic violence) is a discretionary ground. It applies where a partner (ie spouse, civil partner or cohabitee living as husband and wife or civil partner), have left the dwelling due to violence or threats of violence from the tenant to self or family. The tenant need not be living at the dwelling.

9.11 As regards other grounds, problems arise in connection with the overlapping grounds for non-payment of rent. Ground 8 is a mandatory ground applying if the rent is more than eight weeks in arrears if paid weekly or fortnightly, or two months unpaid if payable monthly. Other periods apply to longer terms. Ground 10 is a discretionary ground applying to any rent arrears; and ground 11 is also discretion-

---

6 Housing Act 1985 Sch 2.
7 Housing Act 1985 Sch 2 Part V para 6.
8 Housing Act 1988 Sch 2.

ary applying to persistent non-payment of rent. Where a tenant falls within Ground 8, some housing associations use this draconian power to evict the tenant rather than a discretionary ground. Here once again, the competing models of the housing association come to the fore – namely the commercial and the social/paternalistic.

9.12 In extreme cases, reaching first for Ground 8 may violate Article 8 of the European Convention on Human Rights (ECHR) (right to respect for family life) as being disproportionate (below) since a less extreme option is available. Indeed, this was the origin of *R (Weaver) v London and Quadrant Housing Trust*[9] the leading case on the application of the Human Rights Act 1998 to housing associations. Unfortunately the substantive issue was not decided in that case. The choice of Ground 8 might also be challenged by judicial review if the landlord has adopted a policy of providing maximum security. While earlier Housing Corporation guidance required the use of Ground 8 only as a last resort, apart from requiring policies to be published, the RSH's tenancy standards do not engage with the matter.[10]

9.13 The same grounds apply to tenancies of dwellings in Wales. There is, however, an additional mandatory ground applying to dwellings in Wales – this is where a fully mutual housing association of any kind has opted into the assured tenancy regime under the Housing (Wales) Act 2014. The ground is that the association has defaulted on its mortgage. The tenant must have been notified before the tenancy was granted that this ground is available.[11]

Rents

Introduction

9.14 Rent levels of social housing tenants are subject to limited direct statutory controls. However, they are subject to considerable indirect control by the government by means of public funding incentives and to control by the regulator through the imposition of standards under the Housing and Regeneration Act (HRA) 2008. These controls are discussed together with other sources of finance in chapter 14. In this chapter, we shall outline the legal framework.

---

9 [2009] EWCA Civ 587.
10 See generally Tenant Services Authority, *Rent arrears management practices in the housing association sector*, 2010.
11 Housing (Wales) Act 2014 ss137, 138 adding Ground 2A to Housing Act 1988 Sch 2 Part 1.

9.15 Surviving residual regime tenancies of PRPs, charitable housing trusts in the special sense defined in chapter 2, and co-operative housing associations (other than co-ownerships), are subject to a special housing association fair rent regime under the Rent Act 1977.[12] In the main, this mirrors the private sector regime under that Act.

9.16 Issues remain unresolved as to the extent, if at all, that public subsidy can be taken into account in assessing the level of fair rent and whether comparison can be made with similar private sector dwellings. It was held in *Royal British Legion HA v East Midlands Rent Assessment Panel*[13] that it was irrelevant that the association had received a grant for the dwelling in question since this was a 'personal circumstance' excluded by the Act. However, the general nature of social housing rents can be taken into account not merely economic matters.[14] It is likely that the rent levels for the surviving tenancies under this regime have by now converged with contemporary regime rents since, in deciding what is a fair rent, comparison can be made between the two and with other similar dwellings in the locality.[15]

9.17 As far as the general law is concerned, contemporary regime tenancies being assured tenancies are not subject to external control. An assured periodic tenancy is subject to the protection of a rent tribunal but only if there is no rent review provision in the tenancy agreement.[16] Fully mutual tenancies and licences, not being assured tenancies, are not limited at all.

9.18 As regards rent increases, the statutory requirements that a rent review can take place after 52 weeks and is subject to at least one month's notice, can be replaced by a provision in the tenancy agreement.[17] This creates the risk, magnified in the practice of standardised tenancy agreements, of faulty drafting. For example, attempts to reassure tenants by stating that rents will not be increased within a year have backfired by specifying an annual increase date of 1 April each year – the notorious '364 days' issue.[18]

---

12 Rent Act 1977 ss15, 16, 86, 87.
13 (1989) 21 HLR 482.
14 See *R (Spath Holme Ltd) v Secretary of State for the Environment, Transport and the Regions* [2000] 1 All ER 884.
15 See *Re Leeds Federated HA* (1981) 260 EG 813; *Re Heathview Tenants Cooperative* (1980) 258 EG 645; *Spath Holme Ltd v Greater Manchester and Lancashire Rent Assessment Committee (No 1)* (1996) 28 HLR 107.
16 Housing Act 1988 ss13, 14.
17 Housing Act 1988 s13(1)(b).
18 See *Riverside Housing Association v White* [2007] UKHL 20.

Statutory limits: the rent reduction regime

9.19 Temporary limits on rent levels for registered providers in England were imposed by the Welfare Reform and Work Act (WRWA) 2016.[19] This scheme is due to end in 2020/21. It applies only to rented accommodation, as opposed to shared ownership and other low-cost home ownership schemes.[20] Housing associations have to *reduce* rents of their social housing in each 'relevant year' from 2016 until 2019 by one per cent. This is based on the rent payable on 8 July 2015, although the secretary of state could and has consented to a different date in particular cases.[21] These provisions are enforceable by adding them to the grounds on which regulatory action can be taken under the HRA 2008.[22] The Act also introduces an implied term into the relevant tenancy agreements enabling the use of its powers without notice.[23] These provisions will be discussed in more detail in chapter 14.

9.20 For the last few years, until temporarily displaced by the WRWA 2016, it has been government policy to permit housing associations to raise social and affordable rents by an average of Retail Price Index (RPI) plus one per cent. When the WRWA 2016 scheme ends in 2020, the government intends to revert to the lower CPI (Consumer Price Index) plus one per cent for five years.[24]

9.21 In addition, under Housing Act 1996 ss219, 220 the secretary of state can cap service charges made by PRPs, and charitable housing trusts in receipt of government funding. The Welsh Ministers exercise the same power in respect of RSLs. There is a cap in England (originally £15,000 in London and £10,000 elsewhere) from 12 August 2014 on service charges relating to government-funded works of repair maintenance or improvement. Social landlords my also reduce or waive such service charges on the ground of exceptional hardship.[25]

---

19 WRWA 2016 s23.
20 WRWA 2016 s24.
21 MCHLG, *General social housing rents permitted review date consent*, 2016.
22 WRWA 2016 s30.
23 WRWA 2016 s28.
24 See below para 14.21.
25 Social Landlords Mandatory Reduction of Service Charges (England) Directions 2014; Social Landlords Discretionary Reduction of Service Charges (England) Directions 2014.

Regulatory rent controls

9.22 Within the broad envelope of the law, the Homes and Communities Agency (HCA, now Homes England) has imposed detailed rent controls through its funding powers, implemented by the regulator as binding standards. The government has designated particular rent regimes, which in turn are used in subordinate legislation.[26] As well as being used for the allocation of public funding, these apply to the rights of tenants relating to transfers and the 'right to acquire'.

9.23 The main categories are 'social rents' and 'affordable rents'. There are also 'intermediate rents' (see paras 1.61–1.64). The terms 'social rent' or 'social rented housing' refers to the lowest rent levels. A social rent is intended to approximate to a local authority rent and is about 50 per cent of market value (excluding any service charge). For political purposes, both general needs housing and supported housing of various kinds are the subject of social rents.

9.24 'Affordable' rents are rents subject to an agreement under specific programmes dating from 2011 between an association and the HCA or Greater London Authority (GLA) as funders. They must be not more than 80 per cent of market rent level or the social rent level if this is higher.[27] 'Affordable rents' also apply to shared ownership.

9.25 An 'intermediate' rent can be above 'affordable' level but still below market levels – for example, the former 'key workers' housing policy. All these rent levels therefore constitute 'social housing'. A variation of the intermediate rent – the 'mortgage rescue rent' which enabled struggling home owners to sell their dwellings to a housing association – was terminated in 2014. Housing associations were also permitted to use intermediate rents accompanied by assured shorthold tenancies as a temporary holding mechanism when letting properties, which were intended for sale, which could not be sold following the market collapse in 2008.

9.26 Housing associations can apply for government funding in each category. Government allocations have recently been directed towards more affluent tenants, possibly with a view to influencing swing voters, a policy reminiscent of the Westminster council house gerrymandering of the 1990s.[28]

---

26 See Wilson, *Rent setting: social housing in England*, HC Briefing Paper, November 2017.
27 Social Housing Rents (Exceptions and Miscellaneous Provisions) Regulations 2016 reg 19.
28 See *Porter v McGill* [2002] 1 All ER 465.

9.27　In 2016/17, government-funded social housing starts in England for affordable housing was 17,159 and for social rents 1,409. This was the lowest share of state-funded housing since records began in 2009. Shared ownership starts increased by 52 per cent from the previous year to 9,184 and there were 7,147 full market value projects.[29] In October 2017 the government announced a proposal to increase funding for affordable rents.[30] However, in a recent policy shift, more attention seems to have been given to the social rent level.[31]

Rents in Wales

9.28　The approach is broadly similar for Welsh bodies. The Welsh government's *Policy for social housing rents*[32] is based upon fairness in the distribution of housing. This applies both to general needs and sheltered housing at 'social' rents, provided by RSLs with more than 100 dwellings and is irrespective of funding. A social rent means a rent within the policy and is based on the average weekly rent charged by all social landlords including local authorities. Under the policy until 2018/19, rent increases are limited to CPI plus 1.5 per cent. A target band of the various types of housing is set for each association subject to the policy.

9.29　Affordable housing does not feature, but outside the rent policy 'intermediate' housing includes rents above social levels. Accordingly, social housing in Wales is classified by the Welsh government as 'social renting' under the rent policy; 'other social housing' meaning special types of housing specifically excluded from the rent limits these being self-contained supported housing, bedsits, hostels and high care provision. Of Welsh social housing, 95 per cent falls within the rent policy.[33]

9.30　There is also 'non-social housing' which includes intermediate rents; home purchase schemes; shared ownership; market rents; flexible tenancies for the elderly; various home purchase schemes; and investment property.[34] Again these are not subject to rent limits. (This classification does not relate to the statutory definitions of

---

29　See Homes England, *Housing statistics*, 1 April 2017 to 31 March 2018.
30　MHCLG Press Release, 4 October 2017.
31　See Homes England, *Shared Ownership and Affordable Rent Homes Programme 2016 to 2021: addendum to prospectus*, June 2018, paras 7–8.
32　2017.
33　See Welsh Government, *Social landlords housing stock and rents*, 2017.
34　See Welsh Government, *Social landlords housing stock and rents*, 2017.

social housing discussed in chapter 2 under which in Wales all housing provided by an RSL is social housing.)

Succession

9.31 There are no special statutory provisions for housing association *secure* tenants in respect of the (diminishing) rights of succession available to members of a tenant's family when the tenant dies.[35] In the case of assured tenancies, including those granted by housing associations, a spouse, civil partner or unmarried partner[36] can succeed to a *periodic* tenancy. However, many housing associations grant wider rights of succession in their tenancy agreements. The RSH's tenancy standard (2012) requires only that associations publish clear and accessible discretionary succession policies that take account of the needs of vulnerable household members.[37]

9.32 There are special statutory provisions relating to assured tenancies in England, where the landlord is a PRP. These are slightly more generous than for other assured tenancies. They apply to a tenancy created on or after 1 April 2012 when the relevant parts of the Localism Act 2011 came into force, and are similar to the rights of secure tenants:[38]

1) In the case of a fixed-term tenancy for not less than two years (thus excluding some assured shortholds and corresponding to a flexible tenancy) – the tenant's spouse, civil partner or unmarried partner occupying the premises as his or her only or principal home immediately before the tenant's death, qualifies as a successor.
2) In the case both of a periodic tenancy and a fixed-term for not less than two years – a sole tenant can nominate a successor without there being a spouse, civil partner or unmarried partner occupying the premises, but only if the tenancy agreement expressly authorises this.
3) If the deceased tenant is a successor – there is no further right of succession. Instead, the tenancy agreement itself can designate a person 'to succeed a successor to the tenancy'.[39]

---

35 See Housing and Planning Act 2016 Sch 8 (not yet in force).
36 Housing and Planning Act 2016 s17(4).
37 RSH Tenancy Standard para 2.2.1, i.
38 Housing Act 1988 s17(1A)–(1E).
39 Housing Act 1988 s17(1E)(b).

9.33 Depending on the level of rent, a shared ownership tenant might be an assured tenant. However, as a fixed-term, a shared ownership tenancy is not subject to the general statutory right of succession and the Localism Act 2011 provisions do not apply.[40] The law regarding succession to a shared ownership tenancy therefore has no special housing association provisions and depends on the general law and the terms of the lease itself.

9.34 It might be noted that, under the general law, succession to a shared ownership lease is complicated by the possibility that, if there is no specific nomination clause in the lease, any established right to a payment, being only a contractual right, could be left by will to a different person (maybe accidently if land is left separately) from the lease itself. This would also apply if the deceased had an assured *periodic* tenancy (ie if the term of the lease had expired).[41] In the case of a residual regime shared ownership tenancy, the lease devolves under the general law since there are no statutory succession provisions. At present, few if any leases are near their expiry date.

9.35 Older shared ownership leases may provide for the lease to be terminated on the tenant's death. Such leases are converted to 90-year terms which can be brought to an end by at least one month's notice after the tenant's death.[42] However, since the tenancy will be an assured tenancy or, if at a low rent, a 'long tenancy',[43] this can be only be brought to an end on the statutory grounds.

Transfer/exchange of tenancies

9.36 An exchange of tenancy can be an assignment of the existing tenancy, in which case, if the new landlord's legal structure is the same, the same status continues. Alternatively, there can be a surrender of the tenancy followed by the grant of a new tenancy. Here, a previous secure tenant can remain a secure tenant only if the exchange is within the same landlord.[44]

9.37 As regards the residual regime, a secure tenancy cannot generally be assigned except under certain statutory family provisions and also to a family member who would qualify as a statutory successor to the

---

40 Housing Act 1988 s17(7).
41 Above para 8.26.
42 Law of Property Act 1925 s149(6).
43 Above paras 8.58 and 8.60.
44 Above para 8.40.

tenancy on the tenant's death.[45] However, a residual secure tenant, other than an introductory or flexible tenant, has a right to exchange dwellings by way of assignment to another secure tenant subject to the consent of the each landlord. An exchange can also be between a secure and an assured tenancy where the assured tenancy landlord is a PRP, RSL or charitable housing trust in the special sense defined in chapter 2.[46]

9.38 Consent to an exchange by the landlord of a secure tenancy can be refused only on certain grounds, similar to those for obtaining possession including the same special housing association grounds (above).[47] In addition, where a housing association of any kind manages local authority housing under a management agreement on a 'semi-mutual' basis (ie at least half the members are tenants and vice versa), consent can be refused if a proposed assignee is not a member and refuses to become one.[48]

9.39 An assured tenant is not required to obtain consent from its landlord under these provisions. However, it is an implied term of a periodic assured or assured shorthold tenancy that assignment requires the landlord's consent subject to specific arrangements in the tenancy agreement.[49] Consent must not be unreasonably refused.[50] The difference between the two forms of consent is important, since under the implied term provision the assignment is valid but there is liability for breach of contract.[51] Moreover, where the landlord association is acting in a public law capacity, as will be the case where the tenancy is part of a government sponsored scheme, there is an interaction between this private law contractual power to consent and its public law duty to act fairly and reasonably. We discussed this in chapter 7.

9.40 A fixed-term tenancy can be assigned unless the tenancy agreement requires the landlord's consent. As regards the contemporary regime, therefore, assignments depend primarily on the tenancy agreement.

9.41 Localism Act 2011 s158 is intended to deal with the new generation of fixed-term tenancies. This applies where one of the

---

45 Housing Act 1985 s91 as amended.
46 Housing Act 1985 s92.
47 Housing Act 1985 Sch 3.
48 Housing Act 1985 Ground 10.
49 Housing Act 1988 s15(1).
50 Landlord and Tenant Act 1988 s1.
51 See *Sanctuary Housing Association v Baker (No 1)* (1997) 30 HLR 809.

tenancies concerned is an assured shorthold tenancy or local authority 'flexible tenancy', one other is a secure tenancy or an ordinary assured tenancy, and all other tenancies, if any, also fall into these categories. Exchanges made after the Localism Act 2011 came into force (15 January 2012 in England) do not involve an assignment of the existing tenancy but a surrender followed by the grant of a new tenancy on the same terms. Each tenant must first request the existing landlord in writing to consent to the arrangement and all relevant landlords must consent.

9.42 A landlord can refuse to comply with a request only on certain grounds.[52] Two of these are peculiar to housing associations: first, where the landlord is a charity and the new tenancy would conflict with its charitable objects; second, where the tenancy is provided to cater for a housing need, other than a financial need that is especially difficult to meet.[53] Other grounds for refusal relevant to a housing association are briefly as follows: unpaid rent or other breaches of the agreement; possession proceedings in progress, or various other court orders in force; the new dwelling is unsuitable or is designed to meet the need of the disabled, or is supported housing. The new tenancy must be either an old style secure tenancy or an ordinary assured tenancy depending on the landlord's capacity to grant either kind.

9.43 However, as part of a continuing policy of weakening the rights of tenants the Transfer of Tenancies and Right to Acquire (Exclusion) Regulations 2012[54] removes the Localism Act 2011 right from many assured shorthold tenancies. The exclusions are as follows:

a) assured shortholds for less than two years;
b) periodic assured shortholds;
c) assured shortholds where the rent payable is an affordable rent, an intermediate rent, a 'mortgage rescue rent' (a scheme now defunct to help people who could not afford to keep up their mortgage repayments following the 2008 financial crisis), or a shared ownership rent.[55]

---

52 Localism Act 2011 s159, Sch 14.
53 This also applies to a housing trust in the special sense defined in chapter 2 even if not charitable.
54 Transfer of Tenancies and Right to Buy (Exclusion) Regulations 2012 SI No 696 reg 3.
55 This would be where the fixed-term tenancy comes to an end – see Housing Act 1988 ss19A, 20.

9.44 The Housing and Planning Act 2016, the relevant provisions of which are not yet into force, will make further changes in England to the disadvantage of tenants. In particular the new tenancy can be granted on whatever terms the landlord decides. The tenant may therefore have less security than before. To prevent retroactivity, if the existing tenancy was an 'old style' secure tenancy or an assured tenancy created before the relevant provisions of the Housing and Planning Act 2016 come into force and at least one of the landlords concerned has not yet complied with the request, the existing position (above) remains. The secretary of state can exclude particular kinds of assured shorthold tenancy from these provisions.

9.45 The RSH's 'Tenancy Standard' (2012)[56] links assignments with allocations generally in particular with issues of under occupation and overcrowding. PRPs are required to cooperate with local housing authorities for example by having a system of common registers. The emphasis is on process without any substantive rights. In particular polices must be published and the criteria for decisions clearly set out. Reasons must be given for decisions and advice provided. Tenants must be given free access to a comprehensive internet mutual exchange service and there must be 'reasonable support' in using the service to tenants who have no internet access. Most associations follow a similar practice. Housing associations usually exclude starter tenancies and other assured shortholds from the right to exchange.

Shared ownership

9.46 The assignment of a shared ownership tenancy depends on the terms of the lease. The regulator's model leases are intended to ensure that the dwelling or its value stays within the social sector. They prohibit assignment of part of the dwelling, and any underletting or parting with possession. They prohibit other assignments without the landlord's consent. Unless the lease is sold at a reduced price this being the portion of the value already acquired and to a person nominated by the landlord, the seller must pay the landlord on demand the portion not 'staircased'. There are, however, exceptions to the latter requirement. They include assignment by will or intestacy, assignment under certain statutory family provisions and mortgages. Thus shared ownership leases are marketable.

56 Para 2.1.

9.47 Where a shared ownership lease began on or after 1 January 1995, if the landlord transfers the dwelling to another body, the shared ownership obligations and rights automatically pass to the new landlord under the Landlord and Tenant (Covenants) Act 1995 since, under that Act,[57] a covenant includes any term, condition or obligation of the tenancy. If the tenancy began before that date, the position is more complex since the term requiring a money payment may not automatically attach to the lease and rank only as an ordinary contract. If this is so, the original landlord remains liable after any transfer unless the obligation is specifically transferred.

The right to buy: secure tenants

Overview

9.48 Some housing association sitting tenants have a right to buy their dwellings, but this is somewhat random depending both on the type of housing association and on the shifts in government policy since the right was first created by the Thatcher government in 1980.

9.49 The right to buy in common with local authority secure tenants applies to some secure tenants of PRPs and RSLs. It does not apply to tenants of charitable housing associations,[58] nor to fully mutual associations,[59] nor to housing associations that have never received public funding from the main statutory sources.[60] Thus if an association changes its status from mutual to non-mutual, or charitable to non-charitable, or vice versa, the tenant will gain or lose the right to buy accordingly.[61] Unlike the case where a dwelling is transferred to another landlord (below), there seem to be no specific provisions protecting established rights in this kind of case. Some housing associations have made their own schemes to sell dwellings to sitting tenants.

9.50 The right to buy does not usually apply to shared ownership tenancies since they are not secure tenancies.[62] Dwellings particularly suited for the elderly are also exempt. In this case, there is a

---

57 Landlord and Tenant (Covenants) Act 1995 s28(1).
58 Housing Act 1985 s118.
59 Housing Act 1985 Sch 5 para 2.
60 Housing Act 1985 Sch 5 para 3.
61 See *Bhai v Black Roof Community Housing Association Ltd* [2001] 2 All ER 865.
62 Above para 8.73.

right of appeal, in England to a tribunal and in Wales to the secretary of state.[63]

9.51 There is no longer any accompanying right to a mortgage or to shared ownership terms, but there is provision for 'rent to mortgage' schemes under which the former landlord takes a lower payment and holds a charge over the property and the former tenant makes repayment at a rate equivalent to the former rent.[64] A dwelling subject to this scheme remains 'social housing' under the HRA 2008 until the full amount is paid off.[65]

The preserved right to buy: change of landlord

9.52 The 'preserved right to buy' applies to a 'qualifying person' who is entitled to a right to buy, where the dwelling-house is disposed of to a private sector body – that is, a body not capable of granting a secure tenancy.[66] This seems to include a housing association other than in the special cases where a new secure tenancy can be granted.[67] Most housing associations which are excluded from the ordinary right to buy, namely charities and non grant aid bodies, are subject to the preserved right to buy.[68] A fully mutual association is exempt.

9.53 A qualifying person is the previous secure tenant or a joint tenant. A family member who is a statutory successor (above) is also a qualifying tenant, if the deceased tenant was an assured tenant with a preserved right to buy. A person to whom the dwelling is transferred in matrimonial proceedings also qualifies.[69] The preserved right to buy carries with it whatever requirements of residence etc have been met at the date of the transfer.

9.54 As an obvious safeguard against manipulation, a private sector landlord cannot dispose of part only of its interest without the approval of the secretary of state. Somewhat illogically, this does not apply to a PRP even though the exception was inserted as part of an

---

63 Housing Act 1985 s10 and Sch 5 para 11; Housing Act 2004 s181.
64 Housing Act 1985 s143 inserted by Leasehold Reform, Housing and Urban Development Act (LRHUDA) 1993.
65 Above para 1.67.
66 Housing and Planning Act 1986 s8; Housing Act 1988 s127; Housing Act 1985 ss171A–171H, Sch 5 paras 1–3 as amended by SI 1993 No 2241.
67 Above para 8.40.
68 Housing (Preservation of Right to Buy) Regulations 1993 SI No 2241; Housing (Preservation of Right to Buy) (Amendment) Regulations 1999 SI No 1213. But this cannot override the trusts of a particular charity, HA 1988 s127(3).
69 Housing Act 1985 s171B.

agenda designed to make housing associations more like private sector bodies.[70]

9.55 The preserved right to buy therefore arises if a local authority or housing association tenant with a right to buy (but not the dwelling) is transferred after 1 April 1989 to a housing association or to a private landlord at any time since, in such a case, the tenant becomes an assured tenant.[71] Where the original landlord was exempted from the right to buy (above), then, whatever the position of the new landlord, the preserved right to buy is of course also excluded, as it may be in other cases specified by the secretary of state.[72]

9.56 The preserved right to buy continues while the qualified person remains in occupation of the dwelling as his or her only or main residence. It is not affected by any further transfers of the dwelling to another landlord unless it is transferred to a secure tenancy landlord, in which case it may be replaced by a new right to buy.[73] It is registerable with the Land Registry, and failure to do so attracts compensation. Thus, the preserved right to buy may bind subsequent purchasers or inheritors of the dwelling indefinitely. However, if the landlord has only a leasehold interest the preserved right to buy is lost if the lease ends.[74]

9.57 Where a tenant moves to a different dwelling, either by assignment or where a new tenancy is created, the following principles apply. Where there is a right to buy or a preserved right to buy, previous uninterrupted periods of residence in qualifying social housing can be aggregated:

1) If the *same* landlord grants a new tenancy to a tenant with the preserved right to buy, the carries this over to the new tenancy which becomes the 'qualifying dwelling' house for the purposes of the preserved right to buy.[75] (It may or may not be recalled that a *secure* tenant who moves within the same landlord remains a secure tenant and so keeps the original right to buy.)

2) If the tenant is granted a new tenancy by a different housing association or a private landlord, there is no right to buy since the tenancy will not be a secure tenancy because under the

70 Housing Act 1985 s171D(2ZA), inserted by Housing and Planning Act 2016 Sch 1.
71 Above para 8.39.
72 Housing Act 1985 s171A(3).
73 Housing Act 1985 s171D.
74 Housing Act 1985 s171E (if the landlord's act or omission caused the termination, the landlord must pay compensation).
75 Housing Act 1985 s171B(6).

contemporary regime the new landlord cannot create a secure tenancy. There is no preserved right to buy since the dwelling has not been disposed of. There is some protection. In proceedings brought on the ground of suitable alternative accommodation the court must refuse to make a possession order unless the accommodation offered falls within 1) (above) or the new landlord is a secure tenancy landlord.[76]

3) If a secure tenancy is assigned then, assuming the landlord's position is unchanged, the assignee will have his or her own right to buy. Except where the assignment is a statutory exchange made after the original tenant has served notice claiming to exercise the right to buy, the new tenant is treated as if the notice had been given by him or her.[77]

The right to acquire: assured tenants

9.58 An assured tenant has no right to buy but a watered down version – 'the right to acquire' – applies to some assured tenants of PRPs and RSLs.[78] It also applies to secure tenants of these bodies thus giving rights to some of those excluded from the right to buy itself. In particular, it does apply to charitable PRPs. Accordingly, the general restriction on charities selling land below market price does not apply to a PRP, although this does not override any specific restriction in the terms of the charity itself.[79] However, as with the right to buy, the right to acquire does not apply to fully mutual tenancies, nor to most shared ownership tenancies.

9.59 The dwelling must have at all times been owned by a PRP or public sector landlord and must have been 'publicly funded' in England or 'provided with public money in Wales'. (This includes a stock transfer from a local authority after 1 April 1997, when the Housing Act 1996 which created this right came into force. The difference between England and Wales relates to a power of the HCA in England to regard certain assistance as public funding.)[80]

9.60 The detailed provisions are similar to those of the right buy. However, the discount provisions are more flexible. The level of discount is set by the secretary of state or the Welsh Ministers and

---

76 Housing Act 1985 s171F.
77 Housing Act 1985 s136.
78 HRA 2008 ss180–191 (as amended); Housing Act 1996 s16 (as amended).
79 HRA 2008 ss188, 189.
80 HRA 2008 s181; Housing Act 1996 s16(2).

can vary locally. It cannot be greater than 50 per cent in England or 25 per cent in Wales.[81] The secretary of state and the Welsh Ministers have power to exclude the right to acquire in rural areas where they decide that there is a social housing shortage.[82]

9.61 As part of a continuing policy of weakening the rights of tenants, the Transfer of Tenancies and Right to Acquire (Exclusion) Regulations 2012[83] removes the right to acquire from certain assured shorthold tenancies. The exclusions are as follows:

a) assured shortholds for less than two years;
b) periodic assured shortholds;
c) assured shortholds where the rent payable is an intermediate rent or a 'mortgage rescue rent' (a scheme now defunct to help people who could not afford to keep up their mortgage repayments following the 2008 financial crisis).

The 'voluntary' right to buy

9.62 The Conservative government of 2012–15 proposed to extend the right to buy to housing association tenants. This could be achieved without primary legislation by voluntary arrangements. The proposal was highly controversial and resisted by most housing associations. Apart from a few pilot schemes, it was not pursued. However, the Housing and Planning Act 2016, the swansong of that government, enacted watered down 'voluntary' right to buy provisions under which the government can give financial assistance to a PRP that chooses to implement its own right to buy scheme. A pilot scheme is currently in place in the West and East Midlands.

Wales

9.63 The right to buy in Wales is more restrictive. The qualifying residence period is five years, as opposed to three years in England.[84] More drastically, a local housing authority after consultation can apply to the Welsh Ministers for a direction that the right to buy, the preserved right to buy and the right to acquire be suspended for up to five years.[85] While an application is being considered and while

81 Housing Act 1996 s17(1)(a); HRA 2008 s184.
82 Housing Act 1996 s17(1)(b); HRA 2008 s184.
83 SI 2012 No 696 reg 3.
84 Housing Act 1985 s119(A1), (1) as amended.
85 Housing (Wales) Measure 2011 ss1–6.

a direction is in force, any claims to exercise the right to buy and the other rights are suspended.[86]

9.64 An authority can apply for a direction only where it considers there to be a shortage of social housing in the area: 'the housing pressure condition'. For this purpose, all housing provided by a housing association (and indeed by a private body) is social housing in Wales as long as the body provides some housing below market rates.[87] The direction can relate to the whole or part of the area or to particular types of housing including a particular type of provider or even an individual provider.

9.65 Before applying for a direction, the authority must consult every social housing provider in the area concerned; representatives of tenants who the authority 'considers' to be affected; and other local housing authorities. Its application must include a draft directive, reasons for its application, proposals for other action which it intends to take to deal with the shortage of social housing in its area and details of its consultation. It can later apply following the same process for the scope of a direction to be enlarged or reduced, its time limit extended or for it to be revoked. However, if an application of any kind has been refused, the authority cannot reapply for two years.[88]

9.66 Unlike English housing law which is led by a central bureaucracy, this power is led at local level. The discretion of the Welsh Ministers is limited. They have no power to initiate action, they must consider an application if they think it contains all the information required by the measure and must refuse it if it does not unless the omission is 'immaterial or insignificant' in which case they have a discretion to consider it. They have a discretion to require the authority to provide further information.[89] The local authority must 'have regard to' any guidance issued by the Welsh Ministers'.[90]

9.67 The Welsh Ministers *must* make a direction if they are satisfied that the local authority has consulted properly, they agree with its

---

86 Housing Act 1985 ss122A, 122B; Housing (Preservation of Right to Buy) Regulations 1993 SI No 2241; Housing (Right to Acquire) Regulations 1997 SI No 619, as amended in both cases by Housing (Wales) Measure 2011 (Consequential Amendments to Subordinate Legislation) Order 2012 SI No 2090.
87 Housing (Wales) Measure 2011 s33.
88 Housing (Wales) Measure 2011 s29.
89 Housing (Wales) Measure 2011 s27.
90 Housing (Wales) Measure 2011 s30; see *Guidance for local housing authorities on applications to suspend the right to buy and related rights*, Welsh Government, 2012.

conclusion in favour of a direction and they consider that the authority's other proposals are likely to be effective.[91] However, they can refuse to make a direction if the authority fails to provide any further information requested or if the Welsh Ministers consider the authority's statutory Housing Strategy[92] to be inadequate in relation to the shortage of social housing. They seem to have no discretion to make or refuse to make a direction in any other circumstances.

9.68 These powers seem to be vulnerable to a Human Rights Act 1998 challenge in so far as they restrict an established right to buy. There seems to be no safeguards other than the general law of judicial review or the ombudsman's limited powers. On the other hand, under Protocol 1 of Article 2 of the ECHR, a property right can be overridden in the general interest provided that this is proportionate.

9.69 A much more drastic measure is the Abolition of the Right to Buy and Associated Rights (Wales) Act 2018. Under this Act, the right to buy, and the right to acquire, are abolished for all tenancies granted after the Act comes into force. This provision is to be brought into force by the Welsh Ministers, but for existing tenancies. Final abolition will be on 26 January 2019.

9.70 Before full abolition tenants of 'previously let social housing stock' – what the Welsh government calls 'new homes' meaning dwellings not let as social housing[93] during the six months before 24 March 2018 – are excluded from exercising the right to buy and the preserved right to buy.[94] There are, however, certain exemptions. These concern transfers of people with existing rights to buy. There is one specific housing association exemption where the dwelling was let by a PRP or RSL on an assured tenancy, other than a long tenancy and a person with a preserved right to buy in respect of another dwelling becomes the tenant after the Act takes effect.[95] (See *Information about the Abolition of the Right to Buy and Right to Acquire*, Welsh Government 2018).

---

91 Housing (Wales) Measure 2011 s5(4).
92 If this has been required by the Welsh Ministers under Local Government Act 2003 s87(1).
93 This means let on secure, introductory or demoted tenancies or where the dwelling was subject to the preserved right to buy.
94 Housing Act 1985 ss121ZA, 171B7 and Abolition of the Right to Buy and Associated Rights (Wales) Act 2018 ss2, 3.
95 Housing Act 1985 s121ZB.

Human rights

9.71 As we saw in chapter 3, the Human Rights Act 1998 applies directly to a decision by a housing association only where it is both exercising a public function and the particular act complained of it is public in character. This means either that the tenancy must either be integral to a function of the landlord that is enmeshed in central or local governmental activities or policies or the decision must involve the use of special statutory powers not available to a private landlord. Market rent schemes are unlikely to qualify even if they are promoted by government.

9.72 In respect of the particular *act*, even if the function is part of a public project, the particular act complained of must also be public. Thus a power deriving from a private law source such as the termination of a tenancy agreement is s a public act where it is inseparable from the public function.[96] By contrast, matters such as repairs may not qualify. We also saw in chapter 3 that the Human Rights Act 1998 can sometimes apply 'horizontally' even to a private function. However, in a private law context, even if the Human Rights Act does apply, the landlord's contractual rights appear to trump human rights grounds.[97] Thus a tenant's rights appear to be depend on the particular scheme under which he or she is housed in particular whether, 'social rent', 'affordable rent' or market rent. The main Human Rights Act 1998 ground protecting a tenant is provided by ECHR Article 8, which concerns respect for the enjoyment of a home that a person already has but does not give a right to be housed as such, nor to a right to stay in the home for any particular time.[98] Thus, although it does not depend on the existence of a property right, Article 8 may apply only once the occupier has taken possession of the home or perhaps when a tenancy or licence agreement is completed.

9.73 ECHR Article 8 gives a right not to be interfered with in the home, except on the specified grounds of public interest or the protection of the rights of others. The interference must be justified under clear rules of domestic law and must be proportionate. The most prominent Article 8 cases concern evictions. Article 8 also concerns poor housing conditions which raise health and safety concerns.

---

96 *R (Weaver) v London and Quadrant Housing Trust* [2009] EWCA Civ 587.
97 *McDonald v McDonald* [2016] UKSC 28, and *FJM v UK*, Application No 76202/16, 29 November 2018, above para 3.35.
98 *Chapman v UK* [2001] 10 BHRR 48 at [99].

9.74   In respect of evictions, there are comprehensive statutory provisions which are intended to balance the interests of landlord and tenant. It is often suggested, that compliance with these should be enough. However, after earlier vacillation it is clear that the circumstances of the individual case at the time of the, trial, including disputed facts, can be examined on human rights grounds in any possession proceedings.[99] In the case of an assured shorthold tenancy, Article 8 is particularly important because in domestic law the court has no discretion to refuse a possession order and the landlord does not have to give reasons.

9.75   The statutory shorthold tenancy provisions in themselves have been held to be compliant with both Article 8 and Article 6 (right to a fair trial) of the ECHR. In *Poplar HARCA v Donoughue*[100] a tenant challenged her eviction on the ground that the assured shorthold tenancy provisions violated her rights under the Human Rights Act 1998 by making her homeless. The Court of Appeal held that the Act applied, but it would nevertheless not interfere. Lord Woolf CJ said[101] that:

> ... the economic and other implications of any policy in this area are extremely complex and far-reaching. This is an area where ... the courts must treat the decisions of Parliament as to what is in the public interest with particular deference.

Thus a tenant only has a limited chance of success. There is a 'high threshold', meaning that, provided that the statutory procedures are followed, it is only where the tenant raises a 'seriously arguable' case that a decision is challengeable.[102] Thus in most cases the landlord association does not have to justify its decision to evict beyond compliance with relevant statutory requirements. The court will balance the whole range of the landlord's public responsibilities in assessing compliance with Article 8, including allocation priorities against the tenant's circumstances and conduct.[103]

---

99 *Manchester City Council v Pinnock* [2011] 2 AC 104; *Hounslow LBC v Powell* [2011] 2 AC 186; *Southend-on-Sea BC v Armour* [2014] EWCA Civ 231.
100 [2001] 4 All ER 604.
101 At [69].
102 *Powell* (above note 99) at [33], [90]–[94]; *Pinnock* (above note 99) at [52]; *Riverside Group Ltd v Thomas* [2012] EWHC 169 (QB); *West Kent Housing Association Ltd v Haycraft* [2012] EWCA Civ 276; *R (JL) v Secretary of State for Defence* [2013] EWCA Civ 449; *Lawal v Circle 33 Housing Trust* [2014] EWCA Civ 1514.
103 See *Powell* (note 99) at [37]; see eg *Armour* (note 99 above); *Turner v Enfield LBC* [2018] EWHC 1431 (QB); *Thurrock BC v West* [2012] EWCA Civ 1435.

9.76 As we saw in chapter 7, Article 8 does not usually apply to an application for a tenancy but may in exceptional circumstances apply to an application or to decision to refuse consent to an exchange of tenancy or to a transfer or renewal. This is where a tenant may face serious disruption to family relationships such as separation from children or parents.

9.77 Article 8 also requires that the tenancy agreement enables the tenant to exercise the normal amenities associated with occupying a home. Thus while transfer or subletting or taking in lodgers other than family members may be prohibited, lawful visitors cannot be restricted. The tenancy agreement cannot authorise entry to the premises by the landlord or others without reasonable notice or on reasonable grounds such as an emergency or to protect the vulnerable or to safeguard the landlord's property. Thus the various 'review' practices instituted by housing associations which involve visiting the tenant at home may be vulnerable to challenge under Article 8. A visit must be carefully tailored so that its purpose does not go beyond protecting the legitimate interests of the landlord and its conduct is proportionate.

9.78 Article 8 is not concerned with meeting prescribed standards of amenities and repair as such. Thus a breach of regulatory standards is not in itself relevant. However, in an extreme case where the home lacks basic amenities or protection against the elements, or creates a health risk or the special needs of an elderly or disabled tenant are not met, Article 8 may be invoked.[104] Article 8 also applies to a failure to prevent noise or other anti-social behaviour and to a failure to prevent environmental hazards in areas subject to the landlord's control. Finally, Article 8 applies where measures to collect arrears of rent go beyond what is proportionate, namely the usual lawful procedures, for example by 'naming and shaming policies'. The keeping of pets as such does not fall within the ECHR.[105] However, it has been suggested that the imposition of a new restriction on existing pets might do so as would a provision preventing assistance dogs.[106] Article 5 (deprivation of liberty), raises difficult issues in connection with secure accommodation for mental patients concerning the thin line between deprivation which is a violation and 'restriction' of liberty which is not. This overlaps with Article 8 since both

---

104 See generally, Equality and Human Rights Commission, *Human rights at home: guidance for social housing providers* (2011) and *Bernard v Enfield LBC* [2002] EWHC 2282 (Admin).
105 *Artingstoll v UK* (1995) 19 EHRR CD92.
106 Equality and Human Rights Commission, above notes 15,16 and 104.

Particular rights 211

deprivation and restriction of liberty may interfere with normal social relationships. The courts have been troubled by the variety of conditions involved, ranging from supervised freedom to complete confinement. The Strasbourg cases are uncertain. It is likely that Article 5 applies to a housing association even if it is acting in a private capacity since this right is so fundamental as to have direct horizontal effect (above). This is discussed in chapter 10.

9.79 Other provisions of the ECHR may come into play. Article 6, right to a fair trial in relation to 'civil rights and obligations', applies to the eviction of a tenant and to other decisions affecting the rights under the tenancy agreement. This broadens the scope of the ECHR into, for instance, transfer decisions. Article 6 requires procedural fairness looked at in the context of the process as a whole including the existence of other safeguards such as judicial review and the ombudsman.

9.80 There must be adequate reasons for decisions, an opportunity to cross-examine, the assistance of a lawyer and an independent assessment of issues of fact. An internal review by a person other than the original decision maker may satisfy this as long as there is a further independent safeguard in the shape of an appeal to the court or judicial review.[107] However, the scope of judicial review of facts may be too limited for this purpose in a case where the decision depends on findings of particular facts such as breach of a tenancy agreement.[108]

9.81 *R (Gilboy) v Liverpool City Council*[109] concerned a decision to downgrade a secure tenancy into a demoted tenancy. The Court of Appeal held that a combination of an internal review and judicial review satisfied Article 6. This was due to the primarily discretionary nature of the process which did not depend on any specific findings of fact.[110] It was held that the same would apply to an 'introductory tenancy' and so, we might infer, to a housing association starter tenancy.

9.82 In particular Article 3, prohibition of 'inhuman or degrading treatment', could apply where housing conditions are intolerable and the victim would otherwise face destitution.[111] Banning meetings on premises controlled by the landlord might infringe Articles 10 and

---

107 See *Runa Begum v Tower Hamlets BC* [2003] 1 All ER 731; *R (McLellan) v Bracknell Forest BC* [2001] EWCA Civ 1510.
108 See *Tsfayo v UK* (60860/00) (2009) 48 EHRR 18.
109 [2009] 3 WLR 300.
110 At [51].
111 See *Anufrijeva v Southwark LBC* [2004] QB 1124; *R (Limbuela) v Secretary of State for the Home Department* [2005] UKHL 66 (asylum-seeker).

11: freedoms of expression and assembly. Restrictions on aerials or satellite dishes might infringe Article 10 or even Article 9, freedom of religion, if the tenant is unable to receive significant transmissions.[112] Article 1 of Protocol 1 of the ECHR, enjoyment of property, may also come into play. However, it is doubtful whether this adds anything to an Article 8 challenge since it also requires a fair balance between the property right and the public interest.

9.83 The Human Rights Act 1998 also applies to allocation decisions, albeit in a limited way. Since there is no right or entitlement to housing as such, neither Article 8 nor Article 6 apply directly.[113] However, Article 14 (protection against discrimination), applies when an issue is 'within the ambit' of (meaning substantially connected to), another Article of the ECHR.[114] The grounds of discrimination are widely defined and open-ended. They include grounds 'such as sex, race, colour, language, religion, political or other opinion, national or social origin, association with a national minority, property, birth or other status'.

9.84 The meaning of 'other status' is obscure. Apart from characteristics imposed by law such as marriage, nationality, residential or immigration, it has been held to include matters which broadly fall within the notion of 'personal identity' such as age, sexual or gender orientation and family membership.[115] It may also include membership of an organisation such as a profession or trade union.[116] Thus allocation procedures must not discriminate directly or indirectly, for example by creating language or internet access problems.

Judicial review

9.85 A tenant, or indeed anyone with a genuine interest in the matter, can apply for judicial review, but only where the association is exercising a 'public function'. This is the case where the association is

---

112 See Equality and Human Rights Commission, above note 104.
113 *Dixon v Wandsworth LBC* [2008] EWCA Civ 595 at [11]; *Tomlinson v Birmingham City Council* [2010] 2 All ER 175; *Ali v Birmingham City Council* [2010] 2 All ER 175.
114 See *Secretary of State for Work and Pensions v M* [2006] UKHL 11; *Wandsworth LBC v Michalak* [2002] 4 All ER 1136; *Ghaidan v Godin-Mendoza* [2004] 3 All ER 411.
115 See eg *Wandsworth LBC v Michalak* [2002] 4 All ER 1136; *Ghaidan v Godin-Mendoza* [2004] 3 All ER 411.
116 See *R (A) v Secretary of State for Health* [2016] 1 WLR 331 at [32].

carrying out a function which is 'enmeshed' with government in the same sense as with the human rights cases (above). In *R (McIntyre) v Gentoo Group Ltd*[117] the High Court expressed the matter broadly by suggesting that the functions of managing and allocating social housing were inherently public functions. We also saw in chapter 3 that one difference from the human rights cases is that in the context of judicial review there is no requirement to distinguish between an 'act' and a function.

9.86 There are other differences between judicial review and human rights cases. Judicial review concerns only the quality of the particular decision at the time it was made, whereas a human rights challenge more broadly concerns the circumstances at the time of the trial since the issue is whether the court should at that time exercise its powers. Judicial review is also discretionary, and the court may not grant a remedy where the claimant has another suitable remedy such as the social housing ombudsman or an ordinary private law action. The grounds of judicial review require that a decision must comply with any relevant legal rules, must take into account all relevant factors and exclude irrelevant ones, must be fair and unbiased and must be reasonable in the sense of rational. This overlaps with the human rights standard of proportionality, but is a higher threshold for a claimant to get over. Short of perversity, disputed facts cannot be investigated, although a clear error of fact will invalidate a decision.[118] It is unlikely that failure to comply with 'standards' or 'guidance' from the regulator will suffice since this is not intended to be legally binding.

9.87 Further important grounds for judicial review under the general head of 'unfairness' are, first, that a decision-maker must not 'fetter its discretion', for example by a blanket refusal to consider exceptions to a policy or repeated applications to renew or transfer a tenancy. However, this requires only that the decision-maker is willing to consider exceptional circumstances.[119] Second, if an association departs from a published policy affecting a tenancy a person affected has a right to make representations.[120] As we saw in chapter 7, this may be enhanced by a 'legitimate expectation' where a specific undertaking or promise has been given to a tenant.

---

117 [2010] EWHC 5 (Admin).
118 See *R (A) v Croydon LBC* [2009] 1 WLR 2557; *Adan v Newnham LBC* [2002] 1 All ER 931.
119 See eg *British Oxygen Co Ltd v Minister of Technology* [1971] AC 610 at 625.
120 See *R (Trafford) v Blackpool BC* [2014] EWHC 85 (Admin).

9.88 In the context of a shortage of housing, the courts are reluctant to interfere with the discretion of a housing authority, on the basis that the latter is more aware of the local circumstances.[121] Indeed, in *R (McIntyre) v Gentoo Group Ltd*[122] the High Court stressed that, in view of the non-profit nature of a housing association and its experience, the court will give great respect to its decisions. The court will therefore give the landlord a 'margin of discretion', meaning that the court will override the landlord's decision only if it is clearly and seriously flawed, as was the case in *McIntyre* itself (below).[123] However, where a tenant is substantially prejudiced, procedural unfairness will attract judicial intervention.[124]

9.89 Where a tenancy agreement is involved, public and private law principles may interact thus focusing on the ambivalent nature of a housing association. An initial difference is that, in public law, once the existence of power is established, the onus is on the claimant to show that the decision being challenged is invalid whereas in private law a person asserting a right must establish it to the full.

9.90 Public and private law might not coincide and the aggressive commercial dimension might be at odds with the public interest dimension. In private law, a landlord can of course act for its own self-interest and motive short of fraud is usually irrelevant. In public law, by contrast, there must always be a public interest motive and a fair procedure.

9.91 Where the two dimensions interact, the private law position is a relevant factor in public law, but where they conflict, it seems that public law prevails. For example, in *R (McIntyre) v Gentoo Housing Group Ltd* (above), the High Court held that it was unreasonable as a matter of public law for the association to refuse consent to an assignment because the tenant's husband had a historic debt for rent arrears on a different property. In private law, arrears on another property is not a valid ground for refusing consent to an assignment. The association had misunderstood its private law powers and this tainted the public law aspect as well. However, if the private law refusal had been valid, the decision would also have been justified in public law since conservation of public money is a legitimate factor to take into account. Thus the two perspectives were in harmony. In the end, judicial review was refused as a matter of discretion because the claimant had an alternative private law remedy.

121 See *R v Hillingdon LBC ex p Puhlhofer* [1986] AC 484.
122 [2010] EWHC 5 (Admin).
123 See also *McDonald v UK* [2014] ECHR 492.
124 See *Eastlands Homes Partnership Ltd v Whyte* [2010] EWHC 695.

9.92   *R (Macleod) v Governors of the Peabody Trust*[125] is similar. The landlord refused to consent to a mutual exchange of the claimant's tenancy. The tenant claimed in public law that by putting his name on its transfer list, Peabody had led him to believe that he could arrange the exchange. As we saw in chapter 3, the High Court held that the matter was one of private law because there was no sufficient government connection. However, even if the matter had been one of public law the claim would have failed since, under the tenancy agreement, the tenancy could be assigned only to an approved key worker. This invalidated any undertaking in public law since the landlord had no power to give such an undertaking. Peabody's administrative arrangements were criticised but did not constitute illegality.

9.93   In *Eastlands Homes Partnership Ltd v Whyte*,[126] by contrast, the two perspectives conflicted. A tenant faced with eviction established a legitimate expectation that a housing association would adhere to its published rules in connection with its appeals procedure relating to a refusal to convert a starter tenancy into an ordinary assured tenancy. This overrode the private law right to terminate the tenancy.

9.94   Similarly in *R (Trafford) v Blackpool BC*[127] the council refused to renew a tenancy held by a solicitor in its Enterprise Centre on the ground primarily that the solicitor brought many claims against it on behalf of tenants of the Centre. It was held that the council's decision was invalid in public law since its purpose was to punish the claimant. It was not entitled to rely on self-interest alone, and accordingly it had failed to take into account broader public interest factors and acted unreasonably. Moreover, it had consistently failed to consider applications for a new tenancy and so fettered its discretion.

9.95   Thus in the event of a conflict between private law and public law, the latter prevails. On the other hand, if a decision-maker has considered both public and private law factors and the balance struck between the two is not irrational, the court is unlikely to interfere. The non-profit nature of a housing association suggests that public and private law will often be in harmony. However, there is older authority which still has some judicial support that a contractual relationship cannot be a public law matter at all.[128]

---

125 [2016] EWHC 737 (Admin).
126 [2010] EWHC 695 (QB).
127 [2014] EWHC 85 (Admin).
128 See *Peabody HA v Green and others* (1978) P & CR 644; Lord Scott in *YL v Birmingham City Council* [2007] UKHL 27; and Rix LJ dissenting in *Weaver* (para 3.28).

CHAPTER 10

Supported housing problems

10.1 Introduction

10.3 Supported housing, residential and nursing care: costs in a time of austerity

10.3 Background

10.6 Undermining of 'extra care'

10.9 Legislative and statutory guidance framework: the integration of health and social care?

10.14 Challenging decisions: recent case-law
R (Sefton Care Association) v Sefton Council • *R (JM & NT) v Isle of Wight Council* • *Summary*

10.22 Residential care: deprivation of liberty

Introduction

10.1 Housing associations, along with providing general needs housing, provide supported housing for vulnerable people with additional care and support needs. This has been a key part of the sector's work for many decades. Sometimes the provision of a home is not enough and additional support is needed for people to live independent lives in the community.

10.2 In recent years, due to governmental economic austerity measures, supported housing has had to respond to a challenging operating environment. However, with the funding regime for supported housing likely to be settled now that the housing benefit cap is no longer to be applied (following government announcements towards the end of 2018), many associations are committing to build new projects, after years of stalemate.[1] Even though housing benefit will now apply in full, there remain considerable impediments to progress with viability of future schemes and of existing projects. Housing benefit is only one part of the funding equation. Care or support costs are met either through payment from local authorities or from the NHS. Budgets of both care funding sectors have been put under serious pressure as a result of government cuts, but also significant growth in demand for services.

Supported housing, residential and nursing care: costs in a time of austerity

Background

10.3 There is a serious crisis in care due to the twin problems of unprecedented demand and the impact of austerity measures tightening public spending on care. There are growing and unprecedented demands on the provision of care, with people in residential and nursing care schemes and in their own homes requiring increasing amounts of support. This is primarily due to the societal impact of an aging population and the bulge in needs which will come through especially with the so called 'baby boomers' reaching retirement. This places further pressure on social care and health care budgets administered by local authorities and the NHS, with increased

---

1 See Peter Apps, 'Housing associations plan more supported housing following LHA cap U-turn', *Inside Housing*, 17 August 2018.

10.4 hospital admissions, length of hospital stays, stresses on GP services, ambulance and other emergency call outs.[2]

10.4 A typical response by local authorities has been to look at ways to reduce the costs of care. This has had a damaging impact on housing associations providing care, undermining their ability to continue to run services and to maintain appropriate quality within such tight budgetary constraints. Two relatively recent cases (below), throw light on how 'reasonable' commissioners should consider key issues before trying to reduce the costs of care.[3]

10.5 Work in the care sector is poorly paid, evidenced in part with hourly rates often barely above the minimum wage and people often employed on zero-hour contracts. This very skilled, difficult and at times unpleasant work, which should be paid at appropriate rates and with job security, has not surprisingly led to difficulties in recruitment and retention of care workers.

Undermining of 'extra care'

10.6 Of particular concern amongst housing and care professionals is the undermining of the very successful 'extra care' model. Extra care is where a person is provided with self-contained accommodation within a specially designed scheme where care is available on-site 24 hours a day to meet whatever changing needs might arise. The care is funded by commissioners on a block or scheme basis, and can enable the management of unplanned care incidents as well as planned care. This ensures that issues and problems are addressed locally rather than leading to hospital admission.

10.7 The roll-out of personal budgets (where funding is provided to the service user rather than to the provider to enable the service user to make a choice about their individual care provider) has been mixed with slow results. In theory, of course, empowering people to make their own choices is excellent. However, in practice it creates

---

2 For general background on the relationship between housing, health and care see: C Handy, 'Housing, health and social care – an introduction', *Journal of Integrated Care*, Vol 22, no 1 2014, pp4–9.

3 *R (Sefton Care Association) v Sefton Council* [2011] EWHC 2676 (Admin); and *R (JM and NT) v Isle of Wight Council* [2011] EWHC 2911 (Admin). These case have been followed in a series of further High Court challenges: *R (East Midlands Care Ltd) v Leicestershire CC* [2011 EWHC 3096 (Admin); *R (South West Care Homes Ltd) v Devon CC and another* [2012] EWHC 2967 (Admin); *R (Members of Committee of Care North East Newcastle) v Newcastle City Council* [2012] EWHC 2655 (Admin); and *R (Members of Committee of Care North East Northumberland) v Northumberland CC* [2013] EWHC 234 (Admin).

problems around viability of the extra care model. Even where all those individuals still choose the housing association/care provider to deliver their care, the overall funding package leading to a reduced overall funding of the service. As a consequence, the underlying funding which makes extra care a success is no longer there, resulting in extra care providers are being financially forced to drop the 24-hour and unplanned extra care service.

10.8   If social care is not provided at the right level within such projects, the NHS inevitably picks up the consequences and cost through increased hospital admissions.[4]

Legislative and statutory guidance framework: the integration of health and social care?

10.9   The legislative framework for the provision of social care is complex and has been extended by the Care Act 2014. This creates a new duty for local authorities in promoting well-being in all decisions regarding an individual's care needs. It also creates a requirement for local authorities when carrying out their care and support functions to integrate services with those provided by the NHS and any other health-related services, such as housing provision.

10.10 In deciding *R (JM & NT) v Isle of Wight Council*[5] Lang J cited the summary of the relevant legislative framework given by Rix LJ in *R (McDonald) v Kensington and Chelsea RLBC*[6] which is worth stating here.

> 28. The Statutory framework is to be found in provisions of the National Health Service and Community Care Act 1990 ('NHSCCA 1990'), the Chronically Sick and Disabled Persons Act 1970 ('CSDPA 1970'), and the National Assistance Act 1948 ('NAA 1948').
> 29. Section 47 of the NHSCCA 1990 imposes a statutory duty on local authorities to assess those who appear to be in need of community services. It requires 'an assessment of his needs' and then a decision 'having regards to the results of that assessment ... whether his needs call for the provision by them of such services.' Subject to any directions given by the Secretary of State as to the manner in which

---

4 National Audit Office, 31 October 2013, paras 11, 22. In the 2013 report, *Emergency hospital admissions, managing the demand*, it was found that one-fifth of emergency admissions were avoidable as they were for existing conditions that primary, community or social care could have managed. Research has also indicated that investment (increased spending) in social care reduces both emergency admissions and delayed discharge in hospitals.
5 [2011] EWHC 2911 (Admin).
6 [2014] EWCA Civ 2464.

an assessment is to be carried out or the form it is to take, it shall be carried out and take such form as the local authority consider appropriate.

30. Section 29 of NNA 1948 places a duty on local authorities to 'make arrangements' for promoting the welfare of (among others) persons who are substantially and permanently handicapped by illness or injury.

31. Section 2(1)(a) of the CSDPA 1970 extends the provision of welfare services required by Section 29 of the 1948 Act to 'the provision of practical assistance for that person in his home', where that is necessary to meet the needs of that person.

32. Thus these Acts require a local authority to assess needs, then to decide by reference to such an assessment whether the provision of relevant services are called for, and then to make arrangements for the provision of the services which have been decided upon as being called for . . .

33. Section 7(1) of the Local Authority Social Services Act 1970 ('LASSA 1970') authorises the Department of Health to issue guidance to local authorities which the authorities are bound to follow unless they can provide clear and adequate reasons for not doing so . . . The Department has issued such guidance in *Fair Access to Care Services*.

34. Relevant jurisprudence has determined the extent to which a local authority is entitled in the assessment of needs and the provision of services to meet such needs to have regards to resources. It is entitled to have regards to them in assessing needs (R v Gloucester County Council ex parte Rixon[7] (and in choosing between different means of meeting assessed needs (*R v Kirklees MBC ex p Daykin*[8]). Subject to that, however, a need once assessed, has to be met by the provision of services . . .

10.11 In *Savva v Kensington and Chelsea RLBC*,[9] Kay J said:

> It is axiomatic that local authorities do not have a bottomless pit of funds at their disposal. It is permissible for them to take account of the relative severity of individuals' needs and the availability of resources when determining whether it is necessary to make arrangements to meet an individual's needs. However, once a local authority has decided it is necessary to make such arrangements, it has an absolute duty to provide the individual with services or the personal budget with which to meet the assessed needs.

10.12 Statutory guidance (subject to reissue as a result of the enactment of the Care Act 2014) is currently contained in *Prioritising need in the*

---

7 (1997) 95 LGR 638.
8 (1997–98) 1 CCLR 512.
9 [2010] EWCA Civ 1209.

context of putting people first (2010)[10] and builds on earlier guidance in Fair access to care services (2003). In R (W, M and others) v Birmingham CC[11] Walker J found the council's decision to fund only 'critical' needs to be 'potentially devastating' and ruled the decision to be unlawful due to the lack of regards to the disability equality duty and an inadequate consultation process. Guidance was issued as Care and support statutory guidance (2014) under the Care Act 2014 which sets out eligibility criteria and assessment requirements including the controversial capital and income arrangements for personal and family contributions.[12]

10.13 Integrating social care and health care is according to some part of the solution in the provision of better holistic care and achieving better value for the taxpayer. The creation of the Better Care Fund (to assist with meeting the costs of health and social care) helps pool budgets and ensure that integration happens. However, progress has been limited.

Challenging decisions: recent case-law

10.14 A number of recent cases in the High Court emphasise the difficulties and dilemmas faced by those in need of the right level of care and also by care providers and care commissioners. The cases provide a number of 'guiding principles' commissioners should follow. They also highlight a number of important grounds for legal challenge by care users and care providers if what is commissioned is inadequate in extent or nature or standard to meet the required care needs of the individual in question.

R (Sefton Care Association) v Sefton Council[13]

10.15 The claimants in this case asked the court to review a decision by Sefton Council in December 2010 to freeze fees paid to care homes for residential and nursing care for a second year. The claimants (Sefton Care Association, an unincorporated care association with around 40 members), had seven grounds for judicial review and effectively cited lack of due process, asserting that the council had failed to take a number of required factors into account when

---

10 *Prioritising need in the context of Putting People First: A whole system approach for eligibility for social care*, Department of Health, 2010.
11 [2011] EWHC 1147 (Admin).
12 See pp75–112 and 169–230.
13 [2011] EWHC 2676 (Admin).

making its decision. Thus, they felt, the council was unable to show that it had reviewed relevant factors to demonstrate fee levels were sufficient to meet required levels of care. The court quashed the decision to freeze fees because the council had not taken into account the actual cost of care required by statutory guidance. Raynor J stated:[14]

> In my view, taken as a whole, the statutory Guidance and the Agreement do not contemplate there will be any significant imbalance between the usual cost of care and the actual cost. If a local authority consciously fixes the usual cost in a sum significantly less than actual costs, then I do not see how it could be said to be having 'due regard to the actual costs of providing care' as required by paragraph 2.5.4 of the Guidance.

10.16 Raynor J went on to say that in setting fees, a local authority should take into account the 'legitimate, current and future costs faced by providers, as well as the factors that affect those costs', and went on to say that if fee levels are set significantly below actual cost then there will be 'inevitable reduction in the quality of service provision', which 'may put individuals at risk'.

10.17 In addition, the court held there had been no 'meaningful consultation' about the proposal to freeze fee levels and that even though the care providers expressed concerns about the level of fees, the council did not take those concerns into account. The inadequacy of central government funding cannot excuse a failure to properly consult.[15] The court also ordered that risk assessment should be revisited in the light of its decision.[16]

10.18 However, the court did not find that the freezing of fees was a breach of Disability Discrimination Act 1995 s49A. Raynor J in reaching his decision took great care to follow the principles set out in the judgment of Walker J in *R (W and others) v Birmingham City Council*[17] (above).

10.19 It is clear, then, that financial pressures on their own cannot justify a reduction in care cost, they must be considered in the context of the care needs of individuals and whether levels of care are sufficient to meet the individual's needs, including undertaking any appropriate risk assessments. Councils must undertake meaningful consultation, regardless of government funding levels, and properly

14 At para 70.
15 See para 71.
16 See para 81.
17 [2011] EWHC 1147 (Admin).

take the view of care providers into account when making a decision on the appropriate level of fees.

R (JM and NT) v Isle of Wight Council

10.20 In this case, the Isle of Wight Council proposed making savings by changing eligibility criteria for access to adult care social services. This meant a potential shift from a policy of providing services to people assessed as being at 'critical' or 'substantial' risk and moving to one of restricting people in the 'substantial' risk category to those who were placed 'at the greatest risk of not being able to remain at home and safe'.

10.21 The case concerned two young men with autism. Lang J held that the statutory guidance made it clear that there was no hierarchy of needs – all areas of life must be considered, including the right to dignity and respect, quality of life and freedom from discrimination. Thus the council had acted unlawfully by prioritising the risks of not being able to remain at home and be safe. In addition, the council had used criteria relating to frequency, likelihood and immediacy of risk, instead of focusing on 'severity of risk' as required by the guidance. The council's consultation was also seen by the court as inadequate due to its lack of detail on the number of people likely to be affected, the costs and potential savings or the types of services included. The court also found that the council had failed to comply with its equality duties.

Summary

10.22 These cases are important in establishing principles, especially in relation to the statutory guidance, which commissioners should follow when making decisions on the provision of care and support services in the light of funding restrictions and cuts. It is very clear from the case-law that councils should not fetter their discretion and should consider the care needs of individuals carefully and set the provision of service in relation to those assessed care needs and not take blanket decisions based upon budgetary constraints. It is important to properly consult with relevant bodies to enable appropriate opportunity for considered responses for care users and care providers. Councils should also take into account an accurate assessment of the legitimate, current and future costs faced by care providers which recognise these costs in full.

Residential care: deprivation of liberty

10.23 Except in prescribed cases, liberty is an absolute right that cannot be overridden. Article 5 of the European Convention on Human Rights (ECHR) provides an exhaustive definition of when a person can be deprived of liberty and must be given a strict construction.[18] The main exceptions are criminal convictions, disobedience to a court order, control of children, infection, mental health, alcoholism, drug addiction, vagrancy and in order to prevent illegal immigration or with a view to deportation or extradition (Article 5(2)). Any detention must be in accordance with a procedure 'prescribed by law' and so there must be safeguards.

10.24 Following a number of relatively recent pivotal Supreme Court decisions, providers of nursing, residential care and supported housing need to be particularly careful not to inadvertently deprive a resident or customer of their liberty. The rulings are important for housing associations due to the extensive provision of residential, nursing and supported housing across the sector giving rise to the possibility of particular settings which could have deprivation of liberty implications. Care workers could unintentionally deprive someone of their liberty believing they are acting in their 'best interests'.

10.25 In two landmark cases, considered together, by the Supreme Court it was held that all people a) who lack the capacity to make decisions about their care and residence; and b) who are under the care of the state (whether or not directly provided by the state or placed into care by the state regardless of the provider of that care); and are c) subject to continuous supervision and control, effectively in all practicality lacking the option to leave their care setting, are deprived of their liberty.

10.26 In *P v Cheshire West and Chester Council; P and Q v Surrey CC*,[19] the claimants were mental patients who had been placed in residential care with different degrees of supervision and support. One claimant was fostered in an ordinary home but could not leave alone. Another required 24-hour care but could leave his staffed bungalow frequently with one-to-one support. Another living in a residential home was subject to occasional restraint and medication. They did not object and were happy with their placements. It was held that all

18 *Zenati v Commissioner of Police of the Metropolis* [2015] EWCA Civ 80 at [17].
19 See, for example, *P v Cheshire West and Chester Council and another; P and Q v Surrey CC* [2014] UKSC 19.

were nonetheless deprived of liberty. The test should be the same for everyone, namely that the person concerned was under continuous supervision and control for a not-negligible time and was not free to leave.

10.27 This ruling set aside the previously well-grounded concept of 'relative normality' taken by the Court of Appeal, ie in deciding whether an incapable person was deprived of their liberty depends upon the situation faced by someone in similar circumstances. However, Lords Carnwath, Hodge and Clarke, dissenting in different degrees in each case, took the view that living under benign supervision for one's own good in a domestic setting was not a deprivation of liberty. However, as the majority pointed out, this leads to uncertainty and blurs the question of whether liberty is removed with whether this is justified.

10.28 There is also a subjective element in that positive consent prevents deprivation of liberty. However, the person's passive compliance or lack of objection is not consent. Importantly the purpose of the detention is irrelevant whether good or bad and whether or not it is intended to benefit the person (although this may be relevant when assessing the proportionality of safeguards). Whether conditions are 'normal' or comfortable is also irrelevant. Lady Hale remarked[20] that the whole point about human rights is their universal character and that 'in the end it is the constraints that matter'.[21]

10.29 Under the Mental Capacity Act 2005 a person living in a 'hospital' or 'care home' can only be deprived of the liberty in very strict circumstances. Care homes or hospitals must get the permission of a local authority, a health body or the court to allow someone to be deprived of their liberty under the 'standard authorisation'. In settings such as supported living (including adult placement, small group settings and domestic settings, ie a person's own home) an application has to be made to the Court of Protection.

10.30 These arrangements effectively amount to deprivation of liberty safeguards (DOLS) and must be followed. It is not enough to act in a person's best interests. Lady Hale said, stressing the inextricable links between safeguards for vulnerable adults and human right considerations, that 'it is axiomatic that people with disabilities, both mental and physical, have the same human rights as the rest of the human race'.[22] Furthermore she states the 'whole point about human

---

20 *P v Cheshire West and Chester Council; P and Q v Surrey CC* at [36].
21 At [56].
22 At [45].

rights is their universal character'. The rights set out in the ECHR are to be guaranteed to everyone (Article 1). They are premised on the inherent dignity of all human beings whatever their frailty or flaws.[23] It is also important not to confuse a wish to help a vulnerable person, ie benevolent justification with the concept of deprivation of liberty. On this point, Lady Hale went onto say:

> We should not let the comparative benevolence of the living arrangements with which we are concerned blind us to their essential character if that indeed constitutes a deprivation of liberty.[24]

10.31 Being kind, then, is not a defence, and the types of interventions or practices which are inadvertent or seen to be in the best interests of a client might include, for example:

- provision of supervision outside a scheme where a person does not want to be supervised;
- restricting access to the things a person wants to do in order to protect from apparent risks;
- locks or electronic devices on a person door or window which can have the effect of restricting that persons freedom of movement;
- placing restrictions on a person's freedom to exit and enter premises;
- restraining a person, whether through physical or psychological means in order to administer mediation or treatment;
- placing restrictions on room furnishings or fitments taking away a person's choice.

10.32 In providing care and support, with or without accommodation, care providers must apply the proper safeguards before depriving someone of their liberty.[25] The critical test is whether a person is under 'constant supervision and control and is not free to leave'. As a result of the Supreme Court findings, there is a likely to be an increase in the number of DOLS applications (including those relating to people living in more domestic settings), the need to appoint more fully trained 'best interest' deprivation of liberty assessors, greater focus on the 'least restrictive' care regime in relation to care planning and the need for more periodic checks to ensure living arrangements remain in a person's best interests.

---

23 At [36].
24 At [35].
25 See also the more detailed 'Deprivation of Liberty Safeguards 2008' along with its detailed Code of Practice; also CR Handy, 'Deprivation of liberty', *Journal of Housing Law*, Vol 17, Issue 6, pp112–117.

10.33 Although Lady Hale's judgment provides some clear guiding principles, there is no formula or algorithm which can be applied to determine with certainty whether a person has been deprived of their liberty or whether safeguards are adequate. The case does though provide a duty to ensure vulnerable people have their special needs addressed to ensure they are not deprived of their liberty.

PART 4

Governance and investment

CHAPTER 11

Governance generally

11.1 Introduction

11.4 Current governance issues

11.12 Governance principles and practice

11.21 Governance and regulatory framework

11.26 The membership
11.26 Overview
11.32 Powers of the membership
11.47 Composition of the membership

Introduction

11.1 In governance we encounter the underlying tension between the different strands of housing association law. In this case the third strand, namely the voluntary sector, comes to the fore (the other strands being private commerce and public law). Increasing focus has been placed on the governance of housing associations particularly since 2008. Regulatory focus has stressed the importance of effective governance. In the light of wider governance disasters, especially in the financial sector and in the co-operative movement and recently the Grenfell Tower disaster, this greater emphasis does seem appropriate.

11.2 However, there is a balance to be struck between governmental requirements on the one hand, and freedom of purpose and operation on the other. Whenever the Queen's shilling is taken, there is a price to be paid by way of enlistment. Housing associations are, in law, independent bodies; they are not directly state-controlled despite receiving funding from the state and at times undertaking tasks which would ordinarily be undertaken by government or local government. Yes they are subject to direction by the state when in receipt of state funding, and yes they are also subject to direction if they are carrying on the role of the state through a delegation or contractual obligation such as housing homeless persons.

11.3 The law is complicated by the different structures adopted by housing associations, namely the co-operative and community benefit society under the Co-operative and Community Benefits Societies Act (CCBSA) 2014, the company and the charitable trust. It is arguable that a tailor made corporate structure would be desirable. This argument has sometimes been resisted on the ground of 'flexibility'. In fact, although the different structures are technically diverse, there is considerable overlap which we shall try to identify.

Current governance issues

11.4 Quite rightly there has been increasing focus on housing association governance due to the growing scale and complexity of these organisations. They have grown considerably in recent years, with the largest, Clarion, owning over 120,000 dwellings, and even the smallest accessing quite complex funding arrangements in order to build new homes. The range of activities as well as their scale can be extensive, with organisations such as Places for People deeply engaged in running what were public sector services such as leisure centres; and others, such as Accord, running factories which manufacture off-site timber homes and providing extensive care and support services. The range and complexity of activities is now well beyond the provision of housing, with the pace of change also rapid.

11.5 These factors mean significant governance challenges for the boards and shareholders of housing associations. Key issues are addressed by the National Housing Federation's (NHF) code of governance. This has no binding force as such, but can be incorporated into an association's constitution and may influence standards developed by the courts. It is therefore important that such a code keeps up to date. We now have a revised 'combined code of governance' and, bearing in mind housing association activities are often firmly within the private realm, it is important that boards keep a keen eye on what it advises.

11.6 Key issues going beyond direct legal liability are terms of office; size of boards; and executive membership and the balance between that and the total of non-executives on boards. (There is a growing tendency for smaller boards of executive and non-executive members, increasingly reflecting PLC land.) Skills mix, representation and involvement, especially concerning customers and service users and diversity, all need to be addressed. For housing associations which provide care, there is also need for clinical governance and safeguarding management.

11.7 There are issues with group structures. The unequivocal control of subsidiary boards is vitally important, with some recent failures in this respect within the sector. There are also issues when considering mergers, amalgamations, joint ventures and other strategic alliances. The NHF have developed a voluntary code on mergers which contains good advice but which does not have any official weight.[1] These issues will be discussed in chapter 15.

11.8 Board pay is less of an issue than it was a decade ago, since most board members are now paid and the Charity Commission in particular accepts that payment is needed to attract qualified members. Non-charitable bodies can pay what they like, but a charitable trustee can be paid only where this is necessary to advance the objects of the charity.[2] As a regulatory requirement, from a value-for-money and taxpayer interest point of view, the rate of pay needs to be transparent

---

1 See NHF, Voluntary Merger Code, 2016.
2 See *Trustees expenses and payment*, CC11, 2012. This is distinct from paying a trustee for specific services to the charity which is considered below.

and objectively justifiable. Independent review every couple of years of remuneration levels for chairs and other board members is important and now routine. There are readily accessible resources to check comparable levels of board member pay across the sector. The Charity Commission also requires clear disclosure of any payments to a trustee.

11.9 From the perspective of direct legal liability, risk identification, control and management and from a consumer point of view a focus on safety around such concerns as fire assessments and works and gas servicing are directly in the regulatory and public eye and must be taken seriously by boards. These governance issues are a constantly moving agenda against a highly politicised background especially of housing shortage and safety standards. The key decisions and balances in relation to some of them need to be addressed and decided upon by boards and shareholders within the constitution and rules of their individual organisations. No one solution is right for all housing associations. However, decisions have to be taken within the statutory framework and the administrative requirements of the regulator. It is a complex brew which is subject to constant evolution and development.

11.10 Housing associations are internally accountable to their members and externally accountable to the regulator, and through the regulator to parliament. As we have seen, many powers of the Regulator of Social Housing (RSH) directly to intervene are limited to breaches of the law. The Charity Commission's reach is more extensive, but in practice it often defers to the regulator.

11.11 The existence of adequate mechanisms to deal with wider governance issues is a factor that affects funding decisions not only by the government but also by providers of private sources of finance. Moreover, the claim that housing associations are primarily private bodies carries with it the unfortunate implication of lack of accountability especially in the prevailing cultural climate of market freedom. Beyond legal liability and regulatory enforcement, the grading system applied by the regulator which we discussed in chapter 4 is an effective means of encouraging compliance with high governance standards, its sanction being loss of reputation and disadvantage in obtaining both private and public funding. The 2018 housing green paper[3] proposes to introduce league tables of the performance of housing associations comparable to those for schools.

3 Cm 9671 ch 3.

Governance principles and practice

11.12 During 2017 some £251.5bn of taxpayers' money went to private, charity and voluntary organisations to provide a variety of services. Payments to housing associations were included within this overall sum. Again illustrating the ambivalent status of the sector, the Committee on Standards in Public Life (CSPL) sees housing associations as public service organisations and stresses the importance of following the seven 'Nolan' principles, namely: selflessness, integrity, objectivity, accountability, openness, honesty and leadership.[4] Continuing concerns over the effective governance of public service providers stresses that more should be done 'to encourage strong and robust cultures of ethical behaviour' with a reinforcement of the importance of the seven principles.[5]

11.13 The CSPL commented specifically on the dilemma at the heart of the profit motive of some private sector providers and its ethical conflict with the principle of selflessness where directors of such an organisation will, by virtue of company law, owe a primary duty to their shareholders.[6] This raises a similar dilemma for housing associations where the RSH and government are encouraging the increase of surpluses in order to maximise the production of new homes, although there is public good in the latter outcome since the surpluses are being reinvested.

11.14 Because of a number of governance failures within the housing association sector, in recent years the RSH has placed much emphasis on the importance of good governance. In just over a decade, housing associations have moved from a voluntary model of governance devoted to self-help and altruistic motives of meeting need often on a purely local scale, to a model which is highly commercial and mimicking that of PLCs in the private sector.

11.15 This of course is not true of all housing associations, but increasingly where they have entered into private sector borrowing arrangements the skills of board members have had to be developed along more commercial lines. Associations have also moved from a situation where boards were unpaid to one where the majority of boards now receive some payment for the roles of individual board members.

---

4 See in particular, Committee on Standards In Public Life, *The continuing importance of ethical standards for public service providers*, May 2018, pp6–7.

5 Committee on Standards In Public Life, *The continuing importance of ethical standards for public service providers*, May 2018.

6 See Committee on Standards In Public Life, *The continuing importance of ethical standards for public service providers*, May 2018, pp33–34.

This development in itself inevitably commercialises the sector, by turning the board membership relationship into a contractual transaction. For example, it is now regular practice for board members to have an annual performance appraisal.

11.16 To fully understand the governance of housing associations, it is important to see where power lies. There are very substantial organisations in the sector. Some of the largest housing associations own and manage more than 100,000 properties. Nevertheless a single, simple and somewhat crude governance model applies to almost all housing associations irrespective of their formal structure, role or size. This model places the ultimate governance power and responsibility in the hands of the governing body be it board, management committee or trustees. Where a corporate form is adopted, there is accountability to members.

11.17 However, power is often devolved, necessarily, to sub-committees and executive officers in order for the work of the organisation to be carried out on a day-to-day basis. There is rhetoric that the board sets direction through a corporate strategy, business plan or similar mechanism; requires its executive officers to deliver against that plan; and then holds them to account for their performance. So power sits with the board but then is devolved or distributed through officers, usually the chief executive officer. In practice, of course, as with any large organisation, policies and plans can be (as well as generated by the Board itself) generated from below and are formally approved, amended or rejected by the board. In many cases, executive officers are full board members, thereby tying them in to the accountability and liability principles of the board.

11.18 However, it is a little more complicated because power is fettered by government in a number of ways. First, there is direct control through formal statutory and regulatory requirements; such limitations on powers and freedom are clear, open and transparent since they are published and associations are judged on their compliance. Second, and very often, there is informal influence which in practice can be very powerful. An example of this is the exercising of power through the provision of grant funding backed up by the practice of grading associations. The informal threat of withdrawal of grant funding is a major persuader. Very often if there are governance problems with an association one of the first steps would be to suspend grant fund and effectively freeze an association's development programme.

11.19 Almost all housing associations are constituted as corporate bodies. A key characteristic is that they are ultimately controlled by their members. Excepting a charitable trust which is not a corporate body, membership control is exercised through three elements, namely: 1) control over the constitution (for example, agreeing or otherwise proposed constitutional changes); 2) control over management (appointment of the board); and 3) control over finances (the approval of accounts). Whether or not there is a significant wider membership other than the board members themselves determines whether or not this has any real significance. Housing associations often carefully manage wider shareholder membership and therefore the scale of shareholding can often be quite small.

11.20 Back in 1995, the Hancock Committee (which undertook a fundamental review of corporate governance in the private sector)[7] did not regard membership as a realistic and appropriate method of accountability, suggesting that wider membership was more appropriate to ensure greater participation and consultation. More recently, the NHF has produced a comprehensive governance code which takes into account the changing nature of housing association and the changing policy and operating environment.[8] The code mirrors the Nolan seven principles and emphasises the importance of: ethics; accountability; a customer-first approach; openness; diversity and inclusion; review and renewal of boards; clarity; control; and structures.

Governance and regulatory framework

11.21 The RSH insists on housing associations adopting a code of governance and then in annual returns and annual accounts providing a statement of compliance. Most associations adopt the NHF's code of governance, but that is not a requirement and other codes can be adopted. The NHF code, though, is the one most geared towards the context and nature and operating environment of the sector and therefore the most relevant. The NHF also provides model sets of rules and other specimen documents.

11.22 The requirement to adopt a code and to report on compliance against it is a regulatory requirement but does not have the full force of the law and so is not directly enforceable by the regulator. However, the regulator has taken indirect action against associations who do not comply with their chosen code. This often takes the form of a

---

7 See *Competence and accountability: the report into the inquiry into housing association governance*, p16, Annex 6.
8 See NHF, *Code of governance: promoting board excellence for housing associations*, revised 2015.

downgrade of an association's governance rating. It is accepted that there can be justifiable reasons for non-compliance and therefore the RSH takes the view an association must comply or explain. In fact, the NHF code itself has a requirement that associations must provide a statement in their annual financial statements on compliance. Moreover compliance with the code is a factor relevant to the performance of a governing body under its general legal duties (below chapter 12).

11.23 Key recommendations of the code of governance include:

1) effectiveness of strategic leadership and control and ensuring members act in the best interest of the organisation;
2) clarity on the duties and responsibilities of the board with effective leadership by the chair with duties clearly defined;
3) recruitment to board vacancies should be open and transparent taking into account the board's view on the skills and attributes required to discharge the duties of the board;
4) clarity and effectiveness of board decision-making based upon timely and accurate information with appropriate delegation to committees of the board;
5) formal and transparent arrangements ensuring financial viability, effect internal controls, risk management and audit;
6) clarity in the working relationship between the board and its chief executive with clear and appropriate delegations of authority;
7) conduct, probity and honesty with appropriate dialogue and accountability to tenants and key stakeholders.

11.24 Such overarching mechanisms are helpful in determining the governance approach of a housing association. It is, though, primarily important to follow its own rules or memorandum and article or trust deed, since otherwise the association may act ultra vires. However, apart from statutory model provisions which are not binding, there are no legal requirements as to the selection of members and directors of companies, nor as to their powers and functions. For co-operatives and community benefit societies (CCBSs) the provisions as to their constitutions, the powers and roles of members, governing body and or officers are also open ended and so depend on the governing instrument. The NHF has produced model rules for CCBSs and also model memoranda and articles for companies. However, the RSH may impose obligations and requirements or else registration as a private registered provider (PRP) may be challenged or prevented. In certain circumstances, the regulator may appoint persons to the governing body of a housing association (see chapter 5).

11.25 The RSH has issued a standard in relation to Governance and Financial Viability. There are two kinds of regulatory standard, the economic standard and the consumer standard which must be followed by PRPs. In particular, the RSH may set standards for matters relating to the financial and other affairs of PRPs.[9] The standard may require PRPs to comply with specified rules about the management of their financial and other affairs and their efficiency in carrying out those affairs.[10]

The membership

Overview

11.26 Subject to statute, the composition and powers of the membership are determined by the rules or articles. These are intended to provide a two-tier governance system controlled by the board with the membership playing only prescribed roles. In the case of a CCBS the rules must contain provisions relating to committees (by whatever name), managers and officers and their respective powers and remuneration.[11] For initial registration there must be at least three members or if the members are registered societies then at least two members.[12] In the case of a company, there must be at least one director and one member.[13] Regulatory requirements would prevent these being the same person.

11.27 Membership is largely in the hands of the governing body. Model rules provided by the NHF used by many housing associations give the board an absolute power to admit new members. Membership automatically ceases on certain events notably non-attendance at meetings and a member can be expelled by a special general meeting called by the board.

11.28 In the case of a charitable trust, there are no individual beneficiaries or members as such. There are simply trustees, who can be

---

9 Housing and Regeneration Act 2008 s94(1).
10 Housing and Regeneration Act 2008 s194(1A).
11 CCBSA 2014 ss2(2)(c) and 14.
12 CCBSA 2014 ss2(2)(b), 3(1)(a); see also s5(3)(b) where the Financial Conduct Authority (FCA) can cancel a registration under Condition B where a society no longer meets the minimum registration requirements on membership numbers.
13 Companies Act 2006 s154(1).

unlimited in number appointed in accordance with the trust deed. The trustees' duties are owed to the abstract purposes of the trust, enforceable ultimately by the Crown, through the Attorney-General, the High Court or the Charity Commissioners. This can be done on the application of an individual interested in the trust with the permission of either the Charity Commissioners or the High Court.[14]

11.29 Do board members have significant control or are they simply observers of their fate, this largely resting in hand of others, deciding key actions but with their hands tied loosely behind their backs giving them a false sense of freedom? Then as for members more generally, maybe they have no more than 'walk-on' roles. This is primarily because the rules adopted by the organisation are largely in the control of the governing body. Except in the case of a fully mutual co-operative association, there is no legal requirement that any particular interest group be represented in the membership although some associations do have published membership policies which guide appointments. The statutory 'criteria' for registration prescribed by the RSH concentrate on financial matters and do not prescribe any particular form of membership.

11.30 As we saw in chapter 6, members of community benefit societies have various powers to invoke regulatory action but this presupposes that the membership is much wider than the governing body itself. Since the late 1990s, the emphasis on having wider membership has almost evaporated from the days of *In the public eye* where wider membership especially amongst tenants was seen to be good practice.[15] Often the membership is identical to the membership of the governing body.

11.31 However, in the NHF governance code there are requirements for renewal of board members to avoid the self-servicing self-perpetuating oligarchy situation which existed many years ago in the sector. Long gone are the days when the same membership year-on-year re-elected themselves unopposed. Shares in a CCBS are non-transferable, so it is not possible for hostile take-over by the acquisition of shares by people associated with another housing association. Nor is the wider market mechanism influence possible of the 'voice' and

---

14 See *R (Heather) v Leonard Cheshire Foundation* [2001] EWHC Admin 429; *Construction Training Board v Attorney-General* [1971] 1 WLR 1303 at 1309. Where charity commission proceedings are available, then ordinary judicial review proceedings cannot be brought: see *RSPCA v Attorney-General* [2001] 3 All ER 530.

15 See HMSO, *In the Public Eye*, 1986; and *A Poke in the Public Eye*, 1998, which focused on wider public and tenant involvement and membership.

'exit' of membership. Although recently out of kilter with the rest of the sector, a small number of housing associations have opened their membership to all tenants.

Powers of the membership

11.32 The members usually appoint the governing body at an annual general meeting (AGM). This may be a formality since membership may be no wider than the existing board. The power to remove the governing body usually depends upon a special majority of two thirds of those voting, usually at the AGM or a special general meeting if called.

11.33 The rules or articles normally place governance exclusively in the hands of the board reserving certain powers to the membership at a general meeting as required by statute. In the main, constitutional issues such as rule changes, winding up and appointment of the governing body are controlled by the membership with operational matters decided by the governing body. In all cases, members of the governing body owe their duties to the association and therefore to its social housing objectives and not to the members as such.[16] The governing body is not the agent of the members.[17] The governing body and the members must act in the best interests of the association and not in the interests of other groups.

11.34 The will of the association is expressed annually at the AGM. The principle of 'one member, one vote' usually applies. However, this arguably may be inflexible, precluding weighted votes in favour of particular interests, for example tenants. In certain cases a decision must be made by a special resolution for example of 75 per cent required by statute such as in cases of amalgamation, transfers of engagement, conversion to a company or dissolution.[18]

11.35 In the case of a co-operative association where membership is confined to tenants and prospective tenants it does seem appropriate that equal participation is required. According to the Financial Conduct Authority's (FCA) guidance[19] a co-operative society must be a jointly owned and democratically controlled enterprise (one member, one vote). Similarly a community benefit society (CBS) must be controlled democratically and is accountable to its members.

---

16 See *Fosse v Harbottle* (1843) 2 Hare 461, which applies to all corporate bodies; see *Cotter v National Union of Seamen* [1929] Ch 58.
17 See *Automatic Self-Cleansing Filter Syndicate Co Ltd v Cuninghame* [1906] 2 Ch 34; *Howard Smith Ltd v Ampol Petroleum Ltd* [1974] 1 All ER 1126, at 1136.
18 CCBSA 2014 ss111, 112, 119 and 144.
19 FCA, *Finalised guidance* 15/2, November 2015, paras 4.10–4.16, 5.2.

Any departure from the 'one member, one vote' principle must be justified as being in the interests of the community.

11.36 The constitutional power of the membership is subjected to important restrictions. Under the usual rules, members can vote only on matters specifically assigned to them by statute or the rules. Where the rules allocate a matter to the governing body, the membership cannot override a decision. Indeed members have no general right to inspect board minutes or papers. Instead the membership can elect board members, normally at an annual general meeting, and can remove board members at a special general meeting. The regulator's powers to set governance criteria for registration may ensure an appropriate structure that can deliver accountability.

11.37 The detailed distribution of powers and duties of, and between, members, the governing body and officers is also a matter for the rules or articles of the association. The rules of a CCBS must have the following content: name, objects, registered office, membership, meetings, voting, rule changes, committees and officers, maximum shareholding, borrowing powers, shares, audit, withdrawal of membership, application of profits, seal and investment of the society's funds.[20] Similar provisions apply to a company under the Companies Act 2006.

11.38 There are certain other requirements worth mentioning:

1) Amendment to the rules – any amendment to a society's rules is not valid until registered;[21] an individual member cannot be bound by any changes to rules made after becoming a member with prior written consent, where the rules in question requires an increase in financial stake.[22]

2) A society is required to keep a register of its members and officers containing specified particulars such as member's or officer's name and postal address, any electronic address, number of shares held and the amount paid, a statement of other property held in the society (loans, deposits etc), date became a member or officer and if the case ceased to be such.[23] A duplicate register should be open for inspection at the society's registered officer in a way which does not reveal members shares or other property held in the society and this should be open for inspection by members.[24]

---

20 CCBSA 2014 s14.
21 CCBSA 2014 s16(1).
22 CCBSA 2014 s15(2).
23 CCBSA 2014 s30(2).
24 CCBSA 2014 s30(7) and also s103.

3) A society must keep books of account, giving a true and fair view of its affairs, explaining its transactions and have a satisfactory system of control;[25] a copy at all times of its latest balance sheet must be displayed in a conspicuous place at its registered office.[26] Each society is under a duty to appoint auditors[27] and auditors must report in accordance with the provisions of the Act.[28]

11.39 The FCA as regulator has certain limited powers to intervene (see chapter 6).

11.40 In a CCBS the question of who can change the rules is also left to the rules. A special resolution with a weighted majority is required for certain matters including the ratification of acts outside the rules,[29] constitutional changes and dissolution The same applies to a company under the Companies Act 2006 in relation to a similar range of matters. The NHF model rules require that constitutional changes require at least three quarters of those voting which generates a similar outcome.

11.41 A corporate charity cannot alter its constitution to cease being charitable in relation to its existing property and assets unless acquired for full consideration in money or money's worth.[30] A trust can alter its constitution only with the permission of the court or Charity Commission.

11.42 In some circumstances rule changes and also mergers and winding-up require notification to the regulator. This replaces former statutory consent requirements so as to present housing associations as 'independent'. The relevant provisions are discussed in chapter 5.

11.43 The members of a company have stronger statutory rights than CCBS members, particularly relating to changes in objects or rules (both contained in the articles of association) and against decisions which are alleged to be discriminatory or contrary to the interests of the company as a whole. A change in the articles must be carried by special resolution or unanimously where the company's constitution has 'entrenched' the article in question.[31] In the case of a charitable company, the consent in writing of the Charity Commission is required

---

25 CCBSA 2014 s75.
26 CCBSA 2014 s81.
27 CCBSA 2014 s83.
28 CCBSA 2014 s87.
29 CCBSA 2014 ss43, 44.
30 Charities Act 2011 s197.
31 Companies Act 2006 ss21, 22.

where the change affects the objects of the company or its property on winding up or benefits the directors, members or their associates.[32]

11.44 Under the common law, the majority may not exercise their votes in a manner which is 'illegal, oppressive or fraudulent'. In *Clemens v Clemens Bros Ltd*,[33] Foster J held (although the precise focus of the case is a little unclear) that the majority shareholder enjoying 55 per cent of the shares must exercise 'equitable considerations' when they vote. It may be that the courts would be willing to mould Foster J's approach to the CBS member, in effect placing such a member somewhere nearer to the position of directors when considering the nature of the obligations which, as members, they owe to their society. The courts may be the readier to adopt such an approach given the absence, in the CBS sphere, of any statutory provision comparable to the Companies Act 2006 s994, which empowers the court to intervene where a shareholder has been subjected to unfairly prejudicial conduct, and to redress that conduct by whatever means seems to the court to be appropriate.

11.45 The presence of Companies Act 2006 s994 obviously provides a backdrop against which companies must conduct their affairs, in effect subjecting the legal powers of the majority to equitable constraints. Since there is no suggestion that Parliament's omission to introduce a provision in the CCBSA 2014 comparable to Companies Act 2006 s994 was an act of deliberate policy, but rather of lack of parliamentary time, the court may be the more readily persuadable to regard the policy behind section 994, as pointing the direction in which to develop the common law.

11.46 In practice the RSH takes no action to ensure that the members of a co-operative and CBS or for that matter the shareholders of a company are active with much reliance placed on the adoption of an appropriate code of governance and self-assessment of governance arrangements once a year.[34]

Composition of the membership

11.47 The membership of a CCBS comprises its shareholders. These shareholders are selected according to the rules, usually by the board in the case of a non-profit company membership usually comprises nominal guarantors again selected by the board. In view of their

32 Charities Act 2011 s198.
33 [1976] 2 All ER 268.
34 See HCA, 'Governance and Financial Viability Standard', April 2015, para 2.1.

co-operative or community benefit nature, shareholders have an equal nominal holding and there are no transferable or tradable shareholdings. The duties of members are owed to the society and its objects, and unlike the case of a trading company there is no obligation to the economic interests of shareholders.

11.48 The rules themselves specify the composition of the membership, the powers of members and how those powers are exercised. The membership depends on the historical roots of the particular association formed as it was by a group of volunteers the original governing body choosing its successors and so on indefinitely.

11.49 Some members, including members of the governing body, may be representatives of other organisations, such as a local authority or NHS body, a tenants' organisation, a parent or a subsidiary. Those representative members do not owe a duty to the organisation which nominated them. Instead their duties are owed to the association. Moreover, as we saw in chapter 3, in order to present a housing association as a private sector body, the influence of local authority members has been severely restricted by law.

11.50 The FCA as the regulator for CBSs asks several questions prior to registration: who are the community the society intends to benefit; how will the society benefit that community; how will the society use any surplus or profit; and does the society intent to have a statutory asset lock. It also asks whether the society will have charitable objects. The notes on registration also stress that it is unusual for a CBS to issue more than nominal share capital, ie one £1 share per member.[35]

11.51 In the case of a company, membership is more flexible with the members either being shareholders or guarantors in both cases holding only nominal interests. There are no legal requirements for equal participation. The rights attached to shareholding may well be uniform. If so, all shares are ordinary shares. On the other hand, companies may have different classes of shareholding, for ordinary and preference or voting and non-voting shares. A company limited by guarantee can have voting and non-voting members. In the case of a charitable company, these distinctions must of course be justified in the light of the company's charitable purposes.

---

35 FCA, *Societies Information Note: new registrations and conversions*, April 2017.

CHAPTER 12

The governing body

12.1	Introduction
12.5	Powers of the governing body
12.14	Composition of the governing body
12.18	Regulatory requirements
12.29	**Liability of the governing body**
12.29	Overview
12.36	Companies: standard of care
12.42	Co-operative and Community Benefit Societies Act 2014: standard of care
12.45	Charities standard of care
12.51	**Enforcing director's liability**
12.51	Introduction
12.53	Duties to third parties
12.54	Exemption from liability
12.57	**Conflicts of interest: fiduciary duties**
12.63	Statutory requirements
12.77	Wales

Introduction

12.1 Apart from powers reserved by statute or the rules to the membership collectively, all the powers of an association are concentrated under rules approved by the National Housing Federation (NHF) in the governing body. The governing body is appointed by the members under the rules of the association.

12.2 The governing body usually comprises about 12 persons selected for their professional skills or knowledge and paid. Senior managers may also be members of the governing body thus sharing its legal responsibility. However, few if any housing associations have adopted a board structure with a minority of non-executive members and to that extent have not moved fully into the private sector model. There is a diminishing number of unpaid volunteers to be found mainly in smaller associations and representing the traditional origins of the sector. Most associations have tenant board members albeit, except for mutual associations, usually token only. Many larger associations advertise publicly for new board members and conduct the appointment process in an open manner. Others prefer to rely on personal connections. Although in theory the board is accountable to the members of the association, the board itself appoints the members who in turn appoint the board in a manner more akin to a private club than to a body acting on behalf of the public. The membership often comprises only the board members themselves. Even where there is a wider membership, model rules approved by the NHF limit its powers to matters required by statute or conferred by the rules themselves, although admittedly this varies considerably from association to association. These are mainly constitutional changes: expulsion of a member; election or removal of board members; and winding up powers.

12.3 Thus the Regulator of Social Housing (RSH) is the essential source of accountability for housing association governing bodies. Board members individually and collectively owe the normal duty under the general law to exercise due care and diligence and have the fiduciary duty to act independently in the best interests of the association and not to have any conflict of interest or personal gain. There are also some special statutory rules concerning personal gain.

12.4 There is a link between these general principles and the specific powers of the regulator in that the powers of the English regulator to intervene often depend on the board, acting unlawfully. However, the equivalent powers of the Welsh Ministers are limited to breach of an 'enactment', although many of the duties of board members other than those of a company are common law or equitable duties.

Powers of the governing body

12.5 The RSH in its required outcomes of the 'governance and viability standard' states that registered providers 'shall ensure effective governance arrangements that deliver their aims, objectives and intended outcomes for tenants and potential tenants in an effective, transparent and accountable manner'.[1] This is a good starting point in looking at the obligations, role and powers of the governing body of a housing association. Oddly, this opening statement does not cover other customers or refer to stakeholders, although a later reference is made to the latter under the RSH's specific requirements section of the standard.

12.6 There are no statutory requirements as to the mode of governance of co-operative and community benefit societies (CCBSs) other than that of the appointment of a 'committee' (by whatever name) the decisions of which are binding on the society.[2] It makes no difference whether the governing body is called a committee of management or a board or trustees or indeed anything else. It is sometimes claimed that a 'committee' can be one person. However, in *R v Secretary of State for the Environment ex p Hillingdon LBC*[3] Woolf J held (in the context of an elected local government committee) that there must be at least two members. NHF model rules for Co-operative and Community Benefits Societies Act (CCBSA) 2014 societies (2015) suggest between five and 12 members.

12.7 It could be argued that, irrespective of size, in order to boost their self-importance, governing bodies often refer to themselves as 'boards' irrespective of the absence of any legal provenance for such a term. However, perhaps this fits well, sending out accurate signals, with the more recent direction of travel for associations in becoming increasingly like commercial organisations in both their own nature and in terms of the scale and scope of their transactions. This is now a highly commercialised sector, light years away from its roots of voluntarism and altruistic endeavour.

---

1 See HCA, 'Governance and Viability Standard', April 2015.
2 CCBSA 2014 ss14, 45.
3 [1986] 1 WLR 192.

12.8 In practice all governance and management powers are vested by the rules in the governing body subject to any delegated authority. It is of course essential for the governing body to delegate functions. These may include delegation to the chair of the committee, to managers, to specialised sub-committees or to other bodies such as a subsidiary. Powers of delegation, other than routine administration must be clearly specified in the rules or decisions must be ratified by the committee. The same considerations apply to a company.

12.9 Trustees, of whom there can be any number, control a charitable trust. As with other bodies, routine administration can be delegated. Otherwise trustees have restricted statutory powers of delegation and appointment of agents.[4] These include implementing decisions taken by the trustees, investment including managing land, fundraising and other functions prescribed by the secretary of state. However, raising money by means of profit from a trade which is an integral part of the trust's charitable purpose cannot be delegated.[5] A trustee is liable for the acts of the delegate only where he or she is in breach of a duty of care (below) in appointing the delegate or reviewing its actions.[6]

12.10 It is important in principle to distinguish between acts which are outside the objects of the association and so ultra vires and acts which, although within the objects, are nonetheless outside the authority of the governing body to make. However, there are provisions which protect someone dealing with an association. In the case of CCBSs, the validity of an act of the society cannot be challenged as being outside its rules.[7] Moreover, in favour of a person dealing with the society in good faith (ie without collusion), the committee has power to bind the society even where that person knows that the act is outside the society's powers.[8] However, in the case of a *charitable* society, these provisions applies only to a person who gives full consideration in money or money's worth and who is unaware either that the transaction is ultra vires or that the society is a charity.[9]

12.11 Although this makes clear that a duty exists toward a third party who has acted in good faith, the matter may not end there. These provisions do not absolve an individual committee member from

---

4 Trustee Act 2000 s11(3) (see also Trustee Act 1925 s25).
5 Trustee Act 2000 s11(3)(c).
6 Trustee Act 2000 s23.
7 CCBSA 2014 s43(1).
8 CCBSA 2014 ss45, 46.
9 CCBSA 2014 s47.

complying with the rules and a society can be restrained in advance from breaking them[10] in the case of a charity by the Charity Commission.[11] Moreover, the committee members who authorised the transaction may be subject to action by the society. The obligation to comply with the rules is a strict obligation, and individuals are jointly and severally liable even if they acted without fault.[12]

12.12 A breach of the rules can be ratified by a special resolution of 75 per cent of those who vote. There must be a separate special resolution to absolve the individual committee members from liability.[13]

12.13 Similar provisions apply to a company under the Companies Act 2006 and to a charitable incorporated organisation (CIO) under the Charities Act 2011. (In relation to a company, the position at common law was that a transaction beyond the company's powers was void even if ratified by its members.[14]) In the case of an ordinary charitable trust, there is individual liability for violating the terms of the trust but a transaction, at least with a person in good faith, is valid since an individual trustee has unlimited capacity. A failure by a trustee properly to delegate a function does not invalidate the acts of the delegate.[15]

Composition of the governing body

12.14 The composition of the governing body depends upon the association's constitution. This normally requires that the governing body is elected at the annual general meeting, with a third of members retiring by rotation. Bear in mind, however, that the membership of the society may comprise only the members of the governing body who therefore elect each other. The rules should be specific on the length of tenure of a board member and there will also be guidance in the respective governance code adopted by a particular association. The RSH expects associations to comply with their respective codes which state up to two or more terms of office of three years, with three terms of office seen to be the exception.[16] The regulator is not

10 CCBSA 2014 s43(2), (4).
11 CCBSA 2014 s43(2), (4).
12 See *Re Sharpe* [1892] 1 Ch 154.
13 CCBSA 2014 ss43(5), 44.
14 See *Ashbury Railway Carriage & Iron Co Ltd v Riche* (1874–75) LR 7 HR 653.
15 Trustee Act 2000 s24.
16 National Housing Federation Code of Governance, para D2, 2015.

supportive of the idea of a so called 'fallow period', ie a period where someone ceases to be a member of a board and returns to membership after an appropriate gap, usually a term of office (in most rules a third of the board members retire each year, which means a term of office would be three years). Instead the RSH, anecdotally, tends to take a view on the cumulative service regardless of gaps.

12.15 The appointment of trustees depending on the terms of the particular trust instrument is similar. Often the existing trustees appoint their successors. In the case of a charitable body, an employee can be a member of the board only if authorised by the rules or by the Charity Commission or appointed by the RSH under its powers to intervene.

12.16 There are usually restrictions on age, often involving special election requirements once a member reaches the age of 75. There is usually a power of co-option which can include non-members. Under particular rules, a parent association or a public body, for example, might have power to nominate a member. However, as we shall see in chapter 13, local authority membership is severely restricted. In the case both of a CCBS and a company, the governing body is subject to the Company Directors Disqualification Act 1986[17] which enables a director to be disqualified for misconduct or for association with an insolvent company or society.

12.17 The standard insists upon accountability to tenants, the regulator and relevant stakeholders.[18] As we saw in chapter 5, the regulator has a range of powers to intervene in the governance of a registered provider and can make appointments to the governing body, remove governing body members and where necessary manage the affairs of the association through the appointment of a manager.

Regulatory requirements

12.18 What are the regulatory requirements for governing bodies? The 'governance and viability standard' prescribed by the RSH focuses generally on required outcomes. As with its predecessor the Housing Corporation, stress is placed on requirements to produce plans and other documentary evidence describing what the association is doing to minimise risks of every kind. The standard states that:

---

17 See s22E.
18 HCA, 'Governance and Financial Viability Standard', para 1.1(c).

Registered providers shall ensure effective governance arrangements that deliver their aims, objectives and intended outcomes for tenants and potential tenants in an effective, transparent and accountable manner.[19]

12.19 It goes on to say that registered providers:

1) adhere to all relevant law;
2) comply with their governing documents and regulatory requirements;
3) are accountable to tenants, the regulator and relevant stakeholders;
4) safeguard taxpayers' interests and the reputation of the sector;
5) have an effective risk management and internal controls assurance framework;
6) protect social housing assets.[20]

12.20 In the accompanying *Governance and financial viability code of practice*, further emphasis is placed on boards being 'responsible holders and stewards of social housing assets'.[21] Tellingly, the code reveals the regulatory concern about the reputation of the sector stating that reputation 'is key in maintaining confidence in the sector' stressing the need to manage businesses and risks in a way which does not negatively impact on the reputation of the sector.[22]

12.21 There are a number of specific expectations in the standard. There is a need to adopt and comply with an appropriate governance code with governance arrangements establishing and maintaining clear roles, responsibilities and accountabilities for the board, chair and chief executive and ensuring that appropriate probity arrangements are in place. Any areas of non-compliance with the chosen governance code need to be explained. The effectiveness of governance arrangements should be reviewed at least once a year and boards must certify in their annual accounts their compliance with the standard.[23]

12.22 The associated code adds little to this requirement. Registered providers are required to ensure they manage their affairs with an appropriate degree of skill, independence, diligence, effectiveness, prudence and foresight[24] communicating with the regulator in a timely manner on any material issues which relate to non-compliance

19 HCA, 'Governance and Financial Viability Standard', para 1.1.
20 HCA, 'Governance and Financial Viability Standard', para 1.1.
21 HCA, 'Governance and Financial Viability Code of Practice', para 6.
22 HCA, 'Governance and Financial Viability Code of Practice', para. 7
23 HCA, 'Governance and Financial Viability Code of Practice', paras 2.1, 2.8.
24 HCA, 'Governance and Financial Viability Code of Practice', para 2.2.

or potential non-compliance with the standards (ie the economic and consumer standards) generally.[25] Here the code does elaborate stating that compliance 'will include both behavioural aspects, such as ensuring that the board and executive foster a culture of constructive challenge and debate, and good governance practices'.[26] Further guidance is given also on requisite skills of boards and their executives, which should:

- have an appropriate skills strategy to address the needs of the business;
- regularly assess whether boards and management have the right competences, experience, and technical knowledge appropriate to the size, scale and risk profile of the organisation (looking at current and future business as well as the changing operating environment);
- ensure that all material decisions are made with appropriate impartial internal/external expertise or advice;
- have plans to address any skills gaps identified (including bringing in external skills) and monitor those plans.[27]

12.23 Independence is singled out for special attention in the code stating that in some structures 'influence' is inherent in the very corporate structure itself giving the example of a profit-making registered provider which is a subsidiary within a group structure. The code goes on to say that influence can arise out of close associations between the registered provider and other organisation and individuals. Thus it is important that board members should exercise independence of judgement and act at all times in the best interests of the registered provider with mechanisms in place ensuring the highest degree of probity and value for money and preventing undue influence from third parties.[28]

12.24 There is strong attention given to financial governance and control with a focus on appropriate, robust and prudent business planning, risk and control framework.[29] The financial governance arrangements and requirements are set out in chapter 14. It is, though, worth drawing out some points which have significance for board accountability.

---

25 HCA, 'Governance and Financial Viability Code of Practice', para 2.3.
26 HCA, Code of Practice, para 14.
27 HCA, Code of Practice, para 15.
28 HCA, Code of Practice, paras 16–18.
29 HCA, Code of Practice, para 2.4.

12.25   First, the governance and control framework emphasises the need for it to be approved by the board itself, stressing the importance of business planning and systems which monitor delivery and risks with the need to review the framework at least once a year.[30] Second, there is also emphasis placed upon the need before taking on new liabilities that these are understood and that the likely impact on future business and regulatory compliance be carefully considered and managed.[31]

12.26   Third, the associated code stresses the need for business planning and organisational objectives to cover all aspects of the registered provider's business and also demonstrate there is full understanding of the operating environment.[32] Indeed, registered providers need to build their businesses on robust and prudent assumptions looking at past performance, market conditions, deliverability and forecasts of possible future conditions.[33]

12.27   While the standard and the code offer an impressive set of principles and requirements, their degree of detail does raise the serious question about the independence of the sector and what exactly are the freedoms and tolerances owned by individual housing associations. Gone are the days when associations used grant funding to meet housing need, supporting government in addressing housing shortages or poor housing conditions but still seen by the state as independent organisations and part of the 'third (voluntary) sector'. Housing associations have gone through a period of adoption by the state, the increasing sequestering of the sector as a delivery mechanism through which the state can further its policies, whether that be to build more homes, to further home ownership or to reduce public spending.

12.28   When looking at these detailed regulatory requirements, the days of true independence of the sector seem very far behind. Yet the sector does feel comfortable with this close directing relationship with the state. Individual housing associations in their droves continue to bid for state funding, and rarely is there open evidence that associations take on the regulator for its decisions. In fact, in recent consultation over key policy and regulatory documents which undoubtedly have a serious day-to-day impact on the work of housing associations, the tone of responses is generally supportive

---

30 HCA, Code of Practice, paras 2.4.1, 2.4.2.
31 HCA, Code of Practice, para 2.5(c).
32 The Code, para 21.
33 The Code, para 25.

and challenge, what there is of it, tends to be in the detail.[34] What freedoms exist are at the operational level and the local policy level, and even with the latter there are significant restrictions and interferences by central or local government. This is a sector which some might argue is gradually giving up its soul.

Liability of the governing body

Overview

12.29 The members of a company and a CCBS have limited liability for the association's debts in the same way as ordinary company shareholders. Trustees are fully liable unless the trust is constituted as a CIO. Members of the governing body are, however, liable for their personal faults.

12.30 The question of personal liability is controversial. There are competing obligations and imperatives. On the one hand, the growing commercialisation of the sector and contractual obligations to banks and financial institutions require a high degree of equivalent skill. On the other hand, the origins of the voluntary housing movement suggests if this skill set goes too far then the traditional values of altruism and volunteering for a worthy cause may be threatened. Thus some board members may consider themselves to be buccaneering entrepreneurs, while others may be cast in the mould of prudent trustees or public servants.

12.31 The matter is complicated because of the different structures of housing associations. Governing bodies, often within the same group, may have different levels of liability. At the one end with the highest standards there are trustees of charities, at the other end directors of non-charitable companies and in the middle, the most amorphous category, there are committee members of CCBSs, some charitable. There is also, although increasingly rare now, the distinction between paid and unpaid members.

12.32 All owe duties to act in what they consider is the best interests of the association but the level of skill expected of them depends on the structure of the association. In the past, trustees have been subject to a higher more objective standard of skill and care than have company directors even though the burden on the latter are usually greater. However, various statutory provisions have raised the standard in

---

34 Eg see Responses to the proposed changes to the 'Value for Money Standard'.

both cases possibly imposing an unrealistic burden on volunteer board members, especially tenants. A basic problem is that there are no statutory provisions, nor, as far as we can ascertain, case-law explicitly governing the board members of a CCBS. We therefore have to explore company and trust law to seek a valid analogy. We cannot be certain that such analogous legal principles can exactly apply in any given circumstances.

12.33 There are three overlapping areas of liability: the duty at common law to exercise due care and skill; the fiduciary duty in equity, primarily to act without self-interest; and duties under statute spanning both aspects. All concern the duty owed by the board member to the association itself as a separate entity, or, in the case of a trust to its charitable objects, and all derive from a basic duty to act in the best interests of the association. This of course usually means the public interest, certainly in the case of a charity and a community benefit society (CBS). In the case of a fully mutual society, the membership itself is the focus, while the objects of a non-charitable company depend on its articles.

12.34 All persons in positions of responsibility owe a common law duty in relation to managing the affairs of the association. These principles focus on the degree of care and skill required of the board member. They were developed in the context of an ordinary trading company so that some of the cases concerning the need to allow an element of risk must be treated with caution.[35] The equitable or fiduciary duty derives from trusteeship and has been extended to company directors. Fiduciary duty applies to persons entrusted with responsibilities in the interests of others, so that it should equally apply to all governing bodies. It concerns in particular a duty to be 'above suspicion' that is to avoid conflicts of interest and not to profit from the member's relationship with the association, Equity also imposes its own standard of care on trustees. We shall discuss the fiduciary duties in the later section on conflicts of interest.

12.35 There is an important and mutually reinforcing link between the general law and the powers of the regulator. Firstly, as we saw in chapter 5, the regulator's more serious powers of intervention depend on mismanagement. As part of the government's policy of reducing regulation, this now means only 'managed in breach of any legal requirements imposed by or under an Act or otherwise'. Mismanagement in this sense does not directly include violations of regulatory standards and guidance since these are not legally

---

35 Eg *Re City Equitable Fire Insurance Co Ltd* [1925] Ch 407 at 408 and 409.

enforceable as such. However, in as much as they depend upon 'reasonable expectations' (below), regulatory standards and guidance enable the courts to take into account the requirements of the regulator thus helping to unify the law. This may be less effective in Wales since the Regulation of Registered Social Landlords (Wales) Act 2018 triggers the regulator's powers only by breach of an 'enactment', thus excluding the common law and equitable duties.[36] In any event, compliance with regulatory standards does not in itself satisfy legal duties.

Companies: standard of care

12.36 The common law duty was originally a low and subjective one, namely to exercise the degree of care and skill that the board member actually possesses or claims to possess bearing in mind such matters as time to attend meetings and to prepare for them. According to this test, a member need not be proactive in seeking out problems. For example, in *Re Cardiff Savings Bank*[37] the Marquis of Bute was held not to be in breach even though he only attended one meeting of the board. Thus only a self-aggrandising volunteer member might attract a heavier burden. On the other hand, a conscientious member might be at risk.

12.37 Modern statutory provisions have introduced a more objective standard. Chief among these is the Companies Act 2006 which applies to all companies. The Act codifies the duties of a company director. These embody the existing common law and equitable duties: to act within powers, to promote the success of the company, to exercise independent judgment, to avoid conflicts of interest, not to accept benefits from third parties and to declare interests in proposed transactions or arrangements.[38]

12.38 The standard of care and skill is defined as follows: the care skill and diligence that would be exercised by a reasonably diligent person with:

a) the general knowledge and experience that may reasonably be expected of a person carrying out the functions carried out by the director in relation to the company; and

b) the general knowledge, skill and experience that the director has.[39]

---

36 Section 18(2).
37 [1892] 2 Ch 100.
38 Companies Act 2006 ss170–173, 175.
39 Companies Act 2006 ss174, 178(2).

12.39 The objective test in a) normally applies. It is replaced by the subjective test b) only if this is a higher standard. Thus the volunteer board member is at risk. The question of what is a reasonable expectation must be assessed in the light of all the circumstances including the nature of the association's work, and the particular role of the board member concerned. The regulator has exacting requirements which the courts may consider in setting the required level of skill and care, although these are not conclusive and compliance in itself is no defence.

12.40 Insolvency Act 1986 s214 applies a similar standard to cases of 'wrongful trading', that is where, before the company was wound up, the board carried on business and the director in question knew or should have known that the company would become insolvent.

12.41 In company law also, the same provisions apply to 'shadow directors'. A shadow director is:

> ... a person in accordance with whose directions or instructions the directors of the company are accustomed to act. However, a person is not deemed a shadow director by reason only that directors act on advice given by him in a professional capacity.[40]

So a lawyer or accountant, for example, simply giving advice is not a shadow director. The same may apply to a member of the executive staff who is not a board member.

Co-operative and Community Benefit Societies Act 2014: standard of care

12.42 The CCBSA 2014 under which most housing associations are formed is silent on the question of the standards to be expected from the governing body. The Companies Act 2006 (above) does not directly apply. The old, 'subjective', common law duty may therefore still apply, reflecting perhaps the history of these bodies in voluntary endeavour. This would of course protect the relatively few remaining unpaid voluntary board members and also tenant members.

12.43 However, since many CBSs are at the forefront of large-scale commercial activities, this relaxed standard may no longer be appropriate and the Companies Act standards may be applied by analogy. The low standard, requiring that board members do no more than their incompetent best, originated during Victorian laissez faire which encouraged risk-taking. This is a long way from the standard needed in a contemporary housing association which is publicly

40 Companies Act 2006 s251.

funded. Arguably the higher objective standard should apply generally, its stringency based on the nature of the association's work rather than the person. Regulatory requirements in favour of expert and well qualified board members underlie this.

12.44 Indeed, there is authority that independently of the Companies Act 2006 (above) a similar partly objective test also applies under the general law.[41] If this is so, then in a CCBS as well as a company, the primary test is that of the particular role to be reasonably expected of the board member enhanced by any higher abilities he or she may claim. Moreover, in the context of winding up, by virtue of CCBSA 2014 s223, the Insolvency Act 1986 provisions (above) apply to a CCBS as if it were a company. Thus the wrongful trading standard of care also seems to apply since this is parasitic on a winding up.

Charities standard of care

12.45 Whatever the position as regards a company and a CCBS, under the general law trustees have a higher standard of care which is entirely objective. Board members of charitable bodies that are CBSs or companies, although not strictly trustees, are probably treated as analogous to trustees ('quasi-trustees') for the purpose of their duties under the general law.[42] A trustee's liability was traditionally expressed as the standard of a reasonable business person managing their own business affairs.[43] The actual skill a person possesses is therefore not relevant. Paid professional trustees, though, are subject to a higher standard still, that owed to persons for whom they are morally bound to provide.[44] In the latter case, at least the board member must be proactive in the sense that he or she must take positive steps keep informed within the sphere of the board's responsibilities.

12.46 Under Trustee Act 2000 s1, in respect of certain functions, a trustee must exercise such care and skill as is reasonable in all the circumstances, having regard in particular to any special knowledge or experience that he or she has or holds himself or herself out as having. This seems to mean that the trustees own level of competence may require a higher standard. Unlike the similar test

---

41 See *Dorchester Finance Co v Stebbing* [1989] BCLC 498; *Re Barings plc (No 5)* [2000] 1 BCLC 523.
42 See *Liverpool and District Hospital for Diseases of the Heart v Attorney General* [1981] Ch 193; Charities Act 2011 s353(1).
43 *Speight v Gaunt* (1883) 9 App Cas 1 at 19.
44 *Bartlett v Barclays Bank Trust Co Ltd* [1980] 1 Ch 515.

in company law (above) this seems to include the case of a self-promoting member who claims greater competence than they have.

12.47 The Act applies only to certain duties and not to the full range of a trustee's functions which remain subject to the general standards (above). It applies to investing trust property, acquiring land, appointing agents and insuring trust property.[45] Moreover, this duty can be excluded by the trust instrument. The Charity Commission has suggested that the duties of charities under the general law are comparable to those under the Trustee Act 2000.[46]

12.48 In the end, this proliferation of standards seems to require a broad common sense approach, informed in particular by the membership and work of different kinds of housing association, by regulatory requirements and by the accepted practices of the sector endorsed by its representative bodies. The original subjective standard may be appropriately flexible in the case of co-operatives where all the board members, except perhaps for co-optees, if appointed, are likely to be tenants. And equally, a higher standard would be apposite where members of a governing body are appointed as professionals, which is increasingly the case.

12.49 Hence members appointed for their particular expertise must be judged by the standards of reasonably competent persons having that expertise. Similarly a person who takes on special responsibility, such as a chair or the chair of a specialist committee, may be subject to a higher standard. Therefore it is important that an association through its recruitment process of board members determine the standard of skill and competence in appointing board members and filtering out those applicants who don't make the grade.

12.50 The rules or articles, or indeed agreements made outside the constitution may also define expectations about attendance of board members. Standard rules usually provide that board membership is terminated after the absence from three or other defined number of consecutive board meetings. It is possible that membership is a civil right within Article 6 of the European Convention on Human Rights (ECHR), to automatic cessation of membership may be unlawful under the Convention. A member should therefore be given the chance of explaining or justifying their absence with the safeguard of a right of appeal to an independent arbitrator. However, a defence to such a challenge to an automatic forfeiture rule is that this is

45 Sections 1, 2, Sch 1.
46 See Lloyd (ed), *Charities: the new law*, Jordans, 2007, para 10.20.

part of the definition of member's rights under the contract which is constituted in the rules and articles themselves. Nonetheless repeated failure to attend meetings will undoubtedly amount to a breach of the terms of any service agreement between the member and the association.

Enforcing director's liability

Introduction

12.51 In the case of a company, with the permission of the court, a member may bring a derivative action on the company's behalf on the ground of negligence, default, breach of duty or breach of trust by a director or former director.[47] (Any damages are paid to the company and not the person who brought the action.) These provisions are intended to bring some protection to the minority since most decisions are made by a simple majority and thus enable a majority to exploit a minority. By using this procedure a member can gain access to the Board's papers. There is also a personal remedy whereby a member of a company can petition the court on the ground that the company's affairs are being or have been conducted in in a way which is unfairly prejudicial to the membership generally or to some part of it which includes himself.[48]

12.52 These protections do not apply to the ostensibly public spirited world of the CCBS. However, there is a similar common law derivative action which can no longer be brought by a company member but still applies to a CCBS.[49] Under this, the so called 'fraud on the minority' principle, a member on behalf of the company or society can bring a claim where the persons in control have committed an ultra vires act or a fraudulent or negligent breach of duty. This form of protection may be most appropriate to an association with tenant representation especially a fully or part mutual society. However, there is a high threshold in that actual fraud or unlawful personal gain is required.

---

47 Companies Act 2006 Part 11.
48 Companies Act 2006 s994.
49 See *Harris v Microfusion 2000–3 LLP* [2016] EWCA Civ 1212.

Duties to third parties

12.53 Irrespective of corporate form, members and especially board members also owe a duty to third parties. This is normally based on the common law standard (above). An advantage of the corporate form is that it confers limited liability on a member for the entity's debts. Moreover, the wrongful acts of a member of the governing body are attributed to the association if the member was acting within their powers. They may be liable individually and along with other members if they acted outside their powers or where under the law of tort they exercised their power, or gave advice, negligently.[50] An example of this was mooted both in relation to the *Cosmopolitan* and the *Gallions* cases.[51] An individual may also be criminally liable, either alone or with other members or jointly with the association, under particular legislation for a breach of duty where the governing body is responsible. Statutory duties are many and various and in general they cannot be diluted by agreement between parties and the obligation cannot be excluded.

Exemption from liability

12.54 A key question arises as to whether liability can be excluded. There are several statutory provisions. Members of a non-charitable CCBS are less protected than trustees of charities and company directors. In the latter two cases, the courts have the discretion to offer relief from personal liability if the person has acted honestly and reasonably and ought fairly to be excused.[52] The Charity Commission has a similar power in relation to the governing bodies (and auditors) of any charitable association.[53] A member of a charitable association may also protect themselves from legal liability by seeking the advice of the Charity Commission and relying on that advice.[54]

12.55 Companies are prohibited from exempting directors from liability or indemnifying them although insurance can be purchased.[55] However, the members can ratify a breach of duty either by a formal

---

50 See *Mill v Hawker* (1874) LR 10 Ex 92; *Campbell v Paddington Corporation* [1911] 1 KB 869; *Palmer Birch (a partnership) v Lloyd* [2018] EWHC 2316 (TCC).
51 See HCA, *Cosmopolitan Housing Group Lessons*, 2014. See also *Halifax Building Society v Meridian Housing Association* (1995) 27 HLR 123.
52 See Trustee Act 1925 s61; and Companies Act 2006 s1157.
53 Charities Act 2011 s191.
54 Charities Act 2011 s110.
55 Companies Act 2006 ss232, 233.

resolution or unanimous consent.[56] A CCBS and a trust can rely upon provisions in its rules exempting members or officers from liability. In the case of a CCBS, the unanimous consent of the members can ratify a breach of duty. We saw above that the duty of care which applies to some functions under the Trustee Act 2000 can be excluded by the trust instrument.

12.56 Exemption clauses will be construed by the courts very strictly and therefore need to be worded carefully. This is particularly so in the case of trustees and therefore analogously by board members of charitable bodies. Whether the courts would accept an exemption no matter how well and carefully worded for reckless or deliberate wrongdoing is questionable.[57] Membership of the NHF provides board members with insurance protection for wrongdoing but such cover would not include recklessness or criminal activity.

Conflicts of interest: fiduciary duties

12.57 Equity is primarily concerned with fiduciary duties in relation to the management of property and so is of especial importance to housing association boards. The fiduciary duty focuses on loyalty to the association and conflicts of interest. Fortunately the duty seems to apply equally to all the forms of housing association. The trustee of course is the architype fiduciary but the directors of a company and committee members of a CCBS also stand in a fiduciary relationship to their associations.[58] However, they do not owe a fiduciary duty to anyone else. Moreover, a company does not owe a fiduciary duty to its members.

12.58 Board members must so act as not to abuse that position of trust but also to be above suspicion. A board member must firstly act exclusively in the interests of the association as a whole and secondly must not profit from his or her relationship with the association or let a conflict of interest arise. Any personal profit arising, even indirectly, out of the member's relationship with the association, belongs in equity to the association, a very strict standard.[59] Powers are given to a director in order for them to manage the association and for no other reason. Equity demands, therefore, that such powers are only

---

56 Companies Act 2006 s179.
57 See *Rae v Meek* (1889) LR 14 App Cas 558.
58 *Regal (Hastings) Ltd v Gulliver* [1967] 2 AC 134 at 159.
59 See *Boardman v Phipps* [1967] 2 AC 46.

exercised for that purpose otherwise those powers are tainted and equity will require appropriate restitution.

12.59 Regulatory requirements reflect this. Under the specific expectations of the 'governance and viability standard', clear accountabilities must be in place and boards should also ensure appropriate probity arrangements are in place.[60] The standard goes on to say that registered providers should manage their affairs with an appropriate degree of independence.[61] In the associated code of practice, members should exercise independence of judgement and act at all times in the best interests of the registered provider and appropriate mechanisms should be in place to manage any conflicts of interest to demonstrate probity.[62]

12.60 Members of the governing body are sometimes chosen as representatives of stakeholders, such as tenants or local authority members or officers. (However, the declassification of housing associations as public bodies in 2017 (see para 3.12) means that only very limited involvement of local authority members is allowed.) That they have been appointed via this route does not change the scope and nature of their fiduciary duty. They would be in a strong position to put forward views from those they represent or bring that representative perspective to the discussion but they must act in the best interests only of the association itself. Importantly, any interest must be openly and fully declared. Any new interest must be declared as soon as it is known.

12.61 In this respect, the law is more developed in relation to a company than it is to a CCBS with detailed consideration of conflict of interest covered in the Companies Act 2006.[63] In the case of a charitable company, the Charity Commission can authorise dealings in breach of these duties.[64] In the gentler world of the CCBS, there are no corresponding statutory provisions the matter being left to a society's own rules and procedures. However, these typically require a similar declaration of interest.

12.62 Charities Act 2011 s185 enables a charity to pay a trustee or 'connected person' (defined relative or business associate), for services to the charity under an agreement in writing (such as professional

---

60 See HCA, 'Governance and Financial Viability Standard', para 2.1.
61 HCA, 'Governance and Financial Viability Standard', para 2.2.
62 See HCA, 'Governance and Financial Viability Standard' Code of Practice, April 2015, para 17.
63 Companies Act 2006 ss175, 177, 182–185.
64 Companies Act 2006 s181(4).

advice) provided that the level of pay is reasonable, that payment is in the best interests of the charity and that those so paid are a minority of the trustees. This applies to all charities not only to trusts proper. These provisions do not apply to payment of a trustee as such, nor to a contract of employment. In the case of a company, the consent of the Charity Commission is required for any change in its articles that authorises benefits to be paid to directors, members or persons connected with them such as families.[65]

Statutory requirements

12.63 That takes us nicely to specific legislation and regulatory requirements relating to conflicts of interest in housing associations. For all organisational forms, these requirements would seem to be equally if not more stringent than company law in that they extend beyond the members themselves to family and business associates.

12.64 Historically, effectively since the Housing Finance Act 1972, there has been a very strict statutory set of requirements. Following the introduction of the Housing Act 1964 which created the Housing Corporation, loans were given to housing associations to support cost-rent and co-ownership schemes. During the mid-1960s, a number of housing associations were set up by professional people in particular (lawyers, accountants, surveyors, architects and the like) to build these schemes and through governing bodies which comprised themselves, awarded themselves the associated professional work. When grants were introduced, it was felt politically inappropriate for these professionals to earn income from grant-funded projects – there were clear financial conflicts of interests. So a quite stringent regime was introduced, first in rudimentary form under the Housing Finance Act 1972 and then more fully formed in the Housing Act 1974. This regime and its successors go beyond the requirements of equity since they apply to all members not just to those owing a fiduciary duty such as the board. The latest incarnation of this statutory set of requirements under Housing Act 1996 Sch 1 is now applicable only to registered social landlords in Wales. It effectively ensured and still ensures in Wales that members, officers and their families cannot benefit over and above the relationship they may have as a board member or through a contract of employment. Hence there were restrictions on board members and officers receiving payment for services, getting benefits such as the provision

---

65 Charities Act 2011 s198.

of housing accommodation for themselves or their close relatives. Although there were enacted a number of exemptions to these restrictions since they were deemed too draconian compared to other conflict of interest regimes in the public sector.

12.65 Housing and Regeneration Act (HRA) 2008 Part 2, which created the Homes and Communities Agency (HCA), repealed the application of Sch 1 to England and established a narrower regime. Unlike the earlier regime, this does not apply to benefits or payments in general. Nor does it apply to officers and employees unless they are members. HRA 2008 s122 restricts 'the making of gifts', and the payment of dividends and bonuses (all undefined), by a non-profit making registered provider to:

a) a member or former member of the registered provider;
b) a member of the family of a member or former member;
c) a company which has as a director a person within paragraphs a) or b).

12.66 These provisions may not apply to trusts, since a trust has no members as such. However, given that section 122 applies to all non- profit registered providers but the enforcement provisions (below), such as they are, are specifically confined to companies and societies, 'member' here could be interpreted to include a trustee. A gift may be made, and a dividend or bonus may be paid, only if it falls within one of the following classes:

- Class 1 is payments which are:
  a) in accordance with the constitution of the registered provider; and
  b) due as interest on capital lent to the provider or subscribed in its shares (the latter being nominal only).
- Class 2 is payments which are:
  a) paid by a fully mutual housing association (within the meaning of Housing Associations Act 1985 s1(2);
  b) paid to former members of the association; and
  c) due under:
     i) tenancy agreements with the association; or
     ii) agreements under which the former members because members of the association.
- Class 3 is payments which are:
  a) in accordance with the constitution of the registered provider making the payment ('the payer'); and
  b) made to a registered provider which is a subsidiary or associate of the payer.

- Class 4 is payments which are:
  a) in accordance with the constitution of the registered provider;
  b) paid for the benefit of tenants of the provider; and
  c) in any particular case paid to the tenant to obtain other accommodation by acquiring a freehold, or long-leasehold interest in a dwelling.

12.67 If a registered provider, which is a company or registered society, contravenes these requirements, then it may recover the wrongful gift or payment as a debt and may be required by the regulator to do so.[66] Indeed, the only enforcement mechanism seems to be the regulator on the ground of 'mismanagement' apart from the unlikely event of a member bringing an action against the association or board members. The Localism Act 2011 amended the HRA 2008 to include powers of the secretary of state, with appropriate consultation requirements, to issue an order adding, removing or modifying the permitted classes.[67]

12.68 HRA 2008 s272 says that a person 'is a member of a family of another' if:
  a) they are, or live together as if they were, spouses or civil partners; or
  b) one is the parent, grandparent, child or grandchild, brother, sister, uncle, aunt, nephew or niece of the other.

12.69 To make it perfectly clear, HRA 2008 s272(2) says for those purposes:
  a) a relationship by marriage or civil partnership shall be treated as a relationship by blood (and in particular, the person's step child shall be treated as the person's child); and
  b) a relationship by half-blood shall be treated as a relationship of full blood.

12.70 The NHF code of governance says that family member should be given a very wide interpretation and extends the conflict of interest to 'close connections or associations' which can include friends, colleagues, neighbours, business associates and other social contacts.

12.71 Effectively the wider conflict of interest requirements, originally applying to the sector under the Housing Act 1996 and earlier legislation, are now more fully catered for in the 'governance and financial viability standard' and its specific requirement to adopt an appropriate code of governance and compliance with that code. This appears to apply to trusts as well as to companies and CCBSs.

66 HRA 2008 s122(6).
67 HRA 2008 s122(7), (8).

12.72 Most housing associations have adopted the NHF's code of governance.[68] In many ways by extension of the standard this ensures appropriate checks and balances regarding conflicts of interest. Not following the code and therefore the standard could potentially open up an individual board member and the association to regulatory intervention (albeit amounting to 'mismanagement' only if the standard was adopted) by the courts as part of the fiduciary duty (above).

12.73 The code states (section H) that:

> Organisations must maintain, and be seen to maintain, the highest ethical standards of probity and conduct. Boards must operate in an open and transparent manner, having dialogue with and accountability to tenants and other stakeholders.

12.74 The code of conduct elaborates further covering areas relating to:
A) Probity;
B) Loyalty and conflicts of interest;
C) Remuneration;
D) Personal benefit;
E) Prevention of bribery and corruption;
F) Respect.

12.75 Here we will focus on the requirements relating to conflicts of interest. The code says that all 'actual or potential conflicts or dualities of interest must be openly declared and resolved'.[69] Accordingly, rules for CCBSA 2014 societies prohibit a board or committee member from having any financial interest in a contract or transaction with the society and from being granted any benefit from the society other than interests or benefits expressly permitted by the rules or by statute or authorised by the regulator or under the association's own code of practice. Any interest in an arrangement between the association and someone else must be disclosed before it is discussed. There must also be a register of membership of or interests in other bodies.

12.76 Expenses and, subject to independent advice, 'reasonable' remuneration, fees, liability insurance premiums, allowances and payment for loss of earnings can be made as can 'reasonable and proper benefits' (although these may fall foul of statute (above)) and payments to which the member may be entitled as a beneficiary of the society on the same terms as any other beneficiary. This seems mainly to concern fully mutual societies.

---

68 NHF, *Code of Governance: Promoting board excellence for housing associations*, 2015, and the associated Code of Conduct, 2012.
69 Page 8.

Wales

12.77 For Wales, the old more stringent requirements still apply. Broadly speaking, ordinary members and their families are not allowed to receive gifts or share in profits. In addition, officers (essentially board and committee members), other than employees, must not be paid for their work and officers and employees and their close relatives must not receive benefits from the association. The restrictions extend for 12 months after the officer or employee left the association. Historically, the Welsh government and the Housing Corporation had the power to grant exemptions to Housing Act 1996 Sch 1, making most of them meaningless in operation. The same applies today. As in England, apart from the Welsh Ministers' power to require the association to recover the payment,[70] there is no enforcement mechanism against the association.

12.78 The main provisions are as follows (Housing Act 1996 Sch 1 Part I):

1) No gifts or payments by way of dividend or bonus can be made by a registered social landlord to members or past members, to the families of such persons or to companies in which the member is a director or member, unless:
   a) the payment is in accordance with the constitution or rules of the landlord and represents interest on capital lent or subscribed by way of shares;
   b) the payment is by a fully mutual housing association to a person who has ceased to be a member and represents the sum due in accordance with an agreement with the association;
   c) the payment is in accordance with the constitution or rules to a registered social landlord (RSL) which is a subsidiary or associate.
2) No payments or benefits of any kind can be granted by a registered housing association which is also a CCBS or a company registered under the Companies Act 2006, to:
   a) an officer or employee of the society or company; or
   b) a person who at any time within the preceding 12 months has been a person within paragraph a); or
   c) a close relative of a person within paragraph a) or b); or
   d) a business trading for profit of which a person falling within paragraph a), b) or c) is a principal proprietor or in the management of which such a person is directly concerned. There are exceptions to this as follows:

---

70 Housing Act 1996 Sch 1 paras 1(3), 2(4).

i) payments or benefits granted to officers or employees by way of a contract of employment with the society or company;
ii) payments of remuneration or expenses to officers not having a contract of employment with the society or company;
iii) payments by way of interest on capital or shares and payable in accordance with the rules of the society and payments by a fully mutual housing association to persons ceasing to be members in accordance with the tenancy or other agreement;
iv) the grant or renewal of a tenancy by a co-operative housing association;
v) the grant of a tenancy to a person, or a close relative of a person, who later becomes an officer or employee of the society or company; this provision includes the grant of a new tenancy to such a person;
vi) payment, made or benefits granted in accordance with any determination by the Welsh Ministers. The usual consultation and publication requirements apply to the issue of such determination.

The Welsh Ministers can also fix the level of any fees or expenses paid to a member who is not an officer or to an officer outside a contract of employment.

12.79 The Housing Act 1996 provides a definition of 'family'.[71] The definition includes spouses and persons 'living together as husband and wife'. There is also a defined collection of relationships of blood and marriage. An illegitimate child of a person's mother and 'reputed father' is included. Cousins and remote collaterals are not. Grandparents, children, grandchildren, brothers, sisters, uncles, aunts, nephews and nieces are included.

12.80 'Close relatives' is not defined in the Act but is clearly narrower than family. Whether a relationship is 'close' must depend on the facts of each case. However, it will normally include a person's spouse, parent, grandparent, child, grandchild (including illegitimate children and grandchildren), brother and sister. The term 'relative' may not include any relationship that is not by blood or marriage, however close. This interpretation appears somewhat anomalous. The old Housing Corporation guidance advised that associations

71 Housing Act 1996 ss61(1), 62(2).

should treat non-blood relations as 'close' and act as if the provisions apply.

12.81 There is no definition of committee member, or employee, although a 'co-opted member' in relation to the committee (ie the committee of management or other directing body) includes any person co-opted to serve on the committee, whether he is a member of the society or not.[72] It is easy to draw from this a definition of committee member. Given the purpose of the Act it would seem unduly literal to limit its scope to the main committee. On the other hand, in other statutory contexts committees and sub-committees are distinguished.[73]

---

72 Housing Act 1996 s57(2).
73 Eg Local Government Act 1972 s101(1).

CHAPTER 13

Accountability

13.1 Introduction

13.5 Accountability to the regulator

13.10 Accountability to local authorities

13.24 Accountability to tenants

13.44 Accountability to the community and general public

13.53 The Housing Ombudsman

Introduction

13.1 Housing associations – due to their wide range of functions and their roles within communities, in their stewardship of taxpayers' money and their range of contractual obligations – are accountable to a variety agencies, groups or individuals. These include:
- regulatory bodies such as the Regulator of Social Housing (RSH), the Care Quality Commission (CQC) and the Charity Commission;
- local authorities in a range of ways;
- tenants, customers and service users;
- local communities; and
- the public in general.

These multiple forms of accountability are not entirely consistent with the rhetoric of housing associations as independent businesses driven by the market.

13.2 'Accountability' has different meanings to different people and in different contexts. Perhaps the most useful distinction is between 'accountability' in its literal sense of a duty to explain and inform; and 'responsibility' in the legal sense of a liability to sanctions and performance of obligations. In these senses, a housing association as such is both accountable and responsible to statutory regulators and accountable and sometimes responsible to tenants and customers and to persons such as lenders or local authorities with whom it has a contractual relationship.

13.3 Under the general law, the governing body is both accountable and responsible to the association itself. Individual members of the governing body are responsible to the association, accountable to the governing body and sometimes accountable to statutory regulators. The association and sometimes individual officers may also be subject to criminal liability or obligations in tort. As we saw in chapter 11, under the general law, board members owe a high 'fiduciary' standard of duty to the association, but the accountability of other members weaker.

13.4 In this chapter we shall discuss accountability provisions specific to housing associations.

Accountability to the regulator

13.5 The regulator's general powers of monitoring, inspection and to require information were discussed in chapters 4 and 5. Here we will outline statutory requirements to provide accounts. The regulator can give directions to registered providers concerning the way in which their accounts must be presented for the purpose of ensuring 'a true and fair view' of the association's social housing activities and the use of assets relating thereto. Annual accounts must be submitted to the regulator, together with an auditor's report or any other report required by statute.[1]

13.6 These requirements are on top of any requirement imposed by other legislation upon a charity, a company or a Co-operative and Community Benefits Societies Act (CCBSA) 2014 society to give information to the regulator concerned, although there are sometimes co-ordinating provisions especially in the case of a charity. In the case of a charity registered with the Charity Commission, the regulator's directions can require it to use a specified method to distinguish between its social housing activities and its other activities.

13.7 The accounting provisions aim to lighten the burden on smaller bodies while still ensuring accountability. Thus, where under other legislation, no formal audit is required, an accountant's report rather than a full audit must be .submitted to the regulator. These cases are as follows: small companies under the Companies Act 2006, small CCBSs such as co-operatives where there is a resolution at a general meeting to exclude the requirement[2] and smaller charities under the Charities Act 2011. However, in all cases the regulator can require an extraordinary audit.[3]

13.8 These powers are enforced by criminal sanctions, albeit only the summary offence of failing to comply without reasonable excuse. In addition to the association itself, every officer is liable subject to the defence of reasonable care.[4] 'Officer' has a wide meaning including all members of the governing body, managers, and, in the case of a CCBSA 2014 society, the treasurer, secretary and every employee.[5] Prosecution must be by or with the consent of the regulator or the Director of Public Prosecutions (DPP). The regulator can also apply to the High Court for an enforcement order.[6] Finally, the relevant accountant or auditor can pass on information to the regulator

---

1 Housing and Regeneration Act (HRA) 2008 s128.
2 CCBSA 2014 s84: societies with assets not exceeding £2,800,000 and turnover £5,600,000 (in the case of a charity, gross income not exceeding £250,000).
3 HRA 2008 ss133, 134, 139.
4 HRA 2008 s141.
5 HRA 2008 s270.
6 HRA 2008 s242.

whether or not requested concerning any of its functions without liability for breach of confidence.[7]

13.9 Auditors and reporting accountants must be accredited by specified professional accountancy bodies. This involves the risk of conflict of interest, since members of these same bodies may be used as consultants and advisors or be part of an informal network of personal or professional relationships. There is a limited safeguard in that the auditor cannot be an officer or employee of the body audited, nor of its parent or subsidiary.[8] Other safeguards for independence depend primarily on the codes of conduct of the professional bodies.

Accountability to local authorities

13.10 Housing associations should be accountable locally for the work they undertake. Is there, though, any legal standing for this desirable duty or does it purely exist on moral grounds? Certainly at the local level there is a relationship between local authorities and housing associations. At a simple level there may well be nomination agreements in place whereby the local authority nominates from its housing waiting list applicant for housing associations vacant properties. Such nomination agreements, if agreed by both sides and signed, will amount to a contract which is enforceable in law. For a contract to exist, there must be consideration so unless there is some kind of consideration by the local authority for the benefit of housing people from its waiting list then arguably the legal basis of the apparent contract may fail. In many cases, however, there is no formal agreement, but only a mutual understanding.

13.11 Where a local authority provides land to a housing association for new homes, a provision will be included in the sale of the land giving a local authority the right to nominate from its waiting list usually to 50 per cent of the available properties in perpetuity. For such an arrangement, a local authority will sometimes discount the open market price of the land to get the benefit of nominations. Where it does not do that, though, it is arguable there is no consideration and such an arrangement, if challenged, may well be void. A housing

---

7 HRA 2008 s243.
8 HRA 2008 s131; CCBSA 2014 ss91, 92.

association is, though, under a statutory duty to co-operate with a local authority in relation to homeless persons in particular.[9]

13.12 There are, however – often beyond housing people from the waiting list – other levels to a relationship. The relationship between a housing association and a local authority, then, is often complex and multi-layered. For example, where a housing association providing housing and care – such as in the provision of extra care for people with dementia – as well as the link between nominating people for the available housing, there will be provisions relating to care. There may also be arrangements to pay for benefits directly to the housing association where people are in arrears with their rent and service charges. Housing associations may be able to provide important information when local authorities are statutorily considering the housing needs of their districts and how these may be met. Housing associations may also be deliverer affordable housing under planning agreements for the development of new homes. There is a growing trend where housing associations are called to local authority scrutiny committees to give evidence on a wide range of issues. The basis upon which the demands to attend such committee is a little questionable, but nonetheless housing associations in the main comply with such requests.

13.13 Associations and local authorities should be careful not to enter into arrangements formal or otherwise which amount to restrictive practices or restrict or distort competition. Arrangement can also fall foul of the prohibition of agreements and concerted practices which have as their object the prevention, restriction or distortion of competition under Article 85 of the Treaty of Rome. Furthermore, a crucial aspect of the Office for National Statistics (ONS) decision in 2017 to de-classify housing associations as public sector bodies was that local government influence over housing associations had been reduced (below). Any increase in local influence might therefore trigger a further reconsideration of the matter.

13.14 At one time, special considerations applied to 'stock transfer associations' which have acquired local authority tenanted stock. The governing body of a stock transfer housing association was typically constituted as one-third local authority representatives, one-third tenants and one-third independent members. It is sometimes stated that a community benefit society (CBS) must be constituted on the basis of equality in terms of voting participation. This is not necessarily so. Votes and representation can be weighted provided that

9 Above para 7.12.

13.15 control is not weighted in accordance with the members' financial interests. For example, there can be a tenant majority, or a parent association owning a single share can have a controlling interest created by the rules of the association in a subsidiary. It must be emphasised that members of the governing body, as fiduciaries, owe duties only to the association and must not regard themselves as bound by the interests of their nominating body.

13.15 However, special considerations apply to local government members. Under Local Government and Housing Act (LGHA) 1989 Part V, certain 'companies' in which local authorities have an interest are subject to special controls exercised by the secretary of state who can 'by order, make provision regulating, forbidding or requiring the taking of certain actions or course of action'.[10] Companies within this regime are subject to local authority financial controls. A CCBSA society is a company for this purpose.[11] Charitable trusts are not affected but non-charitable trusts can be brought within the notion of 'influenced' companies by the secretary of state.[12] 'Local housing companies' set up by councils themselves are subject to these provisions and must not be dominated by the local authority in other ways.

13.16 Three types of body fall within this power. A company can either be a) 'under the control of the authority'; or b) an 'arm's length' company;[13] or c) a company subject to local authority 'influence'.[14] A company is under the control of the authority if the authority can appoint or remove a majority of its board or committee or control a majority of votes at a general meeting. In other words, it is a subsidiary of the local authority. The same applies if the company is a subsidiary of another company which is itself under the control of a local authority.[15] However, the authority can resolve that a controlled company be an arm's length company provided that a list of prescribed conditions is complied with which illustrate that the company is in practice independent of the authority, eg no financial influence or 'networking'.[16]

10 LGHA 1989 s70.
11 LGHA 1989 s67.
12 LGHA 1989 s72.
13 LGHA 1989 s68.
14 LGHA 1989 s69.
15 LGHA 1989 s68(1)(d).
16 LGHA 1989 s68(6).

13.17   A company is subject to local authority 'influence' if more than half of its assets derive from the authority, or it occupies land obtained from the authority (or a controlled company) at below market value. At least 20 per cent of voting rights or 20 per cent of the directors must be persons 'associated' with the authority – ie members, officers, or employees who are also officers of controlled companies. A person who was a member of the authority within the last four years is also associated with the authority for this purpose.[17] The secretary of state can make regulations bringing certain employees of bodies contracting with the authority into the net of associated persons.[18] This applies (among other things) to contractors concerned with giving advice to the authority about the management of an undertaking or the development of land by a company to which it is proposed that the authority should make any grant or loan. It also applies where the employee holds office in a political body represented on the council in question. There may also be lesser degrees of local authority involvement where a local authority is a member of a free standing association or nominates individual members to its board.

13.18   Many of these bodies are now subject to the statutory provisions which we discussed in chapter 3 restricting local government influence over housing associations. This was in order that the sector could be treated as part of the private sector for the purpose of government finances. Accordingly, Housing and Planning Act 2016 s9 gives the secretary of state the power to issue regulations limiting or removing local authority influence, especially in relation to limiting the appointment and removal of officers and limiting influence through local authority voting rights. Similar provisions apply in Wales under the Regulation of Registered Social Landlords (Wales) Act 2018.

13.19   This is especially relevant to Large Scale Voluntary Transfer (LSVT) associations. The concern that LSVTs might continue to be regarded by the ONS as public bodies while the rest of the sector was deregulated was removed by the regulations: Regulation of Social Housing (Influence of Local Authorities) (England) Regulations 2017.[19] These do not apply to associations 'wholly controlled' by a local authority, meaning that it has no members apart from the local

17 LGHA 1989 s69(5).
18 LGHA 1989 s69(6).
19 Regulation of Social Housing (Influence of Local Authorities) (England) Regulations 2017 SI No 1102.

authority itself or a subsidiary or persons acting on their behalf.[20] Otherwise the regulations treat all English housing associations on a similar basis.

13.20 Regulation 3(1) states that 'the percentage of officers of a private registered provider [PRP] who are local authority officers may not ... exceed the designated percentage of the total number of officers who are members of the board'. A 'local authority officer' means an officer appointed to the board of a PRP by a local authority.[21] The 'designated percentage' is 24 per cent.[22]

13.21 The relevant local authority must nominate which local authority officers are to be removed in order to comply with the requirement[23] and if it doesn't do so those Board members who are not local authority officers are required to select by majority votes the persons who are to be removed.[24] Any appointment of a new local authority officer which would result in the designated percentage being exceeded will have no effect.[25] In addition, any quorum requirements relating to local authority officers shall have no effect.[26] Thus these provisions ensure that a local authority officer or officers will have no more than 24 per cent of any representation on a board so being unable to block a special resolution.

13.22 In some cases, agreements entered into on stock transfer conferred 'golden shares' in the form of special voting rights to, or a veto by, a local authority where it is a member in its own right. Under reg 5, local authorities as such lose all voting rights. (This does not affect the position of individual members of an association who are local authority nominees.) An association must amend its constitution to pro rata the voting rights of local authorities among the other members of the association.

13.23 In addition, to prevent local authority blocking votes, reg 6 requires that, where there is a local authority officer on a board, voting provisions can require a majority of no more than 75 per cent. Any provision requiring a local authority's consent to a constitutional change is void. The regulations override any agreement. Whether these limitations will curtail local authority stock transfers to housing

20 Regulation of Social Housing (Influence of Local Authorities) (England) Regulations 2017 SI No 1102 reg 1(3).
21 Reg 2(c).
22 Reg 3(5).
23 Reg 3(4).
24 Reg 3(3).
25 Reg 3(2).
26 Reg 4.

associations we will have to wait and see. Arguably, what transfers were going to happen have now largely happened so that little new activity is likely. However, a key benefit of stock transfer – over and above getting the housing stock improved and a local authority gaining a capital receipt – was the continued degree of influence over the new sponsored housing association. The de-regulation provisions were created by subordinate legislation and can easily be removed by a future government more sympathetic to local authorities.

Accountability to tenants

13.24 Perhaps those housing associations which operate at a very local level are better placed than local authorities to encourage tenant involvement, participation and control. They are smaller, less bureaucratic and relatively free of political whim. Indeed, housing co-operatives are the embodiment of local democracy and control.

13.25 There are statutory obligations imposed on registered social landlords to provide certain information to and to consult with their tenants. These strictly apply only to secure tenants thus discriminating against occupiers of hostels and shared housing. Moreover, co-operative housing associations are exempt from these obligations.[27] Similar arrangements arguably apply to contemporary regime assured tenants by virtue of custom and practice following what was once Housing Corporation regulatory guidance, namely the 'tenants' guarantee'.

13.26 Under Part IV of the Housing Act 1985 which applies to secure tenants, section 105(1) requires a landlord authority including a PRP and a registered social landlord (RSL) to 'maintain such arrangements as it considers appropriate to enable those of its secure tenants who are likely to be substantially affected by a matter of housing management' to be informed and to make their views known.

13.27 The arrangements must provide:

1) that information be given to tenants about the matter;
2) that tenants be given the chance to make their views known within a specified period; and
3) that the housing association should consider any representations made by tenants before coming to a decision on the matter.

---

27 Housing Act 1985 s109.

13.28 A matter is one of housing management if, in the opinion of the social landlord:

1) it relates to the management, maintenance, improvement or demolition of dwelling houses let by the landlord under secure tenancies, or the provision of services or amenities in connection with such dwelling houses;[28] and
2) it represents a new programme of maintenance, improvement or demolition, or a change in the practice or policy of the landlord; and
3) it is likely to substantially affect either its secure tenants as a whole or a group.[29]

13.29 The Act therefore only deals with changes in practice or policy which are likely to have a substantial effect, and this is left to the social landlord to determine. Little guidance is given on what amounts to a change or what measure should be applied to see if it is substantial.

13.30 Expressly stated as not being matters of housing management are those relating to the rent payable or any charge for services or facilities under a secure tenancy.[30] However, a secure tenant may have a right to make representations to the Rent Officer in respect of these matters.

13.31 If a matter of housing management which is a qualifying matter is likely to affect the social landlord's tenants as a whole or a group, then there is a duty to consult before the decision is made. Where all tenants are affected by a change, the duty to consult would apply to all the secure tenants of the landlord equally and this obligation must form part of the landlord's consultation arrangements. What amounts to a group of tenants is somewhat more obscure. Housing Act 1985 s105(3) offers some guidance in that it suggests a group should be defined by reference to:

1) tenants who form a distinct social group; or
2) tenants who occupy dwelling houses which constitute a distinct class (whether by reference to the kind of dwelling house, or the housing estate or other large area in which they are situated).

13.32 The arrangements should enable tenants affected to be informed of the proposals and to let tenants make their views known within a reasonable specified period. Holding public meetings and providing a questionnaire for responses would be adequate as long as time

---

28 Housing Act 1985 s105(2).
29 Housing Act 1985 s105(3).
30 Housing Act 1985 s105 (2).

scales were reasonable alongside those arrangements.[31] The landlord authority must take into account any representations before taking a decision on the matter. A landlord authority is not required to provide a method for tenants to make their views known.[32] It is not necessary to set out the disadvantages of a proposal.[33]

13.33 A registered provider is required to send a copy of any published arrangement and proposals to the RSH. Any application to look at the arrangements by tenants or members of the public should be free of charge and available at all reasonable hours for viewing.[34] Similarly to the publication of allocation policies, housing association tend to apply these arrangements to all their tenants even though in law the arrangements only apply to secure tenants.

13.34 This sprang out of two primary reasons: first, it amounts to good practice to have consultation arrangements in place which are the same for all tenants regardless of the specific nature of the tenancy; and second, due to tenancy churn, tenants within specific scheme or localities will have different tenancies and should be consulted on the same rather than a differential basis.

13.35 A landlord also has a duty to publish information about its secure tenancies and to provide individual secure tenants with copies of such information with a written statement of the terms of the secure tenancy.[35]

13.36 The RSH has published a 'tenant involvement and empowerment standard'[36] which has a number of required outcome relating to customer service, choice and complaints; involvement and empowerment; and understanding and responding to diverse needs of tenants. Specifically the involvement and empowerment outcome requirement states[37] that registered providers shall ensure tenants are given a wide range of opportunities to influence and be involved in:

a) the formulation of their landlord's housing-related policies and strategic priorities;
b) the making of decisions about how housing-related services are delivered, including the setting of standards;

---

31 *R v Gatesehead MBC ex p Smith* (1999) 31 HLR 97, QBD.
32 *R v Brent LBC ex p Morris* (1998) 30 HLR 324, CA.
33 *R (Beale) v Camden LBC* [2004] EWHC 6 (Admin), [2004] HLR 48.
34 See Housing Act 1985 s105(1)–(7).
35 Housing Act 1985 s104.
36 HCA, July 2017.
37 Para 1.2.1.

c) the scrutiny of their landlord's performance and the making of recommendation to their landlord about how performance might be improved;
d) the management of their homes, where applicable;
e) the management of repair and maintenance services, such as commissioning and undertaking a range of repair tasks, as agreed with landlords, and the sharing in savings made; and
f) agreeing local offers for service delivery.

13.37 Nothing in the standard refers to the statutory requirements to consult secure tenants, it relates more to involvement rather than consultation obligations.

13.38 Thus the standard[38] goes on to say that:

Registered providers shall support their tenants to develop and implement opportunities for involvement and empowerment, including by:

a. supporting their tenants to exercise their Right to Manage or otherwise exercise housing management functions, where appropriate
b. supporting the formation and activities of tenant panels or equivalent groups and responding in a constructive and timely manner to them
c. the provision of timely and relevant performance information to support effective scrutiny by tenants of their landlord's performance in a form which registered providers seek to agree with their tenants. Such provision must include the publication of an annual report which should include information on repair and maintenance budgets
d. providing support to tenants to build their capacity to be more effectively involved.

13.39 Apart from these basic requirements it is up to the social landlords to determine their own consultation arrangements. The arrangements once established are required to be published and:

1) to be given, on payment of a reasonable fee, to any member of the public who asks for one;
2) a copy sent to the regulator and the council of any district or London borough in which the association has secure tenancies.[39]

13.40 These provisions exist to ensure that social landlords, along with other public sector landlords, maintain consultation arrangements. The law lays down some basic requirements which must be incorporated in these arrangements. However, the vagueness of the

---

38 Para 2.2.1.
39 Housing Act 1985 s105(6).

statutory language gives social landlords a wide discretion to make their own arrangements. In practice, when these measures were originally introduced, few associations took advantage of the positive opportunity available but simply published arrangements complying with the basic provisions of the Act.

13.41 A failure to comply with the consultation arrangements could arguably be subject to enforcement by injunction in the county court, on the basis of a breach of statutory duty. However, in the case of the secure tenancy provisions, the width of the statutory discretion involved suggests that private rights are not intended to be conferred on individual tenants.

13.42 Moreover, other than rights in respect of service charges, assured tenants have no statutory right be consulted but at best a legitimate expectation based on the old Housing Corporation guidance. If this is the case then the only remedy is an application for judicial review thus raising the question whether the function is one of public law (above chapter 2). It is arguable that an ordinary landlord and tenant matter even where, as here, it involves statutory requirements is not one of public law. On the other hand, the consultation provisions are primarily concerned with public sector tenants with whom registered providers have been assimilated.

13.43 The consumer standards therefore place emphasis on the importance of communication, engagement and involvement. However, in practice, in recent years very little emphasis has been placed on these requirements, with an increasing focus on governance, financial viability, risk and value for money. The impact of the Grenfell disaster in June 2017 may well place renewed focus on the importance of tenants, their views, opinions and needs. The voice of the tenant must take a renewed centre stage. Indeed, in order to enhance accountability to tenants, the recent housing green paper[40] proposes a new system for publishing league tables of performance indicators related to the quality of housing and responses to complaints.

Accountability to the community and general public

13.44 The main purpose of a housing association is to provide housing for those who need it. If a social landlord has few properties in a given area, the effect of its work will be relatively unnoticed. However,

40 *A new deal for social housing* Cm 9671 (2018) 3.1.

where a social landlord is highly active in a particular area, it can provide a major focus of community involvement. This has particularly been the case in Wales. There is also a very good example of this in Accord Housing Association and its community involvement in specific areas of the West Midlands.

13.45 Community involvement is achieved in many cases by formal consultation arrangements with local interest groups or by representation on a reciprocal basis on relevant committees. Unfortunately there are no legal requirements relating to these matters, and as we saw above it is a fundamental principle that the members of a corporate body owe a duty to the association as such and not to others. Subject to this reservation, the NHF's constituency model for members may provide a useful basis to ensure community interests are heard.[41]

13.46 Company accounts and other information held by the Companies Registrar are available to the public. At the other end of the scale, documents held by a trust are available only at the discretion of the trustees. However, the Charity Commission must make accounts, audits and reports of registered charities (trusts and companies) that it holds available for public inspection.[42]

13.47 There is no systematic provision for transparency in the sense of public access to information held by housing associations. The ambiguity of their status means that they are not public bodies under the Freedom of Information Act 2000 and their different legal forms makes for confusion. The RSH's registration documents which include audited accounts and annual returns or their equivalents are available for public inspection[43] and its circulars and main policy documents are published.

13.48 There are provisions in the Companies Act 2006, the Insolvency Act 1986 and in EU law regarding the transparency of company information. There are no special housing association rules. For example, in the case of companies employing more than 250 persons the director's report must include information about the employment of disabled persons and employee consultation.[44] Annual accounts and 'confirmation statements' (similar to the annual returns of a CCBSA society) must be submitted to the Companies Registry.

41 See *Governance and accountability*, Annex 6 option 2.
42 Charities Act 2011 s169.
43 HRA 2008 s111(2).
44 SI 2008 No 410 Sch 7 paras 10, 11 – see EU Directives 2009/101/EC Art 2; 2013/34/EU Art 19(2).

The requirements are relaxed in a graduated way for smaller companies.[45] However, where there is a relaxation, the RSH has power to require information. The Registrar of Companies must make basic information available for public inspection and copying, and company registers, such as that of members, must in be available for public inspection.[46] The Financial Reporting Council, a non statutory body, regulates compliance with various company accounting requirements.

13.49 In the case of a CCBSA society, public access is limited. Its balance sheet must be displayed in a conspicuous position at its registered office[47] but there is no general statutory obligation to make information available to the public. There is no right to inspect the books even by members.[48] There are three limited exceptions. First, a society must supply on demand to a member or anyone interested in the society's funds a copy of its latest annual return, which includes its revenue accounts and balance sheets and of its auditor's report.[49] Second, there are rights of a member and a person with a financial interest to inspect their own account and the register of members and officers.[50] Third, there are certain public rights of inspection when a charge is attached to the society's property.[51] A society must also provide a copy of its rules to anyone on demand (for a fee of up to £5 or as specified by the Treasury).[52]

13.50 There are stronger requirements for a charity. Annual reports and related documents kept by the Charity Commission (which it can require) must be available for public inspection at all reasonable times.[53] The governing body of a charity must provide to any person on request a copy of the charity's annual report and accounts. A reasonable fee can be charged.[54] Thus non-charitable CCBSA societies have a lower level of public accountability than other housing associations.

13.51 There are no other formal statutory mechanisms for public complaints about the conduct of a PRP or RSL. Judicial review

45 Companies Act 2006 ss382, 384A, 384B, 465.
46 Eg Companies Act 2006 s114.
47 CCBSA 2014 s81.
48 CCBSA 2014 s108.
49 CCBSA 2014 s90.
50 CCBSA 2014 s103.
51 CCBSA 2014 s59(4).
52 CCBSA 2014 s18.
53 Charities Act 2011 ss165(1), 170.
54 Charities Act 2011 ss171, 172.

depends upon the particular function being classified as a public function (above chapter 2). Alternatively judicial review might be sought in respect of a failure by the regulator to exercise its statutory duties. However, given the RSH's wide discretion this seems only a remote possibility. The regulator has no statutory obligation to consider complaints from the public, and its relationship with the government may pose problems. Moreover, the complainant must have 'sufficient interest' in the matter.[55] While the modern standing rules are generous it is questionable whether a member of the public as such would have standing to challenge a decision of an RSL (see *National Association of the Self Employed and Small Businesses v Inland Revenue Commissioners*[56]).

13.52 There is a further consumer standard, the 'Neighbourhood and Community Standard' which states a number of required outcomes in relation to the wider community:

1.1 Neighbourhood management
Registered providers shall keep the neighbourhood and communal areas associated with the homes that they own clean and safe. They shall work in partnership with their tenants and other providers and public bodies where it is effective to do so.

1.2 Local area co-operation
Registered providers shall co-operate with relevant partners to help promote social, environmental and economic wellbeing in the areas where they own properties.

1.3 Anti-social behaviour
Registered providers shall work in partnership with other agencies to prevent and tackle anti-social behaviour in the neighbourhoods where they own homes.

The Housing Ombudsman

13.53 The Housing Ombudsman investigates complaints against a social landlord in respect of its housing activities. Under the Housing Act 1996[57] all PRPs must subscribe to an independent Ombudsman Scheme approved by the secretary of state. Other landlords (not limited to social landlords) can voluntarily subscribe. The Act does not designate who can make a complaint to the ombudsman. Under the only approved scheme, tenants, former tenants and applicants

---

55 See Senior Courts Act 1981 s31.
56 [1982] AC 617.
57 Section 51, Sch 2 as amended by HRA 2008 s124 and Localism Act 2011 s180.

for tenancies or their representatives are eligible to do so.[58] The regulator investigates individual complaints from tenants only where they indicate wider systematic failures. Under a memorandum of understanding with the Housing Ombudsman (below) there are reciprocal arrangements to refer complaints to the appropriate body.

13.54 However, Localism Act 2011 s180 has made the ombudsman process more difficult. Under the so-called 'democratic filter', a complaint cannot normally be made directly but must be made by a 'designated person' in writing. A designated person is an MP, a member of the local housing authority or a 'tenant's panel', this being a group of tenants approved by the landlord. The ombudsman then reports back to the designated person, giving reasons if it refuses or discontinues the investigation or as to the outcome. This filter is difficult to fit in with the rhetoric that housing associations are private bodies. There are plans to provide for direct complaints to the Ombudsman in future without this filter process.

13.55 A complaint can be made directly to the ombudsman in two cases. The first is where the designated person refuses to refer the complaint or agrees to it being made directly; the second is where the complainant uses the landlord's internal grievance process and the ombudsman is satisfied that at least eight weeks have passed after that process has been exhausted.

13.56 The 2018 housing green paper[59] acknowledges that the filter is unsatisfactory in that it may have made the process too long and led some designated persons into exaggerating their roles. Moreover, tenants panels were sometimes underused or non-existent. The green paper suggested reducing the waiting time to four weeks or removing the filter altogether.

13.57 The ombudsman must publish an annual report, and can publish a report on an individual investigation. It can order payment of compensation and the alteration of contractual rights and obligations. As with other ombudsmen, its decisions are not legally binding, but the PRP in question must publish a statement that it has failed to comply. However, under Localism Act 2011 s180, the secretary of state can authorise the ombudsman to apply for a court order enforcing its decision.

13.58 The ombudsman is independent of the regulator who places stress on the ombudsman in relation to its consumer standards. The regulator does not deal with individual complaints against a

---

58 *Housing ombudsman service scheme*, February 2013.
59 *A new deal for social housing* Cm 96 71 (2018) Paras 46–49.

landlord. There are two specific links between the ombudsman and the regulator. First, the regulator must consult the ombudsman, along with various other public bodies when deciding whether to enforce the consumer standards against a PRP.[60] Second, the regulator cannot order a PRP to pay compensation where the ombudsman has done so thus giving the latter priority.[61]

13.59 In Wales, the Public Services Ombudsman deals with complaints against RSLs, replacing the Housing Act 1996 scheme.[62]

---

60 HRA 2008 s198A.
61 HRA 2008 s239.
62 Public Services Ombudsman (Wales) Act 2005.

CHAPTER 14
Capital and revenue: investment, grants and income

14.1	**Part 1: Housing development investments and grants**	
14.1	Funding programmes	
14.4	Social housing assistance: Housing and Regeneration Act 2008 s19	
14.9	Shared Ownership and Affordable Homes Programme	
14.30	Other sources of finance	
	Overview • Private finance • Loan capital • Types of private funding	
14.40	Covenants, constraints and consents	
14.41	Private finance initiative	
14.43	Disposals Proceeds Fund	
14.46	**Part 2: Revenue, rents and service charges**	
14.46	Introduction	
14.47	Overview: current rent framework	
14.51	Rent control	
14.59	Rent reduction	
14.75	The Rent Standard	
14.77	Supported housing and supporting people funding	

continued

Part 3: Taxation and fiscal privileges

14.87 Introduction

Tax on income

Charities • Co-operatives, co-ownerships and self-build societies • Unregistered non- charitable non mutual housing associations • Grants and corporation tax liability • Tax on sales of property, including capital gains • Charities • Co-operatives, co-ownership and self-build societies • Non-charitable non-mutual housing associations

14.117 Group structures and tax liability

Part 1: Housing development investments and grants

Funding programmes

14.1 A key activity for housing associations is to build more homes and undertake regeneration projects. The vast majority of associations exist to meet need as their raison d'etre. As well as re-letting the housing units they already own, they build new units to add to the housing stock. The sector in recent years has collectively developed some 40,000–80,000 new units per year, although this has reduced during the period 2014–2016 due to the impact of the rent reduction regime and the cessation of the Affordable Housing Programme (AHP) with new housing development taking a dip until a new programme – the Shared Ownership and Affordable Homes Programme (SOAHP) – was introduced. New programmes have been recently introduced by the government, including Homes England's New Ways of Working initiative and an extension of funding beyond 2022.[1]

14.2 Housing associations build new homes for rent and for sale and use a variety of financing mechanisms to meet the costs of development. They receive grants from the Homes and Communities Agency (HCA) and also in London the Greater London Authority (GLA). In theory, they can also obtain grants and other forms of funding from local government, but this is now quite rare except in relation to discounted or free land. They raise private finance and use their own resources, or internal reserves. They fund development agreements under the planning system. Housing associations use sale receipts from the outright sale of property to fund on-going sales programmes. Accord in the West Midlands runs a factory which manufactures timber homes which it sells internally and also to other providers, and reinvests profits from the activity back into its core purpose of meeting housing need.

14.3 Housing associations have since the late 1990s diversified their range of activities in order to extend their roles but also to generate additional income. They also use sale and leaseback and other alternative funding mechanisms to extend their financing options.

---

1 See 'Sector hails "huge significance of speech"', *Inside Housing*, News Team, 21 September 2018, giving details of Theresa May's announcement of an extension to the Homes England funding programme and the need to tackle stigma attached to social housing.

Social housing assistance: Housing and Regeneration Act 2008 s19

14.4 At the heart of the funding regime for building new affordable housing is the financial assistance which can be given to housing associations and other persons by the HCA (now renamed Homes England). With the secretary of state's consent, Homes England may give financial assistance to any person and in any form.[2] Under previous funding regimes, such assistance was almost exclusively reserved for housing associations, although this was widened to some degree to include developers and builders back in 1998. Now, though, the power is much wider.

14.5 It is a statutory condition of Homes England funding that the *landlord* of sub-market rental homes (including 'affordable rent' and 'rent to buy' homes) must be a 'registered provider' (RP).[3] However, the Homes England operates a successful 'agreed transfer' model allowing unregistered bodies to build such homes, and receive grant, ahead of onward transfer to an RP. This statutory requirement does not apply to shared ownership homes. Financial assistance may be in any form. The Housing and Regeneration Act (HRA) 2008 gives the examples of grants, loans, guarantees or indemnities, investment or incurring expenditure for the assisted person's benefit.[4] Homes England can impose such terms and conditions it thinks appropriate, including provisions for repayment, with or without interest.[5]

14.6 Homes England now has considerable flexibility in how it can provide financial assistance and to whom it may support with such range of powers supporting its much wider investment role in getting Britain building again.

14.7 At the heart of this building activity is the grant system run by Homes England (under SOAHP; the previous programme was the AHP; both of these overlapped to some degree). This is a competitive bidding programme open to housing associations and other housing providers, including private sector builders and developers and local authorities. It has replaced the previous programme run by what was the Housing Corporation, the Affordable Development Programme, to which it bears a close resemblance.[6] Periodically

---

2 HRA 2008 s19(1), (2).
3 HRA 2008 s31.
4 HRA 2008 s19(3).
5 HRA 2008 s19(4).
6 See Housing Corporation, *A new approach to investment*, 2001; and *National Investment Strategy, 2002/03*, 2002.

there is a bidding process, after which funds are allocated to successful bidders. More recently there has been supplementary bidding under a new approach called New Ways of Working.

14.8 However, there is a further means of accessing funds through a process called continuous market engagement which allows open bidding on interesting schemes as long as Homes England has sufficient money to support projects. It is estimated that about 30–50 per cent of total funds were held back in the initial bidding round to support this open continuous bidding mechanism. The programme actively encourages housing associations to offer additionality such as non-grant funded housing which can be added to the unit numbers of the overall programme and the sale of property in order to generate capital receipts to build more new homes.

Shared Ownership and Affordable Homes Programme

14.9 The financial assistance provided under HRA 2008 s19, which built upon the earlier principles relating to the social housing grant regime, represents one of Homes England's key programmes for affordable housing.

14.10 The aims of the SOAHP, the government stated, through its provision of £4.7bn of capital grant between 2016 and 2021, were to deliver starts on-site for at least:

- 135,000 homes for Help to Buy: Shared Ownership;
- 10,000 homes for Rent to Buy; and
- 8,000 homes for supported and older people's rental accommodation.[7]

14.11 The new programme marked a decisive political shift towards support for home ownership, a return to the property-owning democracy years of Thatcherism.[8] Bids were encouraged where 88 per cent of homes built would support Help to Buy: Shared Ownership; five per cent for homes for older, disabled and vulnerable people; and seven per cent for Rent to Buy.[9] The SOAHP complemented related government initiatives, such as Starter Homes and the voluntary extension of the Right to Buy to housing associations.

---

7 See HCA, *Shared Ownership and Affordable Homes Programme 2016 to 2021: Prospectus*, 13 April 2016, para.1.
8 See M Daunton, *A property owning democracy*, 1987.
9 See HCA, *Shared Ownership and Affordable Homes Programme 2016 to 2021: Prospectus*, 13 April 2016, para. 3.

14.12 The government wanted to see greater involvement by the commercial housing sector in delivery, particularly in relation to shared ownership. New entrants were encouraged and included the following measures:

- removing restrictions on the type of organisation which can hold an interest in shared ownership properties in the long term;
- promoting the agreed transfer model that makes it administratively easy to bid for grant for those that do not want to hold the investment for the long-term;
- offering extra support for those unaccustomed to bidding for grant;
- removing restrictions on accepting indicative bids (ie where full scheme details have yet to be worked up by the bidder) which will make it easier for new entrants to bid and receive feedback and support.[10]

14.13 For the first time, the government encouraged the use of modern and innovative methods of construction, including offsite construction. It was felt this would potentially 'raise the bar for quality in house building ... through the precision and quality control available through such approaches'.[11] Other perceived benefits included speed of delivery; cost efficiencies; and minimal disruption to communities adjacent to development sites.

14.14 Other hopes for the new programme included strengthening further the partnerships that were developing between the HCA and local areas to bring forward public land for development and deliver on housing, local growth and regeneration priorities and facilitating to the 'overall regeneration of an area, or assist more rapid build out of substantial urban extensions or regeneration'.[12] There was also support for devolution deals under the Localism Act 2011.[13]

14.15 There was still a strong focus on bidding and cost cutting, ensuring:

> ... best value is obtained for the grant available, maximising the number of new homes built within the Programme and addressing

---

10 HCA, *Shared Ownership and Affordable Homes Programme 2016 to 2021: Prospectus*, para.4.
11 HCA, *Shared Ownership and Affordable Homes Programme 2016 to 2021: Prospectus*, para.5.
12 HCA, *Shared Ownership and Affordable Homes Programme 2016 to 2021: Prospectus*, para.6.
13 HCA, *Shared Ownership and Affordable Homes Programme 2016 to 2021: Prospectus*, para.7.

housing affordability. Bidding is competitive and we will allocate only to those bids offering a significant contribution to the government's housing policy for the amount of grant sought.[14]

14.16 Not all the funding available would be allocated, unlike in previous programmes but further bids would be considered through a process of Continuous Market Engagement.[15]

> The change of government in 2016 led to a significant change in policy. The Chancellor's autumn statement, delivered on the 23rd of November, reaffirmed the Government's commitment to extending home ownership, including through the SOAHP 2016 to 2021 but also emphasised the Government's determination to increase overall housing supply and to meet the needs of those who are 'just about managing'. This resulted in a volte face in policy terms in relation to housing for rent albeit not for social rents. Thus the needs of the poorest were excluded.

14.17 The Chancellor announced:
- an additional £1.4bn to deliver a further 40,000 affordable homes (some of this budget will be allocated by the GLA for homes in London, rather than through the SOAHP 2016 to 2021);
- the availability of grant for affordable rent schemes.[16]

14.18 This change of direction required that homes for rent must be let under the tenancy and rent setting arrangements required by HCA guidance for affordable rents. Affordable rents can be used only under a specific 'housing supply delivery agreement' with the funding body. An 'affordable rent' (including service charges) is set at or below 80 per cent of the local market rent for an equivalent property (unless the social housing 'target rent' is higher).[17]

14.19 The addendum temptingly suggested 'that bidders with existing social rented stock may wish to generate financial capacity to support new build through planned conversions to Affordable Rent, when these homes become vacant'. Any such proposal as part of a bid needed to outline:

---

14 HCA, *Shared Ownership and Affordable Homes Programme 2016 to 2021: Prospectus*, para 8.
15 HCA, *Shared Ownership and Affordable Homes Programme 2016 to 2021: Prospectus*, para 9.
16 HCA, *Shared Ownership and Affordable Homes Programme 2016 to 2021: Addendum to the Prospectus*, January 2017, paras 2–3.
17 Above para 9.22.

- the number of homes to be converted;
- the additional financial capacity generated.[18]

14.20 It went on to say that bidders 'with existing social rented stock may also wish to generate financial capacity to support new build through disposals of vacant homes', asking bidders to estimate the financial capacity generated by disposals.[19] Also where disposals of stock took place and under the regime for the Disposal Proceeds Fund (DPF) were reminded that such 'funds, as directed by the regulator, can be allocated to the acquisition and development of homes for rent and they are therefore encouraged to utilise DPF balances as part of their financial contribution to Affordable Rent schemes costs'.[20]

14.21 Such a change of policy enabled housing associations to bid for affordable rent projects to support 'hard working families' and those 'just about managing' at the expense of those in greater need. However, there was an expectation that resources generated through the sales of vacant property as well as the application of any other available funds would be applied to help build new supply.

14.22 With affordable rents higher than social rents it was felt that associations would generate extra income which could be ploughed back into the funding of new homes (including social homes). The sale of empty homes would also generate capital receipts which equally could be used to supplement private finance and grants. Associations were also expected to use their own resources to help build more new homes. The issue here was to increase housing supply to tackle the growing housing shortage that existed across the country.

14.23 Access to the programme is through qualification in gaining 'investment partner' status by one of two routes, either in its own or as a member of a wider consortium.[21] Key assessment criteria for gaining investment partner status includes: an organisations financial and technical capacity to undertake a programme of new supply and also

---

18 HCA, *Shared Ownership and Affordable Homes Programme 2016 to 2021: Prospectus*, para 13.
19 HCA, *Shared Ownership and Affordable Homes Programme 2016 to 2021: Prospectus*, para 14.
20 HCA, *Shared Ownership and Affordable Homes Programme 2016 to 2021: Prospectus*, paras 15–16.
21 HCA, *Shared Ownership and Affordable Homes Programme 2016 to 2021 Prospectus*, paras 30 and 34.

its good financial standing.[22] Emphasis was placed on joining existing investment partner consortia which were set up as a requirement of the earlier bidding under the AHP. It was stressed that this was the usually the best approach for 'small, specialist, rural community led or new bidders', helping with efficiency and delivery.[23]

14.24 Bid assessment under the programme is undertaken by Homes England using two primary criteria, value for money and ability to delivery taking into account costs of building and over the lifetime of the property, maximising other cost contributions from wider non grant funded developments such as cross-subsidy from market sales and minimising land costs, for example by encouraging local authorities to provide free or discounted land to support development. The primary metric, though, is grant per home: 'a lower grant request per home will score more highly'.[24]

14.25 However, on its own that is not enough. Homes England places great emphasis on schemes which offer certainty of delivery. The delivery aspects of assessment will include evaluation of the planning stage achieved at the time of the bid (full planning offers a significant advantage in being given grant) and the status of the land ownership.[25]

14.26 A further addendum has been published outlining a process of agreeing deals and also extending the SOAHP to 'social rent', which the addendum defines as low cost accommodation that is typically made available at rent levels that are set in accordance with the rent component of the Regulator of Social Housing's (RSH) 'Tenancy Standard' and complying with the requirements of the *Capital funding guide*.[26] This means that rents should be set on the formula based on relative property values and relative local earnings.[27] A social rent is usually lower than an 'affordable rent'.

---

22 HCA, *Shared Ownership and Affordable Homes Programme 2016 to 2021 Prospectus*, para 35. See also HCA, *Shared Ownership and Affordable Homes programme 2016-2021: Investment partner qualification application form guidance*, 2016, which set out the requirements in more detail and also the assessment criteria.
23 HCA, *Shared Ownership and Affordable Homes Programme 2016 to 2021 Prospectus*, paras 38, 39.
24 HCA, *Shared Ownership and Affordable Homes Programme 2016 to 2021 Prospectus*, paras 81–84.
25 HCA, *Shared Ownership and Affordable Homes Programme 2016 to 2021 Prospectus*, paras 86, 87.
26 See Homes England, *Shared Ownership and Affordable Rent Homes Programme 2016 to 2021: Addendum to Prospectus*, June 2018, paras 7–8.
27 See discussion later in the chapter on rent control.

14.27 Social rent should also be focused on areas of greatest need that can demonstrate they are areas of high affordability pressure.[28] The key metric in determining this high affordability pressure is 'the difference between average social rents and private rents . . . where the difference between these is £50 per week or more'.[29]

14.28 A key part of the 'New Ways of Working' deal making approach is that bidders will need to provide qualitative information on the use of innovative housing construction methods. These are effectively off-site manufacturing methods of which there are a number which attempt to address the need for in-factory construction methods which eliminate some of the labour shortage problems which increasingly are being found with traditional construction methods.[30]

14.29 As to the what are referred to as the Wave 1 'deals' themselves, there will be discussions with RPs on their ability to deliver at pace and scale over and above existing commitments. Deal propositions will be taken forward on a 'bespoke' basis which responds to local needs, with a focus on targets for delivery on a quarterly and annual basis.[31] This is a response to the need to build 300,000 homes a year, the most recent target set by government. It is expected that a range of deals will be announced and rolled out over 2018 and 2019. At the time of writing, a number of deals (15 in all) have been agreed and further waves of these deals are being considered.

Other sources of finance

Overview

14.30 The financing model for new development of affordable housing involves a cocktail of funding: grant, private finance and, more often than not, a contribution from an association's own finances. Although the amount of grant which is available has varied over the years (some 100 per cent in the 1970s, down to 20 per cent or so during the early 2000s), the fundamental financing model has not altered. Instead we've simply seen a change in the relative proportions.

14.31 Proportions during 2018 were approximately, 20–30 per cent grant, 60–70 per cent private finance and the remainder, anything from zero to 20 per cent from an association's own cash reserves or

---

28 HCA, *Shared Ownership and Affordable Homes Programme 2016 to 2021 Prospectus*, paras 10–12 and such areas are listed in Annex A.
29 Para 23.
30 Para 25.
31 Paras 26–27.

annual surpluses. (This differs from scheme to scheme and in different parts of the country.) Obviously where accommodation is developed without grant all of the cost comes from private finance and reserves.

14.32 We have seen significant building for sale across the sector with the intention that profits be generated which are ploughed back into building affordable homes. We have seen the proliferation of multi-tenure housing developments which offer housing for rent, for sale and shared ownership and even in some cases including a private market rent element as well as affordable rent. This has generated more risk for associations which are diversifying in such ways and governance and viability rating undertaken by the regulator take into account the degree of market exposure.

Private finance

14.33 The original principle guiding housing association development was that subsidy met the gap between net rental income after assumed management and maintenance costs, the amount that could be raised by way of debt finance and the total cost of development. So, for example, if the total costs including land, administration and on-site costs such as design, legal fees etc were £150,000 to build a house and the net rent after management and maintenance costs could raise a £100,000, then grant would be provided to cover the remaining £50,000.

14.34 In many ways this 'mixed funding'[32] regime is still how housing associations consider the funding of projects even in a competitive bidding regime. However, it is now far more likely in order to win grant that a housing association would not expect grant to fully balance any funding gap. It would more likely use internal funds, such as reserves, or raise finance against other assets in order to win enough grants for an overall reasonably sized build programme. Nonetheless, this underlying concept is still an important way to judge and consider overall programme and individual scheme viability.

Loan capital

14.35 The amount of loan capital a housing association can raise will usually be prescribed in its rules or memorandum and articles. This

---

32 For the historical background to this, see David Garnett, *Housing finance*, Chartered Institute of Housing, 2000, chapter 14.

is compulsory in the case of community benefit societies (CBSs),[33] although it is very similar for companies. Both can raise loan capital by way of fixed or floating charges. Floating charges are not open to trusts and therefore when trustees want to borrow, very careful consideration is needed in relation to security. Unless the trust deed says otherwise, charitable trustees can borrow only for prescribed purposes.[34] Sometimes the court or the Charity Commission has to sanction a mortgage or charge by way of security against charitable property.[35] In relation to other housing associations, until recently the formal consent of the HCA was needed. Under the provisions to deregulate housing providers, in the Housing and Planning Act 2016 and the Regulation of Registered Social Landlords (Wales) Act 2018 this is no longer required. However, there are still notification obligations in relation to the RSH and the Welsh Ministers.[36]

14.36 Homes England has the power to guarantee, although the practice has not yet been used. If an association has adopted the National Housing Federation (NHF) 'model rules' (most have) then the rules will allow for borrowing under a wide range of financial products including swaps and other derivatives.

14.37 There are detailed programme management arrangements and a framework agreement which providers have to agree to if in receipt of a programme. They include signing up to a standard form of delivery contract, a grant agreement, regular monitoring and programme management, publication of data, transparency and an open book approach on spend and payment arrangements.[37]

Types of private funding

14.38 Housing associations have borrowed using a wide range of financial products, much like any other organisation. Perhaps the three most widely used approaches would be the following:

1) *Standard commercial mortgage products* – such as long-, medium- and short-term secured loans through typically banks and building societies. Those from building societies have often been very similar products to domestic mortgages. Terms in recent years have reduced from 30- to 40-year durations to less than ten years

---

33 Co-operative and Community Benefit Societies Act 2014 s11.
34 Settled Land Act 1925 s71.
35 Charities Act 2011 s105.
36 Above para 5.55 and more generally chapter 4.
37 These are too complex to go into here, but there is greater detail in the *Capital funding guide* on the Homes England website.

in the main. This has been due to banks and building societies not wanting to be tied into long-term arrangements, especially since they lent at very low rates during the late 1990s and early 2000s. Where housing associations have required consents from the lending institutions under the agreements, this has led to a reduction in lending term and also an increase in rates, the banks and building societies claiming they have been 'under water' in terms of what they could have lent in lending in the current market place.

2) *Unsecured development finance* – such standard lending as described under 1) has also very often been coupled to unsecured development facilities which have been used by housing associations to develop properties before they are put into charge. These are usually no more than five years in duration and can be called in at any time. The scale of the facility will usually mirror the size and flow of the costs of a housing association's development programme after taking into account the advance payment of any grant.

3) *Bond and private placement finance* – bond finance has been around a while for housing associations. It has in the main been the privilege of larger associations wishing to take on significant finance since it tends to be for sums more than £100m. However, it has also been available through consortium deals such as those overseen by the Housing Finance Corporation where a number of housing associations go to market collectively. Private placements have appeared increasingly since around 2008 which operate similarly to bond issues but which are put together privately with no need to go to the open market. Arrangement costs are often lower, smaller sums that can be obtained (perhaps around £50m is usual, occasionally even smaller and more suitable for smaller providers), but interest rates are often above those for a bond issue. On both of these approaches, funds are borrowed for longer period which better match the nature of the long life of the property and can be for a period as long as 40 years, but more usually 25–30 years in duration.

14.39 There are restrictions placed on lenders by the Bank of England and by their own lending rules on the amount to be lent to any one sector and the amount to be lent to any one organisation. This has created the need to refinance where mergers of housing associations, or for that matter, financial institutions have taken place which would have meant overexposure against those restrictions.

Covenants, constraints and consents

14.40 As the raising of private finance has rolled out ubiquitously across the sector, it has created another layer of regulation, the so called 'discipline of the market'. Housing associations at all times must comply with loan requirements and covenants. A breach would need to be reported to the regulator unless the particular financial institution had given prior permission not to comply. Common covenants include requirements on: gearing, annual surplus, interest cover and asset cover, to name but a few. There are also accounting and financial return requirements for monitoring purposes. However, the requirements are not special to the sector, they are very similar to those being applied to a private sector organisation borrowing money.

Private finance initiative

14.41 During the early 2000s there was a real push to maximise investment to renew infrastructure and to encourage public/private partnerships to achieve this end. The public private partnerships which emerged were at the heart of the private finance initiative (PFI) which was employed to provide hospitals, schools, university facilities and the improvement of the rail network amongst many other initiatives. Inevitably from the outset PFI has been used to build, repair and improve social housing, often local authority housing where capital subsidy credits are given by the government to meet additional revenue costs.[38] This was severely restricted as an approach with local authorities when austerity kicked in following the election of the coalition government.

14.42 A typical example relates to the Harville's Hawthorn Estate in West Bromwich in the West Midlands where a large council estate was transferred into management with Riverside Housing Association. The covenant strength (a specific payment for some 25 years) of the payment from Sandwell MBC enabled Riverside to raise appropriate funding to meet the capital costs of improving the estate. There are a number of PFI projects across the country of this nature. There is no specific housing association law which applies to PFI as such.

---

38 See Local Authorities (Capital Finance) (Amendment) Regulations 1998 SI No 371.

Disposals Proceeds Fund

14.43 Until recently there were complex requirements imposed upon housing associations in the way they accounted for and used funds arising from the disposal of property and in some cases interest earned relating to disposal transactions. A special Disposals Proceeds Fund (DPF) was required. The provisions ensured that funds accumulated as a result of disposals where properties had been provided with the benefit of grant funding were properly accounted for and used for the public benefit, generally through the provision of replacement housing.

14.44 However, following the deregulatory provisions of the Housing and Planning Act 2016 these detailed obligations no longer apply to disposals after 1 April 2017, although there are still some requirements during the 'wind down period' until at the latest 6 April 2020.[39] There is, though, still a need to have a DPF and to properly account and provide information to the regulator in the use of such a fund.[40] Similar landlords apply to Welsh bodies under the Regulation of Landlords (Wales) Act 2018.

14.45 With the new bidding process outlined in the latest Addendum to the 'SOAHP Prospectus 2018 to 2021' registered providers with amounts in their DPF are encouraged to utilise such fund balances as part of their financial contribution to social rent scheme costs.[41] The Recycled Capital Grant Fund (RCGF) did not raise the same issues for public sector classification purposes as the DPF apparently because it only applies to grants, whereas the DPF covers proceeds generally, the latter applying a degree of public sector control over areas of private law.[42]

---

39 See HCA, *Guidance on the effect of the Housing and Planning Act 2016 on Disposal Proceeds Fund requirements*, 2016.
40 See HCA, *Disposals Proceeds Fund guidance*, August 2017, particularly addendum on p3 and paras 7.8–7.10.
41 Homes England, *Shared Ownership and Affordable Rent Homes Programme 2016 to 2021: Addendum to Prospectus*, June 2018, para 13.
42 See discussion in NHF, *Deregulatory measures introduced in response to the ONS reclassification of housing associations*, 17 November 2017.

Part 2: Revenue, rents and service charges

Introduction

14.46 The primary forms of revenue income for housing associations are rents and service charges; Supporting People grants; and payments for care and related accommodation costs. The revenue income for all housing associations in England was some £20bn at the end of the 2016 financial year.[43]

Overview: current rent framework

14.47 By way of overview, the Welfare Reform and Work Act (WRWA) 2016 introduced temporary legislative requirements dictating the rents charged by private registered providers. Those legislative requirements apply primarily to general needs housing, ie housing provided to individual and families where specialised support is not required. In the main that piece of legislation required such rents to be reduced by one per cent per year for a four year period from broadly April 2016 to April 2020.

14.48 Otherwise the RSH 'Rent Standard' applies. This previously applied to most social and affordable rents. It states that rents should be charged in accordance with the government's direction to the regulator in May 2014 and the ensuing Rent Standard guidance issued by the Regulator.[44] These provide for formula rents based upon 80 per cent of market value rents for the accommodation (with five per cent tolerance and ten per cent tolerance for supported and sheltered housing in order to give a degree of rent flexibility) and rent increases of no more than Consumer Price Index (CPI) plus one per cent.[45]

14.49 Since the statutory rent control provisions end after the expiry of four years and there has been no new Rent Standard issued, the rent regime from April 2020 should revert to that prior to the application of the WRWA 2016 requirements. The final year of rent reduction starts from 1 April 2019.[46] Recent announcements in the government's white paper, *Fixing our broken housing market*, issued on

---

43 The HCA, *Global accounts* 2017.
44 See HCA, 'Rent Standard', April 2015; and the government's *Guidance on rents for social housing*, 23 May 2014.
45 HCA, 'Rent Standard', paras 1.1, 2.2.
46 WRWA 2016 s23(6)(b); and also details about certain transitional provisions in s31.

4 October 2017, heralded a return to CPI plus one per cent for five years from April 2020.

14.50 Non-compliance against the Rent Standard and the requirements of the WRWA 2016 would elicit an appropriate regulatory response.[47]

Rent control

14.51 Perhaps one of the key mechanisms that central government has used in recent years to control the finances of housing associations has been through universal rent control. Statutory rent control for assured sector tenants was abolished by the Housing Act 1988 but in the case of registered social landlords (RSLs) and private registered providers (PRPs) has been replaced by administrative arrangements policed by the regulator.

14.52 There is some history to this which we must understand since successive governments have had differing views on housing association rents which have led to central control of rents for those differing outcomes. During the period 2002–2015 the policy was one of 'rent convergence'. There were such differing levels of rents in the social housing sector across housing associations and local authorities that it was desirable that rents should be brought into alignment. Thus a rent formula was developed which took into account average local earnings relative to national earnings and property values with the intention that rents would be fully converged over a period of ten years.[48]

14.53 The Housing Corporation, the then regulator, required all housing association rents and service charges to be set at levels which 'are, on average, below those in the private sector for similar properties and which reflect size, property values and local earnings',[49] with all rents over time becoming subject to rent restructuring and to 'target rents' on the basis of property type and a formula of 30 per cent property values and 70 per cent average earnings for different areas.[50] Exceptions were residual regime tenancies and cooperative tenancies which remained subject to the fair rent regime with rents determined by a rent officer. A failure to adhere to the 'rent influencing'

---

47 See RSH, Regulating the standards, April 2018, para 2.51.
48 For the government of the time's policy intentions, see Office of Deputy Prime Minister, Guide to social rent reforms, 2001; and its green paper, Quality and choice: A decent home for all, HMSO, 2000.
49 Housing Corporation, *Regulatory code*, 2001, para 3.1.
50 See Housing Corporation, Circular R2-27/01, *Rent influencing regime: implementing the rent restructuring framework*, 2001.

14.54 This regime remained intact with annual rent increases of retail price index (RPI) plus either 0.5 or one per cent during the coalition government years. Although a 10-year settlement on CPI plus one per cent was agreed in the 2013 spending round, the deal was reneged on by the new Cameron government in its 2015 summer budget when the Chancellor, George Osborne, announced that social housing rents would be reduced by one per cent per year for four years, resulting in an average rent reduction over that time of 12 per cent. There was an expectation that tenants would save on average some £700 per year.

14.55 Since the majority of tenants were on welfare benefits, this meant a direct saving to the Exchequer of around £1.4bn by 2020/21.[52]

14.56 Thus the Chancellor stated:

> Alongside the freeze in working-age benefits, the government will reduce rents in social housing in England by 1% a year for 4 years, requiring housing associations and local authorities to deliver efficiency savings, making better use of the £13bn annual subsidy they receive from the tax payer. Rents in the social sector increased by 20% over the 3 years from 2010–11. This will allow social landlords to play their part in reducing the welfare bill. This will mean a 12% reduction in average rents by 2020–21 compared to current forecasts.[53]

14.57 Although this policy change was sudden and completely unexpected it was in keeping with other policies of pushing the welfare cost elsewhere. So, for example, with the national living wage an element of previously state-borne costs (tax credit, housing benefit and benefits generally for the low paid) were pushed onto the employer. Here, housing benefit costs relating to rents were passed onto social landlords.

14.58 This approach to rent reduction significantly hit the business plan projections of housing associations and also had an impact on their ensuing housing building programmes with some commentators arguing that some 40 per cent fewer homes will have been built over the five years of the programme than would have been the case. There was also speculation that rent reductions might create a finan-

---

51 Housing Corporation, Circular R2-27/01, *Rent influencing regime: implementing the rent restructuring framework*, paras 7.1–7.15.
52 See Homes of Commons Library, Wendy Wilson, *Rent setting: social housing* (England), November 2017, p26.
53 *Summer budget* 2015, House of Commons 264, July 2015, para 1.140.

cial crisis within the sector with predictions that landlords could go bust.[54] However, no such consequences have yet been seen.

Rent reduction

14.59 The current requirements on rent reduction were set out in detail by WRWA 2016 s23:

In relation to each relevant year, registered providers of social housing must secure that the amount of rent payable is respect of that relevant year by a tenant of their social housing in England is at least 1% less than the amount of rent that was payable by the tenant in respect of the preceding 12 months.[55]

14.60 The baseline or reference date for rent levels is whatever rent was being charged on the 8 July 2015, being applied over the previous 12 months. In certain circumstances with consent of the secretary of state a registered provider could elect a different date, the so called 'permitted review date'.[56] If a tenancy starts or ends during the year then the rent reduction applies on a pro rata basis.[57] The relevant year referred to in section 23(1) is the year beginning on the first review date after the 1 April 2016 and each year thereafter.[58] For social rent properties, the reduction applies to the rent element only, not to service charges. However, for most affordable rent properties the reduction applies to any service charge as well as rent.

14.61 There are a range of exceptions, although somewhat limited in nature or else the reduction in the welfare bill would have been undermined. These exceptions are set out in WRWA 2016 s24 and regulations made under it. The Act itself states that rent reductions do not apply if:

a) the accommodation is low cost home ownership accommodation;
b) the accommodation is both low cost rental accommodation and low cost homes ownership accommodation (see HRA 2008 s71).

14.62 There are also some exclusions for accommodation where there a mortgagee is enforcing its security.[59]

---

54 See, for example, Kate Allen, 'Summer Budget; rent cut pushes social landlords towards financial crisis', *Financial Times*, 10 July 2015.
55 WRWA 2016 s23(1).
56 WRWA 2016 s23(3).
57 WRWA 2016 s23(2).
58 WRWA 2016 s23(6).
59 WRWA 2016 s24(2)–(4).

14.63 Under the Social Housing Rents (Exceptions and Miscellaneous Provisions) Regulations 2016[60] a range of further cases are specified where rent reduction does not apply:

(a) accommodation where total household income meet the income qualification criteria (ie certain high income tenants);
(b) in cases where sub-paragraph (a) does not apply, accommodation where total household income met the income qualification criteria in the previous relevant year;[61]
(c) intermediate rent accommodation (certain accommodation built by a registered provider without the support of any public subsidy or accommodation built under a specific government programme for intermediate rent);[62]
(d) specialised supported accommodation (accommodation designed for people required specialised support);[63]
(e) PFI social housing (low cost rented accommodation provider under a private finance initiative);[64]
(f) temporary social housing;
(g) student accommodation;
(h) accommodation where the rent registered under the Rent Act 1977 is lower than the social rent rate;
(i) in cases where (h) does not apply, accommodation where the Rent Act 1977 rent criteria is met;
(j) care homes;
(k) relevant Housing Act 1996 accommodation (certain accommodation which was not low cost rental accommodation);
(l) accommodation where rent payable by the tenant was temporarily reduced or waived for any period during the previous relevant year.

14.64 Following significant pressure from a range of interested organisations, there were further exemptions for a year only to give time for a review. These were:[65]

(a) supported housing which is not specialised supported housing;
(b) almshouse accommodation;
(c) accommodation provided by a cooperative housing association or a fully mutual housing association;

60 SI 2016 No 390 para 3(1).
61 The Housing Minister Gavin Barwell as at November 2016 announced that the government was not proceeding with a compulsory scheme for what was called 'pay to stay', higher rents for higher income earners. He said that housing associations and local authorities could apply 'local discretion'. See House of Commons, *Social housing: written statement – HCWS274*, 21 November 2016.
62 reg 2.
63 reg 2.
64 reg 2.
65 reg 3(2).

(d) accommodation provided by a community land trust.

14.65 Under the Social Housing Rents (Exceptions and Miscellaneous Provisions) (Amendment) Regulations 2017[66] the original list of exempt cases was extended to permanently include all of those contested cases with the exception of supported accommodation and with the addition of domestic violence refuge accommodation following further extensive pressure:

a) domestic violence refuge accommodation;
b) almshouse accommodation;
c) accommodation provided by a cooperative housing association or a fully mutual housing association;
d) accommodation provided by a community land trust.

14.66 The exemption for supported accommodation lasted only until to 2017. The rent reduction for supported accommodation (other than specialist support accommodation and that providing a refuge for sufferers of domestic violence) has caused grave concern for the social housing sector, since those scheme were already financially challenged due to the impact of austerity on local authority support and care spending. Few new supported housing projects have since been built and many existing ones have been closed due to lack of funding.

14.67 Subject to the consent of the secretary of state, the regulator can issue a direction exempting a registered provider from the need to comply altogether or in part, and subject to such measures prescribed by the regulator. This applies either where the regulator considers that the rent reduction regime would jeopardise the financial viability of the registered provider or the circumstances of the registered provider satisfy the requirements of regulations made by the secretary of state.[67]

14.68 The regulator has specified in considering an application for an exemption the following questions will be considered:

> In a scenario where the legislation applies to the provider, will the rent collected for the stock be sufficient to cover the costs associated with carrying out the basic functions and generating a minimal margin (i.e. the minimum needed to allow the organisation to cope with

---

66 SI No 91.
67 WRWA 2016 s25(1)–(6).

downside risk) such as to allow it to continue to be let as social housing.[68]

14.69 In considering this question, the regulator will look at the following criteria:

- Any further reductions in expenditure would jeopardise the ability of the PRP to maintain the stock at a level sufficient to allow it to continue to be used as social housing.
- The PRP has considered all options for reducing expenditure, including looking at all contractual commitments and providing assurance and evidence of advice around the feasibility of getting out of any commitments where to do so would improve financial viability of the organisation.
- The PRP has considered all possible options to ensure continued financial viability.

14.70 Following some speculation about immediate applications for the exemption, the regulator made it clear that PRPs will need to consider full mitigation arrangements including whether a merger with another provider would resolve the problem.

14.71 More recently a new deal has been struck with government so that from 2020 rents will again increase by CPI plus one per cent.[69] Nonetheless, over the period of rent reduction, some £1.4bn has been removed from the business plans of the sector overall. The Office of Budgetary Responsibility (OBR) predicted an overall reduction in housing investment as a result of the policy. It stated that the:

> ... 1 per cent a year reductions in social sector rents for four years from April 2016 announced in this Budget will directly reduce social landlords' income. We expect that this will reduce their ability and willingness to invest in housing, so we have lowered our forecast for residential investment, proportionate to the expected reduction in rental income. The effect is to reduce the level of private residential investment by around 0.7 per cent by the end of the forecast period, which is broadly consistent with a reduction in housebuilding of 4,000 in 2020-21. Over the forecast period, our assumptions suggest around 14,000 fewer affordable homes will be built.[70]

---

68 See HCA, *Explanatory note for making a formal application for an exemption to the rent reductions in the Welfare Reform and Work Act 2016*, updated April 2016, p2.
69 See the housing white paper, *Fixing our broken housing market*, HMSO, February 2017.
70 OBR, *Economic and fiscal outlook*, Cm 9088, July 2015, para 3.84.

14.72 Such reductions in affordable housebuilding were evident the following year, with a significant turndown in completions. However, in practice different associations have coped with the impact of rent reductions in different ways, not necessarily reducing their house building, but applying significant cost cutting linking back to the requirements of the 'Value for Money Standard'. For example, one survey suggested that housing associations during 2015/16 by cutting their expenditure on major repairs by some £386m, a 7.3 per cent reduction and cutting expenditure on planned maintenance by a further £630m representing a 1.6 per cent reduction.

14.73 Running alongside the rent reduction approach, associations were required to cut costs (the rhetoric was to provide better value for money) in order to enlarge their 'bottom lines', ie surpluses, which in turn would enable them to build more homes, by reinvesting enlarged surpluses, or at least negate the impact of rent reduction on their building programmes and achieving better value for the taxpayer. Some associations cut their housing investment programme on existing homes, (ie such programme as major repairs and planned maintenance) which raised some concerns with the regulator about adequate investment levels to ensure housing conditions and standards were being maintained:

> To compensate for the rent reduction, the majority of providers have reduced costs. The largest reductions have been made in respect of spend on major repairs. Total major repairs' spending was £2.1bn in 2017, a 14% reduction, and management costs decreased by 9% to £2.6bn. We will continue to monitor expenditure on major repairs and expect providers to ensure that their properties continue to be appropriately maintained.[71]

14.74 The sector has also seen considerable job losses since 2015, with more to come before 2020 as housing associations wrestle with the challenge of reducing running costs to meet the impact of the punishing rent reduction regime. At a time when there is a growing housing crisis in all parts of the country, with increasing evidence of street homelessness and low completions of new homes, housing associations should have the flexibility and freedom to set their own rents. They are, after all, a sector which exists to meet needs and historically has been shown to be responsible in its policy decisions. It is unlikely we will see soaring rents within such a sector.

---

71 See HCA, 2017 *Global accounts of private registered providers*, p3.

The Rent Standard

14.75 The current Rent Standard for PRPs is based on government guidance for local authorities.[72]

- 'Social rents', the lowest level of rent, are based on the old Housing Corporation formula (above) which combines local property values relative to national values (30 per cent), relative local earnings (70 per cent) with a weighting for number of bedrooms. Service charges are not included. This applies to all social rents whether or not publicly funded.
- 'Affordable rents' are up to 80 per cent of the estimated market value including service charges, and can be increased on the same basis as social rents.

14.76 There are some special cases requiring greater flexibility. First, in the case of rents of secure tenants and co-operatives still subject to the residual regime, 'fair rent' requirements, any rent fixed by the rent officer is a ceiling (as it must be) but otherwise the formula applies in the same way as to other tenants. Second, there are the following exemptions from the formula (however, there is an 'expectation' that general rent increase guidelines will be followed):

- shared ownership and other low cost home ownership schemes;
- certain specialised supported housing carried out in conjunction with other public bodies but without public funding;
- 'high income' social tenants (HISTs) with household incomes exceeding £60,000 per annum;
- PFI schemes;
- temporary/short-life schemes for the homeless;
- care and nursing homes;
- student accommodation;
- key worker accommodation.

Supported housing and supporting people funding

14.77 Supported housing means:

> ... low costs rental accommodation provided by a registered provider which –
>
> (a) is made available only in conjunction with the supply of support,

---

72 See HCA, 'Rent Standard', 2015; *Rent Standard guidance*, 2015; and Department for Communities and Local Government (DCLG), *Guidance on rents for social housing*, May 2014.

(b) is made available exclusively to residents who have been identified as needing support, and
(c) falls into one or both of the following categories –
  (i) accommodation that has been designed, structurally altered or refurbished in order to enable residents to live independently,
  (ii) accommodation that has been designated as being available only to individuals within an identified group with specific support needs.[73]

14.78 It is important, therefore, to understand what amounts to 'support' since this is an essential component of the statutory definition. This is addressed by a list of qualifying categories of schemes or types of support, so 'support' includes:

(a) sheltered accommodation,
(b) extra care housing,
(c) domestic violence refuges,
(d) hostels for the homeless,
(e) support for people with alcohol problems,
(f) support for people with mental health problems,
(g) support for people with learning disabilities,
(h) support for people with disabilities,
(i) support for offenders and people at risk of offending,
(j) support for young people leaving care,
(k) support for teenage parents,
(l) support for refugees.[74]

14.79 The housing association sector has provided support extensively over many years and is seen by many as part of their core business. Providing a home is not necessarily the full answer for people who have complex problems and messy lives and therefore an underpinning of 'support' enables independent living, whereas the lack of that support may mean greater dependence on the state and deepening personal problems and difficulties for the individuals concerned. The safety net of housing and support is therefore a vital part of the health and social care infrastructure. The political debate has in part been focused on whether housing association and voluntary sector support perpetuates dependency on the one hand or alleviates the demands on the state on the other.

---

73 Social Housing Rents (Exceptions and Miscellaneous Provisions) Regulations 2016 SI No 390 reg 2.
74 Social Housing Rents (Exceptions and Miscellaneous Provisions) Regulations 2016 reg 2.

14.80 So a further primary source of income for housing associations are the differing types of income which flow from providing supported housing and support services. One such in relation to care and support is 'Supporting People' funding, although in recent years this has reduced considerably due to austerity measures affecting local authorities.

14.81 Without going into the tormented history of Supporting People funding, the latest position which is not specific to housing associations but nonetheless has a huge impact on their work with vulnerable people is worthy of mention. 'Supporting People' has been a long-standing and important programme. Originally it was intended to help vulnerable people improve their quality of life through greater independence via a working partnership between local government, service users, support agencies and providers of housing.[75] Supporting People funding came by way of a grant and replaced the old Social Housing Management Grant which was administered by the Housing Corporation back in the day. The budget for such grants was always restricted, initially set of £750m per annum back in 2003 and it has always been strongly argues that such funding was never sufficient to cover the growing costs of care for vulnerable people.

14.82 Supported housing schemes operated by housing associations provide a home and also support needed to vulnerable individuals to live life as independently as possible within the community. Such projects operate through hybrid revenue funding packages which include rents, service charges and Supporting People funding. Rents are still either social or affordable depending on when the project was created and are therefore sub-market rates. Service charges can only be at a level and for services which qualify for housing benefit. However, there is a higher management allowance within housing benefit which acknowledges the higher level of management input and therefore costs into such schemes for the vulnerable. Pure care or support costs are then met by supporting people funding. In theory then all costs are met by this hybrid of funding.

14.83 In practice, though since 2010 less and less Supporting People funding has been available, a number of projects have been closed and few new projects have started. Many housing associations, committed to meeting care as well as housing need have, though,

---

75 See Ministerial Foreword to ODPM, *Supporting people – together towards 2003*, 2001 for the original aims of the programme.

continued to run projects at a deficit. This situation has been made worse by the one per cent rent reduction. The implementation of this was delayed for one year, but has been applied from 1 April 2017. During the first year of the rent reduction regime, providers were still able to set rents for supported housing under the previous policy of CPI plus one per cent. In practice, since CPI was negative on the reference date (ie –0.1 per cent as at September 2015) the actual permitted increase was 0.9 per cent.

14.84 For domestic violence refuges and specialised supported housing, the previous rent setting regime of CPI plus one per cent remains in force. Domestic violence refuges were singled out from the rest of supported housing following extensive political arguments for their exclusion. 'Domestic violence refuge accommodation' means accommodation in a hostel which is wholly or mainly for the non-permanent accommodation of persons who have been victims of domestic violence and have left their homes as a result of violence.[76] The accommodation must usually be staffed 24 hours a day by people providing support to the residents and where access by non-residents is controlled.

14.85 'Specialised supported housing' means supported housing –

(a) which is designed, structurally altered, refurbished or designated for occupation by, and made available to, residents who require specialised services or support in order to enable them to live, or to adjust to living, independently within the community,

(b) which offers a high level of support similar to that of a care home,

(c) which is provided by a private registered provider under an agreement or arrangement with a local authority or a health service within the meaning of the National Health Service Act 2006, with the rent charged must be in accordance with any such agreement or arrangement.[77]

14.86 This puts a further deepening squeeze on funding and more projects will inevitably be closed down.

---

76 Social Housing Rents (Exceptions and Miscellaneous Provisions) (Amendment) Regulations 2017 SI No 91 reg 4(1).
77 Social Housing Rents (Exceptions and Miscellaneous Provisions) Regulations 2016 reg 2.

Part 3: Taxation and fiscal privileges

Introduction

14.87 Housing associations have a number of important taxation privileges, the majority of which are associated with charitable status. The taxation position of a particular social landlord will depend upon its legal nature and its activities. These fiscal advantages have generally developed along with their social role in meeting the needs of the most vulnerable in society. With the exception of fully mutual associations, the notion of public benefit in the provision of housing is central to the tax position of a housing association. Public benefit for this purpose is not necessarily confined to charitable objects but also incorporates to some degree the broader notion of 'community benefit' which is key to registration as a CCBS (a 'Co-operative and Community Benefits Societies Act (CCBSA) 2014 society').

14.88 Historically, housing associations other than charities have been treated as private landlords for tax purposes. The Milner Holland Report, *Greater London Report of the Committee on Housing*,[78] made recommendations which were incorporated in the Finance Act 1965 giving grants for taxation relief to housing associations whose functions were exclusively for the provision, letting or maintenance of accommodation.[79] This recognised the need to discharge the tax liabilities of non-profit-making housing associations undertaking work for the benefit of the community and sat alongside government support with state funding especially in the Housing Act 1964, which also set up the Housing Corporation.

14.89 The present taxation position of housing associations depends upon their status. Charities gain the highest level of taxation privilege. If a housing association is a charitable trust it is liable to income tax or if a charitable company or treated as such (eg a CBS with charitable status) is subject to corporation tax. The exemptions and tax treatments of the two are closely assimilated.[80] Until 1999, non-charitable CBSs (previously industrial and provident societies) received a grant to meet their taxation liabilities.

14.90 The power of the secretary of state to make grants to meet tax liabilities still remains on the statute book but is no longer used in

---

78 Cm 2605.
79 Finance Act 1965 s93.
80 See Income Tax Act (ITA) 2007 ss521–536; and Corporation Tax Act (CTA) 2010 ss466–493.

practice.⁸¹ Except for this possible grant to meet taxation obligations non-charitable associations were originally placed on the same footing as private sector landlords by being denied key taxation reliefs. However, the High Court has determined that where a return, whether or not a full market return, bearing in mind the below market rent policies of housing associations, is sought from rented property, and that is the main business of the association, then it may be treated as an investment company for income and corporation taxation purposes and so gain various privileges.⁸² Co-operatives, co-ownership and self-build societies though can disregard certain forms of income, such as rent payments, and capital gains for tax purposes.⁸³

14.91 In practice, there is little difference between the activities of charitable and non-charitable associations. Some associations however choose not to take on charitable status and it is this difference in status which generates a different taxation position. Arguably all provision of social housing should be free from taxation, as long as surpluses are reinvested for its benefit. Admittedly the mood of public opinion around tax avoidance has altered in recent years due to large multi-national companies being able to seemingly easily to avoid taxation by complex and fluid corporate structures.

14.92 Taxation laws are highly complex, so this section will attempt to give a general overview of the main taxation privileges afforded to housing associations, hence it will focus on income, corporation and capital gains taxes. It is not intended that we cover in detail the intricacies or mechanics of the taxation position of housing associations, since that would take a text all of its own.⁸⁴

Tax on income

Charities

14.93 The law applicable to housing associations is the same as that applicable to charities generally. All charitable housing associations are exempt from income and corporation taxes by virtue of CTA 2010 ss485 and 478 if a charitable company or treated as a charitable

---

81 Housing Act 1988 s54.
82 *Medway Housing Society Ltd v Cook (Inspector of Taxes)* [1997] STC 90.
83 CTA 2010 ss642–657.
84 See a specific text on taxation such as J Kessler, E Wong and M Ashley, *Taxation of charities and nonprofit organisations*, Key Haven, November 2017, particularly chapter 43 on housing associations.

company (such as a CCBSA society) for tax purposes and by virtue of ITA 2007 ss531 and 524 if a charitable trust's income is applied to purely charitable purposes.[85] However, the exemptions do not apply to profits arising from the sale or development of land since this is treated as 'non-primary purpose trading'.[86] Similarly, tax is also chargeable on non-exempt miscellaneous income.[87] Charities also have various other exemptions relating to gifts and donations, small scale trading, income from intellectual property rights telecommunication rights and some relevant foreign distributions.[88]

14.94 Tax reliefs may be relevant where subsidiary or satellite housing associations have been created as part of a group structure. Clearly it is important to avoid the danger of artificial tax avoidance schemes and challenge from the Inland Revenue. Otherwise it could well be that the activities undertaken by the charity itself compromises charitable status. In fact, this is why some housing associations establish such structures.

Co-operatives, co-ownerships and self-build societies

14.95 These fully mutual societies are dealt with under CTA 2010 ss642–657. The effect of section 642 broadly ensures that certain 'approved housing associations' are not treated as entities distinct from their members for tax purposes. These are co-operative housing associations. In order to qualify for these exemptions an association must be approved by the secretary of state,[89] and pass a three-part test: 1) it is a housing association within the meaning of Housing Associations Act 1985 s1(1); 2) it is a registered society within the meaning of the CCBSA 2014; and 3) its rules restrict membership to tenants or prospective tenants and preclude the granting or assignment of tenancies to persons other than members.[90]

14.96 Approval means that: a) rent to which the association is entitled from its members is ignored for tax purposes; b) any interest payable by the association during an accounting period is treated as if it were not payable, except in the case where interest is attributable to a

---

85 See *IRC v Church Commissioners for England* [1977] AC 329.
86 See CTA 2010 s2; and Income Tax (Trading and Other Income) Act 2005 s5.
87 See ITA 2007 s528 for charitable trusts; and CTA 2010 ss491A–496. There is an exemption from taxation for trading profits where the turnover of otherwise taxable trades is less than £5,000 or where the turnover is less than 25 per cent of the gross income of the charity with a maximum of £50,000.
88 See, for example, ITA 2007 s536.
89 ITA 2007 s644(6). This approval process is delegated to the RSH in England.
90 See CTA 2010 s645.

property that is not subject to a tenancy.[91] An approved association is not liable to any corporation tax on chargeable gains accruing on the sale of property which is being or has been occupied by a tenant of the association.[92]

14.97 In the case of self-build societies having as their objective the provision of dwellings for sale to or occupation by their members, built or principally built with the use of members' own labour,[93] the following tax concessions apply:

a) rent received by the society from its members is ignored for tax purposes;[94] and
b) Corporation Tax does not become payable on chargeable gains accruing in respect of disposals of land to a member of the society.[95]

14.98 For such societies there is a similar approval process as for co-operatives, and the following requirements must be met by the society:

a) it is registered or deemed to be registered under the CCBSA 2014:
b) it should satisfy any prescribed requirements and in addition comply with any conditions that may be prescribed in regulations issued under CTA 2010 s657.[96]

14.99 There are very few of these organisations in existence, although there is a growth in interest in community land trusts. The tax concessions are a remnant of the government's wish to promote the development of this type of ownership in the early 1960s. To some degree there is growing interest in 'self-build' and no doubt the concessions will become of increasing importance.

14.100 There are tax concession arrangements for housing associations, including a co-operative, to carry forward any trading loss and set off such a loss not only against its trading income of the same accounting period but also against interest or dividends on investments which would have been regarded as trading income had not they been chargeable as tax under other provisions. Where a housing

---

91 CTA 2010 s642(2)–(4).
92 CTA 2010 s643.
93 Housing Associations Act 1985 s1(3).
94 CTA 2010 s651(1).
95 CTA 2010 s652.
96 Again the secretary of state may delegate powers of approval to the RSH in England where the body in question is a registered social landlord.

association trades by way of undertaking shared ownership schemes any profits that arise should be regarded as taxable income.[97]

Unregistered non- charitable non mutual housing associations

14.101 These organisations receive no special benefits relating to income or corporation tax, or any other taxes for that matter, and therefore are not considered in detail here.

Grants and corporation tax liability

14.102 The receipt of 'financial assistance', Social Housing Grants in Wales and any other historical grants is to be ignored for corporation tax computation purposes, by virtue of CTA 2010 s1284 which states:

> A receipt is exempt from corporation tax if the payment was made:
> - under an enactment relating to the giving of financial assistance for the provision, maintenance or improvement of housing accommodation or other residential accommodation; and . . .
> - if the payment was made by way of a grant or other contribution towards expenses (no matter if it was made to the person incurring the expenses or if the expenses have been, or are to be, incurred).

Tax on sales of property, including capital gains

14.103 Over the last few decades it has become common for housing associations to sell property. Secure and some assured tenants who can fulfil certain qualifying conditions have a statutory 'right to buy' or 'right to acquire' their homes. Regularly housing associations sell properties for outright sale as well as under shared ownership terms. Tenants of charitable housing associations do not have a statutory right to buy or right to acquire. Nonetheless, such associations still have the power to sell property and this has been the foundation for the application of voluntary right to buy scheme introduced by the Housing and Planning Act 2016 to charitable housing association tenants.

14.104 In general terms, disposals of property may give rise to chargeable gains occurring to housing associations and the process by which right-to-buy sales are carried out often give rise to gains. As with the taxation of income the taxation on sales of property needs to be considered with reference to the different types of housing association.

---

97 *Hansard*, HC Vol 47, col 15.

In practice associations do make losses as well as gains on right to buy and voluntary sales.

Charities

14.105 Most charities that are housing associations will have a corporate form and as such will not be subject to the Taxation of Chargeable Gains Act (TCGA) 1992 which applies to individuals.[98] Thus charities which have been incorporated under the Companies Acts, the CCBSA 2014 or by special arrangements will be subject to corporation tax.

14.106 Trustees of non-corporate charities, namely charitable trusts, are subject to capital gains tax under the TCGA 1992. There is, however, a specific exemption under section 256 which states:

(1) A gain shall not be a chargeable gain if it accrues to a charity and is applicable and applied for charitable purposes.
(2) If property held on charitable trusts ceases to be subject to charitable trusts –
   (a) the trustees shall be treated as if they had disposed of, and immediately reacquired, the property for a consideration equal to its market value, any gain on the disposal being treated as not accruing to a charity, and
   (b) if and so far as any of that property represents, directly or indirectly, the consideration for the disposal of assets by the trustees, any gain accruing on that disposal shall be treated as not having accrued to a charity,
   and an assessment to capital gains tax chargeable by virtue of paragraph (b) above may be made at any time not more than 3 years after the end of the year of assessment in which the property ceases to be subject to charitable trusts.

14.107 In the case of non-corporate charities, gains are only exempt on the disposal of the charity's own assets. Where funds are transferred from one charity to another and the recipient charity accumulates funds to be applied for charitable purposes, then such a disposal is regarded as being applicable and applied to charitable purposes, unless the transferor knows or ought to know the funds could be misapplied by the recipient.[99]

14.108 Exemptions available on income tax are carried over to income and corporation tax. Exemption is then given to charities for both income and corporation tax as discussed above. Thus the exemptions

---

98 Section 1.
99 See *IRC v Helen Slater Charitable Trust Ltd* [1982] Ch 49.

from income or corporation tax on chargeable gains (depending on whether the association is a charitable trust or a charitable company), is available to organisations with charitable status in the same way as exemption is available from corporation tax.

14.109 Additionally, a charity may claim exemption from corporation tax on any chargeable gains arising out of the disposal of the charity's assets.[100] Under both provisions for the exemption to arise the charity must apply the proceeds to charitable purposes only. Disposals of land between housing associations are treated as gifts 'for such consideration as to secure that neither gain nor loss accrues on the disposal'.

14.110 The arrangements for charitable trusts are subject to a taxation anti-avoidance provision. Where property ceases to be held for charitable purposes and there occurs an additional disposal at market value by the trustees, any gain becomes chargeable on the basis that the disposal was not carried out by a charity.[101] Timing of the application of funds to charitable purposes is also important.[102] Therefore, no immunity arises for unrealised capital gains built up under the guise of charity.[103]

14.111 Under capital gains tax legislation, a further incentive is available to encourage donors to give to charity. This applies to a gift to any PRP or RSL.[104] Thus where a gift is made the donor incurs no tax liability[105] and is able to donate property upon which large gains subject to taxation could have accrued and as such provides a useful and at the same time altruistic means of mitigating tax liability. Gifts made by charities to other charities and gifts made by individuals to charities are also exempt from inheritance tax without limit to the number or size of gifts.

Co-operatives, co-ownership and self-build societies

14.112 Approved co-operatives and co-ownership societies are able to claim exemptions from corporation tax on chargeable gains resulting from the disposal of property where the property is occupied or has been

---

100 TCGA 1992 s345(2).
101 TCGA 1992 ss145(2), 258(2).
102 See *Guild and others (as Trustees of the William Muir (Bond 9) Ltd Employees Share Scheme) v IRC* [1992] 2 AC 310.
103 Income and Corporation Taxes Act 1988 s505(3), (4).
104 TCGA 1992 s259.
105 TCGA 1992 s259A.

occupied by one of its tenants.[106] Similarly, self-build societies are exempt from corporation tax on chargeable gains accruing in respect of disposals of land to members of the society.[107]

14.113 In the case of co-operatives and co-ownerships the exemptions apply to ensure that double taxation does not arise since members who dispose of property are subject to capital gains tax. However, the disposal depending on the nature of the property interest would presumably amount to a disposal of the principal and main home and be exempt in any case. In the case of a self-build society, the tax disposals of property to members of the society, would strike at the roots and purpose of the society and rather defeat the object of these initiatives. Gains made from currency dealings by co-operative and self-build societies are also exempt from capital gains tax,[108] although it is difficult to see how in practice this might be of benefit.

Non-charitable non-mutual housing associations

14.114 Finance Act 1965 non-charitable housing associations that are registered social landlords in Wales or private registered providers in England are subject to corporation tax on (any) chargeable gains since they are corporate entities in the same way for tax purposes as private companies. In theory, tax payable on such gains can be recovered through the discretionary grant. Since grants are no longer payable to meet taxation liabilities under Housing Associations Act 1988 s54, tax is payable on such gains.

14.115 Because the right to buy is a statutory requirement relating to sales of properties to sitting tenants, these sales are likely to be regarded as sales necessary in the normal course of an association's letting activities. Similarly, capital gains on properties already owned by the association which are sold under the various new initiative headings such as improvement for sale or shared ownership schemes, would also be subject to capital gains tax. Similarly gains from the sales of property acquired for sale under the various home ownership initiatives would be taxable. The Inland Revenue had always regarded these latter sales activities as trading and as such no relief was available under section 54 to offset corporation tax liability.

---

106 CTA 2010 s643.
107 CTA 2010 s652.
108 Finance Act 2000 s79(1)(b).

14.116 Gifts to RSLs and PRPs enjoy a number of exemptions from capital gains tax in the same way as gifts to charities. They are also free from inheritance tax.[109]

Group structures and tax liability

14.117 Where social landlords have a group structure, there may be a number of tax advantages which apply similarly to companies adopting group structures. This may provide housing associations with a degree of flexibility over how they organise their trading activities. Interest and dividends payable between parent and subsidiary and vice versa can be paid gross without the deduction of corporation tax thus easing administration and cash flow. Where the controlling interest can be shown to be greater than 75 per cent trading losses of one body can be offset against trading profits of the other. Transfers between bodies within a group structure are also free from capital gains tax.[110]

14.118 Where two CCBSA 2014 societies amalgamate, or there is a transfer of assets from one society to another, the effective transfer is ignored for tax purposes. However, a tax liability may arise if assets are disposed of at a later date. For corporation tax purposes, the amalgamation or transfer carries with it the assumption that any disposal was at a price causing neither a gain nor a loss to either society.[111]

14.119 However, there are important restrictions on the extent to which a housing association can support a subsidiary particularly if it is not registered with the RSH. Under regulatory requirements, an association must have a controlling interest in a subsidiary. This means holding more than 50 per cent of the shares or controlling the body in other unequivocal ways, such as having power over the appointment of the board of management (below chapter 15).

---

109 Inheritance Tax Act 1984 s24A, amended by Housing Act 1996 Sch 3 para 19.
110 TCGA 1992 s171.
111 TCGA 1992 s486(8).

CHAPTER 15

Mergers, amalgamations, group structures and winding up

15.1	Trends and introduction
15.10	Mergers and merger methods
15.22	A note on group structures
15.22	Key drivers and types of structure
15.33	Constraints, control and cross liability
15.43	Strategic alliances
15.44	Winding up and insolvency
15.61	Insolvency in Wales

Trends and introduction

15.1 Huge structural change is happening within the housing association sector. Almost no week passes without some announcement of a merger or impending merger or indeed significant change to structures. In part this is to do with natural rationalisation, which any sector goes through, and regulatory pressures. Arguably the former has been relatively constant over the years whereas the latter have ratcheted up over the last few years and will possibly escalate further due to the deepening impact of rent reduction and value for money requirements. However, perhaps the key driver at present seems to be a belief that size is critical to success and growth and through larger organisations greater efficiency can be achieved which will lead to building more homes. The data does not suggest that this outcome is strictly true, the benefits and disadvantages of merger and super sizing being varied and complex.

15.2 Larger associations get the bulk of subsidies from Homes England (Homes and Communities Agency (HCA) as was). Since the early noughties, the scale of a housing building programme has mattered to Homes England and only the largest of bidders for funds, either by virtue of the individual size of an organisation or a consortium of smaller organisations coming together in gaining 'investment partnering' status have been able to access funds, although that was to some degree relaxed as a requirement in the last Shared Ownership and Affordable Housing Programme (SOAHP) bidding round in 2015.[1] Even so, most of the subsidy goes to the big associations.

15.3 Historically there has been a process of gradual absorption, whereby smaller associations join larger associations. More recently we have seen a spate of 'mega mergers' which buck this trend, where associations of comparatively equal size have joined forces and created ever bigger organisations. The driver, claimed by many chief executives of merging associations, would seem to be significant cost cutting, generating synergies and increasing surpluses to build more homes. This trend recently culminated for the moment in the creation of *Clarion*, which is an association owning and managing some 120,000 plus homes. Other proposed mergers creating associations of significant scale, seem to be closing in on the heels of this mega-association.

---

1 See for example HCA annual report and accounts 2015/16.

15.4 Certainly there is an increased pace to the number of mergers within the sector at all levels.[2] The National Housing Federation (NHF), the sector's trade body, has issued a *Merger, group structures and partnerships code*[3] which exalts the need for the sector to generate better value for money due to the increased scrutiny of the sector. This 'voluntary code' sets out some principles which associations can follow if considering mergers and alliances.

15.5 Key drivers now or in the past are very similar, and akin to those driving the mergers of banks and building societies in the 1980s and 1990s, namely personal ambition of senior executives and board members, economies of scale (no matter how illusory in practice), sheer size, reducing exposure to risk, acquisition of assets and resources, scarcity of high quality expertise and the simple pursuit and love of growth and the dynamic this brings. The welfare of tenants does not appear directly to feature. Larger associations may be in a better position to lobby government, to assert independence from government and to stand up to the potential pressures and pitfalls of agency capture.

15.6 There had historically been a trend through the creation of group structures where smaller associations could be taken over by larger associations but still have a degree of autonomy by retaining their identities, boards, staff and local office as subsidiaries. Notable examples of this were Circle (a national group of associations which itself became a subsidiary of Clarion) and Accord (a West Midlands based group of associations).

15.7 A more recent trend, though, is for mergers to take place with no group structure arrangements, a simple coming together into a single entity of two organisations with a tidying up of structures if either of those associations previously had a group structure arrangement. The main reason for this is to achieve greater simplicity in governance and operational efficiencies, the holy grail of the regulator's value-for-money regime. Increasing concern around the regulation and control of subsidiaries in group structures arose out of the problematic cases of Cosmopolitan and Circle housing groups.

---

2 See, for example, 'The rise of the medium-merger', *Inside Housing*, 23 February 2017; D Mullins, *English Housing Mergers and Groups*, Third Sector Research Centre, University of Birmingham, 2012; and 'Merger sense', *Inside Housing*, 26 May 2016 which announced the mega mergers of Affinity Sutton and Circle; L&Q, Hyde and East Thames; Genesis and Thames Valley and Sovereign and Spectrum.

3 National Housing Federation (NHF), 2015.

Control of a subsidiary by a parent association has become very important and may even lead to the end of group structures.

15.8 Moreover fewer organisations mean fewer registered providers to regulate and therefore greater efficiency from a regulatory point of view. The latest version of the regulatory 'Value for Money Standard' requires periodic assessment of the status of a registered provider, with an option which must be considered to see whether stand alone is still appropriate to deliver its business objectives.

15.9 Many smaller organisations within the sector either do not develop new homes or develop very small numbers. Absorbing those associations into the operating bases of larger organisations has some apparent advantages, in that significant synergies can be gained through a reduction in running costs and latent assets can be employed to help with the securitisation of debt to build more homes. There is, though, some evidence that larger associations are not the most efficient.[4]

Mergers and merger methods

15.10 Legally there are a number of routes for housing associations to join forces, but in practice a single route through a transfer of engagement is almost exclusively used, sometimes associated with a change of corporate form to make that route possible, ie if one of the associations concerned is a company. Other more complex routes include amalgamation, membership arrangements, rule changes and granting 'golden shares', although the regulator these days frowns upon the latter. The exact route will depend on the legal form of the two associations involved. Mergers will undoubtedly require alterations to the constitutions of the bodies concerned regardless of the route chosen. 'Merger' rhetoric in the sector usually refers to transfers of engagement and 'amalgamations' as the legal means of achieving the combining of two or more bodies.

15.11 In the case of a community benefit society (CBS), constitutional changes can be made according to its own rules since there are few statutory restrictions. The consent of the Financial Conduct Authority (FCA) is required which must be given if the proposed change complies with the legislation.[5] No amendment of the rules is valid

---

4 See for example National Housing Federation and Housemark, *Housing Association operation efficiency 2008/09 to 2014/15* (2016).
5 Co-operative and Community Benefit Societies Act (CCBSA) 2014 s16(4)(a).

Mergers, amalgamations, group structures and winding up 331

until registered by the FCA under the Co-operative and Community Benefits Societies Act (CCBSA) 2014.[6] However, without special provision in the rules, a resolution at a general meeting cannot impact on the rights of nor alter the original purpose of the society when it was formed.[7]

15.12 In the case of a company, regardless of its exact form, a special resolution is required to changes its articles. However, the articles themselves can 'entrench' provisions by setting up additional requirements for changes. These can be overridden only by a unanimous vote or a court order.[8] A transfer of engagements compared to other processes to effect a merger is relatively straight-forward. Effectively the whole of the business activities of one association which is a community benefit society is transferred to another community benefit society, lock stock and barrel, a kind of 'lift and shift'. Members transfer too.[9] The shareholders of the transferring association resolve by 'special resolution' to transfer all assets and liabilities into the receiving community benefit association. There is a second confirmatory special general meeting within 14 days. Such a special resolution must be passed by at least two-thirds of the eligible members who vote at the first meeting, and at the confirmatory meeting must be passed by at least half of eligible members who vote.[10] The process is even simpler for the receiving association in that the resolution is made by the board or shareholders accepting the transfer. The process is beautiful in its simplicity.

15.13 Once the resolutions have been registered by the FCA, all rights, assets and liabilities are automatically vested in the receiving association by operation of law. If a company is involved as the transferring association it must change its form to a community benefit society as a first step and then effect the merger through the transfer of engagements process. There is a similar process for converting a company into a community benefit society.[11] The simplicity of the process means it is still much easier to go through this preliminary stage than pursuing the alternative methods.

15.14 If it is comprehensive, the transfer of engagement process leaves the association as an empty shell. The regulator requires that such a

---

6 CCBSA 2014 s16(1).
7 *Auld v Glasgow Working Men's Building Society* (1887) 12 App Cas 197; *Hole v Garnsey* [1930] AC 472, 500.
8 Companies Act 2006 ss21, 22.
9 See *Sun Permanent Benefit Building Society v Western Suburban and Harrow Road Permanent Building Society (No 2)* [1921] 2 Ch. 438 at 456.
10 CCBSA 2014 s111(2)(a), (b).
11 CCBSA 2014 s115.

body be wound up, in this case by an instrument of dissolution (below).

15.15 The process is not without risk in that shareholders can reject the resolution, which has in fact happened many times with failed merger attempts. It is therefore very important to keep members informed about intentions and timescales. Similarly this is a consideration if pursuing the amalgamation process with a company which we will discuss next.

15.16 Similar considerations are needed where one of the entities is a charity and the other not. There may be a need to undertake the preliminary process of converting a company into a charitable CBS so that again the transfer of engagements process can run smoothly. As a CBS is an exempt charity, registration with the Charity Commission is not required.

15.17 A special resolution process exists also for a CBS to convert into a company or to amalgamate with a company.[12] The difference is that at least three-quarters of eligible members to vote are required to vote in favour at the first special general meeting. This method can be more difficult if the society has charitable status (below). The body remains the same entity in law, so existing claims against it apply to the new company.[13] There is, therefore, a permutation of possible options: CBS to CBS; non-charitable company to a CBS after conversion into a CBS; and a charitable company converted into a charitable CBS. Obviously a non-charitable company will have to demonstrate its activities are charitable in nature to be able to change its form.

15.18 The Regulator of Social Housing (RSH) and its predecessors had a key role in approval of mergers. However, since April 2017 the requirement for the regulator to give consent to mergers, acquisitions and restructuring no longer applies. This was part of the declassification package introduced by government under the Housing and Planning Act 2016 and the Regulation of Registered Social Landlords (Wales) Act 2018.

15.19 Housing associations must now notify the regulator of any significant constitution changes usually within ten working days of passing a resolution, unless the resolution relates to insolvency or viability where the notification must be by the following day. Notification requirements relate to resolutions on mergers, dissolution, changes of rules or articles which affect profit or not for profit

12 CCBSA 2014 ss112, 113.
13 CCBSA 2014 s117; see *Re London Housing Society Ltd's Trust Deeds* [1940] Ch 777.

status, and changes in the objects of a charity. Additional notification requirements include decisions which relate to conversion into a company or into a CBS or such more mundane issues as a change of name.[14] Further, more onerous protections apply to charities. Charity Commissioner consent is required for a change in the memorandum, articles or rules of a charitable company or a CBS under which it ceases to be a charity and which impact on its property.[15] In the case of company changes in its objects also require consent.[16] A change to a trust deed would require the consent of the Charity Commissioners as in the case of any charity. However, a registered charity can probably convert to a CBS with charitable status without the need for consent from the Charity Commissioners.[17]

15.20 Is there a possibility of a hostile take-over of a housing association? Shares are not transferrable, so a member cannot sell their share for gain which in the private sector is one of the main methods of hostile take-over. However, it is theoretically possible that, where an association has an open membership, individuals linked to another association or organisation could apply for shares and achieve sufficient numbers to engineer a take-over through the constitutional approach which has been described in this chapter.

15.21 Certainly, merger activity will continue at a pace. It does feel a threshold point has been reached which will push and accelerate merger and consolidation activities within a sector which has been slow to surrender to such market pressures. Simple mechanisms exist which make this rationalisation of a diverse sector particularly easy.

A note on group structures

Key drivers and types of structure

15.22 Since the 1990s, housing associations for a variety of reasons have formed group structures, partly as a result of the increasing diversity of their activities and exposure to financial risk. Along with these developments, a variety of structures have emerged, perhaps the most common having a non-charitable parent (either a company or a

---

14 Housing and Planning Act 2016 Sch 4 Part 2.
15 Charities Act 2011 s197.
16 Charities Act 2011 s198.
17 See Charities Act 1993 ss53, 64(1).

non-charitable community benefit society) with one or more subsidiaries which perform different activities or work in different geographical areas. Often where a housing association has encouraged another smaller association to join its structure, the smaller association will keep its corporate form and continue to work relatively independently within the larger group.

15.23 Despite recent failures of group structures (and a sub-trend since 2015 to collapse complex structures, due in part to the apparent antagonism of the regulator towards governance complexity), the trend, as with every other sector in the economy, is likely to prevail.[18] This is because there are good reasons for group structures, including growing tax obligations with structures that gift-aid to charitable limbs within a group; isolation of risk; rationalisation of the sector; potential to sell off entities, particularly those that might have a more private sector flavour; and political manoeuvring for growth. On the other hand, the complexity, duplication and inevitable additional costs have to be balanced against the advantages.[19]

15.24 It is felt within the sector that the creation of a subsidiary or satellite organisation can extend the range of the housing association's activities beyond what it can undertake within its objects. Perhaps the legal basis for this is questionable. A 'subsidiary' is defined by Housing and Regeneration Act 2008 s271 as follows: the parent must either control the composition of the board of management or hold at least 50 per cent of the nominal equity. An 'associate' means a parent or another subsidiary. The regulator requires that the parent be in 'unequivocal control' of its subsidiary. Certainly therefore, a subsidiary can be a separate legal entity and not subject to the restrictions of the parent, but the parent is still fettered by its objects when it wishes to exercise control. The parent can act only for the benefit of its own objects.

15.25 Moreover, if there is a close relationship between the parent which is a housing association and a subsidiary and the acts of the subsidiary can be attributed to the parent then the courts in some circumstances are prepared to 'lift the veil' of corporate identity to see where

---

18 See, for example, the report on HCA, *Cosmopolitan Housing Association, Lessons Learned*, 2014.
19 For a discussion of the types of group structures which have emerged within the sector and the primary reasons behind these, see D Mullins, *English housing mergers and groups*, Third Sector Partnership for Service Delivery, University of Birmingham, 2013; and D Mullins, *The evolution of corporate governance structures and relationships in English housing associations*, Nonprofit Governance: Innovative Perspectives and Approaches, Routledge, 2013.

control lies. For this reason, a trend has emerged where a group is often headed up by a company, not registered with the regulator and not having charitable status.

15.26 A group involving companies may be, indeed usually is, constituted by means of companies higher up a chain owning shares in companies lower down the chain. This is in order not to breach Companies Act 2006 s23 which provides that 'a body corporate cannot be a member of a company which is its holding, i.e. parent company'. It would therefore be preferable in a group structure with common membership that the parent be a CBS. CCBSA 2014 s32 in enacting that shares 'in a registered society may be held by any other body corporate (if that body's regulations so permit)' paves the way for making groups of societies. Although an individual member cannot hold more than £100,000 in shares,[20] there is no such limit for another registered society, nor for a local authority which acquired its shares under various statutory powers to assist housing associations or under its general powers.[21]

15.27 Because of the regulation of diverse activities association it is sometimes convenient to put all non-social housing activities in an unregistered association within the group. In such a case, it will be important to have regard to the particular objects of each member of the group. So that, for example, if one object of the unregistered association is to make profits then its directors will have to be astute not to subjugate its interests to other members of the group. This will especially be so where the constituent members of the group have different shareholders[22] with one or more members established for profit. These must not surrender profit-making opportunities to other members of the group, unless that can be clearly seen as in the interests of the surrendering company.

15.28 In the case of a fully mutual housing association, another association cannot be a member (membership is only open to tenants or prospective tenants). Unless the parent is a company, the fully mutual association can be a member of the parent and individual members of a fully mutual association can be members of the parent.

15.29 In the case of charities, Charity Commission guidance states that group structures can take many forms and are likely to have the following features:

---

20 CCBSA 2014 s24(1).
21 CCBSA 2014 s24(2)(a), (b), (c).
22 Or members in the case of bodies which do not have shareholders.

- The group members act as a collective to deliver a range of services to beneficiaries.
- The arrangement is formalised – for example, by contract, service level agreement or memorandum of understanding.
- The group will often include a parent organisation with one or more other charities and non-charitable subsidiaries.
- The group may consist of organisations which are both charitable and non-charitable.
- The group might consist of only incorporated organisations and, as such be subject to the Companies Act 2006.
- All organisations within the group will have their own name and distinct objects (although it is likely that these will be similar in some way).
- The group will produce consolidated accounts.[23]

15.30 The guidance gives the example of the Portsmouth Housing Group, primarily involved in social housing and community regeneration, which has Portsmouth Housing Association, the Portsmouth Foyer, the EC Roberts Centre and the Bill Sargent Trust within its group. It gives examples of affiliated or federal structures and coalition structures.

15.31 The guidance stresses the need to keep the control of charitable and non-charitable activities insulated from each other and to account separately for them, for example by ensuring that any services provided by a charity to a non charity are paid for at a market rate.

15.32 Economic groups may also come about by contract under which one company links itself to another by agreeing to co-operate in specific ventures or generally in specific respects. A parent may also exercise control by means of a power to appoint and dismiss the board. Groups may also arise simply because there are directors common to several companies (sometimes referred to as common boards) so that in practice the decisions of one will be taken in the light of their impact on others.

Constraints, control and cross liability

15.33 Although a governing body owes its duties primarily to its own association, where there is a closely integrated group structure it is important to be alert to the possibility that the exercise of powers by the governing body or the membership affects other members of the

---

23 See Charity Commission, *Guidance – collaborative working and mergers: an introduction* ('Charity Commission Guidance'), August 2017, p9.

group. In that event, for example, members of the governing body might be liable to other bodies for breach of their duty of care or their fiduciary duties. The regulator requires that group parents which are registered providers shall 'support or assist those of their subsidiaries that are registered providers with a view to ensuring compliance with regulatory requirements'.[24] Where there is a group structure with a parent which is not a registered provider, there should be mechanisms in place to ensure that:

a) such parent companies will give appropriate support or assistance as necessary to the registered provider;
b) such registered providers have the ability to require the support or assistance of the parent company concerned;
c) the registered provider's ability to meet the regulator's standards and other regulatory requirements is not and cannot be prejudiced by the activities or influence of the parent company or another part of the group.[25]

15.34 Whichever group structure and controlling mechanism is adopted will provide some insulation for one member of the group not to be saddled with the liabilities of another member of the group. In the ordinary course, there will be no such cross liability since 'the fundamental principle is that "each company in a group of companies (a relatively modern concept) is a separate legal entity possessed of separate legal rights and liabilities": see *The Albazero* ... per Roskill LJ'.[26] This is equally true whether the group comprises exclusively companies or exclusively co-operative and community benefit societies (CCBSs) or a combination, since each company or society is in law a separate entity.

15.35 What is meant by 'control', and where is it to be found? Inevitably there is some overlap in treating these two questions. Control can be de jure or de facto. By de jure in the present context is meant that the person having control has a legal entitlement to require the entity controlled to respond in accordance with the controller's directions. By de facto is meant that the controller, although not having a legal entitlement to require the entity to act in accordance with the controller's directions, nonetheless has such influence as will secure that

---

24 Charity Commission Guidance para. 3.1.
25 Charity Commission Guidance para 3.3.
26 *Owners of Cargo Laden on Board the Albacruz v Owners of the Albazero* [1975] AC 774, at 807; Per Slade LJ in *Adams v Cape Industries plc* [1990] BCLC 479, at 508. *Adams* affords a very clear example of the application of this principle; for a contrasting case see *Creasey v Breachwood Motors Ltd* [1993] BCLC 480.

result. The legal constraint, or the factual constraint, may arise from within or outside either a particular company or the group as a whole. It is often the case in a housing association that the board has de jure control simply by virtue of it comprising a majority of the membership. A parent association may have de facto control by means of a power to appoint the directors of a subsidiary. In the case of a CCBS, control cannot be weighed in favour of financial interests. However, a parent association may have de jure control by means of a golden share.

15.36 It is possible to assert that a parent company is not in a fiduciary position with regards to its subsidiaries. Company or CBS members of a group are separate legal entities.[27] The courts have yet to adopt a consistent jurisprudence in relation to groups. In *DHN Food Distributors Ltd v Tower Hamlets LBC*[28] Lord Denning in one of his customary more radical judgments held that subsidiaries were 'bound hand and foot' to the parent company and in effect the whole was a 'single economic entity'. However, in *Woolfson v Strathclyde Regional Council*[29] the House of Lords limited that interpretation saying that the corporate veil would be upheld unless the company was a façade. The difference between the two cases was that in *DHN* the parent was in practice able to control the subsidiary, whereas in *Woolfson* the parent had no control whatsoever.

15.37 For a parent not to be implicated in the activities of a satellite, then, there must be arm's-length arrangements, and only for the purpose which are in keeping with its own objects or which are reasonably incidental to its objects. In a sense, the primary aim of the regulation of housing associations attempts to confine the activities so as not to put social housing assets at risk.[30] This is because public funds have been used in the creation of those social housing assets. In *Rosemary Simmons Memorial Housing Association Ltd v United Dominions Trust Ltd*[31] a charitable housing association guaranteed the debts of a non-charitable satellite which was legally independent

---

27 See *Saloman v Saloman* [1897] AC 22 HL; Milman, David (as author), in *Regulating enterprise*, Hart Publishing, Oxford, 1999, ed D Milman; *Groups of companies: the path towards discrete regulation*, p232. Some confusion and contradiction has arisen in the context of companies but there is no reason to suppose in this context that the law is fundamentally different where the group comprises or includes CBSs, but there is no clear authority to that effect.
28 [1976] 1 WLR 852, CA.
29 [1978] 38 P & CR 521, HL.
30 See HCA, 'Governance and Financial Viability Standard', April 2015, para 1.2.
31 [1986] 1 WLR 1440; see also *Charterbridge Corp v Lloyds Bank Ltd* [1969] 2 All ER 1185; *Credit Suisse v Allerdale BC* (1996) *Times*, May 20, CA.

but in practice wholly controlled by the association. This was held to be unlawful despite the purpose of the satellite being to build flats for the elderly, which could have been carried out within the object of the parent.

15.38 However, in *Halifax Building Society v Spurzeon; Same v Meridian Housing Association*,[32] Arden J held that a mortgage to the defendant housing association for business purposes was intra vires thus facilitating intra-group funding. Meridian had borrowed money in order to develop a site into commercial offices and dwellings, the offices being necessary in order to give financial viability to the scheme. This was held to be intra vires on the basis that Meridian's rules by implication permitted it to have offices for estate purposes and, under the principle in *Rolled Steel Products (Holdings) Ltd v British Steel Corporation*[33] the actual motive of the directors (in that case to make money) was not relevant. In practice on lending will be restricted by loan covenants in any agreements with financial institutions.

15.39 To add to the confusion, legislation has, for specific purposes, been prepared to treat a group as one entity. The preparation of accounts and the tax treatment of groups of companies provide good examples, along with provisions relating to insolvency. Some principles have emerged from the case-law. Thus, just as the corporate veil may be lifted where there is only one company, so it may also be lifted where there is a group of companies, albeit that the applicable principle is narrow, namely that 'it is appropriate to pierce the corporate veil only where special circumstances exist indicating that it is a mere façade concealing the true facts'.[34]

15.40 There are four other situations which merit a brief mention where a subsidiary might claim against a parent or vice versa, namely: agency; tort; the unfair prejudice provisions of company law; and the position of shadow directors.[35] It is possible that one member of a group may be the agent or shadow director of another and hence incur liability on behalf of that other. Agency will not be inferred lightly, but may nonetheless arise by implication, where one member of a group knowingly allows another member of the group to contract on its behalf;

---

32 [1994] 2 BCLC 540, Ch D.
33 [1986] Ch 246, CA.
34 As in *Jones v Lipman* [1962] 1 All ER 442, where the company was formed by Lipman in an unsuccessful attempt to prevent the court ordering specific performance of a contract; also per Lord Keith in *Wolfson v Strathclyde Regional Council* (1978) SLT 159, supported by Lords Wilberforce, Fraser and Russell.
35 Above paras 12.41 and 12.5.2, and more generally chapter 11.

and it may arise in tort, for example the tort of negligence where one member of the group assumes responsibility for the actions of another.[36]

15.41 Thus a parent who intervenes in the affairs of the subsidiary might become a shadow director and so liable. Bearing in mind the discussion above and the regulatory requirements of the RSH it could be argued that intervention or intrusion by a parent or the regulator was through regulatory necessity and therefore could not be prejudicial in any way. However, conduct can still be unfairly prejudicial – for example, even if those pursuing the conduct had no choice in the matter. There is no case-law on whether the presence of pressure from an outside body, such as the regulator, may prevent the conduct, albeit prejudicial, from being unfairly prejudicial.[37]

15.42 Nonetheless, a safe view, it is submitted, is that a housing association parent, which is a registered provider (especially where that provider in a charity or existing for charitable purposes), can intervene a subsidiary or satellite only for purpose which benefits its own lawful objects.

Strategic alliances

15.43 Groups need not only comprise a parent and its subsidiaries. Arrangements can exist which have two separately owned corporate entities, which are associated to co-operate to further each other's ends. This co-operation can be formalised into a legally binding contract, or may be left loose. Housing associations increasingly undertake joint ventures with other bodies including commercial enterprises as a means of subsidising their housing projects and also as a means of contributing to wider social aims such as urban regeneration or socially mixed developments. Such joint ventures can, as a matter of legal theory, be carried on via a separate body formed especially for the particular joint venture and no other, or to enable joint ventures in general to be executed. In such cases the bodies will have a share structure and governance regime tailor-made to the requirements of the joint ventures. However, joint ventures may be executed simply under contractual arrangements.

---

36 For a more complete list and fuller discussion (including mention of trusts, shadow directors, enemies, tax, companies and other legislation) see B Hannigan, *Company law*, Oxford, Butterworths, 2018; and *Blackstone's statutes on company law 2018–2019*, Oxford University Press.
37 See, for example, the interesting analogous case *Scottish Co-operative Wholesale Society Ltd v Meyer* [1959] AC 324.

Winding up and insolvency

15.44 What was relatively straightforward law relating to insolvency and winding up is now less clear due to the lack of a primary role by the regulator. The regulator had a very clear directional role previously but, with relaxations since 2016 in relation to consents, that no longer exists. Boards now are in the driving seat. Luckily there are very few insolvencies and it is highly likely that associations will maintain a close relationship with the regulator if falling into such difficulty it is likely they will need to consider dissolution or winding up.

15.45 Underlying the insolvency issue is the wider question of the ambivalent nature of a housing association between the public and the private. On the one hand, private funders welcome the security provided by government regulation. On the other hand, they may well fear that the stifling hand of the state may impinge on their control over assets. The law has struggled to find a middle way and the following is the latest incarnation of this.

15.46 A housing association may be dissolved (ie terminating its existence) by two primary routes. The first route is voluntary winding up, although, except where a provider merges with another, such events are rare and is governed by the general law. There are two ways of voluntarily winding up.

15.47 First, the provisions relating to the voluntary winding up of an insolvent company also apply to a CCBSA society as if the society were a company, except that a reference to the registrar of companies is to be read as the FCA.[38] The liability of members and former members is restricted to any amount unpaid on their shares.[39] A corporate charity cannot alter its constitution to cease being charitable in relation to its existing property and assets unless these were acquired for full consideration in money or money's worth.[40] This method is affected by changes introduced by the Housing and Planning Act 2016 (below).

15.48 Second, in the case of a CCBSA 2014 society, three-fourths of members of an *active and solvent* society can vote to use an instrument of dissolution to wind up the society.[41] In the case of a dormant society only two-thirds of members need to vote by way of a special

---

38 CCBSA 2014 s123.
39 CCBSA 2014 s124(2).
40 Charities Act 2011 s197.
41 CCBSA 2014 s119.

15.49 resolution in favour of dissolution.[42] This method is useful in connection with mergers.

Both methods of dissolution are complete only when the FCA, after advertising has cancelled the association's registration.[43] This can be done only after the society certifies that all its property has been properly dealt with.[44]

15.50 The second route, namely the involuntary winding up process involving administration on behalf of creditors, previously applied both to CCBSA 2014 societies and to companies. However, private registered providers (PRPs) are now excluded from these provisions in favour of special 'housing administration' arrangements.[45]

15.51 These were created by the Housing and Planning Act 2016 and take priority over the general law. The main feature is the appointment, by the court by application of the secretary of state or the RSH with the consent of the secretary of state,[46] of a 'housing administrator'. Originally this applied only to companies but in 2018 was extended to all PRPs other than trusts.[47] The core of the regime is that 'the provider's affairs, business and property are to be managed by a person appointed by the court'.[48]

15.52 The court may make an order only if it is satisfied: i) that the registered provider is unable, or is likely to be unable, to pay its debts; or, (on a petition by the Secretary of State under the Insolvency Act), ii) that it is just and equitable to wind up the registered provider in the public interest.[49] A person cannot be appointed as a housing administrator unless qualified to act as an insolvency practitioner in relation to the registered provider.[50]

15.53 The Housing Administration Scheme requires a balance to be attempted between the creditors and the interests of social housing but with the scales weighted in favour of the creditors. It is based on two 'objectives'. Objective 1 is 'normal administration', namely a) to rescue the PRP as a going concern, or, failing that, b) to achieve a better result for the creditors than would be likely if the PRP was wound up in the ordinary way, or, failing that, c) to realise property

---

42 CCBSA 2014 ss120(2), 119(4)(b) and 119(6).
43 CCBSA 2014 s122.
44 CCBSA 2014 s126.
45 CCBSA 2014 ss118(3), 125(2); Insolvency Act 1986 s72G (companies).
46 Housing and Planning Act 2016 s99(1).
47 Insolvency of Registered Providers of Social Housing Regulations 2018 SI No 728.
48 Housing and Planning Act 2016 s95(1)(b).
49 Housing and Planning Act 2016 s100(2).
50 Housing and Planning Act 2016 s101(3).

for the benefit of secured or preferential creditors but without unnecessarily harming the interests of the creditors as a whole. Objective 2 is to keep social housing within the regulated sector.[51] For example, the administrator might transfer some or all of the social stock of the PRP to another PRP, or set up a new PRP for it.

15.54 The administrator must try to fulfil both objectives. Where this is not possible, objective 1 has priority, thus encouraging private funding. So far as is consistent with the statutory objectives, the administrator must act in the interests of the creditors as a whole.

15.55 The administrator has similar powers to those of ordinary administrators under the Insolvency Act 1986.[52] If there is a disposal of land or property, any obligations which were subject to a planning obligation such as a section 106 agreement under the Town and Country Planning Act 1990 will not bind the purchaser or any other successor in title thus enabling requirements to provide social housing to be overridden.[53]

15.56 The ordinary insolvency processes are frozen. The court and the creditors cannot exercise their powers under an ordinary insolvency petition and any petition must be dismissed unless notice in writing of the relevant petition (other than one made by the secretary of state) is given to the regulator and 28 calendar days have elapsed from that date.

15.57 A resolution for a voluntary winding up (above) is also included in this regime. Such a resolution requires the permission of the court which can be only on the application of the PRP.[54] The same 28 days breathing period applies.

15.58 During this 28-day period (which is extendable), if an application for a Housing Administration Order is made, the court can either make the order or carry on with the ordinary insolvency process.[55] However, the Housing Administration scheme cannot be triggered if the PRP in question is already in administration or liquidation.

15.59 At the end of the moratorium, if no housing administrator has been appointed, the court can apply the ordinary processes once more. However, when exercising its insolvency powers the court must act within the objectives of the Housing Administration regime and the secretary of state and the regulator must be given a reasonable opportunity to make representations to the court.[56]

---

51 Housing and Planning Act 2016 s96.
52 Schedule 5; Insolvency Act 1986 Sch 1B.
53 Housing and Planning Act 2016 s103.
54 Housing and Planning Act 2016 s105.
55 Housing and Planning Act 2016 ss104, 106.
56 Insolvency Act 1986 Schs 5 and 6.

15.60   Charitable trusts remain subject to the general law of charities and so to the powers of the Charity Commission and the courts to transfer their assets to other charitable bodies 'cy pres' ('as near as possible'). This enables the dwellings to remain within the social housing sector. (There is a bespoke regime for 'charitable incorporated organisations.[57])

Insolvency in Wales

15.61   The housing administration provisions apply only to a body registered in England with the RSH as a PRP. However, if a PRP owns dwellings in Wales this seems to apply to such dwellings. In the case of an RSL registered with the Welsh Ministers, no corresponding legislation has been enacted. The position remains governed by Housing Act 1996 ss39–50 as amended. This applies to dwellings owned by an RSL both in England and Wales. Unlike the English version, this scheme puts the democratic government at the centre of the process thus providing a policy direction while still giving the creditors ultimate control.

15.62   Under these provisions, notice must be given to the Welsh Ministers of any proposed enforcement of security, winding up or insolvency proceedings. There is an extendable moratorium of 28 days during which the Welsh Ministers, after consulting the landlord and where practicable its tenants, can make proposals for the ownership and management of the land. This included the appointment of a manager with wide powers to implement the proposals including the power to transfer engagements. During the moratorium an interim manager can be appointed without powers to sell or mortgage but not in respect of property wholly in England. The proposals are binding if agreed by the *secured* creditors and enforceable through the court. 'So far as practicable' the proposals must not put the unsecured creditors in a worse position than they otherwise would be. They must not change the priority of secured creditors. The proposals must not override the terms of a charity and occupied dwellings held by a charity must be transferred to another charity with similar objects.[58] If there is no agreement, then when the moratorium ends, the ordinary insolvency process can be resumed.

57   Insolvency Act 1986 Sch 2.
58   Housing Act 1996 s44(5), (6).

Index

Accountability 13.5–13.59
  community, to 13.44–13.52
  general public, to 13.44–13.52
  local authority, to 13.10–13.23
    complexity of relationship 13.12
    designated percentage of officers 13.21
    golden shares 13.22
    local authority influence 13.17
    local government members 13.15, 13.16
    LSVT associations 13.19
    restrictive practices 13.13
    sale of land, and 13.11
    stock transfer associations 13.14
    voting provisions 13.23
  meanings 13.2
  multiple forms 13.1
  Neighbourhood and Community Standard 13.52
  public complaints 13.51
  regulator, to 13.5–13.9
    accreditation of auditors and accountants 13.9
    sanctions 13.8
    statutory requirements 13.4–13.7
  tenants, to 13.24–13.43
    arrangements 13.27–13.33
    consultation arrangements 13.39–13.43
    housing management 13.28–13.31
    RSH tenant involvement and empowerment standard 13.36–13.38
    statutory obligations 13.25
    transparency 13.47–13.50
Accounts, regulation of 4.74
Accreditation 5.43, 13.9
Acquiring information 5.8, 5.9
Affordable housing 1.63, 1.64
Affordable rent 9.24
ALMO 2.56
Almshouse charity 2.36
Almshouses 1.14
Amalgamation 5.54
A new deal for social housing 1.47–1.51
  core principles 1.47
  stigma 1.50
Appeals 5.73–5.76
  decision-making process, and 5.76
  internal 5.75
Appointing officers 5.50, 5.51
Assured shorthold tenancies 8.26–8.32
  fixed-term 8.27–8.30
  specific policies 8.31
Assured tenants 8.19–8.25
  licences 8.21
  public law principles 8.23
Audit 4.74, 5.14–5.24
Austerity 1.27–1.33
  benefit eligibility 1.30
  rent settlement, and 1.28, 1.29, 1.31

Balanced communities 7.44
Bias
  inquiries, and 5.19
  rule 8.45

Board
  composition of 11.47–11.51
  powers of 11.29, 11.30, 11.32–11.46
Bonds 5.64, 14.38
Brexit 1.52–1.56
  availability of labour 1.53
  consumer confidence, and 1.56
  price inflation 1.54
  price of, and 1.55

Capital Funding Guide 14.26
Capital gains tax 14.103–14.116
  anti-avoidance provision 14.110
  co-operatives 14.112, 14.113
  co-ownership societies 14.112, 14.113
  exemptions 14.106–14.109
  gifts, and 14.111
  non-charitable non-mutual housing associations 14.114–14.116
  self-build societies 14.112, 14.113
Care Quality Commission 6.18, 6.19
Cave **Report** 4.3, 4.4
CBS 2.12–2.13
Charitable housing associations 2.26–2.36
  charitable purpose 2.28–2.32
    caring for disadvantaged 2.31
    sheltered schemes 2.32
  features 2.26
  non-charitable purpose 2.33
  objects 2.27
  registration 2.34, 2.35
  structures 2.34
Charitable Incorporated Organisation 2.18
Charitable purpose 2.28–2.32
Charitable trust 2.17
Charity
  accounts and audit 6.16, 6.17
  merger of 11.42
  regulation of 5.16 *see also* Charity Commission
Charity Commission 6.9–6.17
  charity accounts and audit 6.16, 6.17
  collaboration with regulator 6.13
  concurrent jurisdiction of High Court 6.15
  exempt charity, and 6.10–6.12
  objectives 6.9–6.15
  powers 6.9–6.15
  registration of trust 6.10
  removal from list of exempt charities 6.14
Civil partner 8.44, 9.10, 9.31, 9.32
Companies Act companies 2.15–2.16
Companies Registry 6.8
Complaints by tenants 4.45, 13.346, 13.53
Constitutional objectives 7.6
Construction methods 14.13
Consultation 4.60, 4.61
Consumer standards 4.45, 4.54
Continuous market engagement 14.1–14.3, 14.16
Contractual obligations 7.3
Co-operative housing association 9.15
  meaning 2.43
  security of tenure 8.13
Co-regulation 4.40, 4.76, 5.78
Corporation tax
  financial assistance, and 14.102
Covenants 14.40
Criteria for registration 4.22–4.24

Democratic filter 13.54–13.56
Demoted tenancy 8.48, 8.49
Deprivation of liberty
  residential care 10.23–10.33
Deregulation 13.23
Director's liability 12.51–12.56
  duties to third parties 12.53
  enforcing 12.51–12.56
  exemption 12.54–12.56
Disposal of land 5.57–5.65
  disposal, meaning 5.61
  financial and guarantee 5.64
  landlord disposal 5.63
  notice of relevant disposal 5.62
  removal of consent 5.58
Disposals Proceeds Fund 14.43–14.45
DOLS *see* **Deprivation of liberty**

Domestic violence refuges 14.84
Duty of care
charities 12.45–12.50
companies 12.36–12.41
Co-operative and Community Benefit Societies Act 2014 12.42–12.44

Economic standards 4.45
Elderly, leaseholds for 8.88–8.95
exemptions 8.91, 8.92
Housing and Planning Act 1986 8.93
termination 8.89
Enforcement notice 5.31–5.35
appropriate 5.31
contents 5.33
disobeying 5.35
validity 5.34
'English Body' 4.15–4.18
Entry to premises 5.11, 10.31
Equality Act 2010
housing application, and 7.55–7.61
Equity percentage arrangement 8.96
EU law 3.48–3.51
procurement regulations 3.49, 3.50
public bodies, and 3.48–3.51
Eviction 9.5–9.13
Article 8 ECHR 9.12
general protection against 9.6
grounds for possession 9.10–9.13
human rights, and 9.74
statutory grounds 9.8
Excessive payments 1.26
Exchange of tenancies 9.36–9.45
consent to 9.38, 9.39

Fairness 9.86, 8.87
Fair rents 8.17, 8.18
Fair trial 9.75
Family Intervention Tenancy (FIT) 8.50–8.53
Fettering of discretion 9.87, 9.94, 11.18
Fiduciary duty 12.34, 12.57
Finance sources 14.30–14.39

Financial assistance 4.75
conditions attached to 7.4, 7.5
Financial Conduct Authority (FCA) 6.2–6.7
consultation with 6.7
functions 6.2, 6.3
powers of intervention 6.5, 6.6
Fiscal privileges 14.87–14.119
Flats
shared ownership 8.77–8.79
Flexible tenancy 8.46, 8.47
Fraud 1.33, 8.54, 8.55
Freezing assets 5.25–5.28
indefinite 5.27
notice 5.28
temporary order 5.26
Fully mutual housing associations 2.42–2.53
co-operatives 2.47, 2.48
criteria 2.42
management agreement 2.46
privileges 2.44
public benefit element 2.45
registration 2.43
Fully mutual tenancies 8.33–8.37
residual regime co-operatives 8.34
termination 8.37
Wales 8.36
Funding programmes 14.1–14.3
continuous market engagement 14.1–14.3

Governance 11.1–11.51
accountability 11.10
board members, and 11.15
board pay 11.8
code 11.21–11.23
constitution, and 11.24
CSPL 11.12, 11.13
current issues 11.4–11.11
direct legal liability 11.9
funding decisions 11.11
group structures 11.7
key issues 11.6
members, and 11.19
membership 11.26–11.51 *see also* Membership
NHF code 11.5, 11.20
Nolan principles 11.12

power, and 11.16–11.18
practice 11.12–11.20
principles 11.12–11.20
regulatory framework 11.21–11.25
Governing body 12.1–12.81
boards, as 12.7
CCBS 12.6
CCBSA 2014 standard of care 12.32–12.44
charities standard of care 12.45–12.50
common sense approach 12.48
expertise of members 12.49
termination of membership 12.50
trustees 12.45–12.47
code 12.20, 12.22
companies 12.13
companies: standard of care 12.36–12.41
objective test 12.37–12.39
shadow director 12.41
wrongful trading 12.40
composition 12.2, 12.14–12.17
conflicts of interest 12.57–12.81
delegation of functions 12.8
director's liability *see* Director's liability
financial governance and control 12.24, 12.25
governance and viability standard 12.18, 12.19, 12.21
independent 12.23, 12.27, 12.28
liability 12.29–12.50
common law duty 12.34
mismanagement 12.35
personal gain 12.3
personal liability 12.30
powers 12.5–12.13
regulator, and 12.4
regulatory requirements 12.18–12.28
skill, level of 12.32
third parties, and 12.11
trustees 12.9
ultra vires acts 12.10
Government
accounts 3.9–3.13
influence 13.18, 13.19

Government funding
reduction 1.21
Governmental function 3.23
Gradings 4.67, 4.71, 4.72, 11.11
Grants from government 14.1–14.29
Green paper 7.67
Grenfell Tower 1.43–1.46, 7.62, 7,68
Group structures 15.22–15.43
agency 15.40
charities 15.29–15.32
companies 15.26
constraints 15.33–15.42
control 15.33–15.42
cross liability 15.33–15.42
failures 15.23
fiduciary position of parent company, whether 15.36–15.38
group as one entity 15.39
key drivers 15.22–15.32
shadow director 15.41
subsidiaries 15.24, 15.25
tort 15.40
types 15.22–15.32
unregistered association 15.27

'Homebuy' 8.96
Homes and Communities Agency (HCA) 1.38, 1.39, 4.4–4.6
duties 4.9
Homes England 1.38, 1.39, 4.4–4.6, 14.9–14.29
Hostels 4.29, 9.29, 13.25
Housing Act 1974 1.16
Housing Act 1980 1.17
Housing Act 1988 1.20–1.21
Housing Act 1996 1.22
Housing Act 2004 1.23
Housing administration arrangements 15.51–15.60
Housing allocation 7.1–7.68
Housing applications
Equality Act 2010 7.55–7.61
discrimination 7.58
protected characteristics 7.55
Regulating the Standards 7.61
tenancy standard 7.60
vulnerable groups 7.59

Index 349

Human Rights Act 1998 7.46–7.54
  application for tenancy 7.51
  close connection with local authority 7.49
  departure from published lettings 7.53
  jeopardy basis 7.54
  possession proceedings 7.48
  right to home 7.52
Housing associations
  bona fide co-operative society 2.11
  CBS 2.12–2.13
  CCBSA 2014 2.8
  charitable trust 2/17
  CIO 2.18
  Companies Act companies 2.15–2.16
  concept 1.1
  constitutions 2.4
  definition 2.1–2.19
  description 2.3
  different kinds 2.25–2.53
  eligibility for registration 2.9
  English and Welsh 2.20–2.24
  flexibility 1.5
  forms 2.7
  functions 1.4
  historical development 1.14–1.26
  IPSA 2.8
  law 1.8–1.13
  nature of 1.1, 1.2
  'non-profit' 2.9
  objects 2.4–2.6
  private law 1.11
  public law 1.10
  registration 2.9–2.11
  regulation 1.6, 1.7
  'society, body of trustees or company' 2.7–2.18
  socio-economic themes 1.13
  statistics 1.3, 1.5
  statutory provisions 1.8
  themes of law 1.9
  voluntary sphere 1.12
Housing corporation 1.15
Housing crisis 1.40-1.42
Housing development investments and grants 14.1–14.45
Housing management 7.1–7.68

Housing provision 7.1–7.68
Housing quality and safety 7.62–7.68
  green paper 7.67
  home standard 7.65
  serious detriment 7.64
Housing shortage
  effects 1.42
Housing standards
  Grenfell Tower, and 1.43–1.46
Housing trusts 2.37–2.41
  definition 2.37, 2.38
  housing accommodation 2.40
  powers 2.41
  purpose 2.39
Human rights 9.71–9.84
  allocation decisions 9.83
  application for tenancy 9.76
  Article 6 ECHR 9.79
  Article 8 ECHR 9.73–9.78
  evictions 9.74
  housing applications, and 7.46–7.54
  judicial review, and 9.85, 9.86
  'other status' 9.84
  public act 9.72
  public functions 3.19, 3.26, 3.29
  reasons for decisions 9.80
  relevant Articles of ECHR 9.82
  right to a fair trial 9.75, 9.79
  right to family life 9.79–9.82, 9.12
  right to property 9.82
  statutory shorthold tenancy provisions 9.75
  tenancy agreement, and 9.77
Human Rights Act 1998 3.14–3.47
  horizontal effect 3.33–3.35
    arguments for and against 3.33, 3.34
  private law of contract, and 3.35
  public authority 3.14–3.32 *see also* Public authority
  whether housing association can have human rights 3.36, 3.37
Hybrid bodies 3.18

Immigration and Asylum Act 1999
  duty to co-operate 7.14

In-depth assessment 4.78, 4.79
Inquiries
  bias, and 5.19
  Charity Commission, by 6.9, 6.13
  enforcement powers after 5.17
  fairness 5.21, 5.23
  FCA, by 6.2–6.7
  independence 5.18
  mismanagement, and 5.14, 5.15
  procedure 5.21
  public assistance, and 5.16
  publicity 5.20
  regulator, by 5.14–5.24
  report 5.22–5.24
Insolvency 5.71, 5.72, 15.44–15.60
  charities 15.60
  Wales 15.61, 15.62
Inspections 5.10–5.13
  written report 5.13
Intermediate rent 9.25
Introductory tenancy 8.41
Investigatory/monitoring powers 5.7–5.28
Investment partner status 14.23
Investor protection 4.67, 4.71
Involuntary winding up 15.50

Judicial review 3.38–3.47, 9.85–9.95
  housing shortage, and 9.88
  human rights, and 9.85, 9.86
  important issues 3.40
  legitimate expectations, and 7.35, 7.36
  public and private law 9.89–9.95
  public function 3.41–3.46, 9.85
  regulation, and 4.59
  unfairness 9.87

Land Compensation Act 1973 7.15
Law Commission 8.4
Legal framework 2.1–2.59
Legal representation 9.80
Legitimate expectation 7.32–7.45
  balanced accommodation, and 7.44
  clear and unambiguous undertaking 7.39–7.41
  fairness, and 7.32
  housing shortage, and 7.34, 7.40

judicial review, and 7.35, 7.36
legal relationship between applicant and housing association 7.33
public law context 7.42
published policy, and 7.43
Liability of board members 12.29–12.35
Lifetime tenancy 1.42, 8.26, 8.31
Loan capital 14.35–14.37
Loans 2.55, 3.2, 5.16, 5.64, 14.38
Local authorities
  influence 2.55–2.59, 13.16–13.19
  labels attached to housing associations 1.66
  nomination agreements with 7.16–7.20
  requirement to co-operate with 7.12, 7.13
  subsidiary 13.16
Local authority connections 2.54–2.59
  limiting of influence 2.59
  powers 2.55
  stock transfers 2.58
  varieties of participation 2.56–2.57
Local housing companies 2.57
Long tenancies 8.57–8.62
  contemporary regime 8.60–8.62
  residual regime 8.58, 8.59
Low-cost home ownership accommodation 1.58
  equity percentage agreement 1.58
  shared ownership 1.58
  shared ownership trusts 1.58
Low-cost rental accommodation 1.58

Management 5.41–5.43
  appointment of manager 5.41
  powers in respect of 5.41–5.43
  tender for manager 5.41
Margin of discretion/deference 9.88
Market, ideology of 1.19
Membership 11.26–11.51
  amendment to rules, and 11.3
  appointment 5.50, 5.51, 11.32, 11.33, 12.2

changes to rules, and 11.40–11.42
company, of 11.43–11.45
composition 11.47–11.51
functions 11.29
governing bodies, and 11.27
majority votes 11.44
participation 11.35
powers 11.29, 11.30, 11.32–11.46
register 11.38
removal 5.45–5.49, 5.74, 11.32, 11.36
renewals 11.31
restrictions on power 11.36
will of association 11.34
Mergers
approval 15.1
CBS 15.11
CBS and company 15.17
company 15.12–15.16
group structures, and 15.6, 15.7
hostile take-over 15.20
increased number of 15.4, 15.5
mega mergers 15.3
notification 15.19
routes 15.10
trends 15.1–15.9
Mismanagement
meaning 4.50, 4.51
inquiries, and 5.14, 5.15
Mortgage finance 14.38

Natural justice 4.1
Nolan principles 11.12
Nomination agreements with local authorities 7.16–7.20
function of 7.18
legal force 7.17
tenancy standard 7.18, 7.19
Non-profit
meaning 4.25
PRP 5.58, 8.14, 8.78

Office for National Statistics 3.10, 3.11, 3.12
Officer 13.8
appointing 5.50, 5.51
local authority 13.20, 13.21
payment 12.77, 12.78
register 11.38

Old-style secure tenancy 8.39, 9.42, 9.44
Ombudsman 13.53–13.59
annual report 13.57
democratic filter 13.54–13.56
regulator, and 13.58
Ombudsman (Wales) 5.79
Ownership
policy emphasis on 1.4

Participation 11.35
Penalties 5.29–5.39
Penalty notice 5.36–5.38
PFI 14.41, 14.42
Political agenda 1.61
Political changes in 1980s 1.18
Preserved right to buy 9.52–9.57
aggregated periods of residence 9.57
qualified person in occupation 9.56
qualifying person 9.52, 9.53
when arising 9.55
Private finance 14.33, 14.34
bond and private placement finance 14.38
discipline of the market 14.40
standard commercial mortgage products 14.38
unsecured development finance 14.38
Private finance initiative 14.41, 14.42
Private law sources of power 3.26, 3.41, 9.72
Private licensing 3.6
Private registered provider
meaning 1.57
Probationary/flexible tenancies 8.41–8.53
Profit-making bodies 4.16, 4.26, 5.69
Proportionality 4.37, 4.40. 4.56
Public authority 3.14–3.32
act 3.19
act done in pursuance of public function 3.26
act enmeshed in activities of public body 3.22
commercial prism 3.28

core 3.17
factor-based approach 3.21
function 3.19
functional 3.18
hybrid 3.18
indirect contribution to
    mainstream activities 3.32
meaning 3.15, 3.16
paradigm 3.17
relationship with local authority
    3.31
scheme-by-scheme approach 3.30
statutory duty to co-operate 3.25
Public bodies
classification and declassification
    1.34–1.37
Public functions 3.41–3.46, 9.85
Public inspection of registers etc.
    13.46–13.50
Public or private 1.34–1.37
Public or private law 3.1–3.51
Public or private sector 3.1–3.51
contexts 3.8
government, and 3.3
Housing and Planning Act 2016
    3.13
housing associations in
    ambivalent position 3.2
Local Government Act 1988 s24
    3.7
nature of problem 3.1
Office for National Statistics 3.10,
    3.11, 3.12
statute, and 3.6
statutory powers 3.5
Public sector landlord 3.6
Public utility sources 1.14

Quasi trustees 12.45

Reasonable expectation 7.32–7.45
    see also Legitimate
    expectations
Registered social landlord
    meaning 2.22
Registration 4.20–4.34
eligibility for 4.22–4.27
    criteria 4.22–4.24
    social housing 4.22

English bodies 4.20–4.27
    significance 4.20
Regulation 4.1–4.84
audit 4.74
Cave review 4.3, 4.4
constraints on powers of English
    regulator 4.50–4.59
consultation 4.60, 4.61
consultation with HCA 4.13
consumer objectives 4.42
continuous regulation of
    economic standards 4.77
designation 4.25–4.26
disclosure of information
    4.66–4.73
economic objectives 4.42
fee 4.27
financial assistance 4.75
framework 4.37–4.39
gradings 4.66–4.73
growth duty 4.43
guidance 4.48, 4.49
IDA 4.78, 4.79
information 4.60, 4.61
instability 4.1
judicial review, and 4.59
jurisdiction of regulators 4.15–4.19
mismanagement 4.50, 4.51
objectives 4.40–4.43
openness 4.66–4.73
powers of regulators 4.12
practice of English regulator
    4.76–4.81
principles 4.41
registration 4.15–4.19 *see also*
    Registration
regulation of accounts 4.74
removal from register 4.35, 4.36
standards *see* Standards
tenant involvement 4.62–4.65
threshold for intervention 4.52,
    4.53
voluntary undertaking 4.57
Wales 4.14
Welsh bodies 4.28–4.34, 4.82–4.84
    criteria 4.32
    England, and 4.33, 4.34
    expansion of housing
        association activity 4.31

flexibility 4.30
statutory requirements 4.29
Regulatory powers 5.1–5.82
criminal penalties 5.2
Housing and Planning Act 2016 5.5
range of 5.1, 5.2
Wales 5.4
Regulatory rent controls 9.22–9.27
affordable rents 9.24
intermediate rent 9.25
social rents 9.23
Relaxing regulation 5.55–5.70
ONS, and 5.55, 5.56
Relocation 7.7
Rent
current framework 14.47–14.50
Rent control 14.51–14.58
administrative arrangements 14.51
history 14.52–14.54
Rent convergence 14.52
Rent reduction 14.59–14.74
baseline 14.60
coping with impact 14.72
cost cutting, and 14.73
current requirements 14.59
exceptions 14.61–14.70
job losses, and 14.74
OBR prediction 14.71
Rent reduction regime 9.19–9.21, 14.54–14.58 *see also* Rent reduction
Rent standard 14.75, 14.76
Rent to Buy 8.98
Rent to mortgage 9.51
Rent to Own 8.96
Rents 9.14–9.30
direct controls 9.14
fair rent regime 9.15
increases 9.18
indirect controls 9.14
public subsidy, and 9.16
regulatory rent controls 9.22–9.27
statistics 9.27
statutory limits 9.19–9.21
Wales 9.28–9.30
Residential and nursing care
costs in time of austerity 10.3–10.22

Residential care
deprivation of liberty 10.23–10.33
DOLS 10.30, 10.32
'relative normality' 10.27
subjective element 10.28
Restricted contract 8.18
Restructuring 5.66–5.70
Revenue 14.46
Right to acquire 9.58–9.61
Right to buy 9.48–9.70
effect 1.41
preserved 9.52–9.57
rent to mortgage 9.51
scope 9.49, 9.50
voluntary 9.62
Wales 9.63–9.70
RSA 4.7
Rural associations 2.51

Secure tenancy 8.12–8.16
Security of tenure 9.5–9.13
tenancy standards 9.7
Wales 9.13
Selection of tenants 7.21–7.45
constitutional objects 7.27
fully mutual associations 7.31
housing need 7.29
legitimate expectation 7.32–7.45
see also Legitimate expectation
operational freedom 7.25
reasonable expectation 7.32–7.45
see also Reasonable expectation
reasons for criteria 7.26
registered care or nursing care applicants 7.30
RSH Tenancy Standard 7.24
set of rules 7.22
summary of rules 7.21
waiting list, and 7.28
Self-build housing associations 2.49
Shadow directors 12.41
Shared ownership 8.63–8.87, 9.45, 9.47
downward staircasing 8.69
exemption from LRA 1967 8.75
financial arrangements 8.65
flats 8.77–8.79

exemption 8.77, 8.78
right to manage, and 8.79
houses 8.74
Housing Act 1980 8.67
long lease, as 8.64
long tenancy 8.68
model leases 8.71, 8.82
previous regimes 8.72
principles 8.73
protected areas 8.86, 8.87
publicly funded schemes 8.80–8.85
schemes in shortage areas 8.86, 8.87
Shared Ownership and Affordable Housing Programme (SOAHP) 14.9–14.29
affordable rents 14.21, 14.22
aims 14.10
bidding 14.15–14.20
commercial housing sector, and 14.12
construction methods 14.13
continuous market engagement 14.16
cost cutting 14.15, 14.16
investment partner status 14.23
social rent 14.26, 14.27
Wave 1 deals 14.29
Small associations 5.63, 13.7, 13.24, 15.3
Social housing
meaning 1.57–1.59
Wales 1.67, 1.68
Social housing assistance 14.4–14.8
Housing and Regeneration Act 2008 14.5
Social housing regulator, independence of 9.10–9.14
Social rent 1.62
Social renters 7.8–7.11
statistics 7.8, 7.9–7.11
Social tenancy 1.65
Specific housing duties 7.12–7.20
Spouse, rights of 8.44, 9.10, 9.31, 9.32, 12.79, 12.80
Staircasing 8.69–8.75, 8.88, 8.92, 8.93
Standards 4.44–4.47
consumer matters 4.45, 4.54
economic matters 4.45

failure to meet 4.46
Starter Homes 14.11
Starter tenancy 8.44, 8.45
Statutory intervention 1.25
Strategic alliances 15.43
Subsidiary body 13.16, 15.24, 15.25
Succession 9.31–9.35
assured tenancies 9.32, 9.33
shared ownership lease 9.34, 9.35
Support
meaning 14.78
Supported housing
ageing population, and 10.3
Care Act 2014 10.9
care workers 10.5
challenging decisions: recent case law 10.14–10.22
costs in time of austerity 10.3–10.22
extra care 10.6–10.8
guiding principles for care commissioners 10.14–10.22
integration of health and social care 10.9–10.13
legislative and statutory guidance framework 10.9–10.13
meaning 14.77
personal budgets 10.7
reduction of costs 10.4
specialised 14.84, 14.85
statutory guidance 10.12
Supported housing problems 10.1–10.33
Supporting People funding 14.80–14.83
Suspending or removing individuals 5.44–5.49
acting while disqualified 5.46
power 5.45
right of appeal to High Court 5.49
right to be heard 5.48
without disqualification 5.47

Tailored Review of HCA 4.6
Target rent 9.23
Taxation 14.87–14.119
private sector landlords 14.90
privilege 14.87–14.119
status, and 14.89

Tax liability
  group structure, and 14.117–14.119
Tax on income 14.93–14.116
  charities 14.93, 14.94
  cooperatives 14.95–14.100
  co-ownerships 14.95–14.100
  self-build societies 14.95–14.100
  unregistered non-charitable non mutual housing association 14.101
Tax on sales of property 14.103, 14.104
Tenancy agreements 8.5, 8.26, 9.3, 9.17–9.19, 9.32, 9.39, 9.77–9.80
Tenant involvement in regulation 4.62–4.65
Tenant management organisation (TMO) 1.46, 2.46, 2.56
Tenants' rights 8.1–8.96
  administrative regime 8.5
  assured tenants 8.19–8.25
  collision between residual and contemporary regimes 8.38–8.40
  contemporary era tenancies as residual regime secure tenancies 8.40
  contemporary regime 8.19–8.25
  determination on uncertain event 8.25
  licences 8.16
  nature of law 8.1
  particular rights 9.1–9.95
  public and private sectors 8.3
  recent policies 8.6
  residual regime 8.4, 8.12–8.16
  residual secure tenancies becoming contemporary regime assured tenancies 8.39
  secure and fair rent tenants 8.12–8.16
  secure tenancy regime 8.13
  social mobility, and 8.7
  special provisions in tenancy agreement 8.24
  unregistered associations 8.2
  Wales 8.9–8.11
Tenant Services Authority 1.39
Third sector 3.4
Transfer of land 5.52–5.54
Transfer of tenancies 9.36–9.45
  exclusions from Localism Act 2011 9.43
  fixed-term tenancy 9.40, 9.41
  Housing and Planning Act 2016 9.44
  refusal to comply with request 9.42
  residual regime 9.37
  shared ownership 9.46, 9.47
  Tenancy Standard 9.45
Transparency 13.47–13.50

Ultra vires acts 12.10
Unlawful subletting 8.54–8.56
Unregistered associations 8.2, 14.101, 15.27

Voluntary winding up 15.47–15.49

Wales
  conflicts of interest 12.77–12.81
  fiduciary duty 12.77–12.81
  housing association law 2.20–2.24
  insolvency 15.61, 15.62
  power of regulator 5.77
  appointment of manager 5.85
  complaints about performance 5.79
  England, application to 5.80
  insolvency regime 5.82, 8.83
  registration 4.28–4.34
  regulation 4.14, 4.82–4.84
  financial viability 4.84
  governance 4.84
  regulation regime 9.4
  rents 9.28–9.30
  right to buy 9.63–9.70
  security of tenure 9.13
  social housing 1.67, 1.68
  tenants' rights 8.9–8.11
  'Welsh Body' 4.15, 4.18
Winding up 5.71, 5.72 15.44–15.60
Wrongful trading 12.40